Theorizing and Analyzing Agency in Second Language Learning

SECOND LANGUAGE ACQUISITION

Series Editor: Professor David Singleton, *University of Pannonia, Hungary and Fellow Emeritus, Trinity College, Dublin, Ireland*

This series brings together titles dealing with a variety of aspects of language acquisition and processing in situations where a language or languages other than the native language is involved. Second language is thus interpreted in its broadest possible sense. The volumes included in the series all offer in their different ways, on the one hand, exposition and discussion of empirical findings and, on the other, some degree of theoretical reflection. In this latter connection, no particular theoretical stance is privileged in the series; nor is any relevant perspective – sociolinguistic, psycholinguistic, neurolinguistic, etc. – deemed out of place. The intended readership of the series includes final-year undergraduates working on second language acquisition projects, postgraduate students involved in second language acquisition research, and researchers and teachers in general whose interests include a second language acquisition component.

Full details of all the books in this series and of all our other publications can be found on http://www.multilingual-matters.com, or by writing to Multilingual Matters, St Nicholas House, 31–34 High Street, Bristol BS1 2AW, UK.

SECOND LANGUAGE ACQUISITION: 84

Theorizing and Analyzing Agency in Second Language Learning

Interdisciplinary Approaches

Edited by
Ping Deters, Xuesong (Andy) Gao, Elizabeth R. Miller and Gergana Vitanova

MULTILINGUAL MATTERS
Bristol • Buffalo • Toronto

We dedicate this volume to Professor Leo van Lier,
whose groundbreaking contribution to research on
agency has inspired and greatly influenced our work.

Library of Congress Cataloging in Publication Data
Theorizing and Analyzing Agency in Second Language Learning: Interdisciplinary Approaches/Edited by Ping Deters, Xuesong (Andy) Gao, Elizabeth R. Miller and Gergana Vitanova.
Second Language Acquisition: 84
Includes bibliographical references and index.
1. Second language acquisition—Study and teaching. 2. Second language acquisition—Methodology. 3. Language and languages—Study and teaching. 4. Interdisciplinary approach in education. I. Deters, Ping, editor. II. Gao, Xuesong, editor. III. Miller, Elizabeth R.- editor. IV. Vitanova, Gergana, editor.
P118.2.T46 2014
418.0071–dc23 2014025228

British Library Cataloguing in Publication Data
A catalogue entry for this book is available from the British Library.

ISBN-13: 978-1-78309-289-5 (hbk)
ISBN-13: 978-1-78309-288-8 (pbk)

Multilingual Matters
UK: St Nicholas House, 31-34 High Street, Bristol BS1 2AW, UK.
USA: UTP, 2250 Military Road, Tonawanda, NY 14150, USA.
Canada: UTP, 5201 Dufferin Street, North York, Ontario M3H 5T8, Canada.

Website: www.multilingual-matters.com
Twitter: Multi_Ling_Mat
Facebook: https://www.facebook.com/multilingualmatters
Blog: www.channelviewpublications.wordpress.com

The policy of Multilingual Matters/Channel View Publications is to use papers that are natural, renewable and recyclable products, made from wood grown in sustainable forests. In the manufacturing process of our books, and to further support our policy, preference is given to printers that have FSC and PEFC Chain of Custody certification. The FSC and/or PEFC logos will appear on those books where full certification has been granted to the printer concerned.

Typeset by Techset Composition India(P) Ltd., Bangalore and Chennai, India.
Printed and bound in Great Britain by the Lavenham Press Ltd.

Contents

Contributors

Editors' Biographies

Ping Deters is a Professor in the English Language Institute of Seneca College in Toronto, Canada. Her areas of interest include sociocultural perspectives on the role of identity in SLA, the acculturation and integration of immigrants and international students, comparative and international education, pre-service and in-service teacher development, and qualitative and narrative research. Deters has published in journals such as *The Canadian Modern Language Review, The Modern Language Journal, TESL Canada Journal, Contact* and *Activities, Adaptation and Aging*. In addition, Deters has published a monograph, *Identity, Agency and the Acquisition of Professional Language and Culture* (2011) with Continuum.

Xuesong (Andy) Gao is an Associate Professor in the Division of English Language Education, Faculty of Education, the University of Hong Kong. His current research and teaching interests are in the areas of learner autonomy, sociolinguistics, vocabulary studies, language learning narratives and language teacher education. His major publications appear in journals including *Applied Linguistics, English Language Teaching Journal, Journal of Multilingual and Multicultural Development, Language Teaching Research, Studies in Higher Education, System, Teaching and Teacher Education, TESOL Quarterly* and *World Englishes*. In addition, he has published one research monograph (*Strategic Language Learning*) and co-edited a volume on identity, motivation and autonomy with Multilingual Matters. He is a co-editor for *System: An International Journal of Educational Technology and Applied Linguistics*.

Elizabeth R. Miller is an Associate Professor in the Department of English at the University of North Carolina at Charlotte. Her research uses fine-grained discourse analysis in exploring issues relating to identity, learner agency, power relations and language ideologies as they emerge in interactions involving adult immigrant learners of English. She has published in journals such as *Applied Linguistics, Modern Language Journal, Linguistics and Education, Multilingua, TESOL Quarterly, Critical Inquiry in Language Studies* and *Journal of Politeness Research* and is the author of *The Language of Adult Immigrants: Agency in the Making* (2014) with Multilingual Matters. In that book she adopts various kinds of discourse analytic approaches in exploring how immigrant small business owners position themselves as agentic figures in constructing narratives about their language-learning and work experiences.

Gergana Vitanova is currently an Associate Professor at University of Central Florida. Her research interests explore sociocultural issues of second language and focus on the interplay between second language learning, identity, gender and agency. She is particularly interested in Russian philosopher Bakhtin's dialogical theory and its application to the analysis of narrative discourse data. She has published in journals such as *Journal of Language, Identity, and Education, Critical Inquiry in Language Studies* and *Language and Dialogue.* She is also the author of the book *Authoring the Dialogical Self: Gender, Agency, and Language Practices* (2010) with John Benjamins and a co-editor of the volume *Dialogues with Bakhtin on Second and Foreign Language Learning: New Perspectives* with Lawrence Erlbaum (2005).

Chapter Author Biographies

Adnan Ajsic is a PhD candidate in Applied Linguistics at Northern Arizona University. His research interests include language ideology, corpus linguistics, critical discourse analysis, English as a global lingua franca, language policy in post-colonial and post-communist societies and supranational institutions, family language policy, as well as pedagogical applications of corpora and individual differences in second language acquisition. His writing has appeared in *Language Policy, English for Specific Purposes* and the *Journal of Language and Politics.* Adnan is currently working on his dissertation, which investigates language ideologies and ethnonational identities in the Balkans.

Mari Aro currently works as a post-doctoral researcher at the Department of Languages, University of Jyväskylä, in a Science Workshop project 'Agency and Languaging: Perspectives on Learning-in-the-world', funded by the Finnish Cultural Foundation. Aro's doctoral dissertation on Finnish children's beliefs of foreign language learning (Aro, 2009) discussed language learners' beliefs in the dialogical framework, using the concepts of voice and agency in its analysis. Her current research focuses on a follow-up study where she re-investigates the research participants of her former study, now young adults.

Sangeeta Bagga-Gupta is full Professor of Education at the Center for Feminist Social Studies, Örebro University, Sweden. Her transdisciplinary research encompasses traditionally separate fields like literacies, mono-multilingualism, multimodality, learning and identities (gender, functional disabilities, ethnicity). Using multiscale ethnography across time and space, she studies everyday life, policy and sociohistorical dimensions of social practices both inside and outside institutional environments, primarily from anthropological and postcolonial approaches. She has published articles and chapters in different academic domains including Communication Studies, Deaf Studies and Educational Sciences over the past few decades. Her books include *Literacies and Deaf Education* (2004), *Alternative Voices. (Re)searching Language, Culture and Diversity . . .* (co-edited, 2013) and *Literacy-praktiker i och utanför skolan* (co-edited, Swedish: Literacy-practices inside and outside school, 2013). She has since 2008 headed the Swedish Research Council-funded multidisciplinary National Research School LIMCUL (Literacies, Multilingualism and Cultural Practices in Present Day Society).

David Block is ICREA (Institució Catalana de Recerca i Estudis Avançats) Research Professor in Sociolinguistics at the University of Lleida (Spain). His main interests are the impact of political economic, sociological, anthropological and geographical phenomena on multimodal practices of all kinds (including social movements, multiculturalism, bi/multilingualism and the acquisition and use of languages). In his more recent work he has focused specifically on neoliberalism as the dominant ideology in contemporary societies and social class as a key dimension of identity, all of which is reflected in his two most recent books: *Neoliberalism and Applied Linguistics* (2012; co-authored with John Gray and Marnie Holborow) and *Social Class and Applied Linguistics* (Routledge, 2014). He is editor of the Routledge book series Language, Society and Political Economy.

Anna De Fina is Associate Professor of Italian Language and Linguistics in the Italian Department at Georgetown University. Her interests and publications focus on discourse and migration, identity and narrative. She has authored numerous articles in internationally renowned journals and edited special issues on these topics. Her books include *Identity in Narrative: A Study of Immigrant Discourse* (2003, John Benjamins) and the co-edited volumes *Dislocations, Relocations, Narratives of Migration* (2005, St Jerome Publishing, with M. Baynham), *Discourse and Identity* (2006, Cambridge University Press, 2006, with Deborah Schiffrin and Michael Bamberg) and *Selves and Identities in Narrative and Discourse* (2007, John Benjamins, with Michael Bamberg and Deborah Schiffrin). Her latest publication is the volume *Analyzing Narratives* (2011, Cambridge University Press, co-authored with Alexandra Georgakopoulou).

Liam Doherty is a PhD student in Modern Language Education at the University of British Columbia. His research interests include World Chineses, diversity and multilingualism in Chinese as a second/foreign/heritage language education, digital literacy and Chinese learner identity. Topics of his recent research include narrative language socialization through popular television dramas and the digitally mediated agency of Mandarin learners using social media and mobile platforms to aid in their literacy development. He previously completed an MA thesis at the University of Toronto on changing contexts and practices in international Chinese language education.

Patricia (Patsy) Duff is a Professor of Language and Literacy Education at the University of British Columbia, where she coordinates graduate programs in TESL and Modern Language Education and is Co-Director of the Centre for Research in Chinese Language and Literacy Education. Her books and guest-edited issues of journals include the following titles: *Language Socialization* (Vol. 8, *Encyclopedia of Language and Education*, with N. Hornberger), *Inference and Generalizability in Applied Linguistics* (with M. Chalhoub-Deville and C. Chapelle), *Case Study Research in Applied Linguistics, Languages and Work* (with N. Labrie), *Indigenous, Minority, and Heritage Language Education in Canada* (with D. Li), *Issues in Chinese Language Education and Teacher Development* (with P. Lester) and, most recently, *Learning Chinese: Linguistic, Sociocultural, and Narrative Perspectives* (with five co-authors). She has published journal articles and book chapters on these and related topics as well.

Hannele Dufva is a Professor of Language Learning and Education at the Department of Languages, University of Jyväskylä, Finland. With dialogism and the work of the Bakhtin Circle as her theoretical background, she has published numerous articles on applied linguistics and language learning and teaching and edited a number of books. Her research is focused on understanding the role of cognition in learning and using languages, and her current research particularly draws on the notions of distributed language and cognition.

Chatwara Suwannamai Duran is Assistant Professor of Applied Linguistics at the University of Houston, where she teaches courses in linguistics and sociolinguistics. Originally from Bangkok Thailand, and having studied in both Europe and the USA, she has learned to appreciate and explore multilingualism in both local and global contexts. Her current research focuses on transnational families' lived experiences, multilingual repertoires and literacies that are complicated by migration, globalization and contested language ideologies in the sending and receiving nations.

Próspero N. García (PhD, University of Massachusetts, Amherst) is an Assistant Professor of Spanish Applied Linguistics at Rutgers University, Camden. His research interests lie in the fields of Spanish second language acquisition and pedagogy, Vygotsky's theory of mind, second language evaluation and assessment, and technology-enhanced language learning. His most recent works explore the role of agency in the conceptualization of grammatical categories, and the implementation of concept-based teaching in the L2 Classroom.

Christina Gkonou (PhD, University of Essex, UK) teaches linguistics, psycholinguistics and methodology of TEFL to undergraduate students at the University of Essex. She also works as an EFL and EAP teacher at the same university. She holds a BA in English language and philology, and an MA in TEFL. Her main research interests lie in the area of individual differences and the psychology of language learning.

Hayriye Kayi-Aydar is an Assistant Professor in the Department of Curriculum and Instruction at the University of Arkansas, where she teaches courses on ESL/ELL education. Her current research works with discourse, narrative and pedagogy, at the intersections of the second language acquisition, interactional sociolinguistics and social psychology. Her research interests focus on positional identities, positioning, power and learning opportunities in classroom settings.

Man-Chiu Amay Lin received her PhD from the applied linguistics program at Arizona State University and currently works as a community activist. Her research interest focuses on the language education of the ethnic minorities in Taiwan, including the Indigenous and immigrant populations, exploring the relationship among language, culture, identity and oppression in a globalizing world. Her dissertation takes a praxis-oriented stance and uses ethnographic, collaborative methods to re-construct the role of the Indigenous language (Truku) in one Truku village in eastern Taiwan.

Carola Mick works as an Assistant Professor (maître de conférences) at the department of Linguistics of the University Paris Descartes in France. She holds a PhD in sociolinguistics and applied linguistics of the department of romance languages (French, Spanish) of the University of Mannheim (Germany), and worked as a post-doc in the interdisciplinary research group LCMI (Language, Culture, Media, Identity) at the University of Luxembourg. She specializes in the critical analysis of discourses in the areas of migration and education, and is particularly interested in questions of the social, discursive construction of identity and learning in multilingual contexts.

Theron Muller is an Associate Professor at the University of Toyama, Japan. His publications include exploration of TBL and academic publishing. He is also lead editor on two book projects related to EFL, the recently published *Innovating EFL Teaching in Asia* (2012) and *Exploring EFL Fluency in*

Asia (Forthcoming, 2014), both with Palgrave Macmillan. Currently his research interests involve investigating the experiences of authors pursuing academic publication and improvement of journal review systems. He is active with *JALT Publications* and the *Asian ESP Journal* and part of the University of Birmingham English Language and Linguistics Open Distance Learning team.

Peter W. Stanfield (EdD) is Program Chair of Social and Behavioral Studies at the Higher Colleges of Technology in the Western Region of Abu Dhabi, United Arab Emirates. His career in the UK, Denmark and the Middle East spans primary, secondary, undergraduate and graduate teaching within formal classroom settings as well as in community and outdoor places. His research interests center on place-based education and teacher development. He is a reviewer for the *International Journal of Bilingual and Multilingual Teachers of English* and has made contributions to pedagogic books on English language teaching research.

Acknowledgments

We would like to extend our gratitude to Laura Longworth, the Acquisitions Editor and Rights Manager of Multilingual Matters, for her support from the very conception of this volume through the final editing stages.

We are also indebted to the external reviewers who provided insightful feedback on the chapters in this book:

Jennifer Bown, Brigham Young University, Provo, UT, USA

Mingyue (Michelle) Gu, The Chinese University of Hong Kong, Hong Kong

Ruth Harmon, University of Georgia, Athens, GA, USA

Peter Jing Huang, Hong Kong Baptist University, Hong Kong

In Chull Jang, Ontario Institute for Studies in Education/University of Toronto (OISE/UT), Toronto, Canada

Robert Kohls, Ontario Institute for Studies in Education/University of Toronto (OISE/UT), Toronto, Canada

Joshua M. Paiz, Purdue University, West Lafayette, IN, USA

Manka Vargese, University of Washington, Seattle, WA, USA

Julia Menard-Warwick, University of California, Davis, CA, USA

Doris Warriner, Arizona State University, Tempe, AZ, USA

Yongyan Zheng, Fudan University, China

1 Introduction to Theorizing and Analyzing Agency in Second Language Learning: Interdisciplinary Approaches

Gergana Vitanova, Elizabeth R. Miller, Xuesong (Andy) Gao and Ping Deters

Agency Situated Historically

This book showcases how language learner agency can be understood and researched from varying perspectives by providing, for the first time, a collection of diverse theoretical, analytic and pedagogical approaches in one volume. The concept of human agency has generated considerable interest across various disciplines – philosophy, psychology, sociology and anthropology – for some time, and this scholarly conversation regarding how to understand humans' capacity to act shows no signs of abating soon. While the notions of *agency* and *the self* have always seemed inherently intertwined, *agency* has been far more difficult to define, although it has been viewed, understandably, as one of the many facets of the self. Thus, the idea of agency or our understanding of the nature of humans' capacity for agency has been, to a large extent, determined by historically influential models that explain the nature of the self.

At least four different models of selfhood have emerged and influenced scholars' perspectives regarding what constitutes both subjectivity and agency. The traditional understanding of self (for a summary, see Hermans & Hermans-Konopka, 2010) is largely represented in myths and rituals, and these have helped humans understand the most significant events of their lives, such as birth and death. Body and spirit were viewed as two separate entities in this traditional model, and the spiritual reality was viewed as the higher one. The modernist conception of self was strongly influenced by

1

Enlightenment era perspectives, and it was marked by what Hermans and Hermans-Konopka (2010: 87) call 'an unprecedented autonomy' with its different forms of individualism. The self was seen not only as possessing an essential and unchanging core but also as independent and rational. Choice and action, which have come to be closely associated with agency, form an important component of this rational, individualistic self. For centuries, or at least ever since Aristotle, agency has also been associated with consciousness. Contemporary philosopher Korsgaard (2009), for example, illustrates the importance of self-awareness for agency in her statement:

> The identity of a person, of an agent, is not the same as the identity of the human animal on whom the person normally supervenes. I believe that human beings differ from the other animals in an important way. We are self-conscious of the grounds on which we act, and therefore are in control of them … When you deliberately decide what sorts of effects you will bring about in the world, you are also deliberately deciding what sort of cause you will be. And that means you are deciding who you are. (Korsgaard, 2009: 19)

Deliberate, conscious choices and actions that are, at the same time, intrinsically moral underlie most Western perspectives on agency. Korgsaard's excerpt also reflects that, for a long time, and in different disciplines, the relationship between *agency* and *identity* has been perceived as deeply entangled. Human actions and experience have occupied a central role as well.

When outlining the development of self as subject in psychology, Blasi and Glodis (1995: 416) point out that '[i]n every intentional action that we perform, in every experience that we undergo, we experience ourselves, *in the process of acting and experiencing*, as related to our actions and experiences' (emphasis in original). Psychologists see the relationship between subjects, actions and experience as organic. Not all acts exemplify human agency, however. Agency requires not merely the ability to produce a change in the world, but also that acts should be knowingly, consciously undertaken by subjects. Thus, reflexivity has emerged as another significant component of agency (Kogler, 2012).

In contrast, in a movement that opposed modernism and came to be known as postmodernism, the self is viewed as decentralized and unstable. Perhaps most importantly in terms of agency, the self appears stripped of its personal autonomy. For instance, feminist poststructuralism (Weedon, 1997), which prefers the term *subjectivity* to *identity* and accentuates the discursive, languaged nature of selves, has been employed in applied linguistics exactly because of its focus on how discourses offer various positions for subjects. While there are different postmodern approaches, what characterizes them most broadly is an understanding of the self as constituted through language (Foucault, 1972; Lacan, 1977). Unlike the traditional or modern approaches to selves, postmodernists have emphasized the power structures that underlie human relationships. Yet these approaches are not entirely without their critics. A major point of criticism has been that they espouse a relativistic perspective. Another point of criticism that is more directly related to agency is that, while postmodern approaches take into account the larger, social and institutional structures, the role of the individual remains unclear and somewhat bleak. That said, proponents of performativity theory, aligning with poststructuralism, have argued that, while 'some critics mistake the critique of sovereignty [of the self] for the demolition of agency … agency begins where sovereignty wanes' (Butler, 1997: 16). Rather than claiming that subjectivity is 'only language', these scholars have argued that discourse provides the 'epistemological condition' by which we come to know and understand the world and to view ourselves as human actors who are able to act in that world (Vasterling, 1999: 21).

Sociocultural perspectives have been proposed as an alternative to other approaches to the self exactly because of their focus on the complex interactions between individuals and communities, on the one hand, and human cognition and experience on the other. Instead of conceiving selves and agency as individual or autonomous phenomena, sociocultural approaches view them as the result of inter-subjective processes. Largely inspired by Vygotsky's sociocultural theory (1978) and Bakhtin's dialogism (1981, 1984), such perspectives have foregrounded the mediated essence of agency. Psychologists Werstsch *et al.* (1993), for example, argue for redefining the boundaries of agency as they borrow Bateson's (1972) famous affirmation that 'agency extends beyond the skin' (Bateson, cited in Wertsch *et al.*, 1993: 337). Very much like cognition, which is understood to be socially mediated, agency too is regarded as developing in relation to social groups, not as a property of individuals. Language itself, as one of the key mediational means along with the processes of language learning, is regarded as intrinsically social as well.

In cultural anthropology, Holland *et al.* (1998) have employed Vygotsky's and Bakhtin's ideas and applied them to explaining the development of identities and agency. These scholars reject traditional Western conceptions of essential individuals by suggesting, instead, that humans act as socially constructed selves, who 'are subject to positioning by whatever powerful discourses they happen to encounter' (Holland *et al.*, 1998: 27). Holland *et al.* underscore that our identities are sociohistorical constructions and that the symbols of mediation that humans use are produced in active collaboration with other actors. This interdependent nature of agency is summarized in Inden's (1990) definition, which Holland and her colleagues have adopted in their work:

> [Agency is] the realized capacity of people to act upon their world and not only to know about or give personal or intersubjective significance to it. That capacity is the power of people to act purposefully and

reflectively, in more or less complex interrelationships with one another, to reiterate and remake the world in which they live, in circumstances where they may consider different courses or action possible and desirable, though not necessarily from the same point of view. (Cited in Holland *et al.*, 1998: 42)

People's capacity to act purposefully and reflectively as they engage in relationships with other human beings in turn prompts human beings to re-invent their own positions or re-imagine how they can act. Such a perspective seems to constitute the core of what most contemporary scholars believe about agency. In an often-cited article, linguistic anthropologist Ahearn (2001: 112) offers a provisional definition of agency that is not dissimilar from the definition above: 'Agency refers to the socioculturally mediated capacity to act'. As this definition suggests, language plays a central role in current thought on agency. Ahearn explains that linguistic anthropology views language as a type of social action. As she reviews different approaches to agency, she recommends that scholars be careful in how they conceptualize this construct and cautions against one-sided definitions. Instead of one form of agency, Ahearn proposes that perhaps different types should be considered and explored, for instance, oppositional agency, complicit agency or agency and intention, while keeping in mind that these different types of agency may actually overlap during any given action.

Agency and Second Language Acquisition

These approaches to agency, identity and the self have been reflected in the fields of applied linguistics and second language acquisition, and as in other disciplines, one can trace a shift from an essentialist perspective to language learning to one that regards language acquisition as a complex socially embedded phenomenon. While the term *agency* itself was not used in early second language research, kernels of the understanding that learners can act purposefully and have some control over their own learning were expressed in some early research such as in the Good Language Learner Model (Rubin, 1975) and in research on individual learner characteristics (e.g. motivation). Successful learners were portrayed as active learners who possess both intrinsic motivation and autonomy (Ushioda, 2003).

A different body of research, however, largely based on postmodern models of language and identity, has emerged, arguing for the need to acknowledge that second language learning, like other activities, is ultimately a socially mediated process. Such scholars have introduced identity to second language acquisition (McKay & Wong, 1996; Peirce, 1995; Norton, 2000; Toohey & Norton, 2001). They have stressed the significance of the hierarchy in power relations within different discourses and have under-scored that second language learners cannot be viewed as independent from these power structures. Norton, for example, in her work with female immi-grants, has rejected the term *motivation* and, instead, proposed *investment* because the latter illustrates more closely how learners relate to their social environments and to others in their realities. Instead of investigating motiva-tion or individual learner characteristics, these scholars have explored how second language speakers or writers negotiate social positions and power through the use of discourses. The active use of discourses and addressing power relations through language become an aspect of learner agency. Relatedly, scholars who have articulated the relevance of Activity Theory for understanding second language learning have stressed the relational aspect of agency for second language learners. Lantolf and Pavlenko (2001: 148), for example, contend that 'agency is never a property of the individual but a relationship that is constantly constructed and renegotiated with those around the individual and with society at large'.

Although addressed by second language scholars only in the past decade and half, learner agency is increasingly regarded as a fundamental construct in language-learning processes and for language-learner identities (van Lier, 2008). This growing emphasis on learner agency reflects the broader shift in second language research to exploring learners as complex individuals whose language use, meaning-making and actions are mediated by their social and cultural worlds. In summarizing existing research, van Lier (2008) claims that there are three central characteristics when it comes to agency in lan-guage classrooms: the learner's ability to self-regulate, the socially mediated nature of sociocultural context and an awareness of one's responsibility for one's own acts. Although van Lier does not specify it directly, ethics or moral responsibility is an important part of both the modern approaches to agency and Bakhtin's (1984) dialogical framework of the self. Importantly, agency does not always imply active participation by learners in the classroom. Canagarajah (1999) has demonstrated how students can resist discourses in a Sri Lanka classroom and they, thus, employ agency by not participating actively in the classroom as a form of resistance.

As attention to agency has grown and developed in second language scholarship, the approaches adopted and the definitions offered point to diversity rather than uniform understandings of learner agency. In fact, the individual research of the four editors of this volume demonstrates this quite vividly. Deters (2011) examines the interrelationship between identity and agency from a social psychological perspective, drawing upon Vygotsky's sociocultural theory of mind, Lave and Wenger's community of practice framework, and Erikson's psychoanalytic theory of identity. According to this perspective, agency is seen as comprising an individual aspect that is based on the sociocultural history as well as a situated aspect that is context-specific and co-constructed. In addition, Deters uses Erikson's work on the psychological need for identity coherence to make the connection between agency and identity.

Drawing on Margaret Archer's (2003) theorization of 'internal conversation', Gao (2013) conceptualizes language learners' agency as a precondition to learners' efforts to take charge of the learning process. He proposes that close examination of language-learners' reflexive/reflective thinking helps reveal how agency enables them to discern and deliberate on their concerns, desires and visions in the light of contextual and structural conditions before their commitment to particular learning paths (see also Gao, 2010). Miller (2012, 2014) foregrounds the fundamentally mediated and relational aspect of learner agency. To that end, she draws on Vygotsky's notion of semiotic mediation and Bakhtin's concept of dialogic mediation along with research exploring the mediating effects of language ideologies for learner agency. However, her primary theoretical framing is informed by Butler's (1997) performativity theory. Finally, Vitanova (2010) adopts a dialogical, Bakhtinian (1981) framework in exploring how agency is enacted in everyday contexts. Drawing on the experiences of adult immigrants and second language learners, her work suggests a discourse-centered approach to the analysis of narrative as a genre in the field of applied linguistics. Agency, in this context, is portrayed as a creative, responsive and even ethical understanding of one's sociocultural realities.

This volume was developed in light of the increasing importance of the concept of agency in current scholarship in second language learning. In addition, we regard interdisciplinarity as necessary for developing better understandings of agency in second language learning research, and we regard the lack of a single definition for agency as inevitable. Joseph (2006: 240), in fact, argues that 'no single model is adequate' for understanding agency in the larger context of applied linguistics research and contends that what researchers really need to focus on is 'who has and lacks it in what contexts, and to devise ways of restoring it to those genuinely most deprived of it' (Joseph, 2006: 239). We therefore see strength in bringing together a collection of theoretical essays and empirical studies that approach learner agency from a variety of frameworks and approaches.

Overview of the Book

This edited volume presents 13 chapters that explore agency from multiple perspectives. It is organized into three parts: Theoretical approaches to agency; Analytical approaches to investigating agency; and Pedagogical practices for agency. The first part provides an interdisciplinary introduction to theories of agency and second language learning, some of which are new to second language research on agency (e.g. critical realism), while others take well-known theories into new directions (e.g. sociocultural theory and dialogism incorporated with sociocognitive approaches to individual agency; language socialization with a new focus on self-socialization; and language socialization with a new focus on young multilingual language learners as active agents in their socialization process). The second part presents varying analytic approaches to examining agency in empirical studies. Several draw on ethnographic studies and introduce new analytical foci or methods such as artifact–agent symbiosis and introspective autoethnography. Most use some form of discourse analysis, with one author adopting Positioning Analysis and another the use of Systemic Functional Linguistics to explore interview discourse. The last part demonstrates how theory and empirical findings can be implemented into pedagogical practices that support learner agency or enable learner agency to emerge in various learning contexts. These include Greek adult learners of English, a university student learning conversational Spanish, Japanese students in an English for Specific Purposes classroom, and young students learning Truku in a language revitalization program in Taiwan.

Theoretical approaches to agency

This part has five chapters. It begins with David Block's introduction to critical realism as an alternative framework to a poststructuralist take on second language identities, according to which identity emerges in localized, diverse and variable social activity and is about the multiple subject positions that individuals inhabit and/or are ascribed in sociohistorical and sociocultural contexts. Block questions whether agency, understood to be individuals' 'ability to make choices, take control, self-regulate, and thereby pursue their goals ... [of] personal or social transformation' (Duff, 2012: 416), in effect takes over the entire narrative in this decidedly individualistic approach to second language learner identities. He does not argue in this chapter that agency is not important or that individuals have no capacity or ability to act in the presence of structural constraints in their lives. Instead, he reminds readers that 'there is a real world which consists in structures, generative mechanisms, all sorts of complex things and totalities which exist and act independently of the scientist ... [while also] saying that that knowledge is itself socially produced' (Bhaskar, 2002: 211). Drawing on a critical realist perspective to the interrelationship between structure and agency, Block demonstrates how second language identities can be researched in the light of this understanding.

In the following chapter (Chapter 2), Hannele Dufva and Mari Aro bring together sociocultural and dialogical views on agency. In developing further the dialogical sociocognitive approach, they show how the inescapably social aspects of agency intertwine with cognitive/psychological ones, and how both should be attended to when conceptualizing second/foreign-language learning and development from the dialogical viewpoint. Drawing on language learners' experiences, this chapter aims to understand how an examination of agency as both an individual ('subjectively experienced') and a dialogic ('collectively emergent') phenomenon can be accommodated within sociocultural theory and activity theory that have thus far mostly focused on the social and interpersonal viewpoints.

In Chapter 3, Patricia Duff and Liam Doherty note that researchers increasingly underscore the indeterminacy, contingency, bidirectionality and choices involved in learning and using another language (including the choice to *not* study or use the language at all) as they address the important theoretical construct of agency much more explicitly from a language-socialization perspective. In this chapter, they consider the difference between *agency* and *self-socialization*, the latter a concept found in discussions of socialization in psychology but not yet, to their knowledge, in applied linguistics or linguistic anthropology. To make the theoretical discussion somewhat more concrete, they provide examples from recent studies of both English- and Chinese-language learning, where agency (and/or 'self-socialization') is featured prominently, and examine the mechanisms and linguistic (or paralinguistic) manifestations of agency and its significance for learners, their learning environments and interlocutors, as well as for theory.

In Chapter 4, Chatwara Suwannamai Duran theorizes agency among young language learners through the lens of multilingual repertoires. She notes that children are under-represented in the field of second language studies and, for this reason, she offers a view in which children's multilingual repertoires are understood as resources for practicing agency, that is, the right to make and to enact their own linguistic choices, in goal-oriented and context-embedded situations. In this chapter, she develops two conceptual frameworks to conceptualize agency and the language-learning processes that increasingly co-occur with transnational migration and language diversity. The first framework she discusses is an approach that constructs young language learners as multilingual subjects (Kramsch, 2009), who have control of their two (or more) languages in authentic communication. Viewing learners' multilingual repertoires in this way gives us opportunities to see how agency is generated. The second framework discusses how multilingualism as social capital reinforces language learners' agency. Overall, the first framework focuses on an individual level and the second framework sheds light on community-level collaboration. Both are based on the understanding that multilingual repertoires are resources. That is, previously and recently acquired languages foster and strengthen learners' agency, which is anchored in the knowledge of their role in the community and what they can do with their linguistic resources.

In the last chapter of this section, Carola Mick discusses the issue of second language learners' agency from a sociological point of view and considers the results of different approaches in educational sociology in view of their signification for the analysis of 'dispositives' of second language learning

(Deleuze, 1989). The chapter examines the dominant discourses that shape second language learning, including native speaker ideologies, ideologies on second language learning and an autonomous model of literacy. It also explores the possibilities for actors to deal creatively with these discourses and to appropriate, choose, transform or subvert them in daily, interactive learning activities. Mick closes the chapter with a summary of the links between theories on second language learning and agency, as well as an outlook on interesting research questions in the field of agency in second language learning from the point of view of educational sociology.

Analytical approaches to investigating agency

In Chapter 7, the first of the analytically focused chapters, Sangeeta Bagga-Gupta presents a socially oriented perspective on agency, exploring the construct as locally situated (in the here and now) and distributed (across time, space, actors, and tools). This data-driven contribution is based on a complex ethnographic study of the working lives of women in a nongovernmental organization that provides services for migrant communities in Indian megacities. Sangeeta Bagga-Gupta highlights how micro-interactional analysis and the use of time and space can inform issues related to inclusion and marginalization. In addition, her analysis indicates that the status accorded to different language varieties frames accounting practices related to learning.

In Chapter 8, Hayriye Kayi-Aydar turns to Positioning Theory (Davies & Harré, 1990) to explore how identities are constructed through discourse. She argues that these positional identities, impacted by one's cultural and subjective experience, emerge naturally from social interactions and affect one's agency by implicitly or explicitly limiting or allowing certain social actions. In the chapter, Kayi-Aydar adopts a microanalytic approach to reveal how individuals shape discourse and are shaped by discourse through the positions that they take on. Employing Positioning Theory as both a theoretical approach and a method of analysis, the chapter focuses on a case study of one English-language learner in a classroom setting and, at the same time, provides insight into how researchers can study agency empirically. The focal student's (Mounir) experiences with classmates and the teacher show how the conflicting positionings of this English as a second language (ESL) learner constantly interacted with his agency and mediated his access to learning opportunities.

In contrast to the third-person perspective taken in the other analytic chapters, Adnan Ajsic, in Chapter 9, uses autoethnography to explore his own linguistic journey from his childhood in Bosnia to the present. Although deeply personal, his vivid recollections of key language learning and usage experiences allow him to explore the theoretical linkages between agency and ultimate attainment. His retrospective analysis accounts for both internal and contextual 'felicity conditions' that enabled him to 'cross' into the L2 and 'pass' as a native speaker of English. He deftly shows the dialectic relationship between agency and ultimate attainment, noting that full agency in the L2 depends on a high level of L2 proficiency. Just as important, he accounts for the agency in play when his maturing historical and political awareness led him to decide to keep his English self at arm's length. This first-person critical exploration points to the power of autoethnographic and narrative research for identifying nuanced and dynamic moments in the exercise of agency among language learners and in relation to particular moments in time and space.

The most linguistically oriented analytic approach can be found in Chapter 10, Peter W. Stanfield's chapter. In this chapter, Stanfield gives careful attention to the patterned production of five linguistic constructs that were produced in interview conversations with adult learners of English living in the United Arab Emirates. His discourse analytic approach led him to identify how learners' perceptions of agentic possibilities are aligned with different kinds of spaces. In particular, he found that his research participants constructed themselves as more agentic language learners when using language in nonschool spaces and less so in language classroom spaces. His chapter ably demonstrates the power of Systemic Functional Linguistics for identifying how language users can entextualize their assumptions regarding who has agency and in what contexts.

Pedagogical practices and learner agency

This final part begins with Christina Gkonou's chapter, which undertakes a novel exploration of the interrelationship between learner agency and language anxiety. These two aspects of the language learning experience have never before been researched as possible influences on the other. For this study, Gkonou analyzed diary entries written by seven highly anxious Greek adult learners of English as well as their comments produced in semi-structured interviews. She found that learner agency often played a contradictory role in language anxiety. That is, learner agency enabled these individuals to develop strategies for coping with language anxiety. However, learner agency also increased their language anxiety such as in relation to fulfilling professional goals and meeting their own high standards of learning achievement. In discussing the implications of her findings for language classroom pedagogy, Gkonou provides specific strategies that teachers can use to enhance students' awareness of themselves as proactive agents and moderators of their own learning.

In Chapter 12, Próspero García explores the role of agency in the development of the grammatical concept of aspect in the second language (L2) classroom from a Sociocultural Theory approach to SLA. García uses an analytic approach based on Vygotsky's (1978) genetic method to examine case study data involving a student who was enrolled in an advanced college Spanish conversation course. These data include written narrations (performance), verbalization and personal reflection. García introduces the notion of concept-mediated agency and proposes that the development of the learners' conceptual agency promotes awareness and control over the grammatical concept of aspect. García's work has important pedagogical implications for the teaching and learning of grammatical concepts in the SLA process.

Theron Muller, in Chapter 13, addresses learner agency and the call for greater criticality in the field of English for Specific Purposes (ESP). In this chapter, Muller examines and describes three students' written critical reflections during a medical ESP course in a Japanese university, analyzing how they respond to issues raised during the course and how they assert their agency. Muller highlights three objectives of his pedagogical intervention in this chapter. First, Muller focuses on insights that the students' written reflections offer into their agency as enacted in (and in response to) the course. A second objective was to determine through these reflections whether and to what extent the course goals of promoting criticality were accomplished. Finally, Muller also addresses the efficacy of examining of students' reflective assignment writing as a means of revealing learner agency.

In the final chapter, Man-Chiu Amay Lin focuses on an Indigenous village in Taiwan, and incorporates engaged ethnography (Low & Merry, 2010) to carry out a community-based language revitalization plan with the Truku villagers. Lin utilizes the children's special bond with the elders and combines elderly home care with children's Truku language classes in the community. The children, referred to as 'Truku Visiting Angels', become highly motivated to learn songs and prayers in Truku in order to help entertain the elders. This pedagogical experience eventually inspires a relationship-oriented language revitalization framework. Lin argues that, in the challenging context of Indigenous language education, agency is best understood as an emergent process of relationship rebuilding and the restoration of humanity, and proposes a relationship-oriented language revitalization framework that emphasizes the ethics of care and love.

The volume ends with an Afterword by Anna De Fina in which she highlights some of the common refrains found throughout the book: an orientation to the 'social turn' (Block, 2003) in theoretical framing and a preference for qualitative methodologies. She also notes that the collection, when considered as a whole, points to the complexity of agency given the varied definitions offered for the concept throughout the chapters and the theoretical and analytical dilemmas that emerge as a result.

In summary, this volume brings together a collection of works that is diverse in several ways. In addition to examining agency from various theoretical, analytical and pedagogical perspectives, the authors and their works provide an international array of scholarship in diverse research and pedagogical contexts, focusing on learners and users of a variety of languages. Through these unique and multiple perspectives and contexts, this volume contributes to and furthers current discussions and understandings of agency in second language learning.

References

Ahearn, L. (2001) Language and agency. *Annual Review of Anthropology* 30, 109–137.

Archer, M. (2003) *Structure, Agency and the Internal Conversation*. Cambridge: Cambridge University Press.

Bakhtin, M. (1981) Discourse in the novel. In M. Holquist (ed.) *The Dialogic Imagination: Four Essays* (trans. C. Emerson and M. Holquist) (pp. 259–422). Austin, TX: University of Texas Press.

Bakhtin, M. (1984) *Problems of Dostoevsky's Poetics*. Minneapolis, MN: The University of Minnesota Press.

Bateson, G. (1972) *Steps to an Ecology of Mind: A Revolutionary Approach to Man's Understanding of Himself*. New York: Ballantine.

Bhaskar, R. (2002) *From Science to Emancipation: Alienation and the Actuality of Enlightenment*. London: Sage.

Blasi, A. and Glodis, K. (1995) The development of identity. A critical analysis from the perspective of the self as subject. *Developmental Review* 15, 404–433.

Block, D. (2003) *The Social Turn in Second Language Acquisition*. Edinburgh: Edinburgh University Press.

Butler, J. (1997) *Excitable Speech: A Politics of the Performative*. New York: Routledge.

Canagarajah, S. (1999) *Resisting Linguistic Imperialism in English Teaching*. Oxford: Oxford University Press.

Davies, B. and Harré, R. (1990) Positioning: The discursive production of selves. *Journal for the Theory of Social Behavior* 20 (1), 43–63.

Deleuze, G. (1989) Qu'est-ce qu'un dispositif. In *Michel Foucault philosophe, rencontre internationale, Paris 9, 10, 11 janvier 1988* (pp. 185–195). Paris: Seuil.

Deters, P. (2011) *Identity, Agency and the Acquisition of Professional Language and Culture*. London: Continuum.

Duff, P. (2012) Issues of identity. In A. Mackey and S. Gass (eds) *The Routledge Handbook of Second Language Acquisition* (pp. 410–426). London: Routledge.

Foucault, M. (1972) *The Archeology of Knowledge*. London: Tavistock.

Gao, X. (2010) *Strategic Language Learning: The Roles of Agency and Context*. Bristol: Multilingual Matters.

Gao, X. (2013) Reflexive and reflective thinking: A crucial link between agency and autonomy. *Innovation in Language Learning and Teaching* 7, 226–237.

Hermans, H. and Hermans-Konopka, A. (2010) *Dialogical Self Theory: Positioning and Counter-positioning in a Globalizing Society*. Cambridge: Cambridge University Press.

Holland, D., Skinner, D., Lachicotte, W. Jr. and Cain, C. (1998) *Identity and Agency in Cultural Worlds*. Cambridge, MA: Harvard University Press.

Joseph, J.E. (2006) Applied linguistics and the choices people make (or do they?). *International Journal of Applied Linguistics* 16 (2), 237–241.

Kogler, H.-H. (2012) Agency and the Other: On the intersubjective roots of self-identity. *New Ideas in Psychology* 30, 47–64.

Korgsaard, C.M. (2009) *Self-Constitution: Agency, Identity, and Integrity*. Oxford: Oxford University Press.

Kramsch, C. (2009) *The Multilingual Subject*. Oxford: Oxford University Press.

Lacan, J. (1977) *Ecrits. A Selection*. London: Tavistock.

Lantolf, J.P. and Pavlenko, A. (2001) (S)econd (L)anguage (A)ctivity theory: Understanding second language learners as people. In M.P. Breen (ed.) *Learner Contributions to Language Learning: New Directions in Research* (pp. 141–158). Harlow: Pearson Longman.

Low, S.M. and Merry, S.E. (2010) Engaged anthropology: Diversity and dilemmas, an introduction to supplement 2. *Current Anthropology* 51, 203–226.

McKay, S.L. and Wong, C.S. (1996) Multiple discourses, multiple identities: Investment and agency in second language learning among Chinese adolescent immigrant students. *Harvard Educational Review* 66, 577–606.

Miller, E.R. (2012) Agency, language learning and multilingual spaces. *Multilingua* 31 (4), 441–468.

Miller, E.R. (2014) *The Language of Adult Immigrants: Agency in the Making.* Bristol: Multilingual Matters.

Norton, B. (2000) *Identity and Language Learning: Gender, Ethnicity, and Educational Change.* Harlow: Pearson Education.

Peirce, B.N. (1995) Social identity, investment, and language learning. *TESOL Quarterly* 29 (1), 9–31.

Rubin, J. (1975) What 'the good language learner' can teach us. *TESOL Quarterly* 9 (1), 41–51.

Toohey, K. and Norton, B. (eds) (2004) *Critical Pedagogies and Language Learning.* Cambridge: Cambridge University Press.

Ushioda, F. (2003) Motivation as a socially mediated process. In D. Little, J. Ridley and F. Ushioda (eds) *Learner Autonomy in the Foreign Language Classrooms: Teacher, Learner, Curriculum and Assessment* (pp. 90–102). Dublin: Authentik Language Learning Resources.

van Lier, L. (2008) Agency in the classroom. In J. Lantolf and M. Poehner (eds) *Sociocultural Theory and the Teaching of Second Languages* (pp. 163–186). London: Equinox.

Vasterling, V. (1999) Butler's sophisticated constructivism: A critical assessment. *Hypatia* 14 (3), 17–38.

Vitanova, G. (2010) *Authoring the Dialogical Self: Gender, Agency, and Language Practices.* Amsterdam: John Benjamins.

Vygotsky, L. (1978) *Mind in Society: The Development of Higher Psychological Processes.* Cambridge, MA: MIT Press.

Weedon, C. (1987) *Feminist Practice and Postructuralist Theory* (2nd edn). Cambridge: Blackwell.

Wertsch, J., Tulviste, P. and Hagstrom, F. (1993) A sociocultural approach to agency. In E. Forman, N. Minick and C.A. Stone (eds) *Contexts for Learning: Sociocultural Dynamics in Children's Development* (pp. 336–356). Oxford: Oxford University Press.

Part 1

Theoretical Approaches to Agency

2 Structure, Agency, Individualization and the Critical Realist Challenge

David Block

Introduction

> *If this half-learned opposition withstands refutations so well, this is because it is sustained by the purely social force of routine thinking and automatic language; by the logic of the academic oppositions which underlie the subjects of dissertations and lectures (Tarde, or Weber, versus Durkheim, methodological individualism versus holism, ... rational action theorists ... against ... collective action theorists, etc.); by the literary–philosophical tradition of libertarian dissidence against social powers and especially the state; and above all by the potency of the underlying political oppositions (liberalism against socialism, capitalism against collectivism) which unthinking and unscrupulous 'theorists' eagerly adopt in a sometimes barely euphemized form.*
>
> Bourdieu, 2000: 156

These are tough words, as Bourdieu rails against those who waste their time contrasting structure and agency, doing so as an isolated academic endeavor. While Bourdieu is no doubt right that much that is done in academia owes more to 'routine thinking and automatic language' and that there is surely such a thing as 'the logic of academic oppositions', in my view it is still worthwhile from time to time to stop the world and take stock of abstractions created by academics, especially ones that have come to be so much a part of the conceptual furniture that they hardly merit any discussion or even mention. In this chapter my aim is to revisit the interrelationship between structure and agency, which I have discussed previously (Block, 2009, 2012, 2013), and in doing so, I will try to avoid oversimplification and above all being labeled as 'unthinking and unscrupulous'!

I begin with a selective discussion of how structure and agency have (and have not been) defined in the social sciences in general and applied linguistics in particular. I note that, while agency is often glossed in published work, structure normally merits no such attention. I then explore what we might mean by structure, ending with a five-part model designed to help us think about different types of it. I also discuss what I see as a tendency to prime agency over structure in research on language and identity, relating this tendency to the rise of individualization as an all-pervasive concept in late modern societies. I then argue that if we are to give structure its due in discussions of language and identity, and if we are to resist individualizing biases, then we need to reconsider our epistemological bases. At this point, I discuss critical realism, juxtaposing it with poststructuralism. I end the chapter with an examination of how we might relate this return to structure and the turn to critical realism to some life-story interview data that I collected over a decade ago.

Structure and Agency

As I have argued in recent publications (Block, 2009, 2012, 2013), the structure and agency nexus is a vexed and complicated one. However despite being 'the centre of discussions of subjectivity for centuries' (Hall, 2004: 5) and 'one of the most deep-seated problems in social sciences' (Bakewell, 2010: 1689), discussions tend to be either nonexistent or brief and partial in publications in which the two constructs are central (or are, in any case, lurking in the background). Where more attention is devoted to the topic, authors are generally forthcoming when it comes to defining agency, while showing no such disposition when it comes to structure. In practice, this means that it is fairly easy to find definitions like the following ones for agency, taken from social theory, anthropology and applied linguistics, respectively:

> the ability to take action in the light of a conscious assessment of the circumstances. (Layder, 1997: 35)

> the socioculturally mediated capacity to act. (Ahearn, 2001: 112)

> people's ability to make choices, take control, self-regulate, and thereby pursue their goals as individuals leading, potentially, to personal or social transformation. (Duff, 2012: 414)

Meanwhile, there is often a total absence of anything along these lines with reference to structure. Indeed, when writing about the topic recently (Block, 2013), I relied on work dating back some two decades, embedded in a recent article by Blakewell (2010):

> Structure operates in social scientific discourse as a powerful metonymic device, identifying some part of a complex social reality as explaining the

whole. It is a word to conjure with in the social sciences. In fact, structure is less a precise concept than a kind of founding epistemic metaphor of social scientific – and scientific – discourse. (Sewell, 1992: 2)

As I have noted (Block, 2013), Sewell's words only go so far in helping us understand what structure is. Structure is described as a 'metonymic device', 'a kind of epistemic metaphor', 'complex' and as forming part of a bigger 'whole', but it remains unclear to the reader what exactly it is, because in essence, this is not a definition. This lack of clarity is not only characteristic of this particular publication and it may be considered symptomatic of the difficulties encountered by social scientists who might arrive at a reasonably clear understanding of agency, but find that structure proves to be a slippery notion. Something of an exception, Sealey and Carter (2004: 6–7) actually do provide a definition of structure, writing the following:

> [S]ociologists have employed the term in two senses: to refer to normative institutions (the legal system, ideological system and so on) and to relational groupings (capitalist and proletariat, for example). Relational structures and institutional structures are connected but distinct aspects of structure and irreducible each to the other. ... structures are always 'macro' features of society, which persist over time; however, for some ...., the term refers primarily to social institutions – such as the economy, schooling and so forth – while for others the emphasis is on social relations such as employer – employee, teacher–pupil and so on.

This breakdown of structure into two categories – normative institutions and relational groupings – is based on a discussion by Lopez and Scott (2000). Missing here, however, is a third type of structure which the latter authors introduce: *embodied structure*. Adding embodied structure to his examination of structure in the social sciences, Elder-Vass describes what is, in effect, a three-part model:

> *institutional structure* [which] is comprised by the cultural or normative expectations that guide agents' relations with each other. ...
>
> *relational structure* [which] is composed of social relations themselves – causal interconnections and interdependences between agents. ...
>
> *embodied structure* [which] play[s] a key role in reconciling and integrating the earlier institutional and relational views. (Elder-Vass, 2008: 281)

However, as an antecedent to this three-part model, it is worthwhile to posit a still larger social structure that both precedes and shapes the *institutional*, the *relational structure* and the *embodied*. If we adopt a Marxist understanding of societies and how they work (and indeed, how the world works), we see such larger social structure as being about the base and superstructure of societies. Foundational to this approach is the following oft-cited statement from the preface of *A Contribution to the Critique of Political Economy*:

> In the social production of their existence, men inevitably enter into defi-
> nite relations, which are independent of their will, namely relations of
> production appropriate to a given stage in the development of their mate-
> rial forces of production. The totality of these relations of production
> constitutes the economic structure of society, the real foundation, on
> which arises a legal and political superstructure and to which correspond
> definite forms of social consciousness. The mode of production of mate-
> rial life conditions the general process of social, political and intellectual
> life. (Marx, 1904: 11–12)

With these words, Marx introduces the notion of base and superstructure as the ultimate in *structuring structures* (as Bourdieu might put it). In Marxist scholarship, the base of a society is economic and it is constituted by the means and processes of production. The latter can be understood as the activity engaged in to satisfy basic needs in society, such as food cultivation, factory-based commodity production and the construction of housing. Crucially, production engenders particular social relations, that is, modes of interaction among individuals (e.g. the institutional structures cited above). For example, in a feudal, rural, agrarian economy, production was organized around the control over arable land and the exploitation of those who worked it. From this system, particular social groups emerged: the landed nobility/ ruling class, the clerics, the vassal class and the peasant class. In contrast, a later stage of development in societies, capitalism, meant, among other things, the advent of industrial production and the urban, factory-based economy. The latter, in turn, led to the rise of two inherently antagonistic classes (the bourgeoisie and the proletariat), tensions between these two classes owing to the exploitation of the latter by the former (the inherent contradictions of capitalism) and an entirely different set of social relations from those that characterized feudalism. In general terms, then, the social relations arising from production serve as the foundation for the superstruc- ture, that is, the 'social, political and intellectual life' of a society. Ultimately, they condition and shape the legal and political structures that constitute the state. The state therefore emerges as a contingent structure that both depends on and reflects how production is organized. The same can be said of the *institutional structures* cited above.

Finally, although it is not always included in discussions of structure, the physical environment is arguably another type of structure to be considered, for there can be little doubt that the spaces within which we are confined and within which we move, to say nothing of the physical objects that we encounter on a moment-to-moment basis, act as *structuring* elements in our lives. There is, by now, a line of research in applied linguistics that focuses on notions such as landscapes, scales and space (Blommaert, 2010; Collins *et al.*, 2009; Shohamy & Gorter, 2008), mobile language and cultural practices (Canagarajah, 2013; Pennycook, 2012) and displacement (e.g. Baynham & de Fina, 2005). What all of these publications have in common is that they treat physical locations and physical objects as part and parcel of a larger multimodality, which is central to all communication, and of which language is just one component. In one way or another, they are all about physical locations and physical objects as shapers of language and other semiotic practices.

Drawing on the discussion thus far, I suggest a model of structure that looks as follows:

(5)   Sociocultural configurations which emerge in the ongoing interactions among individuals acting collectively in social formations, for example, fields (Bourdieu, 1984), communities of practice (Lave & Wenger, 1991), etc.

(4)   Psychologically based, embodied dispositional formations, such as Bourdieu's (1977) *habitus* or Layder's (2006) *psychobiography* or Lahire's (2011) 'embodied, individualised folds of the social', which act as internalized structuring structures.

(3)   More concrete organizations and institutions (such as religion, education, employment and family), and the abstract, discursive and concrete, material constraints which they impose on thought and behavior.

(2)   The physical environment (including geographical terrain, neighborhood, furniture and other physical objects).

(1)   The material, economic bases of societies and the legal, political superstructure emerging from this economic base (Marx, 1904).

Economic structure (realm 1), physical structure (realm 2), social structure (realm 3) and psychological/embodied structure (realm 4) all have 'anteriority': they have an existence prior to the exercise of agency and therefore in language and identity research there needs to be some attempt to understand how they interrelate with agency (as well as how they interrelate with one another). Otherwise, agency – as the exercise of intentionality, as self-conscious activity, as any number of aspects of individual subjectivity – may be understood to exist in a vacuum. In this case, it would also have no grounding when it comes to life in realm 5, the more immediate and spontaneous interactions in our lives.

A common version of events in applied linguistics is that social structure has traditionally been afforded far too much importance, as the determiner (using strong language) or shaper (using more moderate language) of individuals' life trajectories. As a result, there has been a concerted effort to redress this perceived imbalance by granting far more importance to agency in research. For example, in the following quote, de Fina, Schiffrin and Bamberg (2006b: 7) acknowledge that social structures serve to position individuals but then make clear that individuals may choose how they proceed in life:

> On the one hand, historical, sociocultural forces in the form of dominant discourses or master narratives position speakers in their situated practices and construct who they are without their agentive involvement. On the other hand, speakers position themselves as constructive and interactive agents and choose the means by which they construct their identities vis-à-vis others as well as vis-à-vis dominant discourse and master narratives.

However, if I examine individual publications based on empirical studies in which the relationship between language and identity is central (e.g. publications in applied linguistics journals and edited collections such as Caldas-Coulthard & Iedema, 2008; de Fina *et al.*, 2006a; Lin, 2008; Higgins, 2012; Nunan & Choi, 2010), I detect, on the whole, a tendency to grant much more weight to agency than to structure in accounts of how individuals make their way through social worlds. A good example of this tendency can be found in my 2006 book *Multilingual Identities in a Global City: London Stories*, which contains case studies of people from various national backgrounds (e.g. Japanese, French, Colombian), based heavily on life story interviews. There is a lot of self-citation ('I') in the data that I draw on, and although there is some acknowledgment of structural constraints on individual actions, the general tone is what I would now call 'over-agentive'. The following quote from one of my French informants, followed by my commentary, is fairly typical of what I wrote in this book:

> When I go shopping ... I have a different ... trolley to the people. I have a FRENCH trolley (laughing) I don't have any of these big drinks, weird colour drinks or this big burger bread and stuff. ... there's the way of cooking and the 'aperitif' that I still do every time when I have a friend at home. I drink wine very often ... So I've got this typical French culture thing [but] it is mainly in food ... (Lise, 23 November 2001)

> As Paul du Gay notes, 'commodities ... have importance as signs and symbols' that is, 'they have "identity value" and not simply or primarily "use value"' (Du Gay, 1996: 82). Here Lise tells us about who she is by telling us that she has a 'French trolley' as opposed to an English one, which I presume would have 'weird colour drinks' and 'big burger bread'. She also extends her shopping habits to her cooking and eating habits, citing the 'aperitif' and the drinking of wine as quintessentially French, and presumably, not an English custom. Thus, there is a semiotics of food consumption, involving what is bought and how it is consumed, that Lise invokes here to position herself as French. (Block, 2006: 117)

There is evidence here that, in her interaction with me, Lise is intent on constructing herself as a particular type of person. Within the interaction, she draws on sociocultural phenomena (e.g. what she eats and how) that allow her to position herself as someone who is both conscious of and keen to maintain a 'French identity'. Her 'French trolley' in a London supermarket thus marks her as different from English people and as distinctly French. In my comments about Lise, and indeed in the book in general, I would say that I tend to present the stories of my informants as triumphs of the individual over circumstances.

My point in citing this example is that, although there is often in publications the aforementioned notion that structure is afforded more importance than agency, the contrary has come to be the case. Whether this is an example of the pendulum swinging too far in one direction in an attempt to compensate for past wrongs, the basic reality today is that language and identity research has, if anything, become over-agentive. In my view, one of the chief reasons for this trend is that applied linguists has followed lines of thought emerging from work on social theory, sociology and anthropology that have experienced a shift away from a concern with larger social structures to an interest in the individual agent. Critiquing contemporary sociology, Alain Touraine frames this shift as necessary in the face of the progressive weakening of traditions and stable cultures that have accompanied the complexification of contemporary societies:

> Were a majority of sociologists to continue to support the old representation of social life and the complementary theme of social determination, sociology itself would lose its vigour and perhaps life, for what must be undertaken as a matter of urgency is the study of actors, their relations, conflicts and negotiations. (Touraine, 2006: 89)

In addition, in society at large there has been a certain elevation of the individual over the collective that has become pervasive in late modern societies over the past three decades, a development described relatively early on by Anthony Giddens (1991) in his landmark *Modernity and Self-identity*. It is to the topic of individualization that I now turn.

Individualization

As a way into my discussion of individualization, I take a selective historical journey through ways in which the interrelationship between individual and society has been framed over the years. I start with Karl Marx:

> Society does not consist of individuals, but expresses the sum of interrelations, the relations within which these individuals stand. (Marx, 1973: 265)

These words are taken from *Grundrisse*, where Marx outlined in detail many of the ideas that would appear in more refined form in *Capital 1*. In this sentence, he articulates succinctly the idea that society exists and that it is constituted not by autonomous individuals, but by the practices in which individuals and collectives engage. Many years later, Ayn Rand, a fervent defender of capitalism and the ethos of individualism associated with it, directly contradicted Marx, rejecting the notion that there is anything significant beyond the individual:

> 'The common good' (or 'the public interest') is an undefined and unde-finable concept: there is no such entity as 'the tribe' or 'the public'; the tribe (or the public or society) is only a number of individual men. (Rand, 1967: 20)

Some years later, Margaret Thatcher adopted this individualistic ethos fully as she set out to transform Britain into a society of individuals. She did so while denying the very existence of society, as we see in the following excerpt from a 1987 radio interview:

> I think we have gone through a period when too many children and people have been given to understand 'I have a problem, it is the Government's job to cope with it!' or 'I have a problem, I will go and get a grant to cope with it!' 'I am homeless, the Government must house me!' and so they are casting their problems on society and who is soci-ety? There is no such thing! There are individual men and women and there are families and no government can do anything except through people and people look to themselves first ... There is no such thing as society. There is a living tapestry of men and women and people and the beauty of that tapestry and the quality of our lives will depend upon how much each of us is prepared to take responsibility for ourselves and each of us prepared to turn round and help by our own efforts those who are unfortunate. (Thatcher, 1987)

Moving nearer to the present, we come to the work of David Harvey and his incisive critique of the neoliberal policies and practices which Thatcher and many others in her wake have so enthusiastically embraced over the past 30+ years. In the following quote, Harvey describes the connections between neoliberalism and individualism, in particular the rise of discourses around the individual that have become so pervasive around the world in recent years:

> Neoliberalism is in the first instance a theory of political economic prac-tices that proposes that human well-being can best be advanced by lib-erating individual entrepreneurial freedoms and skills within an

institutional framework characterized by strong private property rights, free markets and free trade. (Harvey, 2005: 2)

In this collection of quotes, we see a move from Marx's notion of society as the sum of the interrelations of individuals in all ambits of their lives to society as a loose collection of individuals acting in relative isolation, to Harvey's linking of neoliberalism to the rise of individualism. Elsewhere, Elliott and Lemert (2006: 15) have written about the increasing ubiquity and pervasiveness of what they call 'the individualist creed of the new individualism' in both the private and public spheres of society. For these authors, individualism is a phenomenon in expansion, riding history on the way to virtual universality. However, this potential universality is mitigated by the fact that true individualism is the privilege of the wealthy nations far more than the less wealthy nations, and the wealthy within single nations more than their poorer fellow citizens. Following a similar line of thinking in his discussion of individualization as a key characteristic of late modernity, Beck provides more detail about how individuals today (and above all, he means individuals in the wealthier parts of the world) are less constrained by social structures than they perhaps once were in more traditional societies. He explains:

> Individualization ... means that each person's biography is removed from given determinations and placed in his or her own hands, open and dependent on decisions. The proportion of life opportunities which are fundamentally closed to decision-making is decreasing and the proportion of biography which is open and must be constructed personally is increasing. (Beck, 1992: 135)

This notion of an individual's biography increasingly dependent on the same individual's decisions has penetrated many corners of the social sciences, in particular where narrative research has become pervasive. The so-called narrative turn in the social sciences (Bruner, 1986; Clandinin, 2007) is nothing if not a turn to individuals and their personal life trajectories and a move away from bigger narratives around macro-level social structures such as the economy and society. Culture, once regarded in a monolithic manner, is now commonly presented as a processual, inchoate and ever-emergent phenomenon (Baumann, 1999). Eschewing the monolithic position is, to be sure, no loss to serious scholarship; however, moving too far in the opposite direction, where culture seemingly has no history, no memory and no structure, is not the best (nor the only) solution. In the end, the virtual abandonment of structure in discussions of identity and the telling of life stories with only a passing reference to possible constraints and issues of power is highly problematic. Thus, while most language and identity researchers actually do acknowledge that individuals are not islands, operating solely on their own volition, they do not back this notion up with any careful or sustained consideration of what structures are, how they might be important and how they work as constraints on and shapers of agency. One big problem, and perhaps the key contributing factor to this state of affairs, is the philosophical base from which so many researchers are working. We might call this base poststructuralist, although quite often this is not made explicit. I now turn to consider a challenge to this way of framing research on language and identity.

The Critical Realist Challenge

If we take on board the previous discussions of structure and agency and individualization, in which it was argued that there is a need to take structure more seriously than is currently the case and to problematize individualization, respectively, we also find that there is a need to rethink how we position ourselves according to two key metaphysical dimensions of our activity as researchers and scholars. On the one hand, there is ontology, or the 'actual reality' that we are researching and writing about; on the other hand there is epistemology, or the origin, the nature and limits of human knowledge and the methods we adopt to obtain this knowledge. In simple terms, we need to consider what it is that we want to know about and how we might come to know about it. In his work on issues around ontology and epistemology, Roy Bhaskar (2002) has identified problems with what he calls 'postmodernism', but which I would term 'poststructuralism'. The latter, as the epistemological position of choice in language and identity research in applied linguistics, has been defined in recent work on identity as:

> an approach to research that questions fixed categories or structures, oppositional binaries, closed systems, and stable truths and embraces seeming contradictions . . . . Poststructural researchers examine how such categories are discursively and socially constructed, taken up, resisted (the site of struggle), and so on. (Duff, 2012: 412)

For Bhaskar, postmodernism/poststructuralism is an epistemological approach to the study of reality which, among other things, primes difference, relativity and pluralism and in general celebrates diversity; views life as a pastiche, a collection of experiences, as opposed to a coherent whole; defines the object of research (its ontology) as discursively constructed, eschewing the idea that there is a material reality out there to be taken on board; shows skepticism about, and even a denial of, the necessity to make reference to the 'real' world; and often involves judgmental relativism, according to which it is impossible to provide a rationale for adopting one belief or action or practice over another.

Not all poststructuralist researchers in applied linguistics necessarily sub-scribe to Bhaskar's version of postmodernism/poststructuralism. However, as we see in Duff's observation about poststructuralism above, language and identity researchers have tended to emphasize difference, relativity and plu-ralism over sameness, the absolute and homogeneity. They have framed iden-tity as pastiche as opposed to something whole or integral and they have, as has already been suggested, primed individual agency over social structure. They have portrayed reality as discursively constructed (with language and culture being an integral part of this view) and they have marginalized the material, avoiding pronouncements about how the world 'really is'. For Bhaskar, all of this is fine if not taken to the extreme that there is nothing beyond the most immediate interaction of individuals and their interpreta-tions and constructions of events and activities in their lives. As he puts it:

> Critical realism is very sympathetic to the politics of identity and differ-ence. Where it takes exception is in suggesting that what postmodernists have done is thrown out the baby of unity with the bathwater of abstract universality. (Bhaskar, 2002: 223)

As an antidote to this state of affairs, he proposes a critical realist perspec-tive. This perspective aims to 'put ontology back on the map and critique ... the idea that [researchers can] reduce being to knowledge' (Bhaskar, 2002: 209). The latter idea is prevalent, for example, in research that frames reality as 'discursively constructed', that is, as existing only in the means through which it is made available to the observer. Taking such a position constitutes what Bhaskar calls the 'epistemic fallacy':

> This consists in the view that statements about being can be reduced to or analysed in terms of statements about knowledge; i.e. that ontological questions can always be analysed in terms of our knowledge of being, that it is sufficient for philosophy to 'treat only of the network, and not what the network describes' [Wittgenstein, 1961: 6.35]. (Bhaskar, 1975: 36)

About the positivist tradition, he writes that it is 'correct to stress that there are causal laws, generalities, at work in social life ... [and] to insist ... that these laws *may* be opaque to the agents' spontaneous understanding' (Bhaskar, 1998: 21). In contrast, he believes that the positivist tradition gets matters wrong when it reduces these laws to empirical regularities, that is, the sys-tematic co-presence of natural and social phenomena and states. For example, the arrival of a large number of migrants from a particular country may coin-cide with a rise in the crime rate in the host community, the assumption being that the presence of these new arrivals and high crime rates are in a cause-and-effect relationship owing to a law of nature. However, there may be many other factors at work, such as the amount of work available for the newcomers when they arrive, the degree to which they are welcome, the type of policing that takes place, and so on. The complexity of such situations acts against attempts to impose easy, shorthand interpretations based on regularities. For this reason, Bhaskar writes that the human sciences (i.e. the social sciences) are about 'the direct study of phenomena that only ever manifest themselves in open systems [in which] invariant empirical regularities do not obtain' (Bhaskar, 1998: 45) and which are 'characterised by both a plurality and multiplicity of causes' (Bhaskar, 1998: 87). All of this makes accurate prediction, a hallmark of positivist research, practically impossible. In addition, social phenomena cannot be accessed at the level at which they are generated, in isolation from the effects which they have, as is the case with some physical phenomena. Thus, if we conduct an ethnography of migrant children coming to terms with English-medium instruction in primary schools in London, we focus on the effects of teaching and learning, that is, phenomena that we can capture via observation, interviews, conversation recording and so. We then move to posit, as causants, social structures that we can imagine and argue for, but which we cannot 'really' access.

As regards what he calls the 'hermeneutic tradition' (but which others would call an interpretivist or social constructivist perspective), Bhaskar writes that it 'is correct to point out that the social sciences deal with pre-interpreted reality, a reality already brought under concepts by social actors' (Bhaskar, 1998: 21). This means that the kind of reality grasped and studied by social scientists, such as the previously cited child and adolescent migrant experience in London schools, has already been grasped by human beings and has passed through their interpretation of it. This occurs because social phenomena are, in the end, the outcome of human activity. In contrast, where the hermeneutic (or interpretivist/social constructivist) tradition goes somewhat wrong is in the conflation of the inability to *show* that social reality exists with social reality itself. To put it another way, in this tradition, there is a tendency to reduce ontology (actual reality, what we want to know about) to epistemology (human knowledge, what we know), the above cited 'epistemic fallacy'. For Bhaskar, the epistemic fallacy is a major error because 'statements about being cannot be reduced to or analysed in terms of statements about knowledge ... [and] ontological questions cannot always be transposed into epistemological terms' (Bhaskar, 1989: 17–18).

Bhaskar's search for a third way through the tensions that arise at the intersection of ontology and epistemology leads him to critical realism, a position he describes as follows:

> What critical realism says is that there is no inconsistency between being an ontological realist ... believing that there is a real world which consists in structures, generative mechanisms, all sorts of complex things and totalities which exist and act independently of the scientist, which the scientist can come to have knowledge of ... [and] saying that that

knowledge is itself socially produced; it is a geo-historically specific social process, so it is continually in transformation in what I call the epistemological, transitive or social dimension for our understanding of science. (Bhaskar, 2002: 211)

Being a critical realist thus means being a realist with regard to ontology (it is intransitive, existing independently of the activity of individuals) and a relativist with regard to epistemology (research and theoretical work are transitive, in that scientific experience changes along with conceptions of the studied world). It also entails a third shift in thinking, to 'judgmental rationalism', which means embracing the notion that 'even though science is a social process and that we know views and opinions change through time, at any one moment of time there will be better or worse grounds for preferring one rather than another theory' (Bhaskar, 2002: 211–212). On a more prosaic level, judgmental rationalism is what allows us to take action in our day-to-day lives. It contrasts with judgmental relativism, which means the inability to take sides in any situation of choosing alternatives because we cannot find better or worse grounds for preferring one theory or explanation for events over another. With judgmental rationalism it is possible to take action, for example engaging in advocacy on behalf of the less fortunate in society, while with judgmental relativism, taking any action is difficult, if not impossible.

What does all of this Mean in Terms of Agency in Language and Identity Research?

I would like to end this chapter by offering a way forward based on the previous discussion of structure and agency, individualization and critical realism. I will do so by examining data collected some years ago in contacts with middle-class migrants from East Asia who were enrolled as full-time students on year-long MA level programs in London. In this research, I conducted relatively informal life-story interviews, during which I elicited from my informants accounts of their contacts with languages in their lives. This meant asking about their first awareness that languages existed, their first experience with a language other than their L1 (which meant English in most cases) and subsequently their development as English language users with an identity as such. What follows is a section from notes that I wrote based on an interview with an informant named Mei (a pseudonym). Mei was a 28-year-old English teacher from Japan who was attending an MA TESOL course in London during the 2001–2002 academic year. These notes were written shortly after the interview took place, in June 2002, and it was my intention at the time that a more refined version of them would appear in publications that I was preparing at the time on the topic of migrants in

London (e.g. Block, 2006). However, in the end, Mei's case did not make it into any publications. Below, I present the notes in edited form, having made minor changes to the text for the purposes of this chapter. The notes are interspersed with transcribed excerpts from the interview. Transcription conventions for these excerpts can be found in Appendix 1.

Mei's story

As regards contact with English, the main focus of our interview, I learned that Mei began studying English at the age of 10. While she reports that she was not particularly taken by English at the beginning, this all changed when at the age of 17, she made a trip to Australia. This was then that she realised the potential of English as a means of communicating with people from different backgrounds.

Mei also spent some time in California two years after her Australian sojourn, but it was not until she lived abroad for an extended period of time that she discovered her cosmopolitanism and her effective displacement from a mono-cultural sense of self. This happened when at the age of 20 she came to Britain on her Japanese university's study abroad program to study at a Winnington University (a pseudonym) for one year.

During the earlier stays in Australia and California, she had come to feel more liberated when speaking English. She said the following about her American experience:

Excerpt 1

I don't have to be / I would say/obedient in the states / I kind of / I felt I had at the time / even if I had some of my own opinions inside me / I felt I shouldn't express everything in front of the people / when I was in Japan / but when I was in the States / I started to express more and more / not the daily things / but the opinions / I think that's because in Japan / maybe as you know / females (.5) there is a notion the female should behave like a female / so I think I felt the pressure in Japan / (.5) and I realised that I am not a very typical Japanese female / because I tend to have a strong opinion / I tend to express that kind of thing overtly / and some people didn't like that / so I felt sometimes very (.5) unhappy with that / but in the states / I felt like I can say what I think / and the people take it in a very natural way / so I think in that sense I felt comfortable with that /. (Mei, 11 June 2002)

As for her year-long stay in Britain, she reports that she socialised with Japanese and other overseas students but very few British nationals. Nevertheless, she further developed an assertiveness that she associated with becoming 'westernised'. When she returned to Japan, she encountered gender bias when job hunting, experiencing what she termed a 'very big reverse cultural shock'. This led her to develop what she called an 'anti-Japanese' attitude. She explains the situation as follows:

Excerpt 2

my crisis was after going to Japan / I think after one year in Britain / I had to do the Japan thing / that was the most difficult part / because I kind of became / kind of became westernised / so I expect / you know / my way of thinking / and what I think abruptly / not strongly / but strongly for a Japanese / I think / and then Japanese men / especially older men / don't like that / so I still remember that I went to a kind of job interview / and they asked me some questions like this / and he kind of asked / *what is most important for you in the job?* / and I said something like / *first of all I need to be brave enough to challenge or try out new things* / and he started to laugh / and he said to me / *oh I think all I expect from female students is just smiling every day* (.5) or something like that /. (Mei, 11 June 2002)

Despite such negative experiences, Mei decided to stay in Japan and find her own way. She explains:

Excerpt 3

I tried to pursue so-called Japanese-ness when I was working / because I didn't want to be seen as a westernised lady / I wanted to be a Japanese / I wanted to understand how Japanese feel / I was Japanese / but I kind of felt some people see / regard me / simply because I studied in Britain for a year / some people (.5) think I'm very westernised (.5) and I didn't want to be seen like that / so I tried to behave Japanese>laughing<more than the normal Japanese / I think / my dress and that kind of thing /. (Mei, 11 June 2002)

Still, she seems unable to take on board the notion that she will never be a mainstream Japanese person, that there is some kind of third-place, cosmopolitan identity that will always be present inside her:

Excerpt 4

if I imagine that I go back to Japan / and get married / children and that kind of thing / I imagine that I will become / I will (.5) start to feel a bit bored / and I may / may (.5) go out from Japan again / so every time if I go one place / I miss something which I can't / what I can't have in that place / if I am here / I / strangely / miss Japan a lot / and I feel my Japanese identity more / but when I go back to Japan / I feel I'm different from mainstream Japanese / that's why I feel very uneasy to do things /. (Mei, 11 June 2002)

Had I managed to find somewhere to publish Mei's case in an article or book over 10 years ago, I would probably have treated her accounts of her experiences as a prime example of someone showing the 'ability to make choices, take control, self-regulate, and thereby pursue ... goals as [an] individual ... leading, potentially, to personal ... transformation' (Duff, 2012: 414), that is, as an active agent in the unfolding of her life narrative. I would have pinpointed the main constraint on her behavior mentioned here, Japanese gender hierarchies, but for the most part, I would have remained at the level of Mei as an individual agent acting in a way that was tempered only slightly by a kind of *structure light*. In this sense I would have treated what Mei said as her construction of herself in response to my questions about who she was. As for the ontological status of her words, I would have made reference to discursive regimes on which she had drawn in her self-positioning. However, crucially, my interpretation would have been about Mei, telling me about how she makes her way through life, who she is, how she is in control of who she is and so on.

Such an approach to Mei's story is all very well as far as it goes. However, what of the model of structure presented above, which moved from the economic base of society to interactions emergent in day-to-day activity, with physical objects and spatial elements, institutions and psychological dispositions derived from socialization processes standing in between? First off, we need to situate Mei's mobility in the context of post-1980s Japan and the internationalization of Japanese business and industry and the rapid increase in its citizens' mobility. Japan is not unique in the world in having internationalization embedded in policies at all levels of society. However, it certainly was something of a pioneer when it moved to the *glocalization* of its business model 1980s, marketing goods and services on a global basis by catering to local particularities (Robertson, 1995), and when it started outreach, internationalizing schemes like the Japanese Exchange and Teaching (JET) Programme. The latter was founded in 1987 by various government ministries with the expressed purpose of 'increasing mutual understanding between the people of Japan and the people of other nations ... [and] to promote internationalization in Japan's local communities by helping to improve foreign language education and developing international exchange at the community level' (JET Programme, n.d.).

Such events took place against the backdrop of Japan's arrival as the third most powerful economy in the world in terms of gross domestic product and prosperity for a large proportion of the population. As I note elsewhere (Block, 2006), from the 1980s onwards, there was a marked increase in the number of Japanese nationals going abroad, not only as tourists, but also as families in which the breadwinner takes up an overseas assignment and as students doing all or a part of their university studies abroad. Therefore, in order to understand Mei's story, we need to see economic deep-structuring at work, whereby the rise of Japan as an economic powerhouse is deep down a shaping and indeed determining factor at the super-structural level of widening prosperity, making travel abroad for tourism, business and study more possible than it had ever been in the past for Japanese nationals. Mei would not have been in London in 2002, talking to me about who she was, had it not been for these developments.

Still, more local discursive regimes deriving from the economic base and social history of Japanese society, such as its discourses of national identity and gender, along with more concrete institutions such as the family and the world of employment, perhaps had not evolved as much as they might have when Mei was moving around the world and looking for a job at the turn of the 21st century (see Itoh, 2000, for an interesting discussion of the resiliency of tradition in the face of economic and social change in Japan). Once again these structures acted as shaping factors in her ongoing narrative. In all four excerpts, but especially in Excerpt 1, Mei makes reference to gendered regimes both inside and outside of Japan, not only how she sees herself fitting into them, but also how they either facilitate or constrain her activity and her behavior. These gendered regimes become conflated with nationalist discourses in Japan, as being Western has both anti-Japanese and anti-Japanese woman connotations. At the family level, Mei reports having encountered resistance to her 'westernised' assertiveness, with the aforementioned national and gendered connotations in the background. She presents herself as conflicted, caught between being a good daughter (being a Japanese woman in a particular way) and her desire to break free of all constraints on her actions. Finally, in the world of employment, she claims to have encountered discriminatory hiring practices, which she understands to be about (older) male domination (Excerpt 2). However, what she describes might be seen as central to the Japanese class system, which is highly resistant to change and which guarantees its own reproduction through particular hiring practices. Ishida and Slater (2010: 19–20) describe matters in Japan as follows:

> Perspective employees self-select the position for which they apply based not only on their qualifications and credentials but also their beliefs about whether it is a good match in terms of dispositions, lifestyles, and demographic attributes ... The selection mechanism thus generates institutional closure by assuring that members of the same class group share not only cognitive traits that may be directly relevant to productivity but also non-cognitive and demographic attributes. The sorting of individuals in this way ensures class closure while the institutionalization of credentials legitimates this selection process.

From her description of events in the interview, it seems that Mei did not take into account such machinations going on behind the scenes of her job interview. In a sense, there were social structures at work, far beyond her ability to transform them, and off her radar at the time, which nonetheless shaped her behavior, her job interviewer's behavior and the outcome of the job interview.

I do not have data that would inform me about how the physical environment and ongoing interactions acted as structuring structures in her life, and I would be hard put to posit much in the way of Mei's habitus, although I do have some information about her embodied behavior when she talks about how her assertiveness acquired through English became incorporated into her repertoire when engaging in Japanese-mediated interactions. In short, there is a lot of work to be done in bringing structure more to the fore in Mei's case and I will have to confess that it would be difficult for me to provide anything like a complete case study for her now, so many years later. As I suggested above, I could take Mei at her word, following the story produced in the interview, and in so doing I could portray her as a free agent (or indeed, a free spirit), making her way through life against whatever obstacles might arise (such as a male chauvinist boss). However, to do so would be to provide a rendering of Mei's story relatively devoid of attention to structure. As I have argued here, this would be a partial – and as such, incomplete – way of going about narrative-based language and identity research. Some years ago, in 'The society of individuals', Norbert Elias (1991: 3) wrote the following:

> [Society] only exists because a large number people exist, it only continues to function because many individual people want and do certain things, yet its structure, its great historical transformations, clearly do not depend on the intentions of particular people.

Elias was writing about the relationship between society and the individual, but what he outlines here also applies for structure and agency and is consistent with Bhaskar's critical realist version of social realities discussed above. Elias's words are also a reminder of how complex social realities are and how we need to avoid Manichean articulations of the issue, the 'half-learned opposition' so disparaged by Bourdieu (2000: 156) in the quote that opened this chapter. Indeed, there is no opposition here; rather there is a constant movement back and forth (see Bourdieu, 1977; but also Giddens, 1984). It is incumbent on those of us who research identity, captured *in situ* and as part of the on-going flux and flow of life, to follow this movement while bearing in mind that all is not on the surface, all is not in the here-and-now, and all is not about the individual and his/her agency.

Appendix 1: Transcription Conventions

/	Indicates the minimal but clear pause between phrases/sentences in normally paced speech.
(.5)	Indicates pause of half a second.
(1)	Indicates pause of one second.

?	Indicates rising intonation (including questions).
Underlining	Words said with emphasis.
italics	Indicates the voicing of self or others, verbatim quoting of self or others when relating past or present events.
>xxx<	Comments describing aspects of extra-linguistic communication, such as voice inflection, laughter, facial expressions, gaze, hand movements, etc.

References

Ahearn, L. (2001) Language and agency. *Annual Review of Anthropology* 30, 109–137.

Bakewell, O. (2010) Some reflections on structure and agency in migration theory. *Journal of Ethnic and Migration Studies* 36 (10), 1689–1708.

Baumann, G. (1999) *The Multicultural Riddle: Rethinking National, Ethnic and Religious Identities*. London: Routledge.

Baynham, M. and de Fina, A. (eds) (2005) *Dislocations/Relocations: Narratives of Displacement*. Manchester: St Jerome Press.

Beck, U. (1992) *The Risk Society*. London: Sage.

Bhaskar, R. (1975) *A Realist Theory of Science*. Leeds: Leeds Books.

Bhaskar, R. (1989) *Reclaiming Reality*. London: Verso.

Bhaskar, R. (1998) *The Possibility of Naturalism* (3rd edn). London: Routledge.

Bhaskar, R. (2002) *From Science to Emancipation: Alienation and the Actuality of Enlightenment*. London: Sage.

Block, D. (2006) *Multilingual Identities in a Global City: London Stories*. London: Palgrave.

Block, D. (2009) Identity in applied linguistics: The need for conceptual exploration. In W. Li and V. Cook (eds) *Contemporary Applied Linguistics*, Vol. 1 (pp. 215–232). London: Continuum.

Block, D. (2012) Unpicking agency in sociolinguistic research with migrants. In M. Martin-Jones and S. Gardner (eds) *Multilingualism, Discourse and Ethnography* (pp. 47–60). London: Routledge.

Block, D. (2013) The structure and agency dilemma in identity and intercultural communication research. *Language and Intercultural Communication* 13, 126–147.

Blommaert, J. (2010) *The Sociolinguistics of Globalization*. Cambridge: Cambridge University Press.

Bourdieu, P. (1977) *Outline of a Theory of Practice*. Cambridge: Cambridge University Press.

Bourdieu, P. (1984) *Distinction*, London: Routledge.

Bourdieu, P. (2000) *Pascalian Meditations*. Stanford: Stanford University Press.

Bruner, J. (1986) *Actual Minds, Possible Worlds*. Cambridge: Harvard University Press.

Caldas-Coulthard, C.R. and Iedema, R. (eds) (2008) *Identity Trouble: Critical Discourse and Contested Identities*. London: Palgrave.

Canagarajah, S. (2013) *Translingual Practice: Global Englishes and Cosmopolitan Relations*. London: Routledge.

Clandinin, J. (ed.) (2007) *Handbook of Narrative Inquiry: Mapping a Methodology*. London: Sage.

Collins, J., Slembrouck, S. and Baynham, M. (eds) (2009) *Globalization and Language in Contact: Scale, Migration, and Communicative Practices*, London: Continuum.

De Fina, A., Schiffrin, D., and Bamberg, M. (eds) (2006) *Discourse and Identity*. Cambridge: Cambridge University Press.

Duff, P. (2012) Issues of identity. In A. Mackey and S. Gass (eds) *The Routledge Handbook of Second Language Acquisition* (pp. 410–426). London: Routledge.

Du Gay, P. (1996) *Consumption and Identity at Work*. London: Sage Publications.

Elder-Vass, D. (2008) Integrating institutional, relational, and embodied structure: An emergentist perspective. *British Journal of Sociology* 59 (2), 281–299.

Elias, N. (1991) The society of individuals. In N. Elias, *The Society of Individuals*. London: Continuum. [Originally published 1939.]

Elliott, A. and Lemert, C. (2006) *The New Individualism: The Emotional Costs of Globalization*, London: Routledge.

Giddens, A. (1984) *The Constitution of Society: Outline of the Theory of Structuration*. Berkeley: University of California Press.

Giddens, A. (1991) *Modernity and Self-identity: Self and Society in the Late Modern Age*. Cambridge: Polity.

Hall, D. (2004) *Subjectivity*. London: Routledge.

Harvey, D. (2005) *A Brief History of Neoliberalism*. Oxford: Oxford University Press.

Higgins, C. (ed.) (2012) *Identity formation in Globalizing Contexts: Language Learning in the New Millennium*. Berlin: Mouton de Gruyter.

Ishida, H. and Slater, D.H. (eds) (2010) Social class in Japan. *Social Class in Contemporary Japan* (pp. 1–29). London: Routledge.

Itoh, M. (2000) *Globalization of Japan: Japanese Sakoku Mentality and US Efforts to Open Japan*. London: Macmillan.

JET Programme (n.d.). http://www.jetprogramme.org (accessed 1 September 2013).

Lahire, H. (2011) *The Plural Actor*. Cambridge: Polity. [Originally published 2001.]

Lave, J. and Wenger, E. (1991) *Situated Learning: Legitimate Peripheral Participation*. Cambridge: Cambridge University Press.

Layder, D. (1997) *Modern Social Theory*. London: UCL Press.

Layder, D. (2006) *Understanding Social Theory*, (2nd edn). London: Sage.

Lin, A. (ed.) (2008) *Problematizing Identity*. Mahwah: Lawrence Erlbaum.

Lopez, J. and Scott, J. (2000) *Social Structure*. Buckingham: Open University Press.

Marx, K. (1904) *A Contribution to the Critique of Political Economy*. Chicago, IL: Charles H. Kerr. [Originally published 1859.]

Marx, K. (1973) *Grundrisse*. Harmondsworth: Penguin. [Originally published 1858.]

Nunan, D. and Choi, J. (eds) (2010) *Language and Culture: Reflective Narratives and the Emergence of Identity*. Cambridge: Cambridge University Press.

Pennycook, A. (2012) *Language and Mobility: Unexpected Places*. Clevedon: Multilingual Matters.

Rand, A. (1967) What is capitalism? In *Capitalism: The Unknown Ideal* (pp. 11–34). New York: Signet. [Originally published 1965.]

Robertson, R. (1995) Glocalization: Time–space and homogeniety–heterogenity. In M. Featherstone, S. Lash and R. Robertson (eds) *Global Modernities* (pp. 25–44). London: Sage.

Sealey, A. and Carter, B. (2004) *Applied Linguistics as Social Science*. London: Continuum.

Sewell, W.H. (1992) A theory of structure, duality, agency and transformation. *American Journal of Sociology* 98 (1), 1–29.

Shohamy, E. and Gorter, D. (eds) (2008) *Linguistic Landscape: Expanding the Scenery*. London: Routledge.

Thatcher, M. (1987) Interview 23 September 1987, quoted by Douglas Keay. *Women's Own*, 31 October, pp. 8–10.

Touraine, A. (2006) *A New Paradigm for Understanding Today's World*. Cambridge: Polity.

Wittgenstein, L. (1961) *Notebooks 1914–1916*. New York: Harper.

3 Dialogical View on Language Learners' Agency: Connecting Intrapersonal with Interpersonal

Hannele Dufva and Mari Aro

Dialogical Views on Agency: Theoretical Starting Points

This paper discusses the dialogical perspective of second/foreign language learners' agency drawing upon Bakhtin (1981, 1984, 1986, 1990, 2004) and Voloshinov (1973, 1976). Agency has been theorized and studied particularly within the Neo-Vygotskian, or sociocultural, point of view, and while the dialogical argument is often consistent with the sociocultural, we maintain that the dialogical perspective also adds to the understanding of agency (for a dialogical approach to language learners' agency, see Vitanova, 2005, 2010). Our view of agency is in accordance with Bakhtin (1986: 87), who urged concretism: to understand the quality of an act one needs to go beyond the *monological* perspective, that is, abstract and reductionist theoretical descriptions. This means going beyond abstractions and such Cartesian dichotomies as social vs individual, or mind vs body and admitting such actualities as *time, space* and *embodiment*. Similar views can also be found in contemporary discussions where human interactivity is analyzed as embodied and socially shared joint actions in which significance is given and meanings are negotiated (e.g. Cowley, 2009; Steffensen, 2013). From these starting points, we analyze agency as emergent in the dynamic, continually fluctuating 'eventing' in time and place.

Drawing on these approaches, our perspective is sociocognitive in nature. This approach contests the cognitivist paradigms of language learning research and the individualist conceptualizations therein. At the same time, the social orientations are judged as myopic as they frequently end up analyzing all individual aspects as mere social constructions. Against this backdrop, we regard agency as a dialogical, or relational, phenomenon that needs to be examined both as subjectively experienced and as collectively emergent, and to borrow Voloshinov's (1973) formulation, considering the incessant interplay between 'psyche' and 'ideology'. At the same time, the sociocognitive view does not exclude embodiment (Dufva, 2011): learners are not to be seen as 'social' and 'cognitive' agents *in abstracto*, but as real persons engaged in real interactions that involve experiences, emotions and values that characterize the particular situation and relationships therein (Thibault, 2011).

To understand and analyze how time and place are involved, we use Bakhtin's (1981) notion of *chronotope*, aiming at regarding the whole where the physical environment, community and dialogues intertwine with the individual's unique experience. According to Clark and Holquist (in Bakhtin, 1981: 279), the chronotope is a bridge between the mind and the world: it is the time–place where meanings are created, and which also connects the past and the present and looks into the future.

Thus, in order to understand agency we should be looking at its fluidity in time and space rather than seeing it as a steady state or a finished product. This view brings together two seemingly opposite ideas. On the one hand, agency is exposed to alteration and change, as it may change over time and also vary across situations. At the same time, agency cannot be genuinely understood without considering the continuity that is involved, that is, persons do not regard their own life-span as a sequence of discrete, random events but as an on-going narrative instead. In how persons see themselves and in how they author their past histories, there are semi-permanent and repeated elements, but on the other hand, new relationships and novel situations constantly challenge their stories and, at the same time, create opportunities for change.

Our analysis of agency is connected to our understanding of language usage and learning as a process in which linguistic resources are *recycled* (e.g. Dufva *et al.*, 2014) – a metaphor that resonates with Bakhtin's idea of appropriation. Because linguistic resources are always embedded with perspectives (Voloshinov, 1973: 70; Bakhtin, 1981), new users also come to recycle ideologies. However, as suggested by dialogical arguments, language learners do not simply duplicate words or ideologies. As Bakhtin (1981: 293–294) says, our words are borrowed from others and are 'half someone else's' – but only half. When 'populated with our own intention', they become appropriated; our own. Thus our own voice – and our own agency – emerges from the interplay between various factors. As learners, we all take words and ideologies from others: from parents, teachers and peers, but populate them with our own intention.

Agency in Second/Foreign Language Learning and Development: Adding Dialogical Overtones to the Discussion

Agency has been discussed fairly extensively, both in the context of language studies (see, e.g. Ahearn, 2001) and in the context of learning and education (e.g. Kumpulainen & Lipponen, 2010). In the field of second language learning in particular, agency has been studied from the Neo-Vygotskian points of view, such as cultural–historical activity theory (e.g. Sannino, 2010) and various socioculturally inspired approaches to language learning (e.g. Gao, 2010; Gao & Zhang, 2011; Lantolf & Thorne, 2006). This discussion suggests that agency comes close to such concepts as, for example, self-regulation, learner autonomy, L2 self, imagined self and also motivation (Breen, 2001; Dörnyei & Ushioda, 2009; Murray *et al.*, 2011).

In sociocultural approaches, the focus has been on socioculturally mediated agency: the agent as a user of sociocultural mediating means. While the dialogical and sociocultural approaches do seem to complement each other in their basic tenets regarding the individual and the social as well as in their view of development (appropriation of voices/other-regulation and self-regulation), they appear to deal with these matters on a slightly different level. As Sullivan and McCarthy (2004) pointed out, a sociocultural view of agency is suitable for studying how an individual makes use of cultural resources, gains power in a community or masters a means of mediation. According to Hicks (2000), the sociocultural approach is biased toward systems and activities rather than individuals and is less suitable for understanding small, personal stories. Therefore, it may miss the affective and emotional aspects of the agentive experience, that is, the viewpoint of the individual agent (Sullivan & McCarthy, 2004). The personally experienced and felt aspects of agency might be better tapped by using such data as language learners' interviews (Aro, 2009), learning histories (Kalaja *et al.*, 2008a) or visual means of self-expression (Kalaja *et al.*, 2008b).

While Sullivan and McCarthy (2004) agreed that cultural, social and historical contexts play a part in agency, they wished to emphasize the individual psychological dimension and suggested that the sociocultural view of agency be enriched with individual sensibility: felt, lived, expressed experience. A dialogically informed view of agency places a responsive individual at the center of the concept, examining how the individual feels and embodies agency (Sullivan & McCarthy, 2004). In addition to the individual's personal perspective and interpretations, feelings and emotions also necessarily come into play. Here, dialogical views can be associated with research on the role of emotion in motivation, language learning and multilingual language use (e.g. Pavlenko, 2006; Ushioda, 2009, 2011).

The shift in focus toward individual sensibility also adds an aspect of choice that is highly relevant for understanding agency. As Morson (1991: 217) put it, 'for Bakhtin it is ultimately people who choose, create and take responsibility'. When Bakhtin's (1990) notion of dialogue and the inevitable presence of the Other are added to the concept of agency, it is possible to discuss an individual's agency in terms of what other voices bring to it. As Sullivan and McCarthy (2004) argued, individuals have a choice over how they value events, Others and their ideological discourses, and so questions of ethics and morality – as well as power and authority – are brought into individual, subjective agency. This is also Marková's (1992) and Linell's (1998) viewpoint to dialogism: individuals are not to be seen as powerless marionettes at the mercy of the external forces. Agency thus becomes, both in actions and in voicework, an individual's choice and creation – not a given from the outside. However, agency will necessarily be influenced and affected by the voices and actions of Others.

Because agency is a relational phenomenon, one needs to take into account the presence of various asymmetries that either constrain or provide affordances for agentivity (e.g. Marková & Foppa, 1991). As individuals encounter various ideological discourses, they can choose to accept or not to accept the viewpoints – and ideological contents – of others. In Bakhtin's (1981) terms, these ideological contents can be dealt with in three ways: individuals can choose to appropriate words and contents that they feel are *internally persuasive* and begin to use them as their own; they can ignore viewpoints that they feel do not concern or interest them; or find that they are faced with *authoritative* views, ideologies and words of the authorities (moral, political, religious) which individuals must either totally affirm or totally reject. Authoritative content rests on a hierarchical differentiation between the power of the speakers and, in Bakhtin's (1981: 342) words, such content 'demands that we acknowledge it, that we make it our own; it binds us ...; we encounter it with its authority already fused in it'. Internally persuasive content invites contact and dialogue; in contrast, authoritative content must either be accepted or rejected totally.

In appropriating Others' words, language learners draw upon the words of various kinds of important Others, including family members, teachers and peers, and also various types of media (textbooks, popular culture), some of which are more authoritative than others. Thus language learners' agency develops in a dialogic interplay that involves power relationships and asymmetry, such as those between students and teachers, or native and non-native speakers. One potential endpoint of such development is *monologue*, a position that produces singularist and essentialist definitions, homogeneity in behavior, hegemonic discourses and dictates. Yet as Bakhtin (1984: 81) indicated, truth is born in contact, at the borderline of consciousnesses; thus in order to find one's own voice, one needs the presence of other voices, not necessarily to be obeyed, but to be negotiated. In communicating, people do not *transfer information*, but *negotiate meanings*, as Rommetveit argued (1990, 1992).

As suggested above, the notion of *chronotope* may add value to the analysis of language learner's agency. As each individual occupies a unique place in time (Bakhtin, 1990), they also construct accounts of their participation from that vantage point. In addition to making sense of things that have happened, Sullivan and McCarthy (2004) pointed out that individuals also experience themselves as always potentially beyond these actions – they rely on their past experiences and acknowledge things to come. Following Sullivan and McCarthy (2004) we understand agency as a chronotopical, time–space bound phenomenon. An agentive individual looks in two directions: to past actions and the responsibility for the actions, and to the future, toward the potential. As language learners, agents have past learning trajectories, but they also have ideal selves: who they want to become and where they want to be. Taking into account the idea of chronotopes means that, instead of a sociocultural 'bird's eye' view of an individual acting within a system, the focus necessarily shifts to the experiences of that individual: to how they experience agency in their unique time–place coordinates (Sullivan & McCarthy, 2004).

The focus on individual emphasizes that language learners and users occupy a unique position, a self, but as they are also historical beings whose lives are continuously unfolding in time, they relate to the cultural–historical flows of our times. Time and place are an integral part of individuals' experiences and thereby their knowledge reservoirs (Dufva, 2003). However, as van Eijck and Roth (2010) note, our unique experience of the world does not mean that we are prisoners of our own time–place coordinates. We build our understanding of the world, of time and place, and of ourselves and others – and share our perceptions and viewpoints with others using language, or as Bakhtin (1981: 332) calls it, *ideological discourses*. Further, as our place in the world is an embodied position (Bakhtin, 1993: 47; see also Dufva, 2004), viewpoints can be negotiated, and possibly shared, precisely because of the shared embodiment of individuals. There is not only intersubjectivity, but also *intercorporeality* (Merleau-Ponty, 1964: 16) between agents. As such, the body is not only a unique place to be, but also 'the one home we share in the world's materiality' (Holquist, 1997: 224; see also Dufva, 2004). By recognizing the Other as one of our own kind, we also understand the possibility of dialogue.

From the point of view of agentive languaging and voicework, the dual tenets of responsibility and potential can also be reflected in the voices that the individual uses. All the dialogues encountered provide individuals with diverse options for whom they consider themselves to be and how they choose to voice themselves. Agency, as it becomes expressed in language, is in this sense seen as rooted in an individual's *response* to the Other (Sullivan & McCarthy, 2004) – individuals *author* themselves in dialogue with others and in the reinterpretations they give; they sort out and orchestrate the various socially marked voices (Holland *et al.*, 1998) in order to make the self knowable in the words of others. Hicks (2000) tied the dialogical notion of agency to the notion of voice and maintained that agency entails the ability to take the words of others and use them in a unique way, that is, to appropriate words and infuse them with one's own intention. In this sense voice and agency become even more intertwined – a view that helps us to see how individuals express their agency verbally.

Individuals are, then, not only inescapably connected with each other and with current time and place, but they are also agents in the historical time. As suggested by Thibault (2011) and Steffensen *et al.* (2010), human interactivity draws upon many different *timescales* ranging from evolutionary and cultural–historical to the very micro-scales of interaction. We are connected to our social, cultural and physical world not only as it is, but also as it was and as we think it will be: we interpret and give meaning as individuals who relate not only to their own individual histories but also to their cultural heritages, and, as members of the same species, to their shared evolutionary past.

In what follows, we discuss the agency of a language learner in the light of examples that illustrate the interplay between the agent, others and the environment.

Data: A Longitudinal Study of Foreign Language Learners' Beliefs and Agency

The data presented here come from a longitudinal study that examined learner beliefs and learner agency from dialogical and sociocultural perspectives (for results, see Aro, 2009, 2012; Dufva & Alanen, 2005). In the study, a group of L1 Finnish learners of L2 English were interviewed on several occasions over more than a dozen years. The first interviews were conducted when the learners were age seven and in Grade 1 of comprehensive school; the next interviews followed when the learners were in Grades 3 and 5 (aged 10 and 12).[1] The findings are reported in Aro (2009, 2012). To study how the research participants' ideas developed further and to give them an opportunity to share a retrospective view of their school years, new data were collected. The most recent interviews were conducted when the learners were around 20 years old.

As is usual in Finnish schools, English as a foreign language was introduced to the research participants as a school subject in Grade 3 (for practices of Finnish language education, see, e.g. Dufva & Salo, 2009). All participants continued to study English throughout comprehensive schooling. Both in the interviews during their school years, and in the recent interviews, the learners were asked about various issues regarding the English language and its learning, the main themes of the interviews being why, how and where English was studied (for a detailed discussion, see Aro, 2009, 2012).

This chapter focuses on interviews with Emma, one of the research participants, to illustrate how she describes her agency and actions as a learner of English. The excerpts are from her interviews when she was in Grade 3, in Grade 5 and an adult, at 20 years of age. From a dialogical perspective, Emma's knowledge reservoir and beliefs are a result of the interactions she has been involved in, and thus marked by perspectivity and positionality. Referring to her past, and looking toward her future, she is constantly authoring herself in dialogue with others, expressing herself and her agency as a language learning agent, acting in the world of language learning and inevitably influenced by and acknowledging the Other and the Others' actions and discourses.

Findings: Emma's Agency on the Move

The first excerpt is from an interview conducted at school when Emma was in Grade 3. Emma was 10 years old at the time and had started to study English a few months earlier. After a discussion about how she had enjoyed her English classes, about what happened in class, and about the kinds of things the group had been studying, Emma was asked if she had noticed that she already knew some English.

Example 1

MA: *No ooksää huomannu vaikka että ku sää vaikka katot televisiosta jotai englanninkielistä sarjaa tai kuuntelet jotai englanninkielistä laulua et sää oisit sieltä jo, niinku ymmärtäny sanan sieltä ja toisen täältä?*
      - No, yleensä ku mä katon englanninkielisiä teeveeohjelmia nii sieltä mä oon oppinu englantii, kauheesti.

MA: *Joo, ku näkee kuitenki sen tekstityksen siinä /ni/,*
      - /nii/ sitte joka sanoissa mää katon aina ku mää katon nauhotetuilta englantilaisilta ni, sitte aina mää siitä, ku mää kuuntelen sen viimesen sanan niin mää sieltä tekstistä katon sen viimesen sanan niin mää sitte niinku tavallaan opettelen lausumaan sitä.

MA: So have you noticed that when you for example watch some series in English on television or listen to some English-language song that you might have already, like understood a word here and there?
      - Well, usually when I watch TV programs in English then I've learnt English, a lot.

MA: Yeah, when you see the subtitles there after all /then/,
      - /yeah/ then every words I always watch when I watch taped English then, there I always, when I listen to the last word then I look the last word up in the subtitles and then like, kind of learn how to pronounce it. (Emma, 10 years, Grade 3)

Even though the interviewer's question dealt more with skills that had already been appropriated than learning, Emma went on to describe how she had used English-language television programs in order to learn English (television programs and foreign films in Finland are not dubbed, but subtitled). She described her actions in detail: 'when I watch . . . I always . . . listen to the last word then I look the last word up in the subtitles and . . . learn how to pronounce it'. Emma's description of her actions here shows how she uses experiences of the past in the present to achieve something for the future, and how she takes words of Others, English speakers, and appropriates them into her own repertoire. Emma's method may not be fool proof – owing to differences between sentence structures in English and Finnish, the last word of the spoken utterance and the last word of the subtitle are not necessarily the same, but it shows remarkable agentivity nonetheless, and makes use of an activity she would probably do anyway, that is, watch television.

What Emma describes seems to be connected with learning English 'in the wild', in informal contexts without any tutor other than herself. In Finland, where English is now often spoken of as the 'third domestic' language – in addition to the official languages Finnish and Swedish – there are plenty of opportunities for learning English informally (for a survey on the position of English in Finland, see Leppänen *et al.*, 2011). In Emma's response, autonomy, self-regulation and motivation seem to be present. A further sign of agentivity is that she provides a kind of self-assessment, saying that she has actually 'learned a lot'. Emma's chronotope of learning is her life-world in its totality: she does not draw a boundary between her school and out-of-school activities.

In the Grade 5, the interview started with questions of why English was useful and why people – and the learners themselves – studied it. The questions then moved on to the question of how: what were the best ways to learn English and how did the learners go about learning English?

Example 2

MA: *No, mitenkäs englantia opiskellaan jos joku haluaa oikei hyvin oppia englantia nii mitä sen kannattaa tehdä?*
      - Lukee niitä sanoja ja harjotella kirjottamaan niitä. (. . .)

MA: *Noh, mitenkäs sää sitte opiskelet englantia minkälaisia asioita sää teet täällä koulussa ja sitte kotona?*
      - No koulussa mää teen tehtäviä ja kotona, sitte mää luen niitä sanoja, ja opettelen kirjottamaan (ne).

MA: Well, how does one study English if one wants to learn English really well what should they do?
      - Read the words and practice how to write them. (. . .)

MA: So, how do you study English what kind of things do you do here at school and at home?
      - Well at school I do exercises and at home, I then read those words and learn how to write (them). (Emma 12 years, Grade 5)

In this excerpt, Emma's agency appears to be very different from what it was in Grade 3. Her voice as a language learner now seems to be controlled by another voice: the *authoritative voice* of the school. First, Emma now seems to connect language learning with the school context and its activities, in particular, its literacy-oriented practices. In her replies, Emma echoes the institutionally sanctioned practices normally followed when English is learned in the school context and gives a list of a few key classroom activities with an emphasis upon reading and writing. The process of learning seems to be led by the teacher and/or regulated by the materials created particularly for instruction, at home as well as at school.

In a way, the change in Emma's responses is not at all surprising. Several studies have indicated that the pedagogical practices in a Finnish classroom are still highly book-centered and literacy-based (see Luukka *et al.*, 2008 for a survey of Finnish teachers) and that the pupils' concept of learning is very closely tied to written language, literacy and books (e.g. Dufva & Alanen, 2005; Kalaja *et al.*, 2008b). Thus, the business of English-learning, to Emma, looks like a function of reading the English textbook and repeating what has been read.

Although Emma may here simply *ventriloquate* an authoritative point of view (Bakhtin, 1981), that of the teachers, it is interesting to speculate on the origins of her words a little further. Emma's literacy-biased views of language learning are almost certainly associated with what Linell (2005) calls a written language bias in Western thought and in linguistic analysis, a bias the large-scale consequences of which for education and assessment have been pointed out by several researchers (e.g. Cummins, 1981; Harris, 1981, 1996; Taylor, 1997; see also Dufva *et al.*, 2010). In a sense, Emma is just another link in the historical chain of language learners who continue to recycle the conceptualization that *one learns languages by studying from books.*

At the same time, we are not convinced that the literacy-centered view is mediated by teachers', or any adult's, explicit *words*. What the children presumably hear at school and at home as well is that *oral communication* is important and that their goal is to learn to speak the language. This explicitly expressed view is so widespread that one can call it a *spoken language bias* (see, e.g. Aro, 2013). It seems likely that it is primarily the repeated practices of the classroom that have given Emma the idea about how to 'correctly' or at least appropriately answer such a question: surely, if this is what you do in English lessons, it must be the best way to learn? Thus it is not only discourses and ways of speaking that mediate views in articulated fashion but also practices and deeds, often in implicit, less articulated ways.

Emma, along with the other children, has appropriated these viewpoints by listening to her teacher and observing classroom practices and now clearly considers them authoritative. Even at home, the things she says she does in order to learn English are closely linked to literary school practices: at school she does 'exercises'; at home she 'reads those words and learns how to write them'. When, later in the interview, Emma was specifically asked about English-language programs and music, she claimed that she did not really watch or listen to them. She obviously has abandoned her earlier view that she could learn English by herself and is renegotiating her agency as a learner. Emma's chronotope of learning is now narrowed into school and educational, 'school-like' activities (Dufva & Alanen, 2005).

Thus, in Grade 5, Emma's expressed agentive actions regarding learning of English were linked to the institutionally sanctioned chronotope of learning. The learning of English takes place at a particular place, at a particular time, and through particular activities. Emma is, in a sense, voicing herself here not so much as an active learner, but as a diligent *pupil* whose future goals revolve more around school-related things, exams and doing well in class – and such goals have an obvious impact on what she says that she does in order to reach these goals. If Emma's agency is now subjected to teacher's instructions and help, she is no exception. When asked how they learn English, some of Emma's classmates responded by saying 'So that the teacher teaches', making the teacher the agent of action, and not referring to themselves at all, even as subjects of the teacher's action (see Aro, 2009, 2012). Between the school and the students' everyday lives, there is now a *boundary* that does not seem to be that easily crossed (for a discussion of boundary crossings, see Akkerman & Bakker, 2011; for a discussion on expanding the chronotope of education, see Rajala *et al.*, 2013).

As Hicks (2000) maintained, agency entails the ability to take the words of others and appropriate them, use them in a unique way, have one's own voice. In this sense, Emma may be ventriloquating ideologies of authority rather than describing her agency in her own words. However, it should be noted that she exhibits the kind of agency she perhaps feels is appropriate for the situation. She is being interviewed at school about English, which is a school subject, so she may well be choosing to show these sides of her agency while hiding others that do not seem compatible with authoritative voices and practices. In part, Emma's responses may also reflect the potential influence of the research method and the researcher as one of the less visible authorities.

When we came back to Emma at the age of 20, now training to become a kindergarten instructor, things seemed to have changed once again. She had learned not only English but also about herself as a learner of English. She could, understandably now, as a young woman, reflect on and discuss her learner agency more in depth in light of her personal learning history.

Example 3

MA: *Miten itse olet englantia oppinut parhaiten, millaisissa aktiviteeteissa?*
- Sillon ku kuuntelee musiikkii tai sitte jos kattoo tosi paljo vaikka telkkaria tai elokuvia missä niitä jää aina kuunteleen niitä ja määki katon... usein englanninkielisillä teksteillä, nii sellasissa tilanteissa opin parhaiten....Ehkä enemmän vapaa-ajalla (nauraa) ku sillee menee

enemmän korvakuuloon mulla paremmin, kuunnella sitä ku sit että mietti
että mihin tulee se ja se ja se ja miten tehään epäsuorat ja tollaset ... Mä
en jaksa keskittyä yhtään niihin niinku että, tohon tulee subjekti ja tohon
tulee, (nauraa) menee ihan sekasi.

MA: What has been the best way for you to learn English, what kinds of
activities?
- When I listen to music or if I watch like a lot of television or
movies where they always catch my ear and I also often ... watch
them using the English subtitles, in those situations I learn the best
... Maybe more in my free time (laughs) cos it is easier for me to
learn by ear, to listen to it rather than to think about where this and
that and that go and how to make an indirect and stuff like that ...
I just can't concentrate at all on things like, here's where the subject
goes and here's the, (laughs) I get all confused. (Emma 20 years)

Looking back, Emma had discovered that the book-centered teaching method
of the school had not been the best way for her to learn. In talking about the
instruction at school and in describing her frustration over its concentration
on grammar and metalinguistic terminology ('indirect', 'subject'), she said
she had learned more in her free time, 'by ear' (for a dialogical notion of
teaching grammar, see Bakhtin, 2004). Again, she renegotiates her agency,
this time dismissing the school as authority. She now describes her own
agentive actions confidently in her own voice, while still contrasting them
with the authoritative voice of the Other, the school world.

Interestingly, her favorite method of learning is very similar to how she
described her learning activities in the third-grade interview: watching
English-language programs and using subtitles – only now, she uses the
English subtitles instead of the Finnish ones. It almost seems as if Emma, in
fact, knew her preference for 'learning by ear' right from the start, but during
her school years, the authoritative practices and the institutional chronotope
got in the way. For a while, she tried to make her authored agency match
what was valued and emphasized at school: books, reading and writing.
Remnants of the authoritative voice of the past still echo in her agency in the
sense that she constantly compares her own viewpoints with the authority
of the past, as an example of what does *not* work for her. While school got to
define the chronotope for learning in the early years of her English learning
trajectory, learning is no longer constrained by a particular time/place and
has now become a more cross-contextual activity, undertaken wherever
English can be heard, at the time and place of her own choosing. Although
she now learns English in informal contexts and incidentally, rather than by
conscious study, once she is asked about this in the interview, she recognizes
the value of her activities and defines it as 'learning'.

Further, emotions that were not discernible in the earlier interviews
appear now, in retrospect. Now, she told the interviewer that seeing herself

as a poor student at school had also led her to consider English (as a school subject) as 'pretty stupid'. In contrast, a recent visit to Scotland had been a revelation: 'I could actually understand what the people were saying'. Here, we see both how her experiences and feelings intertwine with her sense of agency and how her agency is not a finished product, but keeps on changing and developing on a situated basis although it is still given continuity by references to her earlier experiences.

In the latest interview, Emma also told the interviewer that she had been to an English playschool as a child where she 'learned things like, like songs in English that I would then always sing by myself'. She had never mentioned the playschool before in any of the interviews, not even in the first-grade interview where she was specifically asked about her knowledge and experiences of English. It makes one wonder if this was because she did not feel it was relevant for the learning of English during her school years, not something the authoritative others valued. It thus seems as if the retrospective view of her journey as a language learner – her past, present and future – that was renegotiated in the final interview might have given her an opportunity to develop a stronger voice – and thus added to her agency.

Discussion

Emma's answers in the interviews show how her agency emerges differently each time and is constantly renegotiated. In a way, Emma's own personality can be seen each time, as is obvious in, for example, the way she describes her preferences for learning languages, but there are also influences from a variety of sources in her everyday life and at school. There are some explicit Others in her comments, such as parents or teachers, but there are also more implicit comments about the people she has met when travelling. The longer, cultural–historical timescales that are present in the bias toward literacy, teacher-centered traditions and individualist notions of learning are also perceptible in Emma's answers. These cultural–historical flows do enforce a certain conceptualization of learning and a certain kind of agency: that of a pupil subjected to an authority. However, they do not necessarily provide a means for supporting agency that emerges in collaborative activity, or in activities outside the school chronotope.

In Emma's voiced agency, we thus see an influence of intrapersonal and interpersonal factors, and we see how certain important discourses or hegemonic pedagogical practices may have had an impact. We see the chronotopes: we see how learning at school intertwines with various traditions of education and how learning as part of one's everyday life is influenced by other types of traditions, for example, those of popular culture. We see the influence of the interviewer and the situation. Yet we also see Emma herself, her recognition of her own quality as a learner and continuity in the narrative she authors. In all interviews, she renegotiates and partly rewrites her story as a language learner.

Our theoretical arguments on the nature of agency intertwine with pedagogical considerations. Rogoff *et al.* (2003) distinguish between two traditions of learning: one by *intent participation* and the other by *assembly-line instruction*. While the first allows children to learn through their participation in purposive and meaningful activity of the community, the latter is based on transmission of information from experts, and in a way, may leave the students in a receptive – or even passive – role. However, one can argue that intent participation occurs at school also. The children do not learn only by what is explicitly taught, but also by watching and listening, and thus understanding the unarticulated views and hidden agendas embedded in the school practices. Our theoretical starting points suggested that a more holistic approach to agency might be appropriate. What our findings seem to suggest is that new research foci and research questions might also be relevant. For example, we should not only investigate the classroom interaction, or the words and discourses that are recycled there, but also examine how practices may mediate unarticulated views. Further, we need to look more closely into how issues of power, ethics and morality are involved.

Schools around the world may still function very much on the basis of assembly-line instruction, but as we see from Emma's examples, she and many other young people learn by participation in the context of popular culture, media and everyday life. This is not to say that children should be left alone with only the affordances they might encounter in their everyday lives and without systematic language education. The 20-year-old Emma felt that school instruction had provided her with a good, solid foundation on which she could now build her language skills. The scaffolding provided by teachers and peers and the collaborative, purposive activities that engage learners in personally meaningful tasks can be colossally helpful. However, instead of assembly-line instruction, schools need to consider new ways of creating a participatory community in which individual agency is enhanced by raising the students' awareness and by creating collaborative projects in which knowledge is produced together with others (e.g. van Lier, 2008).

When we conducted the first interviews with the group of children that we studied over the years, they almost unanimously looked forward to the beginning of their school years and foreign language studies with warm anticipation. As one of the boys in the first grade told us, he was eager to learn 'fifty-hundred-millions of ways of speaking'. Later on in Grade 3, some of them came to see themselves as poor pupils, illustrated in the comments of one girl whom we interviewed: 'I'm not really good at *remembering* anything'. As both dialogism and contemporary views (e.g. Thibault, 2011) seem to suggest, we need perspectives aiming at more holistic views of not only human interactivity in general but also of learners and their agency. Learners are persons, embodied beings with their own experiences and feelings that are also irrevocably interrelated with their environment and the Others therein. In today's world, in order to encourage agency, and learning of languages, one needs to go beyond the traditional school chronotope. We need to understand the lifeworld of learners as a whole, with its various affordances and learning opportunities, both at school and outside of it.

Note

(1) The data through Years 1–6 was collected as part of the project Situated metalinguistic awareness and foreign language learning (funded by the Academy of Finland with Dr Riikka Alanen as Principal investigator (PI)). The research on dialogism and second/foreign language learning has been carried out within the projects Dialogues of Appropriation (funded by Academy of Finland, with Dr Hannele Dufva as PI, Mari Aro as doctoral student) and Agency and Languaging (funded by Finnish Cultural Foundation, with Hannele Dufva as PI and Mari Aro as postdoctoral researcher).

References

Ahearn, L.M. (2001) Language and agency. *Annual Review of Anthropology* 30, 109–137.
Akkerman, S. and Bakker, A. (2011) Boundary crossing and boundary objects. *Review of Educational Research* 81 (2), 132–169.
Aro, M. (2009) *Speakers and Doers. Polyphony and Agency in Children's Beliefs about Language Learning.* Jyväskylä Studies in Humanities 116. University of Jyväskylä.
Aro, M. (2012) Effects of authority: Voicescapes in children's beliefs about the learning of English. *International Journal of Applied Linguistics* 22 (3), 331–346.
Aro, M. (2013) Kielen oppijasta kielen osaajaksi. In T. Keisanen, E. Kärkkäinen, M. Rauniomaa, P. Siitonen and M. Siromaa (eds) *Osallistumisen multimodaaliset diskurssit – Multimodal Discourses of Participation.* AFinLA Yearbook (pp. 11–28). Jyväskylä: AFinLA.
Bakhtin, M.M. (1981) *The Dialogic Imagination. Four Essays*, (trans. C. Emerson and M. Holquist). Austin: University of Texas Press.
Bakhtin, M.M. (1984) *Problems of Dostoevsky's Poetics*, (ed. and trans.) C. Emerson. Minneapolis, MN: University of Minnesota Press.
Bakhtin, M.M. (1986) *Speech Genres and other Late Essays.* Austin: University of Texas Press.
Bakhtin, M.M. (1990) *Art and Answerability: Early Philosophical Essays.* Austin: University of Texas Press.
Bakhtin, M.M. (1993) *Toward a Philosophy of the Act.* Austin: University of Texas Press.
Bakhtin, M.M. (2004) Dialogic origin and dialogic pedagogy of grammar: Stylistics as part of Russian language instruction in secondary school. *Journal of Russian and East European Psychology* 42 (6), 12–49.
Breen, M.P. (ed.) (2001) *Learner Contributions to Language Learning: New Directions in Research.* Harlow: Pearson Education.
Cowley, S.J. (2009) Distributed language and dynamics. *Pragmatics & Cognition* 17 (3), 495–507.
Cummins, J. (1981) Empirical and theoretical underpinnings of bilingual education. *Journal of Education* 163 (1), 16–29.
Dörneyi, Z. and Ushioda, E. (eds) (2009) *Motivation, Language Identity and the L2 Self.* Bristol: Multilingual Matters.

Dufva, H. (2003) Beliefs in dialogue: Bakhtinian view. In A. Maria Barcelos and P. Kalaja (eds) *Beliefs About SLA, New Research Approaches* (pp. 131–152). Kluwer Publishers.

Dufva, H. (2004) Language, thinking and embodiment: Bakhtin, Whorf and Merleau-Ponty. In F. Bostad, C. Brandist, L.S. Evensen and H.C. Faber (eds) *Bakhtinian Perspectives on Language and Culture: Meaning in Language, Art and New Media* (pp. 133–146). Basingstoke: Palgrave Macmillan.

Dufva, H. (2011) Language learners as socio-cognitive and embodied agents: Dialogical considerations. *Language, Communication and Social Environment* 9 (2011), 6–24.

Dufva, H. and Alanen, R. (2005) Metalinguistic awareness in dialogue: Bakhtinian considerations. In J. Kelly Hall, G. Vitanova and L. Marchenkova (eds) *Dialogue with Bakhtin on Second and Foreign Language Learning: New Perspectives* (pp. 99–118). Mahwah: Lawrence Erlbaum.

Dufva, H. and Salo, O.-P. (2009) Languages in the classroom: Institutional discourses and users' experiences. In J. Miller, A. Kostogriz and M. Gearon (eds) *Culturally and Linguistically Diverse Classrooms* (pp. 252–270). Bristol: Multilingual Matters.

Dufva, H., Suni, M., Aro, M. and Salo, O.-P. (2010) Languages as objects of learning: Language learning as a case of multilingualism. *Apples. Journal of Applied Language Studies* 5 (1), 109–124, http://apples.jyu.fi/index.php?volume=5&issue=1

Dufva, H., Aro, M. and Suni, M. (2014) Language learning as appropriation: How linguistic resources are recycled and regenerated. In P. Lintunen, M.S. Peltola and M.-L. Varila (eds) *AFinLA-e Soveltavan kielitieteen tutkimuksia* (pp. 20–31).

Gao, X. (2010) *Strategic Language Learning: The Roles of Agency and Context*. Bristol: Multilingual Matters.

Gao, X. and Zhang, L.J. (2011) Joining forces of synergy: Agency and metacognition as interrelated theoretical perspectives on learner autonomy. In G. Murray, X. Gao and T. Lamb (eds) *Identity, Motivation and Autonomy in Language Learning* (pp. 25–41). Bristol: Multilingual Matters.

Harris, R. (1981) *The Language Myth*. Duckworth: London.

Harris, R. (1996) *Signs, Language and Communication: Integrational and Segregational Approaches*. London: Routledge.

Hicks, D. (2000) Self and other in Bakhtin's early philosophical essays: Prelude to a theory of prose consciousness. *Mind, Culture, and Activity* 7, 227–242.

Holland, D., Lachicotte, W. Jr, Skinner, D. and Cain, C. (1998) *Identity and Agency in Cultural Worlds*. London: Harvard University Press.

Holquist, M. (1997) Bakhtin and the Beautiful Science: The paradox of cultural relativity revisited. In M. Macovski (ed.) *Dialogue and Critical Discourse, Language, Culture and Critical Theory* (pp. 215–236). New York: Oxford University Press.

Kalaja, P., Menezes, V. and Barcelos, A.M.F. (eds) (2008a) *Narratives of Learning and Teaching EFL*. London: Palgrave Macmillan.

Kalaja, P., Alanen, R. and Dufva, H. (2008b) Self-portraits of learners of EFL: Finnish students draw and tell. In P. Kalaja, V. Menezes and A.M.F. Barcelos (eds) *Narratives of Learning and Teaching EFL* (pp. 186–198). London: Palgrave Macmillan.

Kumpulainen, K. and Lipponen, H. (2010) Productive interaction as agentic participation in dialogic inquiry. In K. Littleton and C. Howe (eds) *Educational Dialogues. Understanding and Promoting Productive Interaction* (pp. 48–63). Abingdon: Routledge.

Lantolf, J.P. and Thorne, S.L. (2006) *Sociocultural Theory and the Genesis of L2 Development*. Oxford: Oxford University Press.

Leppänen, S., Pitkänen-Huhta, A., Nikula, T., Kytölä S. Törmäkangas, T., Nissinen, K., Kääntä, L., Räisänen, T., Laitinen, M., Pahta, P., Koskela, H., Lähdesmäki, S. and Jousmäki, H. (2011) *National Survey on the English Language in Finland: Uses, Meanings and Attitudes*. Helsinki: Research Unit for the Variation, Contacts and Change in English, http://www.helsinki.fi/varieng/journal/volumes/05

Linell, P. (1998) *Approaching Dialogue: Talk, Interaction and Contexts in Dialogical Perspectives.* Amsterdam: John Benjamins.

Linell, P. (2005) *The Written Language Bias in Linguistics: Its Nature, Origins, and Transformations.* London: Routledge.

Luukka, M., Pöyhönen, S., Huhta, A., Taalas, P., Tarnanen, M. and Keränen, A. (2008) *Maailma muuttuu – mitä tekee koulu? Äidinkielen ja vieraiden kielten tekstikäytänteet koulussa ja vapaa-ajalla.* Jyväskylä: University of Jyväskylä, Centre for Applied Language Studies.

Marková, I. (1992) On structure and dialogicity in Prague semiotics. In A. Wold (ed.) *The Dialogical Alternative: Towards a Theory of Language and Mind* (pp. 45–63). Oslo: Scandinavian University Press.

Marková, I. and Foppa, K. (eds) (1991) *Asymmetries in Dialogues.* Hertfordshire: Harvester Wheatsheaf.

Merleau-Ponty, M. (1964) *The Primacy of Perception and Other Essays.* Evanston: Northwestern University Press.

Morson G.S. (1991) Bakhtin and the present moment. *The American Scholar* 60 (2), 201–222.

Murray, G., Gao, X. and Lamb, T. (eds) (2011) *Identity, Motivation and Autonomy in Language Learning.* Bristol: Multilingual Matters.

Pavlenko, A. (ed.) (2006) *Bilingual Minds. Emotional Experience, Expression and Representation.* Clevedon: Multilingual Matters.

Rajala, A., Hilppö, J., Lipponen, L. and Kumpulainen, K. (2013) Expanding the chronotopes of schooling for promotion of students' agency. In O. Erstad and J. Sefton-Green (eds) *Identity, Community, and Learning Lives in the Digital Age* (pp. 107–125). Cambridge: Cambridge University Press.

Rogoff, B., Paradise, R., Mejía Arauz, R., Correa-Chávez, M. and Angelillo, C. (2003) Firsthand learning through intent participation. *Annual Review of Psychology* 54, 175–203.

Rommetveit, R. (1990) On axiomatic features of a dialogical approach to language and mind. In I. Markova and K. Foppa (eds) *The Dynamics of Dialogue* (pp. 83–104). New York: Harvester Wheatsheaf.

Rommetveit, R. (1992) Outlines of a dialogically based social–cognitive approach to human cognition and ommunication. In A.H. Wold (ed.) *The Dialogical Alternative. Towards a Theory of Language and Mind* (pp. 19–44). Oslo: Scandinavian University Press.

Sannino, A. (2010) Teachers' talk of experiencing: Conflict, resistance and agency. *Teaching and Teacher Education* 26 (4), 838–844.

Steffensen. S.V. (2013) Human interactivity: Problem-solving, solution-probing and verbal patterns in the wild. In S.J. Cowley and F. Vallée-Tourangeau (eds) *Cognition Beyond the Brain: Computation, Interactivity and Human Artifice* (pp. 195–221). Dordrecht: Springer.

Steffensen, S.V., Thibault, P.J. and Cowley, S.J. (2010) Living in the social meshwork: The case of health interaction. In S. Cowley, J.C. Major, S.V. Steffensen and A. Dinis (eds) *Signifying Bodies: Biosemiosis, Interaction and Health* (pp. 207–244). Braga: Catholic University of Portugal.

Sullivan, P. and McCarthy, J. (2004) Toward a dialogical perspective on agency. *Journal for the Theory of Social Behaviour* 34, 291–309.

Taylor, T.J. (1997) *Theorizing Language.* Amsterdam: Pergamon Press.

Thibault, P.J. (2011) First-order languaging dynamics and second-order language: The distributed language view. *Ecological Psychology* 23 (3), 1–36.

Ushioda, E. (2009) A person-in-context relational view of emergent motivation, self and identity. In Z. Dörnyei and E. Ushioda (eds) *Motivation, Language Identity and the L2 Self* (pp. 215–228). Bristol: Multilingual Matters.

Ushioda, E. (2011) Why autonomy? Insights from motivation theory and research. *Innovation in Language Learning and Teaching* 5 (2), 221–232.

van Eijck, M. and Roth, W.-M. (2010) Towards a chronotopic theory of 'place' in place-based education. *Cultural Studies of Science Education* 5, 869–898.

van Lier, L. (2008) Agency in the classroom. In J.P. Lantolf and M.E. Poehner (eds) *Sociocultural Theory and the Teaching of Second Languages* (pp. 163–186). London: Equinox.

Vitanova, G. (2005) Authoring the self in a non-native language: A dialogic approach to agency and subjectivity. In J. Kelly Hall, G. Vitanova and L. Marchenkova (eds) *Dialogue with Bakhtin on Second and Foreign Language Learning: New Perspectives* (pp. 149–169). Mahwah: Lawrence Erlbaum.

Vitanova, G. (2010) *Authoring the Dialogical Self: Gender, Agency and Language Practices.* Amsterdam: John Benjamins.

Voloshinov, V.N. (1973) *Marxism and the Philosophy of Language.* New York: Seminar Press.

Voloshinov, V. (1976) *Freudianism. A Marxist Critique.* New York: Academic Press.

4 Examining Agency in (Second) Language Socialization Research

Patricia A. Duff and Liam Doherty

Introduction

Language socialization (LS) represents a growing area of interdisciplinary research, drawing on linguistic anthropology, sociology, cultural psychology and other disciplines. Like many other fields represented in this volume, LS has begun to focus on extensive, often critical, discussions of learner agency. In this chapter, we first provide a brief description of LS, which for our purposes encompasses first, second, bilingual/multilingual foreign and heritage-language contexts, and then examine how and why agency has become increasingly salient in this work. We also analyze the relationship between *agency* and *self-socialization*, the latter representing a construct with origins in psychology (Arnett, 2007; Kuczynski & Parkin, 2007), and consider *self-directed socialization* as a form of self-socialization. These aspects of the personal enactment of agency have yet to be taken up adequately in applied linguistics or linguistic anthropology (a recent exception being Fogle, 2012).

To make the theoretical discussion more concrete, we provide examples from recent case studies of English and Chinese language learning, where learners' agency is foregrounded by participants themselves and by the scholars investigating their learning and sociocultural practices. Also examined are the mechanisms and linguistic (or paralinguistic) manifestations of agency and its significance for learners, their learning environments, their interlocutors and mentors and LS theory. We conclude with a short discussion of some theoretical implications of this research.

Language Socialization and Agency

LS theory and research examine the processes by which newcomers to a culture learn the linguistic and cultural norms and practices required to demonstrate or attain greater participation and competence in the community. Crucial in this form of social experience and learning, according to conventional LS theory, are the more proficient members or mentors in the group and other affordances in the environment, such as textbooks, technology and seating arrangements, that facilitate or mediate the learning process. Through such interactions and mediation, it is claimed, the novices are apprenticed – socially, culturally, cognitively and linguistically – into core communicative practices as well as identities, ideologies, worldviews, stances and knowledge associated with those practices and cultures (see reviews by Garrett & Baquedano-Lopez, 2002; Duff, 2007, 2010, 2012b; Duff & Talmy, 2011; Ochs & Schieffelin, 2008, 2012; Watson-Gegeo, 2004).

Over the past three decades, theoretical accounts of LS have become much more elaborate. The growing number and types of studies and contexts in which LS is being investigated in first-language (L1) and multilingual contexts, and with learners across the lifespan, have provided new insights (e.g. Ahearn, 2001; Duff, 2010, 2012b; Duff & Talmy, 2011; Duranti et al., 2012; Fogle, 2012; Garrett & Baquedano-Lopez, 2002; Morita, 2004; Ochs & Schieffelin, 2008, 2012; Talmy, 2008). There is a growing consensus among LS researchers that a closer analysis and theorizing of agency is warranted to better understand the processes and many possible outcomes of language learning. This 'recent agentive turn', according to Ahearn (2001: 110), 'follows on the heels not only of the social movements of the past few decades but also of postmodern and poststructuralist critiques within the academy that have called into question impersonal master narratives that leave no room for tensions, contradictions, or oppositional actions on the part of individuals and collectivities'. This shift in focus enables researchers not only to document established group members' explicit or implicit expectations with respect to their own and others' linguistic and cultural practices and dispositions (and particularly those of novices or newcomers), but also to show how they are negotiated as people learn (to different degrees) or reproduce cultural forms, innovate or resist certain aspects of their peers' or mentors' behaviors.

In addition, power is increasingly examined in LS treatments of agency in ways that were perhaps less subject to analysis or critique in the past, particularly in anthropological work. Yet power asymmetries and hierarchies are often considered mitigating or complicating factors in learners' and practitioners' ability to exert themselves in terms of their desires, intentions, needs and preferences within a particular sociocultural and linguistic context.

In adolescent and adult language learning, highly motivated learners plan and exert their agency in various ways to achieve their goals. Indeed, learners often display laudable – and sometimes extreme – efforts (as we illustrate below) to direct, control, create and transform their own linguistic/cultural socialization using the myriad social and cultural resources at their disposal, such as new technologies and ubiquitous forms of popular culture. This kind of agency, taken to a heightened level, can be construed as intentional socioculturally mediated *self-socialization* or *self-directed socialization*.

Yet theoretical discussions of LS typically use the passive voice (in English) when focusing on language learners themselves: X *is socialized by* Y into particular linguistic and nonlinguistic domains of knowledge and social practice, where Y, the agent, is typically a teacher, parent, peer or sibling. This usage is not surprising considering that first-generation LS research dealt primarily with very young children, often in non-Western small-scale societies with strong oral traditions, such as Papua New Guinea, Samoa and the Solomon Islands. Furthermore, the notion that teachers or mentors 'teach' and children 'learn' was a common assumption underpinning 20th-century American education and pedagogy. Unsurprisingly, then, early LS research paid markedly less attention to the discussion of infants', toddlers' and young children's agency in their learning of verbal routines and pragmatics. The focus, instead, was on child-directed speech and the forms of accommodation (if any) made by caregivers to scaffold their language learning, acculturation and social maturation, and cross-cultural differences in early LS. Children's capacity for intentionality and action even in their first year was noted, however (Ochs & Schieffelin, 1984).

A misunderstanding sometimes attributed to that early work (e.g. Schieffelin & Ochs, 1986), therefore, was that learners had little apparent opportunity to exercise their agency in the process of learning language and becoming socially competent, and that the 'experts' were the primary socializing 'agents' for novices, although the potential for bidirectional LS influences was acknowledged (Garrett & Baquedano-Lopez, 2002). However, the young novices had what seemed to be relatively little control over the learning process or situation, especially under the authoritative watch of parents, caregivers and teachers (Duff, 2003). Nor were peers or siblings credited with much agency to socialize one another into new communicative practices other than as intermediaries between parent and child (e.g. as parental proxies). In comparison, research on *peer language socialization* now addresses agency much more directly and fully (e.g. Goodwin & Kyratzis, 2012; Kyratzis & Cook-Gumperz, 2008; Mökkönen, 2012).

Looking back, it is clear that the growing concern for agency was broached in some of the earliest explications of LS. Nearly 30 years ago, citing social psychologist George Herbert Mead, Ochs (1986: 1) wrote:

> for Mead, the individual is an *active agent in his own socialization throughout life*; individuals do not automatically internalize how others see them and the rest of the world but rather have *the capacity to select* images and perspectives. In this sense, *individuals and society construct one another through social interaction*. (Emphasis added)

Thus, Mead and, later, Ochs linked agency and (self-)socialization across the lifespan. This notion of agency as highly socially constrained, for both scholars, is also captured in linguistic anthropologist Ahearn's (2001: 112) definition of agency as the 'socioculturally mediated capacity to act'.

More recently, Ochs and Schieffelin (2008: 8) underscored novices' active involvement 'in generating social order', citing sociologists such as Bourdieu and Giddens:

> The active role of the child/novice in generating social order is compatible with social theories that promote *members' reflexivity, agency, and contingency* in the constitution of everyday social life (Bourdieu, 1977, 1990; Garfinkel, 1967; Giddens, 1979, 1984). These approaches favor the study of social actions as at once structured and structuring in time and space, bound by historically durable social orders of power and symbolic systems yet creative, variable, responsive to situational exigencies and capable of producing novel consequences. Even in the maintenance of social regularities, 'the familiar is created and recreated through human agency itself'. (Giddens, 1979: 128; emphasis added)

Seen in this light, children are not passive recipients – literally, grammatical 'patients' or 'experiencers' in certain descriptive theories of grammar – of socializing influences in a pre-constructed social world. Together with their interlocutors, they also negotiate and create their world and 'social order'. They are agents as well as experiencers or beneficiaries. Expanding on this theme of agency and contingency, Ochs and Schieffelin (2012: 4) emphasize that '[a] central tenet of language socialization research is that novices' participation in communicative practices is *promoted but not determined* by a legacy of socially and culturally informed persons, artifacts and features of the built environment' (emphasis added). They therefore contest and refute critiques of LS as being overly deterministic, emphasizing instead the highly (inter)active, emergent nature of social participation and learning, which nonetheless may be subject to an asymmetrical distribution of power that typically favors older or otherwise privileged participants within their local social orders. Ochs and Schieffelin also observe that, particularly in the technological age as noted earlier, certain kinds of knowledge and expertise reside with younger members who socialize their elders or peers into previously unfamiliar and changing practices (e.g. related to technology or other innovations).

Although not concerned with LS specifically, Al Zidjaly (2009), like Ochs and Schieffelin, also sees agency as an interactional achievement (perhaps similar to the conceptualization of identity in poststructural, discursive accounts); and although LS theory has generally featured reasonably compliant learners who take on board the practices and cultures of their mentors, Kulick and Schieffelin (2004) foreground the issue of 'bad subjects', who intentionally and knowingly resist, reject, subvert or transgress traditional ideologies and cultural practices (i.e. displaying their agency), or exert their individuality in non-normative, sometimes counter-cultural or subcultural ways. Kulick, Schieffelin and Ochs, therefore, all assert that cultures are much more fluid and dynamic and that innovation, improvisation, and deviation are in fact an essential part of society, and are thus seen in sociolinguistic interaction, human development and cultural change (see also Garrett & Baquedano-Lopez, 2002).

In summary, linguistic anthropologists and applied linguists increasingly underscore the indeterminacy, contingency, bidirectionality, improvisation and choices involved in learning and using another language (including the choice to *not* study or use the language at all, or to study, internalize and reproduce linguistic routines and ideologies or innovate, creating new ones quite selectively and shedding others; Duff, 2012b; Ochs & Schieffelin, 2012; Talmy, 2008), leading to variable learning/performance outcomes or consequences over time.

Related Constructs: Self-socialization and Self-directed Socialization

Intentionality, volition, motivation, locus of control and investment are other concepts that overlap to some degree with agency and indeed may be used synonymously in some accounts. Until recently (with the exception of investment), these terms were more tied to a psychological discussion of learners' reasonably static dispositions and traits than to a sociological one that takes into account social affordances, structures and situated actions. Greater clarification among these terms is warranted but is beyond the scope of this paper. Here, instead, we consider the relatively recent notion of *self-socialization* in relation to agency.

The discussion of self-socialization or self-directed learning in L1 and L2 literature, as with many other constructs or variables that dominated second language acquisition (SLA) theories in the latter part of the 20th century, has been influenced heavily by cognitive and social psychology. They also reflect aspects of contemporary postmodern 'Web 2.0' do-it-yourself culture that prizes new forms of knowledge creation and social participation in communities of practice. The learners/actors in these new communities are not viewed – nor do they see themselves – as mere consumers of knowledge (e.g. language and culture) or participants in learning communities or affinity groups, but as producers, co-creating, revising and critiquing the knowledge and communities they belong to in highly agentive, time-sensitive and public ways.

Arnett (2007), a psychologist not primarily interested in linguistic aspects of development, describes tensions surrounding individualization and agency that youth in Western cultures grapple with as they come of age and explore their identities and possible future life pathways. Drawing on Heinz's (2002) term *self-socialization*, Arnett's focus is on the shift from *socialization* (by family members, and especially parents, within the home) to *self-socialization* during what he calls 'emerging adulthood' (roughly ages 18–25), when peers, friendships and affinity groups remain important socializing forces but when people often spend more leisure time alone than during adolescence (e.g. when they attended secondary school). He writes that socialization, at that later stage, '[becomes] something that is done by the individual rather than imposed by outside social or institutional forces' (Arnett, 2007: 214). (Recall that Ahearn's definition of agency would see self-socialization as necessarily socioculturally mediated, however.)

In a study of children in Dominica, Paugh (2005) examined how children exercised agency through their use of Patwa, in spite of the fact that the adults in the community disapproved of its use and expected them to speak English. Paugh (2005: 63) found that 'children use Patwa to enact particular adult roles during peer play', that this imaginative play demonstrated that they were 'active agents in their socialization, not simply passive recipients of culture or merely doing what adults tell them to do, despite possible sanctions' (Paugh, 2005: 79), and that children as young as 2 and 3 years old were able to demonstrate knowledge of role- and place-appropriate language use. For Paugh (2005: 68) children's role play is 'a prime context within which children can practice, learn, and socialize Patwa among themselves'.

Arnett (1995, 2007) identifies the role of new media, especially, in the socialization of young adults, made possible by the internet and globalization. This theme has been taken up by some LS scholars in the context of socialization in transnational diaspora settings, in virtual worlds and in online gaming communities (Lam, 2004, 2008; Thorne *et al.*, 2009). Social network sites, such as Facebook or Twitter, were much less widely used or available when Arnett's work was published, and their socializing role and potential has grown exponentially in the interim (e.g. Reinhardt & Zander, 2011). Furthermore, Wang (2012), in her article 'Self-directed English language learning through watching English television drama in China', provides a recent manifestation of the power of new media and popular culture in a foreign-language setting, while Ushioda (2013) considers the possibilities of mobile language learning.

Indeed, the intersections and potential of new media and social networking, agency and self-(directed) socialization into languages, identities and cultures require further exploration and theoretical reflection by applied linguists. To date, much of the research on self-socialization has been conducted by psychologists whose primary concern is not language as either an object or medium of learning. In the following section, we illustrate these themes drawing on recent L2 research which we reframe in terms of L2 socialization and agency.

In L2 research in the 1980s, research connected with *learner autonomy* and *self-access* stripped away many of the social and cultural dimensions and dynamic contingencies that are now of interest to LS researchers (and SLA researchers). Kohonen's (1992: 37) notion of *self-directed language learning* resonates with notions of agency, self-directed socialization and self-regulation but takes this individualistic psychological approach:

> The goal is to enable the learner to become increasingly self-directed and responsible for his or her own learning. This process means a gradual shift of the initiative to the learner, encouraging him or her to bring in personal contributions and experiences. Instead of the teacher setting the tasks and standards of acceptable performance, the learner is increasingly in charge of his or her own learning.

A similar concept, *self-regulation*, is also invoked as a goal in much educational psychology literature. However, unlike self-regulation, we see self-(directed) socialization as highly oriented toward (other) sociocultural groups and their behaviors and values, more so than a form of (internalized) behavioral self-control, although self-socialization presumably requires a high degree of self-regulation as well. We return to the discussion of self-socialization in the following section with a concrete example.

Agency in LS Research in English Language-learning Contexts: Insights and Issues

In her recent book describing agency and second language socialization in American families with transnational adopted children (English L2 learners from Eastern Europe), Fogle (2012) illustrates the forms of contestation and other agentive acts and dispositions of children attempting to create a (monolingual English) social and linguistic order that may be different from the one the parents attempt to socialize them into, such as a bilingual one in which particular narrative activities are valued. In her study of three different families, she illustrates three distinct manifestations of agency by children: (1) *resistance* by children to their father's requests for (English) narratives recounting good and bad aspects of their day, and to his use of Russian, which he had studied in preparation for their arrival; (2) discursive *control* through children's frequent questioning behaviors about language or concepts (e.g. 'What is *wreath*?'; Fogle, 2012: 118); and (3) *negotiation* of language choice (e.g. Russian vs English) in the home in which parents knew Russian and wanted to socialize children into a bilingual home environment and thus assist with L1 maintenance and use among the children, some of whom were older Russian-speaking teens who had recently become members of the family (see also Duff, 2014, for examples of other socializing practices by non-Chinese parents with Chinese adopted children). The roles of 'resistor, questioner or negotiator' in Fogle's (2012: 5) study constitute different forms of agency enacted through particular discursive practices in which children attempt to socialize parents into modified narrative and other verbal behaviors, which parents eventually accommodate to.

Agency should not be equated with resistance or noncompliance, however (Ahearn, 2001: 115). Agentive stances and actions can potentially *facilitate* or *impede* the development of greater normative communicative and cultural competence in new communities. Whereas resistance to particular target practices or communities may be seen as a way of not engaging in expected, privileged ways in that community, it may have other enabling consequences, including the creation of innovative new practices, norms and communities, and effecting other kinds of change that might be quite positive (e.g. disrupting entrenched hierarchical structures or social exclusion; finding more cooperative and compatible communities to engage with). As Fogle (2012) points out, citing relevant literature, the same act can simultaneously have different meanings to the agents and their interlocutors (and others) as well as different consequences (from their own and others' perspectives).

Atkinson (2003) coined the word *dys-socialization* to account for a different type of resistance or contradictory stance toward (English-language) socialization both from the perspective of the newcomers to a community and more socially empowered old-timers. He examined the practices and dispositions of under-privileged Tamil-speaking college students attending 'formerly elite' English-medium college programs in South India which, through efforts to provide more equitable access to higher education, now enrolled students without the same cultural or linguistic capital as traditional better educated and resourced students. By dys-socialization, Atkinson meant that the newcomers 'appear[ed] to be developing and having reinforced social identities that militate[d] against the acquisition of English' (Atkinson, 2003: 148) in a complex co-constructed manner. He concluded that, although the marginalized students were offered access to higher education through the medium of English, their prospects of high educational attainment were in fact modest. As a result, their social and linguistic integration was limited.

Only one article, an extended case study narrative, has fully explored the notion of *self-socialization* (and agency), in a transnational English-L2 learning context. Social psychologists Newman and Newman (2009) reconstructed from their interviews with a UCLA undergraduate student named Lilly her complicated trajectory of English language learning, acculturation, social integration, psychological experiences and academic achievement over the previous 10-year period. Lilly had arrived in the USA originally as a tourist/visitor but had apparently pleaded with her parents to allow her to stay, learn

English and continue her studies in the USA as a 'parachute child', living with her aunt and uncle. Her parents relented, returning to Taiwan without her. Self-socializing, according to Newman and Newman (2009: 523), as in Lilly's case, occurs in a highly agentive and goal-oriented manner when 'an individual is able to reflect on the self, formulate a vision of a future self, set goals, and take actions that create or alter the developmental trajectory'. They explained:

> The idea of self-socialization is illustrated in Lilly's resolve to reach the level of English language competence that would help her achieve her social and emotional objectives, even to the point of overcoming obstacles that might have dissuaded a less determined child. (Newman & Newman, 2009: 528)

In the researchers' assessment, Lilly had 'a profound capacity for personal agency' (Newman & Newman, 2009: 523), which involved also rejecting 'the socialization context of her family' (Newman & Newman, 2009: 524) (both in Taiwan and in the USA as she became a teenager) and even the use of Chinese with them as she claimed and enacted her American identity, particularly when, more than four years later, she returned to Taiwan for her first visit. Because of US visa issues, however, her stay in Taiwan lasted longer than expected. Asserting her American, Anglophone identity, she refused to speak Chinese with her parents, whom she had not seen for more than four years.[1] Through sheer tenacity and self-advocacy, she obtained a new visa after an eight month enforced sojourn in Taiwan, allowing her to return to the USA to complete high school, albeit at a new, private, school that had helped her obtain her study visa.

Newman and Newman describe Lilly's resilience and strategic behaviors seeking out the social and other resources necessary for her to reach her goals (such as consulting the researchers themselves, ultimately, when she was a student in their psychology course years later). However, this case study is not entirely evidence of Lilly's successful integration into the target English-speaking American community she tried to 'self-socialize' into (or any others) because in her later high school years she felt alienated from her (Taiwanese) aunt and uncle's family in the USA, as well as from her US-born peers at both the private and public high schools she had attended, and from her family in Taiwan. For an extended period of time, she had no particular affinity with a peer or family group, although she was in contact with a network of people she could turn to for assistance. In a sense, she had managed to become socialized into English but not into a mutually receptive target or host community. As a final example of her extraordinary agency with respect to her desire to gain in-state residency status to enable her to remain in the USA to study at a state university at reduced in-state tuition rates, and the lengths she would go to do to so, she explained in her narrative that she had 'contacted her congressmen, the chancellor's office, and UC [University of California] legal counsel. She wrote to everyone she could think of to make her case; even Oprah' (Newman & Newman, 2009: 534) and eventually succeeded, thereby becoming an undergraduate 'international' psychology student at UCLA, albeit without the in-state residency she had sought.

The researchers concluded that '[t]his experience of using her network, her persistence, and her understanding of bureaucracies to achieve her goal helped to consolidate Lilly's American identity' (Newman & Newman, 2009: 534). Lilly herself noted: 'This is what I've been taught here being in America. I know that there is this American dream and I know how to ask for the better...you don't say no, you don't back down' (Newman & Newman, 2009: 534). Thus, she had internalized what she perceived to be a cultural norm and set of dispositions – psychological, sociological and pragmatic – to realize her own 'American dream'. Lilly's determination recalls the case studies of some of the Chinese–American first-generation older immigrant women in Li's (2000) multiple-case study examining their socialization into the English language and local American culture(s) and their persistent goal-oriented agency toward their own American dreams.

Agency and Socialization into (or Away from) Chinese Heritage- and Nonheritage Language(s), Communities and Cultural Practices

In contrast to English as a second/first language contexts (or the L2 learning of, say, French, Spanish, German or Dutch in bilingual regions), where students are often expected to learn a particular L2 from a young age rather than choose to learn it of their own accord, the decision to study Chinese in non-Chinese societies (especially outside of a heritage context) may be seen as inherently agentive. Tasker (2012) and Duff *et al.* (2013), among others, cite many examples of learners who began learning Chinese as a form of mild resistance or 'opting out' of more traditional target language study. As Duff *et al.* (2013: 117) comment in describing this phenomenon on the part of several learners, 'their choice to study [Chinese] was a strongly agentive act in itself – often contrasted with other languages such as French'. The choice to learn Chinese thus simultaneously represents both an implicit rejection or turning away from languages that learners may have been required to learn in school or at home, as well as embracing or turning toward a third language that allows them to stand out as unique or special among their mono- or bilingual peers. Both the rejection of other non-self-selected languages and turning toward Chinese are essentially agentive actions (or perhaps the same agentive action, seen from different – negative and positive – perspectives). However, in discussing the agency of these Chinese as an Additional Language (CAL) learners, Duff *et al.* (2013: 117) point out that 'learners' agency does not necessarily lead to positive language learning outcomes', and that conflict and adversity encountered on the road to language proficiency are equally likely to cause learners to retreat into disengagement as they are to lead them to facilitate their own success.

In contrast to contexts in which the learning of a second or additional language might be associated strongly with internally or externally imposed instrumental motivations, and in which a learner's future economic or social mobility may hinge on their success or failure to exert their agency by becoming part of a given target language speech community, Duff *et al.* (2013: 117) note that many of the Canadian CAL learners in their study were learning 'purely out of interest and curiosity' although sometimes with great intensity and optimism. Indeed, the highly agentive transitive verb *conquer* (e.g. *the Chinese language*) was used by at least two research participants to describe their original goals, instead of the more neutral terms *learn* or *study*, or even *master*, indexing their agentive stances. As in the case of the Tamil students in Atkinson (2003), the agency of the CAL learners had both negative and positive valence – in this case a rejection of other compulsory or 'ordinary' (European) languages and a selection of a language representing novelty and symbolic cachet. However, unlike their counterparts in Southern India, the result in the Chinese learning context was not dys-socialization but self-socialization, as the 'target language' and the language 'turned towards' were one and the same.

It may be useful to distinguish between, on the one hand, the ways that a high degree of linguistic and sociocultural competence can enable a learner to be more confident about expressing agency in other areas of their lives, and, on the other, how a learner's strong personal agency may empower them to seek out higher competency in one or more areas of LS, or in other words to 'self-socialize' as part of their linguistic development.

Wong-Fillmore (2000) points out that, in recent US history, very few immigrant groups have been able to successfully maintain their primary languages past the second or third generation. While her study concerns the negative and rejective agency often enacted by younger members of immigrant families as they distance themselves from their heritage languages (HLs) and the older generations who speak them, the renewed interest in heritage language classes among later-generation HL learners raises the question of whether there may also be a positive aspect to agency in this context; in other words, later-generation HL learners may be reconstructing the learning of the HL as an agentive act (i.e. the reverse of early generation rejection-as-agency patterns). Thus, their agentive stances and actions may impede HL retention, at one stage, but facilitate it at a later stage. Presumably, however, only a fraction of those who earlier rejected or were unable to learn and retain the HL go on to (re)learn it later.

He (2012) has devoted a great deal of attention to such give-and-take agentive tensions and misgivings in US Chinese HL communities in particular, both in homes where families seek to cultivate knowledge and everyday use of Chinese and in community HL schools. In such sites, again, children commonly display different (contradictory, cooperative or confrontational) stances toward HL maintenance and toward their parents' and teachers' means of socializing them, and contest the Chinese language and literacy practices and code choice, and even the need to attend supplementary schools. Their agentive actions and stances at once may enable them to develop a sufficient foundation in the language to later build up further proficiency; or their dispositions, in combination with the socializing environments they are in (which they may not appreciate, as in Lilly's case), may lead them to a less positive outcome vis-à-vis maintenance of their HL until they make the choice for themselves to pursue it, with greater agency and self-directed socialization, typically as young adults (e.g. Li & Duff, 2014). Being or becoming empowered through social structures, interactions and relationships to enact one's agency toward a particular language learning goal is one way of conceiving of LS. This learning and sociocultural engagement can be viewed at the level of particular linguistic/pragmatic forms or subsystems (e.g. honorifics, politeness strategies, literacy vs orality) that learners may consciously wish to internalize and use in particular situations, either normatively or counter-normatively. An example of the latter tendency was described in Siegal's (1994) study of Western women learning/using Japanese as an L2 in Japan who made decisions about which grammatical and sociolinguistic practices they would or would not be willing to learn and (re)produce based on their identities as women who had been socialized into English-L1 sociolinguistic sensibilities related to gender and social hierarchy. As Duff (2012a: 412) noted:

> L2 learners might deliberately not accommodate to certain target L2 features, revealing aspects of their identity and agency. Women in Siegal's (1994) study of Westerners learning Japanese in Japan typically resisted very honorific, deferential, and feminine Japanese speech patterns because such forms or registers were incompatible with their identities as assertive Western women.

As discussed above, the interplay of language socialization and agency is bidirectional, iterative and socially situated; learners may feel agentive in one situation and not another. The cycle of interaction between LS and agency (see Figure 4.1) are but two of a variety of factors that both contribute and respond to the emergence of second language (L2) and second-culture (C2) learning.

In this cyclical model of the dynamic relationship between agency and LS, agency emerges nonsequentially, appearing twice (this should be

Figure 4.1 Bidirectionality and contingency of agency and LS, and the emergence of L2 and C2

understood as highlighting the multiple possible ways in which agency might manifest itself, rather than a simultaneous emergence at both ends of LS, although that may certainly also be possible): once as the outcome of the L2 socialization process, and at a different point in the cycle, as the precursor or enabling factor leading to self-directed language socialization on the part of the learner. The (human and nonhuman) affordances and resources available in the learner's environment (including their funds of knowledge and other personal resources) play a key role in tying together the agentive and socializing experiences of the learner, and as the interwoven elements move toward the core, second language and culture acquisition becomes possible and this then further impacts agency and LS.

The inward-pointing directionality of the elements leading toward learning at the centre is reminiscent of Vygotsky's psychological process of *internalization*, which 'ensues from interaction on the social plane' (Duff, 2007: 312). The internalized new knowledge is presumably then acted upon or displayed in social contexts as the process of LS continues. Two broad patterns become prominent in this bidirectional model, namely (1) cases where LS is sought out or made possible by self-directed exertion of learner agency, and (2) the reverse case, where socialization into the L2 culture becomes an empowering experience that increases or engenders the learner's agency across other aspects of their life.

Both forms of LS and agency interaction are in evidence in Tasker's (2012) case study of seven adult learners of Chinese as an additional, nonheritage language. Two of the participants in the study in particular, Stella, a 78-year-old South African–Australian living in a small town, and Brenda, a 61-year-old Australian woman, both exhibited remarkable personal agency in separate decades-long quests to learn Mandarin Chinese.

Brenda's case demonstrates the potential effects of LS on learners' agency, as her learning and immersion into Chinese culture over her lifetime repeatedly enabled her to do and accomplish things (travel, live independently overseas) that she had not previously thought she was capable of. Her gradual immersion into Chinese culture and language learning were thus tied directly to a general increase in agency in areas of her life unrelated to her language learning. Describing a 2004 study visit to Beijing, she said:

> I found it challenged my confidence and in doing so realised my own strength. It also gave me the confidence to travel by myself in China. This has also had a flow on effect for me on other things I do and other places I go to. (Tasker, 2012: 207)

Stella's case, on the other hand, is exemplary of a learner whose personal agency allowed her to find ways to pursue LS opportunities throughout her learning journey, despite numerous obstacles and unfavorable conditions (e.g. living and working on a farm in a small town with limited or nonexistent local resources for second language study, significant family responsibilities, and her husband's disapproval of her study of Chinese).

Tasker (2012: 15) explicitly links Stella's agency with her ability to immerse herself in Chinese language and society and cites Stella's 'characteristic clarity and critical understanding of her learning needs, and the kind of teaching which meets those needs, which has been a feature of her Chinese learning journey from the beginning, and has contributed to her agency in fostering favourable conditions for her learning journey to develop'. After the death of her husband, Stella continued to pursue her Chinese language study as a way of helping her to 'structure her time' (Tasker, 2012: 14), making six short visits to China, studying on a month-long homestay in Beijing and, upon her return to Australia, engaging a teacher in China to tutor her via Skype. In a remarkable example of using personal agency to pursue language socialization opportunities, she requested that the mayor of her town allow her to attend official functions for Chinese business or political delegations, explaining that 'it would be quite nice for visiting Chinese people to know that there are Chinese-speaking non-Chinese people' (Tasker, 2012: 13) in her town. Where many learners might find the lack of opportunities for second language engagement, speaking practice and socialization in a small town discouraging, Stella's agency allowed her to *create* these opportunities for herself where they had not previously existed.

Similarly, one of the authors of this chapter (Doherty) has demonstrated through his own self-efficacy and self-organizing behaviors (as observed by his co-author and others) possibilities for reaching high levels of proficiency in both Mandarin and Cantonese by means of myriad, highly agentive, self-socialization behaviors. To that end, he established several online and offline language learning communities to bring together learners and native speakers, allowing both groups opportunities for co-socialization. In one example, he organized a local Cantonese language group that attracted several hundred members (including L2 learners and native/heritage speakers of all levels) who take part in regular conversation and cultural events (e.g. *dim sum*, hotpot, Hong Kong movies, Cantonese opera, cultural festivals) where they can be exposed to target-language cultural and linguistic norms. In contrast, the other author (Duff), while committed, in principle, to continuing her own learning and use of Mandarin, demonstrates (in her view) more limited forms of agency or concrete actions enabling her to achieve her own language-learning goals, despite possibly having more resources at her disposal and strong incentives to do so (see Duff *et al.*, 2013). On the other hand, she concedes that she has been able (in however limited a fashion) to take agentive actions to facilitate others' socialization into and through Mandarin through programmatic activities she has contributed to. Thus, agency does not necessarily result in one's own (sinophone or other) learning goals but may mediate others' socialization, even when the facilitating or socializing agent is not herself an expert in the Chinese language.

Discussion and Implications

In the preceding sections, we examined how agency has been approached in relation to LS since the inception of this theoretical field, noting that, as in second language acquisition and many other areas of applied linguistics and social life, agency (like power) has assumed a much more central position in both theory and research in the past decade. We also observed synergies and overlap between the construct of agency in LS and the notion of self-socialization, which has been described in the psychological literature for some time, but not yet in studies focusing on *language (and culture)* as a primary medium and outcome of socialization. Given the current trends and opportunities arising from information and communication technologies and new communities of practice, we anticipate much more discussion of self or self-directed socialization in the future as a means by which agency is enacted and oriented.

Indeed, the rise of online self-directed resources for immersive learning (through Massive Open Online Courses, forums, virtual communities such as Second Life, or surrounding shared pop culture interests, in the form of soap operas, movies and music, for example) – in addition to the ease with which learners can move in and out of different speech communities on the Web – has created an environment highly conducive to self-socializing (and other-socializing) behaviors. Although members of online communities interact with one another over the internet, the decision to seek out such communities and the context in which that communication takes place are essentially solitary and self-motivated (when not part of courses). Moreover, while there may be more traditional expert–novice relationships at work among the members of a particular online community, the drive to join a remote or virtual community in the first place can only be internally motivated (i.e. outside of formal education requirements).

In the example of Massive Open Online Courses, dozens, hundreds or thousands of students from around the world independently sign up for online courses that do not provide any traditional form of academic credit. Such new sites for, and modes of, LS and content learning raise new questions and issues, such as why people engage in this form of non-credit-bearing learning; whether students gain cultural or linguistic knowledge from their participation in addition to knowledge about the content (e.g. physics); and whether students are socialized (or self-socialized) into the practices and norms of the online learning community the way that they would be in an in-person classroom, even without direct interaction between and among students and instructors. Addressing these sorts of questions will reveal the intersections between motivation, agency, self-socialization and learning, particularly in the era of new digital literacies and education.

Conclusion

As we have seen, discussions of agency in LS have moved beyond a simplistic, binary novice/expert dynamic to embrace more nuanced portrayals across the learner lifespan, including the possibility that learners are more than just passive recipients of others' agency. It is becoming increasingly clear that agency, LS and learning/participation are co-emergent phenomena that may become manifest concurrently but are nevertheless constantly in flux and interconnected.

This interaction between agency and LS can be seen in the different ways that agentive forces have played out in the learning and socialization trajectories described in the case studies above. Most striking is the way in which highly agentive learners like Lilly were able to empower themselves to 'self-socialize' and alter their own life paths almost entirely by means of personal willpower (and institutions and others willing to accommodate her wishes, pay her fees, etc.). We posit that this kind of self-directed socialization can be the result of learners bringing their agency to bear on the affordances of their personal context and the resources available to them.

There are also aspects of agency involved in the selection or rejection of individual components of a language or its associated culture. In such cases, the learners express their personal agency by deciding not to invest time, energy or attention in aspects of the language that are not valuable to them. While instances of this rejective agency have been recorded frequently throughout the literature on HL learners, it is worth noting that, for learners in noninstrumental language acquisition contexts, the desire to be unique or to have mastered an unusual skill – implicitly or explicitly rejecting more commonplace or socially expected languages – may be just as significant motivating and socializing factors as more traditionally goal-oriented ones. In a way, these factors too have an agentive force, allowing learners to surpass, break out of or otherwise remove themselves from contexts in which they would likely be unable to exert full control over some aspect of their lives or learning paths.

Further research is needed to discover why and more specifically how certain individuals are capable of marshalling great stores of personal agency to the task of their own language socialization. In other words, we need to discover not only why some people are more agentive than others, but also why some learners seem to be able to leverage their agentive resources in creative and empowering ways to create opportunities for learning and change profound enough to fundamentally alter the course of their L2 learning journey and even their entire lifepath.

At the same time, it is important to remember that agency can ebb and flow freely and may be mitigated by other circumstances throughout the different domains of an individual's life, and throughout their learning journey. We must be careful not to make the mistake of imposing too rigid a typology on the classification of agentive personalities; nonetheless, it remains a question worthy of closer inquiry why some learners may be highly agentive in some aspects of their lives but not others. From a more practical perspective, and given the clear relationships between and among agency, LS and second language/culture learning, we should be asking whether agency might be transferable across contexts, and how best to provide scaffolding to learners who struggle with enacting their own agency in pursuit of their language-learning goals.

Note

(1) Rejection of home languages and of attempts by others to socialize them into their home/heritage cultures is a very common and often devastating (for elders) form of agency, peer conformity and choice made by the children of immigrants (or transnational sojourners), who typically shift to socially dominant languages such as English once they enter school (see reviews by Duff, 2014; Li & Duff, 2014).

References

Ahearn, L.M. (2001) Language and agency. *Annual Review of Anthropology* 30, 109–37.

Al Zidjaly, N. (2009) Agency as an interactive achievement. *Language in Society* 38 (2), 177–200.

Arnett, J.J. (1995) Adolescents' use of the media for self-socialization. *Journal of Youth and Adolescence* 24, 519–533.

Arnett, J.J. (2007) Socialization in emerging adulthood: From the family to the wider world, from socialization to self-socialization. In J.E. Grusec and P.D. Hastings (eds) *Handbook of Socialization: Theory and Research* (pp. 208–231). New York: Guilford Press.

Atkinson, D. (2003) Language socialization and dys-socialization in a South Indian college. In R. Bayley and S. Schecter (eds) *Language Socialization in Bilingual and Multilingual Settings* (pp. 147–162). Clevedon: Mulitilingual Matters.

Bourdieu, P. (1977) *Outline of a Theory of Practice*. Cambridge: Cambridge University Press.

Bourdieu, P. (1990) *The Logic of Practice*. Stanford, CA: Stanford University Press.

Duff, P. (2003) New directions in second language socialization research. *Korean Journal of English Language and Linguistics* 3, 309–339.

Duff, P. (2007) Second language socialization as sociocultural theory: Insights and issues. *Language Teaching* 40, 309–319.

Duff, P. (2010) Language socialization. In S. McKay and N.H. Hornberger (eds) *Sociolinguistics and Language Education* (pp. 427–455). Bristol, UK: Multilingual Matters.

Duff, P. (2012a) Identity, agency, and SLA. In A. Mackey and S. Gass (eds) *Handbook of Second Language Acquisition* (pp. 410–426). London: Routledge.

Duff, P. (2012b) Second language socialization. In A. Duranti, E. Ochs and B. Schieffelin (eds) *Handbook of Language Socialization* (pp. 564–586). Malden, MA: Wiley-Blackwell.

Duff, P. (2014) Language socialization into Chinese language and 'Chineseness' in diaspora communities. In X.L. Curdt-Christiansen and A. Hancock (eds) *Learning Chinese in Diasporic Communities: Many Pathways to Being Chinese* (pp. 13–34). Amsterdam: John Benjamins.

Duff, P. and Talmy, S. (2011) Second language socialization: Beyond language acquisition in SLA. In D. Atkinson (ed.) *Alternative Approaches to SLA* (pp. 95–116). London: Routledge.

Duff, P., Anderson, T., Ilnyckyj, R., VanGaya, E., Wang, R.T. and Yates, E. (2013) *Learning Chinese: Linguistic, Sociocultural, and Narrative Perspectives*. Boston: De Gruyter.

Duranti, A., Ochs, E. and Schieffelin, B.B. (eds) (2012) *The Handbook of Language Socialization*. Malden, MA: Wiley-Blackwell.

Fogle, L.W. (2012) *Second Language Socialization and Learner Agency: Adoptive Family Talk*. Bristol: Multilingual Matters.

Garfinkel, H. (1967) *Studies in Ethnomethodology*. New Jersey: Prentice Hall.

Garrett, P.B. and Baquedano-Lopez, P. (2002) Language socialization: Reproduction and continuity, transformation and change. *Annual Review of Anthropology* 31, 339–361.

Giddens, A. (1979) *Central Problems in Social Theory: Action, Structure, and Contradiction in Social Analysis*. London: MacMillan.

Giddens, A. (1984) *The Constitution of Society: Outline of the Theory of Structuration*. Berkeley, CA: University of California Press.

Goodwin, M.H. and Kyratzis, A. (2012) Peer language socialization. In A. Duranti, E. Ochs and B.B. Schieffelin (eds) *The Handbook of Language Socialization*. Malden, MA: Wiley-Blackwell.

He, A.W. (2012) Heritage language socialization. In A. Duranti, E. Ochs, and B.B. Schieffelin (eds) *The Handbook of Language Socialization* (pp. 587–609). Malden, MA: Wiley-Blackwell.

Heinz, W.R. (2002) Self-socialization and post-traditional society. *Advances in Life Course Research* 7, 41–64.

Kohonen, V. (1992) Experiential language learning: Second language learning as cooperative learner education. In D. Nunan (ed.) *Collaborative Language Learning and Teaching* (pp. 14–39). Cambridge: Cambridge University Press.

Kuczynski, L. and Parkin, M. (2007) Agency and bidirectionality in socialization: Interactions, transactions, and relational dialectics. In J.E. Grusec and P. Hastings (eds) *Handbook of Socialization* (pp. 259–283). New York: Guilford.

Kulick, D. and Schieffelin, B. (2004) Language socialization. In A. Duranti (ed.) *Companion to Linguistic Anthropology* (pp. 349–368). London: Blackwell.

Kyratzis, A. and Cook-Gumperz, J. (2008) Language socialization and gendered practices in childhood. In P. Duff and N.H. Hornberger (eds) *Encyclopedia of Language and Education* (2nd edn), Volume 8: Language Socialization (pp. 145–156). New York: Springer.

Lam, W.S.E. (2004) Second language socialization in a bilingual chat room: Global and local considerations. *Language Learning & Technology* 8 (3), 44–65.

Lam, W.S.E. (2008) Language socialization in online communities. In P. Duff and N.H. Hornberger (eds) *Encyclopedia of Language and Education, Volume 8: Language Socialization* (2nd edn; pp. 301–311). New York: Springer.

Li, D. (2000) The pragmatics of making requests in the L2 workplace: A case study of language socialization. *Canadian Modern Language Review 57*, 58–87.

Li, D. and Duff, P. (2014) Chinese language learning by adolescents and young adults in the Chinese diaspora: Motivation, ethnicity, and identity. In X.L. Curdt-Christiansen and A. Hancock (eds) *Learning Chinese in Diasporic Communities: Many Pathways to Being Chinese* (pp. 219–238). Amsterdam: John Benjamins.

Mökkönen, A.C. (2012) Social organization through teacher-talk: Subteaching, socialization and the normative use of language in a multilingual primary class. *Linguistics and Education 23* (3), 310–322.

Morita, N. (2004) Negotiating participation and identity in second language academic communities. *TESOL Quarterly 38*, 573–603.

Newman, P.R. and Newman, B.M. (2009) Self-socialization: A case of a parachute child. *Adolescence 44* (175), 523–537.

Ochs, E. (1986) Introduction. In B.B. Schieffelin and E. Ochs (eds) *Language Socialization across Cultures* (pp. 1–13). New York: Cambridge University Press.

Ochs, E. and Schieffelin, B.B. (1984) Language acquisition and socialization: Three developmental stories and their implications. In R. Shweder and R. Levine (eds) *Culture Theory: Essays on Mind, Self and Emotion* (pp. 276–320). New York: Cambridge University Press.

Ochs, E. and Schieffelin, B.B. (2008) Language socialization: An historical overview. In P.A. Duff and N.H. Hornberger (eds) *Encyclopedia of Language and Education, Volume 8: Language Socialization* (2nd edn; pp. 3–15). New York: Springer.

Ochs, E. and Schieffelin, B.B. (2012) The theory of language socialization. In A. Duranti, E. Ochs and B.B. Schieffelin (eds) *The Handbook of Language Socialization* (pp. 1–21). Malden, MA: Wiley-Blackwell.

Paugh, A. (2005) Multilingual play: Children's code-switching, role play, and agency in Dominica, West Indies. *Language in Society 34* (1), 63–86.

Reinhardt, J. and Zander, V. (2011) Social networking in an intensive English Language classroom: A language socialization perspective. *CALICO Journal 28* (2), 326–344.

Schieffelin, B.B. and Ochs, E. (eds) (1986) *Language Socialization across Cultures*. Cambridge: Cambridge University Press.

Siegal, M. (1994) The role of learner subjectivity in second language sociolinguistic competency: Western women learning Japanese. *Applied Linguistics 17* (3), 356–382.

Talmy, S. (2008) The cultural productions of the ESL student at Tradewinds High: Contingency, multidirectionality, and identity in L2 socialization. *Applied Linguistics 29* (4), 619–644.

Tasker, I. (2012) *The Dynamics of Chinese Learning Journeys* (Unpublished doctoral dissertation). University of New England, New South Wales, Australia.

Thorne, S.L., Black, R.W. and Sykes, J. (2009) Second language use, socialization, and learning in internet interest communities and online games. *Modern Language Journal 93*, 802–821.

Ushioda, E. (2013) Motivation matters in mobile language learning: A brief commentary. *Language Learning & Technology 17* (3), 1–5. Retrieved from http://llt.msu.edu/issues/october2013/commentary.pdf.

Wang, D. (2012) Self-directed English language learning through watching English television drama in China. *Changing English 19* (3), 339–348.

Watson-Gegeo, K. (2004) Mind, language, and epistemology: Toward a language socialization paradigm for SLA. *Modern Language Journal 88*, 331–350.

Wong-Fillmore, L. (2000) Loss of family languages: Should educators be concerned? *Theory into Practice 39* (4), 203–210.

5 Theorizing Young Language Learner Agency through the Lens of Multilingual Repertoires: A Sociocultural Perspective

Chatwara Suwannamai Duran

Introduction

Daw, a 14-year-old Karenni-Burmese girl, was born in a fenced refugee camp on the Burma-Thailand border, where her parents, originally from the highlands of Burma, had been sheltered for more than 15 years. Daw grew up with diverse languages used within her own family and in the camp. She has acquired Burmese as her primary language because Burmese is her parents' lingua franca; however, she has simultaneously acquired Kayan, her mother's primary language, and Karenni, which is spoken by the biggest ethnic group living in the refugee camp. Schooling in the camp allowed her to learn how to read and write in Burmese and Karenni and to pick up some English as a foreign language. In Phoenix, Arizona, where Daw and her family have resettled since 2009, Daw has been required to improve her English proficiency because it is the primary academic and dominant language of her new host country. However, she utilizes all of her previously- and recently-acquired languages daily, depending on various factors: audience, desire, device, domains, modes, proficiency and purposes. For example, Daw speaks with her brother and friends in Karenni because she has many Karenni-speaking friends and neighbors in her current setting. Nevertheless, she continues speaking Burmese with her father. When it comes to religious practices, she reads Bible and prays in Karenni or Burmese with the belief that these two languages facilitate effective communication of her faith and understanding. Concurrently, Daw has used English for a broader communication in her new locale and integrated it in digital communication such as texting, internet surfing and online chat rooms. In all, multilingualism is her preferred method of communication that occurs in a variety of domains daily.

Duran, 2012

73

Daw's vigorous linguistic practices indicate that children's language-learning trajectories get complicated because of multiple settings they are exposed to owing to the rapid flows of people across cultural and linguistic borders, particularly in the last few decades. Children like Daw are engaged in complex, multilingual practices daily but their experiences have been silent and invisible in adult discourses (White *et al.*, 2011). Children are commonly perceived as their caretakers' dependent, passive and vulnerable baggage. They have been left behind throughout our human history (Heath, 2008; Huijsmans, 2011; Orellana, 2009). For this reason, I connect two important calls as a guiding light for this chapter. First, the calls for more research examining children's experiences of migration (Dobson, 2009; Huijsmans, 2011) lead me to focus on children's involvement in diasporic communities. Second, in response to the calls for a more dynamic model of language socialization (Talmy, 2008), this chapter presents children as active agents and highlights how they generate agency in language-learning processes.

Given that this volume strives to scrutinize agency in language learning, I define *agency* as learners' socioculturally mediated right to choose whether to partake in a communication and in what language (see also Ahearn, 2001a, 2001b). I also associate such agency with learners' available *linguistic resources* and their *desire* to participate in constitutive and discursive interactions (Baynham, 2006; Collins, 1993; Miller, 2012). In addition, this chapter emphasizes that the language socialization (LS) process is multidirectional and fluid (Bayley & Schecter, 2003; Kulick & Schieffelin, 2004; Talmy, 2008). It provides theoretical lenses that lead to an understanding of how children who encounter multiple languages perform their contextualized agency (González, 2001; Fogle, 2012; Kulick, 1992; Zentella, 1997, 2005), in contrast with passive novices in the traditional LS framework. This nontraditional view of child agency expands our understanding of children and childhood with regard to questions such as how their role has been historically and socioculturally shaped and reshaped (Aries, 1962; Orellana, 2009) and how the hybridity of the LS process has been complicated by dynamic language contacts over time.

To these ends, I present three interconnected frameworks on children's language learning and agency in the following sections. First, I discuss the concept of multilingual repertoires and propose that learners' existing and emerging linguistic knowledge is a fundamental part of *history in person* (Holland *et al.*, 1998; Lave & Wenger, 1991; Miller, 2012). I argue that, when learners accumulate more linguistic resources through their experiences, they have more control on their agency, or the right to decide whether to engage in a communication and in what language. Second, I illustrate how learning languages, becoming multilingual and enacting agency are related to each other in the light of sociocultural theory, which explains that language learning is enhanced by social contacts through language and language-in-use

(Schieffelin & Ochs, 1986; Talmy, 2008). In addition, I emphasize that coexistence of learners' linguistic repertoires and desire in a particularly appropriate space may set forth agency. Finally, I discuss how the children's role can be transformed from passive receptors to active decision-makers by suitably combining multilingual repertoires, social context and desire. I will use data excerpts from my recent case study of newly arrived Karenni youth and their linguistic choices and practices in the USA to demonstrate such agentive practices.

Multilingual Repertoires

The term multilingual that I characterize here entails both bilingualism and multilingualism – having knowledge of more than one language, either as a second or a foreign language, including both previously and recently acquired languages. Through these inclusions, 'multilingual repertoires' is used in this chapter to accentuate the 'multiplicity' of learners' languages in both oral and textual communications. Such multiplicity is learned from multiple events. They include but are not limited to everyday context, learning an additional language inside and outside language classroom settings, formal and informal interaction, movement or migration and professional training (see also Kramsch, 2009). In addition, I intend to highlight the act of practicing multiple languages as a result of linguistic inventory or resources (Blommaert, 2010).

My agenda is to include 'multilingual repertoires' in *history in person*. According to Holland *et al.* (1998) and Holland and Lave (2001), *history in person* is a theoretical perspective to view individuals' identity as a continuing and transforming process in their participation and local practice. As I exemplify the notion of language as a resource, I use the term *language learners* and *multilingual speakers/individuals* interchangeably in this chapter. This is because language learners are bi- or multilingual, to some extent. Here, it is worth noting that multilingual individuals may not know all of their previously and recently acquired linguistic resources equally well (Canagarahjah, 2009; Kramsch, 2009). However, each language represents a linguistic jigsaw piece of multilingual individual's portraiture – 'life trajectories, their history in person, and their participation in linguistically diverse space' (Miller, 2012: 445). While eliciting history in person by observing what individuals say and do in social contexts, we can trace individuals' unique life trajectories as history 'constituted in the space that encompasses social participation and self-authoring' (Holland & Lave, 2001: 29). That is, each social space frames the way in which individuals play a part and make their linguistic choices to serve their strategic and communicative purposes. As Bakhtin reminds us that every word has a history, I understand that these individuals' linguistic choices in turn tell us about their linguistic autobiography elucidating the languages that they have acquired either as a child or as an adult, either previously acquired or recently acquired (see also Kramsch, 2009). In other words, their past and ongoing experiences of connecting linguistic choice to a contextualized interaction have some impact on the choice they make and the objectives in their present communicative involvement. The construct of language learners as multilingual subjects, who have hard-earned linguistic and sociocultural knowledge, allows us to see their *history in person* when their linguistic resources and practices are set forth in socialization (Talmy, 2008).

It is also important to note that multilingualism can be understood at two levels, individual and societal (Matsuda & Duran, 2013). While I highlight individuals' multilingual repertoires, the individual's communities and institutions such as family members, friends, neighbors and colleagues are all involved in decisions on language choice and practice in a given context. As each language has functions and cannot be separated from social contexts (Ahearn, 2012; Canagarahjah, 2009; Gumperz, 1962; Jacobson, 1960), such relationships impact multilingual individuals' developing ability to move between languages, depending on what language within one's linguistic repertoires is discursively, contextually and functionally needed (Kramsch, 2009). Accordingly, applied linguists and educational anthropologists investigate language learners to examine their sociolinguistic reality, or what learners really do in their daily lives with languages (Blommaert, 2010). This elucidates the way in which learners decide on their language choice and practice in local communities outside school and use it as a bridge to language-learning success in the classroom discourse. Many use the framework to understand how language learners build and maintain social networks and to sustain connections (with people, institutions, ideas, events) within and across linguistic boundaries among transnational and immigrant households, for example, Arabic-speaking families in Australia (Cruickshank, 2006), Chinese-speaking families in England (Wei, 1994), Japanese-and-English-speaking students in the USA (Haneda & Monobe, 2009) and Spanish-speaking immigrants in the USA (Dicker, 2006; Rosolová, 2007; Rubinstein-Ávila, 2007; Zentella, 2005). Their findings demonstrate that the participants were competent and committed to using multiple languages discursively for different purposes and domains.

To understand the process of becoming and being multilingual, recent sociolinguistic and educational research on language choice has explored a wide range of linguistic codes available in multilingual settings and how these individuals learn to choose among these resources to achieve certain strategic goals in multilingual communities (e.g. Baquedano-López & Kattan, 2007; Lamarre, 2003; Miller, 2012; Pease-Avalez, 2003; Schecter & Bayley, 2002; Weldeyesus, 2009). Exploring these language choices helps us to understand how multilingual resources enable multilingual speakers to act linguistically and contextually. In addition, multilingual practices in a community are believed to be a form of multilingual capital that might be used to connect to the past while pursuing goals in the present and the future (Dagenais, 2003: 269; see also Bourdieu, 1977). For example, research on refugees and immigrants' multilingual repertoires shows how contexts, purposes and goals cooperatively influence what choices are made based on available repertoires and activities in particular moments (e.g. Duran, 2012; Weistein-Shr, 1993; Wortham, 2001).

Sociocultural Aspect of Agency

As mentioned earlier, I define agency as learners' socioculturally mediated right to choose whether to partake in a communication, under the framework of language socialization (Ahearn, 2001a, 2001b). Recently, studies on language learners' agency have been guided by multidirectionality and hybridity of LS or the notion that there is no age limit nor predetermined roles for active actors and passive receptors (Bayley & Schecter, 2003; Duff, 2003; Duff & Talmy, 2011; Kulick & Schieffelin, 2004; Talmy, 2008). The multidirectionality and hybridity of LS in these studies include what perspectives to use when analyzing and exploring agency, how and when agency is enacted in such dynamic processes and how to facilitate agency in classroom settings. I suggest adding the notion that learners' agency is desire-driven as the combination of all these inquiries and components. In other words, agency is contextually produced when learners understand their role and what they can do with their linguistic repertoires, and to what extent they want to participate in discourses. Below, I explain the dialogic characteristics of agency by emphasizing (1) the relationship between agency and context; and (2) how an agentive act is desire-driven. Both relationships are explained by incorporating multilingual repertoires that learners have historically and socioculturally acquired.

The definition of language as a social practice (Hymes, 1971) emphasizes *context* as a fundamental factor that shapes (and is shaped by) the way people communicate (Blommaert *et al.*, 2005). *Context* involves sociocultural and discursive norms strongly bound to ideologies, social class, hierarchical relationship (Bourdieu, 1977), gender role, age and a number of cultural and historical factors. For this reason, being a member in a given speech community needs a great deal of multilayered social and cultural knowledge. In reality, such knowledge is even more multifaceted because one can be a member in more than one speech community, depending on needs, interests and the aforementioned multilingual repertoires. For example, a female Mexican-American nurse living in the USA's Southwest region may have multiple linguistic competencies. She may have both social and regional varieties of Spanish and English in her linguistic repertoires because of her upbringing, education, professional training, interests (e.g. gourmet cooking, yoga) and role and responsibility in her family (e.g. as a daughter, as a mother, as a wife), among other things. The better she understands *meaning* and *function* of languages (Blommaert, 2010) within her multilingual repertoires, the more she has the agency or right and flexibility to enact her context-embedded language practices in each communicative domain. When applying this similar view of language learning, it is worth noting that learners' linguistic choice corresponding to the understanding of the participating role, relationships with others and communicative goals can enable their agentive acts. With this definition and focus, learners in this framework are viewed as social actors, whose identity is context-dependent and fluid, 'not a fixed category' (Bayley & Schecter, 2003: 6).

In the field of second language acquisition, *context* guides us to see how social settings encourage individuals to learn and use a second language. Emphasizing learners' participation in the language learning process and engagement in the communities of practice, Lantolf and Pavlenko (2001) proposed that language learning is a social practice. Within such practice, learners need to be viewed as people or what Block (2003: 124–125) defined as 'socioculturally situated human beings' (see also Breen, 2001), whose learning is activated in interactional context and apprenticeship. With a sense of belonging and membership in the community, successful language learning occurs because learners are aware of the relationship between language and function in the community and between themselves and the community (Pavlenko, 2003).

Recently, *space* (Blommaert *et al.*, 2005; Blommeart, 2010, 2013a; Miller, 2012), not merely a location but also all contextual factors that activate social actors' linguistic practices, has been employed as the site to explore how language learners form their agency. With this endeavor, learners' agentive acts are investigated when they practice multilingual acts in the right space – the space where multilingualism is tolerated. This also includes the events when learners communicate about their language-learning trajectories, decision-making and linguistic repertoires, or linguistic 'autobiographical narratives' (Miller, 2012: 449) to connect their past to the present context-embedded purposes (or history in person). Miller (2012: 441) took on the notion that agency is 'discursively, historically and socially mediated' and pointed out through her study that multilingual spaces reinforced agency and multilingualism. In her study, the immigrant small business owners living in the USA learned other languages and carried out agentive acts, driven by their clients being from linguistically diverse backgrounds. At the same time, they subscribed to the ideology of language that prioritizes English. Miller concluded that English-dominant ideology did not stop the immigrants from learning other languages to fulfill their business and communicative goals. Her study suggests that multilingual capacities among the immigrants are shaped not only by the ideology of language that prioritizes the host country's dominant language, but also by the local influences, relationships between multilingual individuals and the *desire* to participate in multilingual networks. From this viewpoint, identifying and locating multilingual space or context, where language learners live in and live with, allow us to see how agency is generated.

Building on the early works of motivation in language-learning theories (Dörnyei, 1998; Gardner & MacIntyre, 1993), I contend that the desire to participate, mentioned above, can be understood as learners' willingness to communicate, which is the self-selected practice. According to MacIntyre *et al.* (1998), desire and level of desire are conditional. Many factors such as linguistic knowledge and communicative competence incorporated 'at a particular time with specific person or persons' (MacIntyre *et al.*, 1998: 547) encourage learners' readiness to enter into a communicative discourse. The specific person or group of people fulfills what I mentioned in the previous section, that multilingual communities, especially the members of such a community, have an impact on the multilingual individual's decision-making. This constituent draws us into the amalgamation of multilingual repertoires, context and space that collaboratively grant learners' agency in language learning. When learners have a *desire* to participate, they are likely to voluntarily use the language to engage in the communication they think fits.

Theorizing Young Language Learner Agency

Several scholars put emphasis on children's language learning in order to understand multiple stages of developmental socialization and how their role is transformed through those stages. They have found that in many cases children actively shape, influence and pass on local language ideologies and communicative norms to adults or to other children (De la Piedra & Romo, 2003; Orellana, 2009; Paugh, 2012). Heath (1982) said the environments children are raised in shape the way they see and understand the world. Although in most cultures children are only allowed to access limited spaces and interactions with certain people (Maynard & Tovote, 2010), the increase in movement and mobility provides more learning experiences to children and encourages them to be regularly exposed to multiple languages within those limited spaces. These accounts have led me to view the process as simultaneous, not the entirely sequential, second language socialization that we usually undertake. That is, multiple languages are, in fact, concurrently used, learned, taught, picked up and intermingled (Blommaert, 2010, 2013a). Thus, deciphering how these multilingual children see and understand their role in their complex language-contact spaces will help disclose the way their agency works in their language choice and use (Paugh, 2012; Schieffelin & Ochs, 1986; Talmy, 2008).

While approaches to children's agency in social settings do not require lenses different from those in the case of adults (e.g. construct them as multilingual individuals and investigate how they utilize their multilingual repertoires in contexts), exploring children's agency requires more of our attention to and participation in the children's world. First, because of a generational gap between adult researchers and children, researchers often overlook and presume children's points of view, rationales and feelings. Influenced by the traditional language socialization that views children as novices, whose language development and ideologies are influenced by adults, children are often invisible. In addition, from my experiences working on the research site, interviewing children is a challenging task. Children have a shorter attention span and we cannot expect them to answer a series of questions the way we expect adults to (see also Orellana, 2009). To access children's world and their agentive practices, Orellana (2009: 17) reminds us to 'prioritize meaning and values assigned to children' and how the meaning and values make children visible. I understand this as our acknowledgment of the children's role and how the children themselves are aware of their existence through linguistic practices with desire to participate.

To identify children's language learning and agency, scholars explore multilingual children's agency and their experiences in three ways: accommodation, participation and resistance (Ahearn, 2001b; Fogle, 2012). Among these three, accommodation and participation lead to successful learning. Serving their families and communities as facilitators, language brokers and knowledge mediators have been emphasized based on this approach. Orellana et al.'s (2001) work in multisited immigrant communities indicated that children's agentive role as brokers does not only bridge their families to a larger community but also makes the children themselves visible. He (2013) also explains that children's agency is produced in numerous ways. Her study on Chinese heritage language learning in the USA discusses how young learners enact their agency through the choices and practices of their Chinese and English communicative competencies. Owing to their understanding of both English-speaking and Chinese-speaking cultures, these children can talk *about* their family, talk *for* their family and talk *with* their family. This emphasizes that children can either participate in a communicative act or accommodate their audience in context because of their multilingual repertoires. Based on Goffman's terms, He concludes that these children play multiple roles: authors, back-up animators, co-authors and editors and self-appointed principals.

While language learners' agency in the classroom and the motivation for language learning and acquisition are studied, more and more sites outside the classroom setting have been investigated because of the sociocultural authenticity they offer. For example, De la Piedra and Romo (2003) examined five siblings in a Mexican-American household to understand the way in which older siblings can be mediators of language and literacy in order to help younger children partake in the literacy events. The older siblings in the study, for instance, creatively adapted pedagogical games learned from school to play in the household. Veléz-Ibáñez and Greenberg (1992) also showed that children's multilingual practices are collective activities incorporated in the family's linguistic repertoires that are transmittable and maintainable among family members. Likewise, young immigrants in Orellana's (2009) study demonstrate that children's agentive linguistic acts are extended to tasks commonly done by adults, because multilingual competence is desired and valued by their family members. For example, these children speak on their parents' behalf when the parents, who have less dominant language competence, need to deal with service providers (e.g. bankers, doctors, salespersons) and teachers. Her study suggests that children's multilingual practices inside and outside the households in a variety of activities give them confidence and reinforce language learning, language maintenance and multilingualism. These studies demonstrate how valuable children's role as language brokers and mediators are since their multilingual competencies empower them and give them agency to dynamically shape the situation.

The second perspective on children's agency is formulated on the basis of *resistance* to or rejection of participation in an interaction or the use of a certain language (see also Norton, 2001). Recently, Fogle's (2012) analysis of data on adopted Russian-speaking children in American families demonstrated that children utilize sociocultural and sociohistorical knowledge not only to make sense of their multilingual world but also to communicate their needs or their disapproval feelings through their linguistic choice and practice. Fogle (2012: 166) concludes that agency produced by these children through both their participation and their resistance 'determines societal processes of language maintenance and shift, as well as cultural transformation and change'. Drawing on these perspectives, I see that children's agency is influenced by and connected to desire, as I discussed earlier. In all, children's agency can be explored and carried out in an authentic social setting. Below, I provide two examples that demonstrate children's agency in language learning, authority and dynamic contribution to the language socialization process by drawing on their multilingual repertoires.

First example

Toh Reh, a nine-year-old Karenni boy, had been in the USA for almost two years and was in second grade at the time when I met him. Karenni is his primary language but he learned English in school after he arrived in the USA. I recruited all of his family members in my study that investigated linguistic and literacy practices among recently arrived Karenni refugee families in Phoenix, Arizona. He was open and friendly, especially when he was at home with his family and four siblings. He always took part in conversations when his family had visitors. On one occasion, I was interviewing Nway Meh, who is Toh Reh's 45-year-old mother and spoke only Karenni. I was being assisted by an interpreter. However, Toh Reh came out from his room to join our conversation when he heard that English was being used. The following exchange was part of the recorded audio when Toh Reh sat beside his mother (Nway Meh), who was being interviewed.

Me (asking Nway Meh):	Can you speak English? (waiting for the interpreter to assist)
Toh Reh:	No!
Me (asking Nway Meh):	So, you are from Burma but from the Karenni village.
Toh Reh:	But, we are Karenni. We are not Burmese.
Me (asking Nway Meh):	But, can you speak Burmese?
Toh Reh:	No!

Toh Reh was not a designated interpreter but decided to join the conversation because his multilingual repertoires that include English triggered his desire to participate. He answered the questions for his mother when the question in English was asked despite the fact that an interpreter was there to assist us. In addition, instead of interpreting for his mother, Toh Reh voluntarily answered the questions and skipped the interpreting stage. His participation transformed the situation from *no need of his presence* to *needed*. Without my request or his mother's request, he chose to respond immediately because he held two authoritative qualities: he owned (1) the information I was gathering from his mother; and (2) English communicative competence necessary to articulate it. As Orellana (2009) suggested, we prioritize meaningful roles assigned to children; here, the child's meaningfulness also covers the unassigned, yet valuable, role that he willingly carried out. Toh Reh decided to talk *about* and *for* (He, 2013) his mother because he had learned the value and functions of English in the situation here and interacted with me on his mother's behalf. His practice demonstrates his desire for his and his mother's voices to be heard. Applying the framework of multilingual space as site (Miller, 2012) and the construct of learners as multilingual individuals (Kramsch, 2009), this authentic setting reinforces Toh Reh's agentive act. The situation accentuates the significance of contextualized, discursive and desire-driven agency. It highlights desire as the product of an amalgamation of factors that include linguistic repertoires that could serve the right person(s) at the right time and space (MacIntyre *et al.*, 1998). Not the child alone but the child's understanding of his social activities with other individuals contributes to his role as a language broker being in charge of his mother's responses. Toh Reh understood that he could be a situated communicative mediator and provide a language service to adults on the site. This shows his acknowledgment of his significant role and his relationship to the circumstance he partook in. According to Blommaert (2013b), language offers an advantaged access to various aspects of social life. In this circumstance, Toh Reh, who is a young English language learner and a multilingual individual according to Kramsch's (2009) construct of multilingual subject, has more access and flexibility to connect his linguistic resources to a wider range of activities than his mother does.

Second example

Based on the notion of *history in person*, this section presents how we may be able to elicit learners' agency in the events when learners discuss and evaluate their language learning trajectories, including their decision to learn a certain language. Owing to her varied experiences that include living in a refugee camp, living in a Christian dormitory, going to a local school in Thailand and managing the transition to living in Phoenix, Arizona, See Meh, a 14-year-old Karenni female, brought with her a rich multilingual background to language-learning endeavors. She was born in a Thai refugee camp where her parents, originally from the Karenni State of Burma, were sheltered. In addition to her native language, Karenni, See Meh had acquired Thai since she was nine years old during her stay outside the refugee camp and her study in the Thai local school sponsored by a nonprofit organization. In the USA, she used Thai with friends from Burma and Thailand who knew Thai. See Meh told me that her multilingual ability includes Karenni, 'Karen, Thai, a little bit of Burmese and a little bit of English'. When I asked her to reflect how she managed her language choice, she said (in Thai),

ถ้านั่งกับคนอินเดีย กับคนดำ หนูก็พูดภาษาอังกฤษ ถ้าอยู่กับเพื่อนกะเหรี่ยงขาว หนูก็พูดกะเหรี่ยงขาว ถ้าอยู่กับเพื่อนคาเรนนี หนูก็พูดคาเรนนี

[When I sit with Indian friends and Black friends, I will speak English. When I am with the White Karen[1] friends, I will speak White Karen. When I am with Karenni friends, I speak Karenni.]

She also added,

ถ้าพวกเขาคุยกันเป็นภาษาอังกฤษหนูก็คุยเป็นภาษาอังกฤษ ถ้าพวกเขาคุยกันเป็นภาษากะเหรี่ยงขาวหนูก็คุยเป็นภาษากะเหรี่ยงขาวค่ะ แล้วแต่พวกเขาคุยก่อน พวกเขาชอบภาษาอะไรหนูก็คุย แล้วแต่เขา ถ้าบางคนกะเหรี่ยงขาวพูดไทยเป็น เขาพูดไทยกับหนู หนูก็พูดไทยกับเค้า หนูรอให้พวกเขาพูดก่อน เขาพูด (ภาษา) อะไรหนูก็พูด เพราะหนูรู้ภาษาเยอะ

[If they talk in English, I will talk in English. If they talk in White Karen, I will talk in White Karen. I let them initiate the conversation ... whatever language they like, up to them. Some White Karen (people) can speak Thai and they speak Thai to me, I will speak Thai to them. I wait for them to start first. I will use the language they use, whatever language they use ... because I know many languages.]

When asked about the Karen language, the language she had learned from a group of Karen children in the refugee camp, See Meh explained that learning Karen was very easy because she had many Karen friends to communicate with. See Meh added that she remembered specific instances where her ability to speak Karen had declined but she added,

พอไปเรียนภาษาไทยไม่มีคนคาเรนค่ะ หนูก็เริ่มลืมๆ มันไป แล้วหนูก็ไม่เคยพูดคาเรนอีก พอหนูมาถึงที่นี่มีเวลาเพื่อนหนูคุยกับหนู หนูเข้าใจแต่หนูพูดไม่ได้ พอหนูมาถึงแล้วประมาณห้าเดือนหนูเริ่มพูดออกมา แล้วตอนนี้ก็พูดออกได้ง่ายแล้ว

[When I learned Thai in the Thai school, there were no Karen people, so I kind of forgot it and did not speak it. When I arrived in the USA, Karen friends talked to me, I understood what they said but I could not talk back in Karen. After five months in the USA, I started speaking Karen again. Now, I speak it. And now, it comes out so easily].

See Meh's Karen language development represents learner's agency. Learning Karen is not typical in her community, even though interethnic communications among refugees from Burma are common. Burmese is usually and preferably used as the lingua franca among these refugees. See Meh explained that her Karen friends, therefore, did not learn to speak Karenni because they believed that learning and using Burmese, an official language of Burma used by a larger group, would be more useful. In addition, Burmese continues to hold a powerful and symbolic status among refugees from Burma. Nevertheless, See Meh chose to learn and use Karen, the language of her Karen friends, to communicate with them, both in school and when they visited her at home (once or twice a week). See Meh believed that learning and using Karen strengthened the friendship between her and Karen friends and expanded her social network in the current setting.

The relationship between See Meh's multilingual repertoires and agency is twofold. First, multilingual repertoires allow her flexibility and a variety of options to select the appropriate language to use in each context, depending on the audience. In many situations, she was the person who spoke more languages than her audience did, so she had more linguistic choices. It brings her pride to be multilingual. That she said, 'I will use the language they use … because I know many languages' indicates that her language choice is not only contextualized, but also desire-driven and accommodative to participate in interactions. Her agency was activated in the context where she has the right to choose one among her available language resources to accommodate her audience and let them use the language they are capable of. While I was interviewing her during the data collection process, I too benefitted and was accommodated by See Meh's unique multilingual repertoires. She spoke to me in Thai, the language I was most comfortable with. Her multilingual practices are shaped by the strong relationship between local influences made up of multilingual members and the space where multilingualism is prioritized and valued (Blommaert, 2010, 2013; Miller, 2012).

Although the larger space is English-dominant, See Meh was aware of the advantage she may obtain by speaking multiple languages and utilizing them when she wanted to.

Second, See Meh's talk about her decision on language learning and choice is an act of communicating her autobiographical narratives (Miller, 2012) that shows how her agency is produced. That is, her case substantiates that 'identity is not a fixed category' (Schecter & Bayley, 2003: 6) but it is a process of becoming in which an individual learns from a variety of settings (home, peer group, school) to practice situated and selective identities. This process, in turn, demonstrates See Meh's agency that is sustained by her linguistic repertoires, the persons involved in that space and the persons' linguistic repertoires. In addition, See Meh's schooling experience in different contexts that included a local school in Thailand, a Christian boarding school in Thailand and a high school in the USA have influenced her strategically social interaction. She told me that the first high school she enrolled in in Phoenix did not have many Karenni students. Consequently, she wanted to be accepted by friends from a diverse background (e.g. American mainstream, African American, Mexican American and Karen). She later joined the school's volleyball team where she used English and Karen to connect with them. Such experiences constituted her linguistic autobiography. In January 2011, her family moved to a new apartment. At the time, there were more than 20 Karenni families in the complex and many Karenni students enrolled at the local high school nearby. Although she enjoyed her Karenni friends, See Meh brought with her the confidence, effort and desire to make more friends outside the Karenni group. Her decision is opposite to that of many newcomers, who feel more comfortable and secure in their native language-speaking community. However, See Meh emphasized the positive aspects of having cross-cultural communication, 'It's good. It helps you make more friends and to practice the language'. She happily told me, 'หนูมีเพื่อนหลายแบบ หลายสไตล์' ['I have all kinds of friends'].

See Meh's multiple identities are discursively produced through social engagement with 'all kinds of friends'. The use of certain languages in certain situations helps produce the identity she wants her audience to perceive and accept in the interaction and that makes her proud of being multilingual. See Meh's experiences demonstrate how an individual's successful language learning might be influenced by discursive forces in the local context as well as personal desire and choices made by the learner. Here, we see that reasons for language learning and decision on language choice in See Meh's experience involve the positive thinking about multilingualism based on her own history. By recognizing usefulness, function and purpose of a language, See Meh understands the potential benefit and adopts a positive attitude toward multilingualism that stimulates her language learning, while confirming that her true self is Karenni, as shown in the following exchange.

See Meh: I am Karenni.

Me: What makes you think you are a Karenni?

See Meh: My father speaks Karenni. My mother speaks Karenni. I speak Karenni. I speak Karenni to my family.

Me: You speak Thai, too. Do you think you're Thai?

See Meh: No.

While See Meh has her self-perception as a Karenni, she takes advantage of being multilingual. Her experiences present the use of multilingual repertoires as resources to create and sustain connections (with people, institutions, events) across linguistic and cultural boundaries. Such connections accentuate the use of multilingualism and produce agency for See Meh, to achieve a wide range of communicative purposes.

Both Toh Reh and See Meh are the representation of multilingual children who have language-learning experiences affected by migration and different languages used in their previous and current locations. The two examples are drawn on the construct of language learners as multilingual subjects (Kramsch, 2009) who have the ability to communicate in two or more languages. With the understanding of the value of languages and their functions in the multilingual spaces they are involved, Toh Reh and See Meh possess and practice agency to participate in a given social setting.

Both examples demonstrate the key ingredients of agency formulation. First, when learners have a *desire* to participate in a given context, they voluntarily use the language necessary to engage in that context, which includes various sociocultural elements. This is because they learn to know their significant role and their relationship to the circumstance they are playing a part in. Second, their *multilingual repertoires* strengthen their capacity to communicate. Both Toh Reh's and See Meh's experiences demonstrate how an individual's successful language learning might be influenced by discursive forces in the local context as well as personal choices made by the learners (e.g. Toh Reh's voluntarily participation in his mother's interview and See Meh's learning Karen to fulfill her personal interest). Above all, agency in language learning and language choice of both children involve their practical multilingualism. Each language has a function and purpose; however, an individual must have a perceived need or reason to undertake language learning. By recognizing a particular language, its usefulness, function and purpose, Toh Reh and See Meh understand the potential benefit, adopt a positive mindset and generate learners' agency that stimulates their language learning and language in use (Talmy, 2008).

Conclusion

In this chapter, I exemplify how children's agency can be investigated by a sociocultural approach with more attention and priority to children's tasks (e.g. language brokering), participation and language practices. In order to visualize children's language-learning agency, I draw attention to children and their agentive roles activated by their multilingual repertoires and a proper combination of sociocultural and sociohistorical factors. As shown in the two examples, language choice and willingness to be involved in socialization are endorsed by the children's readiness and multilingual upbringing and experiences. This collective view of sociocultural and sociohistorical factors in language use allows me to claim that, even at a young age, children have historical influences (Holland & Lave, 2001; Lave & Wenger, 1991; Wortham, 2001, 2005). The influences include their language learning in multiple settings and in their daily participative and communicative practices. They help us approach their agency in a range of social and geographical spaces, especially in the case of our current global state that has expanded multilingual arenas.

It is my hope to encourage researchers and educators to address children's desires, agentive acts and participation as part of language socialization process and as pedagogical rationale. The chapter has implications for many groups of learners and a wide range of educational settings, which I broadly define as including formal language classrooms, community-based language learning and everyday contexts. The chapter also suggests that we recognize and reflect on what linguistic resources learners from linguistically diverse backgrounds already have and bring with them to their learning ventures. We can employ these resources to facilitate learners' agency for both academic and social purposes.

Note

(1) 'White Karen' refers to the Karen people from the Karen State of Burma. They are distinguished from the Karenni people, who are commonly called 'Red Karen' from the Karenni State of Burma.

Acknowledgements

I would like to express my deep appreciation to Andy Gao and all the other editors of this volume. My special thanks also go to two anonymous reviewers and my dear friend, Tanita Saenkhum, who provided constructive feedback in the formation of this chapter.

References

Ahearn, L. (2001a) Language and agency. *Annual Review of Anthropology* 20, 109–137.
Ahearn, L. (2001b) *Invitations to Love: Literacy, Love Letters and Social Change in Nepal*. Ann Arbor, MI: The University of Michigan Press.
Ahearn, L. (2012) *Living Languages*. Chichester: Blackwell.
Aries, P. (1962) *Centuries of Childhood: A Social History of Family Life*. New York: Jonathan Cape.

Baquedano-López, P. and Kattan, S. (2007) Growing up in a bilingual community: Insights from language socialization. In P. Auer and W. Li (eds) *New Handbook of Applied Linguistics* (pp. 57–87). Berlin: Mouton de Gruyter.

Bayley, R. and Schecter, S. (eds) (2003) *Language Socialization in Bilingual and Multilingual Societies*. Clevedon: Multilingual Matters.

Baynham, M.J. (2006) Agency and contingency in the language learning of refugees and asylum seekers. *Linguistics and Education* 17 (1), 24–39.

Block, D. (2003) *The Social Turn in Second Language Acquisition*. Edinburgh: Edinburgh University Press.

Blommaert, J. (2010) *The Sociolinguistics of Globalization*. Cambridge: Cambridge University Press.

Blommaert, J. (2013a) *Ethnography, Superdiversity, and Linguistic Landscapes: Chronicles of Complexity*. Bristol: Multilingual Matters.

Blommaert, J. (2013b) Interview with Jan Blommaert. Max Planck Institute for the Study of Religious and Ethnic Diversity, http://www.mmg.mpg.de/en/online-media/interviews/interview-with-jan-blommaert-tilburg-university-the-netherlands-babylon-center-for-the-study-of-superdiversity/(accessed 24 August 2014).

Blommaert, J., Collins, J. and Slembrouck, S. (2005) Space of multilingualism. *Language and Communication* 25 (3), 197–216.

Bourdieu, P. (1977) The economics of linguistic exchanges. *Social Science Information* 16, 645–668.

Breen, M.P. (ed.) (2001) *Learner Contributions to Language Learning*. Harlow: Pearson Education.

Canagarajah, S. (2009) The plurilingual tradition and the English language of South Asia. *AILA Review* 22, 5–22.

Collins, J. (1993) Determination and contradiction: An appreciation and critique of the work of Pierre Bourdieu on language and education. In C. Calhoun, E. Lipuma and M. Postone (eds) *Bourdieu: Critical Perspectives* (pp. 116–138). Cambridge: Polity Press.

Cruickshank, K. (2006) *Teenagers, Literacy and School: Researching in Multilingual Contexts*. New York: Routledge.

Dagenais, D. (2003) Accessing imagined communities through multilingualism and immersion education. *Language, Identity, and Education* 2 (4), 269–283.

De la Piedra, M. and Romo, H.D. (2003) Collaborative literacy in a Mexican immigrant household: The role of sibling mediators in the socialization of pre-school learners. In R. Bayley and S. Schecter (eds) *Language Socialization in Bilingual and Multilingual Societies* (pp. 44–61). Clevedon: Multilingual Matters.

Dicker, S.J. (2006) Dominican American in Washington Heights, New York: Language and culture in a transnational community. *International Journal of Bilingual Education and Bilingualism* 9 (6), 713–727.

Dobson, M.E. (2009) Unpacking children in migration research. *Children's Geographies* 7 (3), 355–360.

Dörnyei, Z. (1998) Motivation in second and foreign language learning. *Language Teaching* 31 (3), 117–135.

Duff, P. (2003) New directions in second language socialization research. *Korean Journal of English Language and Linguistics* 3, 309–339.

Duff, P. and Talmy, D. (2011) Language socialization approaches to second language acquisition. In D. Atkinson (ed.) *Alternative Approaches to Second Language Acquisition* (pp. 95–116). New York: Routledge.

Duran, C.S. (2012) A study of multilingual repertoires and accumulated literacies: Three Karenni families living in Arizona. PhD thesis, Arizona State University.

Fogle, L.W. (2012) *Second Language Socialization and Learner Agency: Adoptive Family Talk*. Bristol: Multilingual Matters.

Gardner, R.C. and MacIntyre, P.D. (1993) A student's contribution to second language acquisition. Part II: Affective variables. *Language Teaching* 26, 1–11.

González, N. (2001) *I am My Language: Discourses of Women and Children in the Borderlands*. Tucson, AZ: University of Arizona Press.

Gumperz, J. (1962) Types of linguistic communities. Anthropological Linguistics 4 (1), 28–40.

Haneda, M and Monobe, G. (2009) Bilingual and biliteracy practices: Japanese adolescents living in the United States. *The Journal of Asian Pacific Communication* 19 (1), 7–29.

He, A.W. (2013, June) Language choice and language use in Chinese American households. International Symposium on Bilingualism, Singapore.

Heath, S.B. (1982) What no bedtime story means: Narrative skills at home and school. *Language in Society* 11, 49–76.

Heath, S.B. (2008) Language socialization in the learning communities of adolescents. In P. Duff and N. Hornberger (eds) *Encyclopedia of Language and Education* (2nd edn), Volume 8: Language Socialization (pp. 217–230). New York: Springer.

Holland, D. and Lave, J. (eds) (2001) *History in Person: Enduring Struggles, Contentious Practice, Intimate Identities*. Santa Fe, NM: School of American Research Press.

Holland, D., Lachicotte, W. Jr, Skinner, D. and Cain, C. (1998) *Identity and Agency in Cultural Worlds*. Cambridge, MA: Harvard University Press.

Huijsmans, R. (2011) Child migration and questions of agency. *Development and Change* 42 (5), 1307–1321.

Hymes, D. (1971) *On Communicative Competence*. Philadelphia, PA: University of Pennsylvania Press.

Jacobson, R. (1960) Linguistics and poetics. In T.A. Sebeok (ed.) *Style in Language* (pp. 350–377). New York: MIT Press.

Kramsch, C. (2009) *The Multilingual Subject*. Oxford University Press.

Kulick, D. (1992) *Language Shift and Cultural Reproduction: Social, Self, and Syncretism in a Papua New Guinean Village*. Cambridge: Cambridge University Press.

Kulick, D. and Schieffelin, B. (2004) Language socialization. In A. Duranti (ed.) *A Companion to Linguistic Anthropology* (pp. 349–368). Malden, MA: Blackwell.

Lamarre, P. (2003) Growing trilingual in Montreal. In R. Bayley and S. Schecter (eds) *Language Socialization in Multilingual Societies* (pp. 62–80). Clevedon: Multilingual Matters.

Lantolf, J.P. and Pavlenko, A. (2001) (S)econd (L)angauge (A)ctivity theory: Understanding second language learners as people. In M.P. Breen (ed.) *Learner Contribution to Language Learning* (pp. 141–158). Harlow: Pearson Education.

Lave, J. and Wenger, E. (1991) *Situated Learning: Legitimate Peripheral Participation*. Cambridge: Cambridge University Press.

MacIntyre, P.D., Clément, R., Dörnyei, Z. and Noels, K.A. (1998) Conceptualizing willingness to communicate in a L2: A situational model of L2 confidence and affiliation. *The Modern Language Journal* 82 (4), 545–562.

Matsuda, A. and Duran, C.S. (2013) Problematizing the construction of Americans as monolingual English speakers. In V. Ramanathan (ed.) *Language Policy, Pedagogic Practices: Rights, Access, Citizenship* (pp. 35–51). Bristol: Multilingual Matters.

Maynard, A.E. and Tovote, K.E. (2010) Learning from other children. In D. Lancy, J. Bock and S. Gaskins (eds) *The Anthropology of Learning in Childhood* (pp. 181–206). Walnut Creek, CA: AltaMira.

Miller, E.R. (2012) Agency, language learning, and multilingual spaces. *Multilingua* 31, 441–468.

Norton, B. (2001) Non-participation, imagined communities, and the language classroom. In M.P. Breen (ed.) *Learner Contribution to Language Learning* (pp. 159–171). Harlow: Pearson Education.

Orellana, M.F. (2009) *Translating Childhood: Immigrant Youth, Language, and Culture*. New Brunswick, NJ: Rutgers University Press.

Orellana, M.F., Thorne, B., Chee, A. and Lam, W.S.E. (2001) Transnational childhoods: The participation of children in processes of family migration. *Social Problems* 48 (4), 573–592.

Paugh, A.L. (2012) *Playing with Languages: Children and Change in a Caribbean Village*. New York: Berghahn Books.

Pavlenko, A. (2003) 'I never knew I was a bilingual': Reimagining teacher identities in TESOL. *Journal of Language, Identity, and Education* 2 (4), 251–268.

Pease-Avalez, L. (2003) Transforming perspectives on bilingual language socialization. In R. Bayley and S. Schecter (eds) *Language Socialization in Bilingual and Multilingual Societies* (pp. 9–24). Clevedon: Multilingual Matters.

Rosolová, K. (2007) Literacy practices in a foreign language: Two Cuban immigrants. In V. Purcell-Gates (ed.) *Cultural Practice of Literacy: Case Study of Language, Literacy, Social Practice, and Power* (pp. 99–114). Mahwah: Lawrence Erlbaum.

Rubinstein-Avila, E. (2007) From the Dominican Republic to Drew High: What counts as literacy for Yanira Lara? *Reading Research Quarterly* 42 (4), 568–588.

Schecter, S.R. and Bayley, R. (2002) *Language as Cultural Practice: Mexicanos en el norte*. Hillsdale, NJ: Lawrence Erlbaum Associates.

Schieffelin, B. and Ochs, E. (1986) Language socialization. *Annual Review of Anthropology* 15, 163–191.

Talmy, S. (2008) The cultural production of the ESL student at Tradewind High: Contingency, multidirectionality, and identity in LS socialization. *Applied Linguistics* 29 (4), 619–644.

Veléz-Ibáñez, C. and Greenberg, J. (1992) Formation and transformation of funds of knowledge among U.S. Mexican households. *Anthropology & Education Quarterly* 23 (4), 313–335.

Wei, L. (1994) *Three Generations, Two Languages, One Family*. Clevedon: Multilingual Matters.

Weinstein-Shr, G. (1993) Literacy and social process: Community in transition. In B. Street (ed.) *Cross-cultural Approaches to Literacy* (pp. 272–293). Cambridge: Cambridge University Press.

Weldeyesus, W.M. (2009) Language socialization and ensuing identity construction among Ethiopian immigrants in metropolitan Denver. Unpublished Doctoral Dissertation. University of Colorado, Boulder, CO.

Wenger, E. (1998) *Communities of Practice: Learning, Meaning, and Identity*. Cambridge: Cambridge University Press.

White, A., Laoire, C.N., Tyrrell, N. and Carpena-Méndez, F. (2011) Children's role in transnational migration. *Journal of Ethnic and Migration Studies* 37 (8), 1159–1170.

Wortham, S. (2001) *Narratives in Action: A Strategy for Research and Analysis*. New York: Teachers College Press.

Wortham, S. (2005) Socialization beyond the speech event. *Journal of Linguistic Anthropology* 15, 95–112.

Zentella, A.C. (1997) *Growing Up Bilingual: Puerto Rican Children in New York*. Malden, MA: Blackwell.

Zentella, A.C. (2005) *Building on Strength: Language and Literacy in Latino Families and Communities*. New York, NY: Teachers College Press.

6 Sociological Approaches to Second Language Learning and Agency

Carola Mick

Introduction

Learning a language is primarily and fundamentally based on the acquisition of a new linguistic system, but beyond that, it involves socialization into a community's specific ways of representing and living social reality. It is the process through which an individual seeks to appropriate resources that allow her or him to actively take part in the social construction of reality (Berger & Luckmann, 1981) in a community of practice (Lave & Wenger, 2007). Language acquisition is one of the requirements for an individual to become a social actor, and linguistic resources enable her or him to influence the target speech community. Therefore, learning a language is also about negotiating access to a language community and, thus, it is embedded in power relations. All this implies that learning a language is related to agency.

When discussing agency in first-language learning, issues of becoming a member of and an active participant in a given community are prevalent. Sociocultural knowledge is necessary for a language learner in order to use new linguistic resources in socially appropriate ways. Its complexity is demonstrated through the notion of *communicative competence* (Hymes, 1972), and it is variable from one speech community to another (Bernstein, 1972). More specifically, language socialization research is interested in the intersection of language acquisition with socialization practices. It considers learners' verbal statements as active positioning with regard to the activities, knowledge, values and institutions of the target community (Ochs & Schieffelin, 2008). It also conceives of language socialization as a twofold process of a learner's integration into a community and her or his developing active role as a participant in its social practices.

When analyzing agency in second language learning, further dimensions have to be taken into consideration. In addition to the acquisition of new linguistic resources and community-specific sociocultural knowledge, second language learners need to become able to *translate* (Bhabha, 1996) between different language systems and language communities. Second language learning influences the individual's pool of available semiotic means for social practice and creates new opportunities for meaningful encounters. It provides the learner with access to alternative ways of representing and evaluating the world than those that were part of her or his first-language socialization, and it thereby can trigger awareness of the relativity of social realities. As an actor who is situated at the border between coexisting or competing speech communities, the second language learner is exposed to the group-specific representations of the other and has to deal with their mutual relationship. As a mediator and broker, furthermore, she or he may become able to influence the community borders and power relations.

The chapter at hand suggests a way of theorizing these aspects of agency at the crossways of sociology and educational research on second language learning. It discusses second language learners' agency from a sociological perspective in its interactions with linguistic resources (mediational means), sociocultural knowledge and ways of representing social reality (discourses). It also deals with the links between second language learning, the construction of individual and collective identities of communities and community members, as well as power structures. Second language learning, in other words, is viewed as a social practice that mediates and transforms the relationship between speech communities.

The chapter starts by presenting the sociological debate on structure and agency (see also Mick, 2012) and then establishes a link to second language learning by offering Deleuze's (1989) concept of *dispositives*. This heuristic tool allows for focusing on four dimensions of agency in second language learning: the creation of a multilingual pool of mediational means through second language learning; the target community's representations of languages, learning and the language learner; the negotiation of access and membership into this target community; and the learner's participation in the social construction of its reality. This discussion builds mainly on socio-constructivist approaches to language learning and sociocultural theory (see Vygotsky, 1978; Wertsch, 1993; Lantolf, 2000). It provides examples from interactional sociolinguistic studies of different social and cultural contexts of second language learning. The chapter ends with a brief summary of the links between theories on second language learning and agency and provides an outlook on further sociological research questions regarding agency in second language learning.

Agency and Language Learning from the Perspective of Sociology

With regard to agency, sociology is interested in the degree of determination of an individual's actions by the society and the specific position she or he occupies within it, as well as in the possibilities of self-determination. Parsons (1968) defines the two extreme points of a structure–agency paradigm as total determinism of an individual's action by her or his social condition on the one side, and total autonomy of the individual despite her or his social environment on the other. Other sociologists stress the necessary interdependence of structure and agency. Giddens (2009), for example, argues for the possibilities of social and structural change that arise from the individual's capacity for agency within society, and Durkheim (1999) considers socialization (which for him is the primary aim of education) as the precondition for an individual to become a social actor. Sewell's (1992) conceptualization of agency takes into account these dynamics and looks on the way in which structurally available tools are used for reconstituting or constituting new forms of social reality (*schemes*). He argues that, 'Agency arises from the actors' control of resources, which means the capacity to reinterpret or mobilize an array of resources in terms of schemes other than those that constituted the array' (p. 20). As such, agency depends on the mobilization of existing social structures, and it implies the transformation of these structures. Relational sociology, as conceived by Emirbayer and Mische (1998), further highlights the temporal relations that characterize agency. As will be explained in the following paragraph, agency depends on the actualization of meaningful social resources of the past (*practical-evaluative element*), which are re-appropriated within specific present social encounters (*iteration*) with the aim of projecting oneself as a member of society into the future (*projectivity*).

As these last-mentioned theories stress, agency is mediated by meaningful devices, in other words, objects or behavior to which society has assigned meaning and which are transformed into structurally embedded cultural artifacts (Holland *et al.*, 1998: 36). The prototypical form of such a mediating device is language (Halliday, 1993: 93), but every element of the social reality can be transformed into a resource for agency. These cultural tools function as archives of meaning that carry with them the specific sociocultural contexts of former uses. Social practices that are mediated by these devices become meaningful by positioning a current activity in relation to past contexts in which the tools appeared (Kramsch, 2000: 134–138). These complex relationships between former and actual social practices are described as dialogism by Bakthin (as cited in Todorov, 1981), and put in relationship to language learning by Holland *et al.* (1998): 'In authoring the world, in putting words to the world that addresses her, the "I" draws upon the languages, the dialects, the words of others to which she has been exposed' (p. 170). This is the dimension of agency Emirbayer and Mische (1998) conceptualize as *iteration*.

By exploiting the available mediating devices in a specific new context, actors do not only carry out current activities but imagine, prepare for future social encounters, redefine their own status and transform the cultural tools they use, too (*projectivity*, Emirbayer & Mische, 1998). Kramsch (2000: 137) emphasizes the transformative potential of mediated agency by stating, 'Because signs point to other signs, the mere act of using signs reorients the whole field of action...and thereby makes things happen. It creates new things, states, and events'. The use of cultural tools creates new meaning and resources, and thus, transforms social reality and structure.

As members of society, individuals are obliged as well as enabled to take part in the meaning-making within and of society (Holland *et al.*, 1998: 272). Their social nature provides them with inbuilt possibilities for (in-/voluntary) improvisation, imagination, disruption and subversion of their own social order (Butler, 1995). As Emirbayer and Mische (1998) emphasize, the conscious engagement in social transformation needs a deliberate mobilization of resources by anticipating, estimating and evaluating their possible social consequences (*practical evaluative element*). It presupposes a dialogic, critical and moral relationship of the self toward its own acts and implies, as Dewey explains (1985), both an element of discipline to structurally provided discourses within society as well as freedom of choice: 'The need for careful assessment of aims, objectives, allegiances, etc., and of the conception of the good, may be important and exacting. But despite this need for discipline, the use of one's agency is, in an important sense, a matter for oneself to judge' (p. 204). The practical evaluative capacity of agency is about deliberately dealing with the structural elements in order to influence them responsibly in a sustainable manner.

The next section reviews and theoretically elaborates on the connection between agency and second language learning by introducing the concept of *dispositives* of learning.

Agency and Dispositives of Second Language Learning

Foucault (1975) introduces the concept of *dispositives* when describing complex socially conceived systems, structures and schemes that become enacted in social practice. They consist of predefined role models, rules of interaction, a given array of legitimated resources, structured activities, spaces and times. As Yurén (2005: 32, 33) argues, learning happens within the dispositives that are socially shaped according to specific educational aims; they can be institutionalized to different degrees, or not. Formal second language learning, for example, often happens within specific school buildings, according to an institutionally defined timetable and by using specifically designed didactical materials. The prevailing role models are those of teachers and students. The learning activities are mainly planned by the teacher or authors of textbooks in accordance with an official curriculum. Only certain cultural tools are legitimated as interactional resources within these classrooms, and interaction is organized by following institution-specific rules. Even in informal learning settings the concerned actors arrange the available resources and elements of the context so that they serve a certain educational goal, whether it is explicitly stated or not. Through the social design of educational dispositives, the community structures the learning process, promotes predefined forms of practice among its new members and thereby guarantees a certain coherence in the knowledge, values, institutions and relations it identifies with (see also Yurén & Mick, 2013).

Deleuze (1989) details the concept of dispositives by characterizing its relation to agency on different levels. He stresses first that dispositives consist of concrete resources – material elements of space, body and linguistic resources, for example – that are put together and designed in a specific way (*lignes d'énonciation: lines of visibility*). These elements become meaningful tools for the interactions that are promoted by the dispositive, mediate the social practice and condition the capacity of agency of the implied learners and teachers. Second, the particular ways in which these resources are arranged in order to shape a dispositive depend on socially prevailing worldviews or discourses (Foucault, 1971), for instance, the context-specific dominant representations of what counts as learning, language and a second language learner's agency. The particular form of these discourses reflects the majority's point of view on second language learning and frames the educational dispositive (*lignes d'énonciation: lines of utterances*). Third, dispositives are not only shaped but are also shaping ensembles; they contribute to the social construction of reality by offering an environment to human beings for developing their agency. More precisely, dispositives of second language learning offer certain social roles and conditions to individuals as potential members of a linguistic community. This means that dispositives promote specific forms of subjectivities that are a prerequisite for individuals to become social actors, or in other words, to actively take part in meaning-making within society (*lignes de subjectivation, lignes d'objectivation: lines of subjectivation, lines of objectivation*). Fourth, dispositives take part in the constitution of the power relations within the social context they are part of. Depending on their characteristics, dispositives can either enhance the reproduction of existing social structures or contribute to a certain degree to their transformation (*lignes de force: lines of force*). In the case of second language learning, for example, dispositives can either deny or facilitate the new language speaker's access to the target language community, and they can thereby control the degree to which she or he may influence the reality and relation of these groups.

The following sections analyze agency in second language learning by presenting theoretical reflections and examples that concern these four dimensions of educational dispositives.

Language learning as mediated action (*lignes de visibilité*)

As we have seen before, agency depends on the use of available semiotic resources and above all on linguistic means. There is broad agreement among researchers that second language learning provokes changes within the linguistic repertoire and the intellectual development of the learner, and thereby influences her or his development of agency. Whereas traditional theories of second language acquisition discuss a potentially positive or negative influence of the first and second languages of learners (*interferences, transfer*), socio-constructivist approaches highlight the intricate relationship between first-language acquisition (L1) and second language learning (L2) with regard to the development of the individual's practical-evaluative competency for agency. As sociocultural research on second language learning effectively shows, bilingual children are not only able to participate in socially meaningful ways in different language communities and to translate content from one language and cultural system into another, but they also display an important metalinguistic awareness, are particularly sensitive to linguistic meanings, develop multiple learning strategies and enjoy remarkable flexibility and creativity in their thinking as well as important verbal and nonverbal communicative competences. As Mondada and Pekarek Doehler's study (2004) demonstrates, in the case of a French second language classroom, second language acquisition interacts with the communicative competence that learners already control, and it can enhance their capability to exploit semiotic resources consciously. Drawing on 'various embedded linguistic, interactional, institutional competencies' (p. 514), students exploit tasks in interactive learning activities in order to create further learning opportunities in the target language for themselves.

Other studies in interactional sociolinguistics illustrate the way in which the interplay of linguistic resources from the learner's several languages serves communicative goals. In a traditionally multilingual context, language alternation can be used to index and introduce a change to the semiotic frame of an activity (see Gumperz, 2000), and thereby can become an important tool for the individual's active participation in reality construction. More than that, language alternation may linguistically create intimacy between speakers and exclude others, and it can accomplish aesthetic functions or evoke specific emotions. Dittmar *et al.* (1998: 126), for example, demonstrate in a sociolinguistic study the way in which learners can linguistically index their emotional stance with regard to the target language community and culture. Mondada and Pekarek Doehler (2003) describe how the participants in a second language classroom define and interpret the functions, structures and context of interaction through their local choice of linguistic resources. The learners thereby actively mediate their own and others' learning processes, interactively construct the reality of the learner community and shape individual or collective identities. Furthermore, as Auer illustrates (1999: 312), agency in second language learning can lead to the creation and even grammaticalization of new semiotic resources or 'fused lects' when language alternation becomes the usual form of interaction within a multilingual community.

In short, second language learning enriches the array of available resources or *mediational means* (Wertsch, 1993; see Kramsch, 2000: 135) for individuals' participation in the social constitution of reality and creates a zone of contact for different language communities. It provides the individual with access to new spheres of society, allowing her or him to get in touch with people, representations and objects that formerly remained out of reach. These new elements can scaffold alternative forms of agency and create further possibilities for learning and participation in social practice.

However, research points to several restrictions to a beneficial development of agency through language learning in the above-mentioned senses. According to Gumperz (1964), the particularities of the performed bi- or multilingual proficiency (*verbal repertoire*) – whether it is compartmentalized ('separate') or overlapping ('common'), exclusive or complementary – depend on social and cultural characteristics of the dispositive of language acquisition and use. He differentiates the communicative requirements in *transactional interactions* (Gumperz, 1964: 149), where social status is at stake, and *personal interaction*, where participants in social encounters perform as individuals. In the first type of interaction, speakers stick to a homogeneous, uniform communicative competence that corresponds to the social role they are expected to perform. In theses contexts, learners are asked to keep the linguistic resources from different languages separate. Contrariwise, in dispositives where the second type of interaction prevails, learners may exploit all their available linguistic resources more flexibly and creatively in order to accomplish multiple communicative goals. Arditty and Vasseur (2003) distinguish and characterize the communicative events in three different dispositives of second language learning: at school, at the workplace, and within a family. The focused classroom communication being characterized by a predominance of a transactional type of interaction, the use and promotion of linguistic resources for social practice is institutionally restricted to the target language. In the example of a medical workplace context, the negotiation of multilingual resources is not institutionally predefined but depends on the situated communicative needs and competences of the actors involved. The family dinner interaction aims at the emotionally driven individual and collective identity construction; speakers exploit and acquire shared linguistic resources in a creative manner, suggestive of Gumperz's category of *performative interaction*. When learning dispositives are exclusively oriented toward very specific communicative functions, topics or contexts, as in transactional interactions within school, or when a restrictive, monolingual environment constrains the pool of legitimate semiotic resources, it might be difficult for learners to develop more complementary forms of agency in their respective languages that would be transferable to other contexts.

The section below discusses further the discursive restrictions of agency in dispositives of second language learning that can also interact with ideologies on race, gender, age, social status, occupation or origin.

Representations of second language learning (*lignes d'énonciation*)

The forms of agency that are promoted through second language learning depend on what counts as learning, language and agency in a specific educational dispositive (*orders of discourse*, Foucault, 1971). Historically contingent *languages of education* (Tröhler, 2009) shape learning; for instance, the discourses that mainly characterized Western educational systems from the past are the republican ideas of public virtue and political freedom, the Augustinian model of education as a process of inner mental exercise and spiritual experience, and the ideals of scientificity and rationality. These three discourses influence dispositives of learning and the teaching of second languages too. Learning and teaching Latin and Greek in the 16th century, according to the Augustinian model of education, was considered as an intellectual exercise that promoted the learner's sophistication. Contrariwise, learning and teaching the main European lingua franca, French, in the 17th century aimed at communicational purposes and was used by a societal elite to construct their collective identity as cosmopolitan, educated, urban citizens. During and after the Second World War, learning and teaching second languages became a field of scientific study for political reasons (Block, 2003: 12), and current theories on the 'knowledge society' stress the links between language-learning and economy (see Heller, 2010). Each of these historically situated discourses of dispositives of learning shaped specific forms of agency in second languages.

When discussing this embedment of language-learning and teaching in a specific sociohistorical context, Giroux (1983) considers schools as sites where socioeconomic and political interests meet and struggle for power over discourse and meaning. He notes, 'schooling must be analyzed as a societal process, one in which different social groups both accept and reject the complex mediations of culture, knowledge, and power that give form and meaning to the process of schooling' (p. 62). He raises awareness of discursive mechanisms (*hidden curricula*) that contribute to the reproduction of established social hierarchies.

Gogolin (1994), for example, reconstructs a persistent *monolingual habitus* in today's educational systems. She demonstrates that, even though schools value formal language learning, educational dispositives are generally conceived as monolingual spaces. There are very few languages that actually have legitimated status within the educational institutions, and the language choice is based on geopolitical and economical strategies. As Calvet (2002) illustrates, languages are profoundly unequal, not only from a statistical point of view but also with regard to the social functions and the representations they evoke. Many languages that are present in today's diverse societies – for example regional languages, minority languages – are excluded from the schools' curriculum. Hélot (2004: 188–193) observes that there are various forms of 'migrant bilingualism' that are invisible, ignored or even prohibited within formal educational dispositives that tend to promote exclusively an 'elite bilingualism'. Whereas the multiple languages spoken by migrants are interpreted as an accident and a handicap for intellectual development, schooling, professional careers or social integration, schools promote bilingualism in the internationally most visible languages. Knowing and using such languages is conceived as a privilege and is socially valued (see also De Mejía, 2002).

Second, dispositives based on academic language teaching and learning through textbooks aim at a decontextualized language competence and exclude other existing varieties of these languages. By analyzing language-learning activities of two children in the trilingual Luxembourgish school system, Maurer-Hetto (2009) illustrates the way in which an idealized representation of a standard-conform native speaker competence (see Davies, 1991) legitimates the marginalization of the vernacular linguistic resources children may already know and use.

As Hornberger's (1989) model of the *continua of biliteracy* demonstrates, a school's monolingual habitus, negative representations of migrant bilingualism and the normative view of language-learning interact with a *literacy myth*. This literacy myth promotes a restricted interpretation of what counts as literacy and considers written, formal and abstract language exercises as more prestigious than oral, naturally acquired competences. It consequently stigmatizes the linguistic competences of (migrant) bilingual learners and devalues the use of the resources they already use. Street (2006) labels this ideology as the *autonomous literacy model* because it suggests that only one form of literacy – the one that is bound to institutional aims – is legitimate, fosters cognitive development and is useful as a social resource. Such a model ignores all the alternative literacy activities that are developed outside educational institutions and majority contexts, such as within families and in different language communities (see for example Gregory & Williams, 2000). Street stresses the relative validity of this model and raises awareness of the political interests it conveys:

> Literacy, in this sense, is always contested, both its meanings and its practices, hence particular versions of it are always 'ideological', they are always rooted in a particular world-view and a desire for that view of literacy to dominate and to marginalise others. (Street, 2006: 2)

Dispositives of second language learning develop context-specific forms of agency; they depend on the historical, socioeconomic and political circumstances and the prevailing worldview at each moment and place, and tend to preserve the existing, context-specific power structures by restricting alternative ways of meaning-making.

The next section deals with the mechanisms through which the above-mentioned discourses frame (learning) activities, shape the identities of second language learners, reproduce power relations between language communities and retroactively legitimate prevailing ideologies of second language learning. Simultaneously, these observations concerning the *performativity* (Butler, 1995) of discourses will also lead us to discuss the inherent possibilities for social transformation that can be enhanced by second language learning, as well as the specific forms of agency it entails.

The social construction of reality through second language learning (*lignes de sub/objectivation*)

Dispositives of learning also shape individuals' actions by socializing them into particular subject positions and by putting specific material conditions for learning at their disposal:

> Human interaction is most often localized, framed, held in check. By what? By the frame, precisely, which is made up of non-human actors. ...Any ego chosen as the reference point finds itself pre-inscribed by the set of egos available to it in the diversified form of durable things. (Latour, 1996: 238, 239)

When designing the material construction of learning dispositives, for example, schools, classrooms, textbooks, worksheets, etc., the creators (in-) voluntarily reify the discourses that underlie their conception of second language learning. The objects they create exceed their immediate action. Once they become resources for social practice, they deploy their inbuilt discursive meaning. Analyzing a language-learning event in a Luxembourg primary school, for example, Portante (2011) illustrates how the teacher's material and didactical design affords children's reconstruction of a 'normative, unitary conception of language and literacy' (p. 524) in their group-work. It predefines the way in which the students engage in the language-learning activity and conditions – facilitates or blocks – their development of 'identities of mastery' (Lave & Wenger, 2007: 29), in other words, their process of becoming a full member of the target language community. As contexts and frames for learning activities, dispositives shape the material conditions of the learning process and the subject positions of the learners at the same time.

Restrictive dispositives whose underlying discourses (for example xenophobic, normative or sexist ones) impede the learners' full engagement, provide few possibilities for students to deploy agency. Freire *et al.* (2009) illustrate the ways in which students' categorization as being 'at risk of educational exclusion' (p. 81) limits their possibilities to participate in the negotiation of the meaning of their own learning experiences. It thereby provokes their further disengagement from school and investment in alternative practices outside the institution, where full participation and positive identity construction is encouraged (p. 86). The same happens when monolingually oriented or xenophobic dispositives of language-learning ignore or exclude some children's cultural resources and thereby hinder their participation in learning practice, as Cummins demonstrates (1996). Maybin (2006) shows that the learner's attempt to discover and exploit *hidden spaces* (Canagarajah, 2004: 118) or spaces that the dispositive does not directly control (*backstage*, Goffman, 1971) is an alternative reaction to restrictive dispositives. Children's peer-talk, for example, that emerges once the teacher turns her or his back to the class, or in the restrooms, or in dead spots of the courtyard '[multicircuits] the exercise of institutional power... and children take an active part in their own institutionalisation into schooling' (Maybin, 2006: 188). As restrictive dispositives only offer very few and limited subject positions to learners and legitimate only a few specific forms of agency, they tend to provoke resistance, truancy and deviance.

Conversely, a learning context that strengthens 'students' developing sense of self' (Cummins, 1996: 2) provides them with opportunities for active participation and promotes their academic effort. Once the learners' previous diverse experiences are legitimated within the target language (learning) community, the individual can develop her or his agency fully; the flexibility of subject positions such a dispositive puts at their disposal enables learners to participate in the language-learning process and to influence the target language community as full members (see also Gregory & Williams, 2000).

In this case, more dialogic forms of negotiation of the social reality can appear, as Li's (2009) study of the language practices of three Chinese students in London illustrates. He analyzes the ways in which their linguistic creativity and play with all of the available resources and their shared multilingual[1] verbal repertoire enables their active identity construction in a culturally diverse context: 'We are not completely Chinese any more. We are British, if you see what I mean. *I think mixing Chinese and English together is us, is what we do*' (Chris, quoted in Li, 2009: 1231, my emphasis). Li classifies the communicative practice of these youths as *translanguaging* because they do not only use resources from different languages but also create a new way of representing their bilingual experiences, for instance by inventing wordplays across languages (e.g. the use of the English interjection *cake sellers* instead of *my god* because of its similar sound to the Chinese translation of *cake sellers*: *mai gao de*). García and Sylvan (2011: 389) consider *translanguaging* as 'a product of border thinking' and as 'complex discursive practices that enable bilingual students to also develop and enact standard academic ways of languaging'. It is not an *interlanguage* (Selinker, 1972) but a complex, elaborate and dynamic language practice that enables students to adapt to the communicative requirements of their social reality as learners. It implies not only the ability to adapt to monolingual, normatively oriented contexts but also creative dealing (*translating*, Bhabha, 1996) with the particularities of their multilingual worlds (see also Weber, 2009). Pavlenko and Lantolf (2000: 174) sum up this processual agency in second language learning as follows: 'crossing a cultural border is about "renarratizing a life"'. By developing these kinds of communicative practices and identities in the *in-between*, as Li (2009: 1234) demonstrates, translanguaging also transforms the contexts within which it appears. The constant moving between languages, language communities and cultures whilst maintaining a strong sense of attachment to the space the learner lives in contributes to the construction of transnational spaces of interaction that transcend traditionally maintained boundaries.

These possibilities, however, depend on the characteristics of the dispositive. Gutiérrez (2008) outlines a pedagogy that transforms dispositives of learning into *third spaces* that build on these creative possibilities of language and particularly on literacy practices. Such learning environments promote the active participation of students in the design of classroom language-learning activities, and invite learners to imagine through their target language and literacy practices the identities and contexts they consider as appropriate for their individual and collective development. In the following quote, for example, the teacher intends to raise students' awareness concerning the projective element of agency by highlighting their possibilities as authors of autobiographic stories. Manuel, as quoted in Gutiérrez (2008: 156), states: 'Maybe, if you start telling your story in a different way you possibly can start living – you know? – differently? You can probably start thinking about the chapters yet to come, you know, because you still have a lot of chapters'. Such a 'transformative learning environment' (p. 148) builds on three elements: first, the dispositive allows for the negotiation of the perspective of the institutional curriculum that imposes writing activities in a target language; second, it builds the learning process on the students' personal history and perspective, marked by experiences of mobility, poverty, violence, exclusion and abandonment; and third, the dispositive is characterized by the perspective of the teacher who believes in the students' capacities as social actors and legitimates their individual stories and voices as tools for accessing academic language. Gutiérrez (2008: 152) observed three types of transformations that are promoted by this kind of pedagogy of a *third space*: (1) the dispositive builds on the mutual enrichment of school-based concepts and everyday concepts from the students' daily lives, thereby contextualizing academic contents and inviting actors to use them within and outside school; (2) the dispositive positions the participants in a range of different pedagogic, interactive situations that allow them to individually choose and try out the forms of mediation and the tools that most suit their individual learning process and developing social practice; and (3) thereby, the dispositive aims at enabling students to become designers of their own futures, *that is*, social actors who consciously participate in the constitution of their social environment and of themselves. Other pedagogical approaches that aim at fostering agency in dispositives of learning are those provided by the *pedagogy of possibility* elaborated by Halasek (1999) or a *pedagogy of performativity* as described by Wulf and Zirfas (2007). By referring to Bakthin's principle of dialogism (in Todorov, 1981) or Butler's concept of performativity (1995), they all target students' practical evaluative, iterative and projective capacities for agency.

As the next section will highlight, dispositives of second language learning that are based on these principles can contribute to the *empowerment* of students in the words of Cummins (1996).

The negotiation of power within dispositives of second language learning (*lignes de force*)

As has been stressed in the theoretical discussion, socialization into existing power structures is a precondition for an individual's meaningful participation in social practice, and *vice versa*, agency provides the actor with a certain power to influence social reality. In the previous sections we saw that whether second language learning contributes to the development of the learner's agency with regard to the target language (learner) community depends on the characteristics of the educational dispositive, namely on the individuals' authorization to participate in social practice, on their possibilities to develop a common, complementary verbal repertoire, as well as their potential to adopt transitional forms of learner identities and practice as fully legitimated members of the target language community. Such authorization depends on the prevailing order of discourses, and it is enacted (performed) in social practice by the personal and material conditions of the learning dispositive. This means that the dispositives of learning tend to filter the learners and only promote an agency that reproduces the prevailing discourses and social relationships (see Bourdieu, 1982). However, there is more and more research that stresses the inherent possibilities of educational dispositives and develops pedagogic approaches that aim at a transformative agency. For instance, Dumenden (2011) discusses the possibilities of changing a disadvantaged learner's trajectory through one-to-one tutoring that aims at consciously passing over symbolic capital from the teacher to the student. Gutiérrez's (2008), Halasek's (1999) and Wulf and Zirfas's (2007) pedagogical approaches have similar goals for the classroom level.

According to Freire and Macedo (1987), for change to become possible, the educational dispositive needs to contribute to awareness-raising among the students concerning the constraints to individual action and the possibilities for the social construction of reality. Questioning would be the first step in the transformation of social hierarchies and power structures because 'it transcends the constituting reality' (p. 49); questioning can happen either when socially disadvantaged students reflect on the conditioning of their action and its reasons, or when socially advantaged students reflect on the social implications of their privileges and on the origins of social inequality. Once students become critically aware of their own participation in the daily construction of power relations, they can start to question, choose, appropriate and elaborate the interactive resources that allow them to put into practice their ideal worldview.

Both steps may depend on some mediating elements, for example on a disparate encounter with the world of objects, discourses or persons. Dispositives of second language learning can provide particularly beneficial contexts in this sense, when they challenge the actors' mediating competences 'at the intersection of multiple temporal-relational contexts' (Emirbayer & Mische, 1998: 1007). Second language learning combines the challenge of socialization in a dispositive with the experience of a new form of making meaning in and of the world; this learning of alternative ways of dealing verbally with social reality can interrupt a routinized course of action and make students question their own worldviews and representations. Under specific circumstances, as we have seen in the previous sections, second language learning can provide the learner with an awareness of the multiple functionalities of the mediational tools she or he uses, with a curiosity and desire to explore the semiotic possibilities of these resources as well as with the capacity to integrate, appropriate and transform them. This consciousness can give rise to the critical, imaginative and creative process of *translating* (Bhabha, 1996), that is, the dialogic authoring of the world (Holland *et al.*, 1998). Of course, transformation does not happen immediately but presupposes a long process of interactive dealing with the tensions that the social negotiation of meaning provokes; it depends on the communicative capacities of the individual and her or his willingness to dialogue, persist, be patient and endure, and in very restrictive dispositives, on her or his resilience.

Second language learning can not only enable a transformative practice, but it can also provide the individual with the necessary tools and positions *in between* discourses that raise awareness of the possibilities for social change and their agentive capacity. It can be a powerful tool for the invention of an alternative social reality.

Insights that a Sociological Approach brings to Agency and Second Language Learning

A sociological perspective on agency in second language learning reflects on the way in which dispositives of second language learning interact with existing social structures and resources and can promote transformative processes within society. More specifically, the contribution could be described as follows:

(1) It accounts for the ways in which second language learning itself is negotiated in the social practices of the implied actors, and uncovers the mechanisms through which educational dispositives promote or hinder learners' progress in the target language. The learning process does not only depend on the structural characteristics of the respective languages or the learners' cognitive capacity to overcome them, but it is also a question of the legitimation of resources and identities, of authorization or denial of access to the target language community, and finally of the social status of the speaker with regard to this community.

(2) It uncovers the opportunities of second language learning in terms of social practice: learning a second language enlarges the pool of resources social actors can use and opens up new possibilities for communicative (social) action. It implies the meeting of language systems, communities and cultures, raising awareness for alternative ways of wording and living together, and opening up possibilities for questioning one's own social reality. The concerned systems change through such interaction, and in-between spaces are developed that can be exploited creatively. Learning a second language, therefore, can significantly enhance a learner's overall agentive capacity and is a potentially critical, transformative social practice.

(3) As a research perspective, a sociological view on agency and second language learning furthermore allows for evaluating dispositives of second language learning with regard to their contribution to social change. It invites us to think about alternative strategies of second language learning and teaching that would meet the challenges society faces. It will be important to analyze the ways in which the innovative language and learning practices change the structural elements of dispositives of learning. Some of the questions that research at the crossways of sociology and second language education could deal with are the following: how far does translanguaging impact on the educational institutions' representation of the target language, the 'standard' that is aimed at and the 'native speaker competence'? How far do the particularities of the spaces, frames and identities that this kind of second language practice creates impact dispositives of second language learning? How far do these translating practices transform globalized discourses, for example, of the new economy's commodification of language?

Of course, a sociological perspective alone is not sufficient either to analyze all the dimensions of agency in existing dispositives of second language learning or to materially create alternatives; interdisciplinary dialogue with pedagogy, linguistics, anthropology, psychology, etc., are needed in order to benefit fully from the insights of each individual discipline with respect to second language learning and agency.

Note

(1) According to the terminology of the Council of Europe (Beacco & Byram, 2007), the adjective 'plurilingual' would be more appropriate when talking about the individual's heterogeneous, complex and composite linguistic competence, whereas the adjective 'multilingual' describes the particularities of interactions in various languages within groups or areas.

Acknowledgments

Thanks are due to Dominique Portante and Teresa Yurén for the rich scientific exchanges we had on the issues of language learning and agency, and thanks also go to the editors of this volume for their review comments.

References

Arditty, J. and Vasseur, M.-T. (2003) Que font les gens de leurs langues? In L. Mondada and S. Pekarek Doehler (eds) *Plurilinguisme – Mehrsprachigkeit – Plurilingualism. Enjeux identitaires, socio-culturels et éducatifs* (pp. 111–122). Tübingen: Francke.
Auer, P. (1999) From code-switching via language mixing to fused lects: Toward a dynamic typology of bilingual speech. *International Journal of Bilingualism* 3 (4), 309–332.
Beacco, J.-C. and Byram, M. (2007) From linguistic diversity to plurilingual education: Guides for the development of language education policies in Europe. Council of Europe See www.coe.int/lang (accessed 29 June 2009).
Berger, P.L. and Luckmann, T. (1981) *The Social Construction of Reality.* Harmondsworth: Penguin Books. [Originally published 1966.]
Bernstein, B. (1972) A sociolinguistic approach to socialization; with some reference to educability. In J.J. Gumperz and D.H. Hymes (eds) *Directions in Sociolinguistics. The Ethnography of Communication* (pp. 465–497). New York: Holt, Rinehart and Winston.
Bhabha, H. (1996) *The Location of Culture.* New York: Routledge.
Block, D. (2003) *The Social Turn in Second Language Acquisition.* Washington, DC: Georgetown University.
Bourdieu, P. (1982) *Ce que parler veut dire.* Paris: Librairie Arthème Fayard.
Butler, J. (1995) For a careful reading. In S. Benhabib, J. Butler, D. Cornell and N. Fraser (eds) *Feminist Contentions: A Philosophical Exchange* (pp. 127–144). New York: Routledge.
Calvet, L.-J. (2002) *Le marché aux langues.* Mesnil-sur-l'Estrée: Plon.
Canagarajah, S. (2004) Subversive identities, pedagogical safe houses and critical learning. In B. Norton and K. Toohey (eds) *Critical Pedagogies and Language Learning* (pp. 116–137). Cambridge: Cambridge University.
Cummins, J. (1996) *Negotiating Identities: Education for Empowerment in a Diverse Society.* Ontario: California Association for Bilingual Education.
Davies, A. (1991) *The Native Speaker in Applied Linguistics.* Edinburgh: Edinburgh University Press.

Deleuze, G. (1989) Qu'est-ce qu'un dispositif. *Michel Foucault philosophe, rencontre internationale, Paris 9, 10, 11 janvier 1988* (pp. 185–195). Paris: Seuil.

De Mejía, A.-M. (2002) *Power, Prestige and Bilingualism: International Perspectives on Elite Bilingualism*. Clevedon: Multilingual Matters.

Dewey, J. (1985) Well-being, agency and freedom. The Dewey lectures 1984. *The Journal of Philosophy* LXXXII (4), 169–221.

Dittmar, N., Spolsky, B. and Walters, J. (1998) Language and identity in immigrant language acquisition and use. In V. Regan (ed.) *Contemporary Approaches to Second Language Acquisition in Social Context. Crosslinguistic Perspectives* (pp. 124–136). Dublin: University College Dublin Press.

Dumenden, I. (2011) Agency as the acquisition of capital: The role of one-on-one tutoring and mentoring in changing a refugee student's educational trajectory. *European Educational Research Journal* 10 (4), 472–483.

Durkheim, E. (1999) *Education et sociologie*. Paris: Presses Universitaires de France. [Originally published 1922.]

Emirbayer, M. and Mische, A. (1998) What is agency? *American Journal of Sociology* 103 (4), 962–1023.

Foucault, M. (1971) *L'ordre du Discours*. Paris: Gallimard.

Foucault, M. (1975) *Surveiller et Punir. Naissance de la Prison*. Paris: Gallimard.

Freire, P. and Macedo, P. (1987) *Literacy: Reading the Word and the World*. Westport, CT: Bergin & Garvey.

Freire, S., Carvalho, C., Freire, A., Azevedo, M. and Oliveira, T. (2009) Identity construction through schooling: Listening to students' voices. *European Educational Research Journal* 8 (1), 80–88.

García, O. and Sylvan, C.E. (2011) Pedagogies and practices in multilingual classrooms: Singularities in pluralities. *The Modern Language Journal* 95 (iii), 385–400.

Giddens, A. (2009) *Sociology*. Cambridge: Polity Press.

Giroux, H.A. (1983) *Theory and Resistance in Education: A Pedagogy for the Opposition*. Amherst, MA: Bergin and Garvey.

Goffman, E. (1971) *The Presentation of Self in Everyday Life*. London: Penguin.

Gogolin, I. (1994) *Der monolinguale habitus der multilingualen Schulen*. Münster: Waxman.

Gregory, E. and Williams, A. (2000) *City Literacies*. London: Routledge.

Gumperz, J.J. (1964) Linguistic and social interaction in two communities. *American Anthropologist* 66 (2), 137–153.

Gumperz, J.J. (2000) Contextualization and understanding. In A. Duranti and C. Goodwin (eds) *Rethinking Context: Language as an Interactive Phenomenon* (pp. 229–253). Cambridge: Cambridge University Press.

Gutiérrez, K.D. (2008) Developing a sociocritical literacy in the third space. *Reading Research Quarterly* 43 (2), 148–164.

Halasek, K. (1999) *A Pedagogy of Possibility: Bakhtinian Perspectives on Composition Studies*. Carbondale: Southern Illinois University Press.

Halliday, M.A.K. (1993) Towards a language-based theory of learning. *Linguistics and Education* 5, 93–116.

Heller, M. (2010) The commodification of language. *Annual Review of Anthropology* 39, 101–114.

Hélot, C. (2004) Bilinguisme des migrants, bilinguisme des élites, analyse d'un écart en milieu scolaire. *Actes de la Recherche: Les perspectives de développement de l'enseignement bilingue* 3, 8–27.

Holland, D., Skinner, D., Lachicotte, W. Jr. and Cain, C. (1998) *Identity and Agency in Cultural Worlds*. Cambridge, MA: Harvard University Press.

Hornberger, N.H. (1989) Continua of biliteracy. *Review of Educational Research* 59 (3), 271–296.

Hymes, D.H. (1972) On communicative competence. In J.B. Pride and J. Holmes (eds) *Sociolinguistics: Selected Readings* (pp. 269–293). Harmondsworth: Penguin.

Kramsch, C. (2000) Social discursive constructions of self in L2 learning. In J. Lantolf (ed.) *Sociocultural Theory and Second Language Learning* (pp. 133–153). Oxford: Oxford University Press.

Lantolf, J.P. (ed.) (2000) *Sociocultural Theory and Second Language Learning*. Oxford: Oxford University Press.

Latour, B. (1996) On interobjectivity. *Mind, Culture and Activity* 3 (4), 228–244.

Lave, J. and Wenger, E. (2007) *Situated Learning. Legitimate Peripheral Participation*. New York: Cambridge University Press. [Originally published 1991.]

Li, Wei (2009) Moment analysis and translanguaging space. *Journal of Pragmatics* 43 (2011), 1222–1235.

Maurer-Hetto, M.-P. (2009) Struggling with the languages of the 'legitimate market' and the 'islets of liberty' (Bourdieu). A case study of pupils with immigrational background in the trilingual school-system of Luxembourg. *International Journal of Multilingualism* 6 (1), 68–84.

Maybin, J. (2006) *Children's Voices. Talk, Knowledge and Identity*. New York: Palgrave Macmillan.

Mick, C. (2012) Das Agency-Paradigma. In U. Bauer, U. Bittlingmayer and A. Scherr (eds) *Handbuch Bildungs-und Erziehungssoziologie* (pp. 527–543). Wiesbaden: Springer.

Mondada, L. and Pekarek Doehler, S. (2003) Le plurilinguisme en action. In L. Mondada and S. Pekarek Doehler (eds) *Plurilinguisme – Mehrsprachigkeit – Plurilingualism. Enjeux identitaires, socio-culturels et éducatifs* (pp. 95–110). Tübingen: Francke.

Mondada, L. and Pekarek Doehler, S. (2004) Second language acquisition as situated practice: Task accomplishment in the French second language classroom. *The Modern Language Journal* 88 (iv), 501–518.

Ochs, E. and Schieffelin, B. (2008) Language socialization: An historical overview. In P.A. Duff and N.H. Hornberger (eds) *Encyclopedia of Language and Education, Volume 8: Language Socialization* (2nd edn; pp. 3–15). New York: Springer.

Parsons, T. (1968) *The Structure of Social Action*. New York: Free Press.

Pavlenko, A. and Lantolf, J.P. (2000) Second language learning as participation and the (re)construction of selves. In J.P. Lantolf (ed.) *Sociocultural Theory and Second Language Learning* (pp. 155–177). Oxford: Oxford University Press.

Portante, D. (2011) Enacted agency as the strategic making of selves in plurilingual literacy events. *European Educational Research Journal* 10 (4), 516–532.

Selinker, L. (1972) Interlanguage. *International Review of Applied Linguistics* 10 (3), 209–231.

Sewell, W.H. (1992) A theory of structure: Duality, agency, and transformation. *American Journal of Sociology* 98 (1), 1–29.

Street, B. (2006) Autonomous and ideological models of literacy: Approaches from New Literacy studies. E-seminar (EASA), http://www.media-anthropology.net/index.php/Download-document/Street-Autonomous-and-Ideological-Models-of-Literacy-E-Seminar.html (accessed 11 February 2013).

Todorov, T. (1981) *Mikhaïl Bakhtine. Le principe dialogique, suivi de ecrits du Cercle de Bakhtine*. Paris: Editions du Seuil.

Tröhler, D. (2009) Beyond arguments and ideas: Languages of education. In P. Smeyers and M. Depaepe (eds) *Educational Research* (pp. 9–22). Dodrecht: Springer.

Vygotsky, L.V. (1978) *Mind in Society: The Development of Higher Psychological Processes* (M. Cole, V.P. John-Steiner, S. Scribner and E. Souberman, eds.). Cambridge: Harvard University Press.

Weber, J.-J. (2009) *Multilingualism, Education and Change*. Frankfurt/Main: Peter Lang.

Wertsch, J.V. (1993) *Voices of the Mind. A Sociocultural Approach to Mediated Action.* Cambridge, MA: Harvard University Press. [Originally published accessed 11 February 2013.]

Wulf, C. and Zirfas, J. (2007) *Pädagogik des performativen. Theorien, methoden, perspektiven.* Weinheim/Basel: Beltz.

Yurén, T. (2005) Ethos y autoformación en los dispositivos de formación de docentes. In T. Yurén, C. Navia and C. Saenger (eds) *Ethos y atoformación del Docente. Análisis de dispositivos de formación de profesores* (pp. 19–48). Barcelona: Pomares.

Yurén, T. and Mick, C. (eds) (2013) *Educación y agencia. Aproximaciones teóricas y análisis de dispositivos.* México: Juan Pablos Editor.

Part 2

Analytical Approaches to Investigating Agency

7 Performing and Accounting Language and Identity: Agency *as* Actors-in-(inter)action-with-tools

Sangeeta Bagga-Gupta

> *Humankind is a languaging species ... 'Languages' are abstractions, they are sociocultural or ideological constructions which match real-life use of language poorly.*
> Jorgensen *et al.*, 2011: 22

Introduction

A sociocultural perspective on communication and development recognizes that artifacts and cultural tools, including language, the most significant of tools (Lantolf, 2000; Perret-Clermont, 2009; Vygotsky, 1962) are in a mediational symbiotic relationship with actors (Säljö, 2012; Wertsch, 1998). A central tenant here is the irreducible actor–tool concert and mediation that frames cognition and agency. Drawing upon a sociocultural 'Mind as Social Action' position (Wertsch, 1998), the empirically framed analysis in this chapter shows that, rather than being a dimension of individual actors, motivations or desires, agency has an intertwined situated, distributed nature (Hutchins, 1993; Lave & Wenger, 1991). Here communication is learning and is seen as 'appropriating and sharing power, a more or less legitimate behavior not independent of social positions, including gender' (Perret-Clermont, 2009: 8). In other words, this locally *situated* (in the here and now) and *distributed* (across time, space, actors and tools) character of agency is embedded in social action.

Taking these sociocultural views as points of departure, a multiscaled approach (Bucholtz & Hall, 2005; Hult, 2010; Scollon & Scollon, 2004) informs my analysis of agency in a couple of specific ways. First, I discuss agency analytically and empirically through the *actors–tools* continuum. Second, I relate it specifically to fields that are conventionally clothed in terms of bi/multilingual and multimodal learning. Finally, the empirical explorations in this chapter highlight the situated and distributed nature of identity-positions and belonging (Antaki & Widdicome, 1998; Krzyzanowaki, 2010; Lave & Wenger, 1991; Näslund, 2013; Rogoff, 1990). My overall aim is to make visible how a theoretically framed analysis of agency and identity can be represented by focusing on multiscaled empirical data.

The next section in this chapter explicates the *webs-of-understandings* that emerge vis-à-vis language, identity and learning issues from sociocultural and postcolonial positions. Thereafter, I theorize my ethnographic stance, including the datasets used. The central empirical section that follows presents analysis at different scales. The final section discusses the nature of agency against the backdrop of language and social dimensions of human existence.

On Languaging, Learning and Identity

The ways in which human beings live in language (van Lier, 2004) and their language-in-use *in situ* or 'languaging' (García, 2009) have an implicit but also an overt bearing upon socialization, including the learning of language-use and identity-positions in different spaces (Antaki & Widdicombe, 1998; Näslund, 2013). Focusing on performatory and accounting practices in terms of the ways in which categories and social positions get talked-into-being (Drew & Heritage, 1992; Goodwin, 1994) and become framed in social actions shifts the analytical lens away from actors' 'pure' intentions and the 'real' meanings that reside in and are ascribed to the irreducible symbiotic relationships between actors and tools (Chaiklin & Lave, 1993; Hutchins, 1993; Rogoff, 1990).

More recent contributions from sociolinguistically framed postcolonial perspectives have highlighted not only the fallacy of equating geopolitical boundaries with specific social groupings or communities (Gal & Irvine, 1995; Hasnain *et al.*, 2013), but also that of a Eurocentric framing of language (Blommaert, 2010; Gal & Irvine, 1995; Rosén & Bagga-Gupta, 2013; Shohamy, 2006). This has been discussed in terms of the one-nation–one-language myth that continues to shape much thinking and theorizing, not least in the language and educational sciences in general and some of their branches in particular. Some of my recent work has called for 'challenging understandings in the language sciences from the lens of research that focuses social practices' (Bagga-Gupta, 2012a), where I highlight that

[the] term bilingualism has become an important area of study in Northern settings and is perhaps one of the most central concepts in the Language Sciences today. It lies at the center of a *web-of-understandings*

and is connected to a flora of concepts in language education. The latter include both areas of research inquiry and subjects that are currently taught in schools and in higher education in Sweden: 'home language', 'mother tongue', 'foreign language', 'Swedish', 'first language', 'second language', 'Swedish as a second language', 'Swedish for the deaf/hard of hearing', etc. (Bagga-Gupta, 2012a: 92, italics in original)

Using an action-based sociocultural perspective as a point of departure, I have argued for (1) an empirically driven focus on the very languaging that is glossed as 'bi/multilingualism', 'second language', 'mother tongue', etc. and (2) an inclusive stance wherein institutional education is recognized as *one of many spaces* where individuals get socialized into their primary multiple language varieties (Bagga-Gupta, 2012a, 2012b). This highlights dominant narrowly selective positions vis-à-vis learning and potentially illuminates issues regarding pluralistic societies and 'the ongoing tension of the multilingual balancing act' in education (Hult, 2004: 196). I focus on languaging in noneducational settings where actors use a range of language varieties and tools in the course of everyday events in part to highlight alternative webs-of-understandings. These alternative ways-of-being-with-words in what gets glossed as bi/multilingualism is significant for reconceptualising issues related to the 'multilingual balancing act' in school settings (Hult, 2004: 196).

Studying languaging, rather than language *per se*, also enables one to give attention to actors' emic perspectives on their identity performances and who they are in relation to one another *in situ* (Benwell & Stokoe, 2006). Thus, '[A]gency, in the sense of an action orientation is ... intrinsic to the analysis without locating it in self-conscious intentionality, cognitive processes, or in abstract discourses' (Widdicome, 1998: 203). Identity – be it gender, ethnicity, abilities – like (social) cognition is oriented to and displayed *in-action*, as dimensions of ascribed membership of and marking actors' meaning-making of categories: '*Guys, girls, mothers, sisters, pastors, real estate agents* ... What roles do these seemingly mundane labels for referring to people play in social interaction? When and why are such categories invoked by participants, how are they oriented to, and what do they accomplish?' (Reddington, 2013: 21, italics in original).

Linguistically framed gender identity is increasingly located within more broadly framed interactional research (see for instance Ochs, 1992; Speer & Stokoe, 2011; Stokoe, 2000; Stokoe & Smithson, 2001; Zimmerman, 1998). Here the situated, distributed or sequential and categorical nature of identity work is framed in analytical fields like Conversation Analysis (CA), Membership Categorization in Action (MCA) and Critical Discourse Analysis: 'CA helps us document the ways in which fields of visibility and modes of rationality are sequentially organized, while MCA provides analytical tools to uncover the categorical work by which subjectivities and identities are morally accomplished in social interaction' (McIlvenny, 2013). While these approaches focus on naturally occurring language data in some form, two issues can be noted for the present purposes. First, ethnographic data are not generally drawn upon in studies where CA approaches are deployed. Second, the data focused on in these theoretically framed works is typically in English, and the literature that focuses on interactional framings of identity or ways-of-being-with-words in other language varieties, particularly in what is glossed as bi/multilingualism is wanting. This chapter contributes to these gaps in the literature specifically.

Furthermore, recognizing the analytical foundations of ethnography necessitates the framing of methods and data theoretically. A fundamental difference between an action-based sociocultural perspective on agency and other views that frame it is related to the mediational role attributed to cultural tools that have emerged phylogenetically and are appropriated ontogenetically (Säljö, 2012; Wertsch, 1998; Vygotsky, 1962). Agency, cognition and knowledge in concert with cultural tools are here at times envisaged in the hyphenated concept 'individual(s)-acting/operating-with-mediational-means' (Wertsch, 1998: 24). This key theoretical irreducible medley gives rise to an important *analytical-methodological stance* significant to the analysis here: in order to understand agency, the research enterprise needs (in a parallel irreducible manner) to focus on the concert of actors-in-(inter) action-with-tools across scales. Actors' naturally occurring *languaging per se* instead of language or some attribute like gender, place of residence, functional ability or elicited information from actors (e.g. interview data or reflective logs), thus becomes the irreducible unit-of-analysis, at both the micro-interactional and macro-ethnographic scales of this attention. The ethnographic framings of languaging in the data explored in this chapter are discussed in the next section.

Doing Ethnography: The Study and Data

The data focused here is taken from my ongoing ethnographic fieldwork in the GTGS project,[1] where issues of communication and identity are explored inside and outside a not-for-profit organization[2] that provides a range of services for migrants in a megacity in the Global South. Following the mobile lives of the diverse groups of women working at this not-for-profit organization in Mumbai allowed me to reflect upon the outcry occasioned by the 16 December 2012 violent gang-rape 2000 kilometers away in Delhi (where the victim's injuries were fatal). Understanding why this rape had attracted widespread publicity and concern glocally (i.e. where the *glo*bal intersects with the *lo*cal) became significant during this specific fieldwork trip (see Blommaert & Rampton, 2011; Husnain *et al.*, 2013; Messina Dalhberg & Bagga-Gupta, 2013). These types of crime are reported as being commonplace in both urban and rural India and, while they constitute issues that need critical academic, political and social engagement in their own right, they are beyond the scope of the concerns here. The analysis presented here does, however, engage with and thus contribute to current framings of gendered spaces.

The specific data include video-recordings of a public event where the screening of a documentary film on gender violence was followed by a discussion, internet resources pertaining to the specific public event, field notes and discussions in the media. Conventional labels used for the language varieties in the data include Mumbaiya-Hindi, North Indian Hindi, English, Angrezi or Indian-English and Marathi. The datasets constitute rich 'inbetween' (Krzyzanowski, 2010: 168) sites of 'Learning at the boundary' (Akkerman & Bakker, 2011) where, as we will see, language modalities and varieties are oriented to and get displayed as complex intertwined-cum-layered action.

A Multiscaled Ethnographic Analysis

This exploration of the performances and irreducible dialectical dimensions of the actor–tool–agency continuum is presented in two subsections: an analysis of the organization of *interactional order* that situates the public event across larger timescales and geographical spaces and the *micro-interactional order* of talk-at-work within the identified phases of the public event. The ethnographic analysis in the first section enables a macro-scale understanding of the public event across time and urban spaces glocally, as well as within the public event itself. The analysis in the second section, contingent upon the macro-scale analysis, allows the complexities of languaging to come center-stage at the micro-scale.

Interlinked event flows in glocal urban spaces

A range of activities, meetings and happenings unfold in public spaces such as parks, malls and road curbs. The 'BMW Guggenheim Lab' (henceforth GL) activities, initiated in 2011 spread out in public spaces of selected megacities across the globe, focus on the 'participatory city' with the overarching aim of 'inspiring innovative ideas for urban design and new ways of thinking about urban life' (http://www.bmwguggenheimlab.org/, May 2013). Led by international, interdisciplinary teams, the GL is described as,

> a mobile laboratory about urban life … From 2011 to 2013, the Lab travelled to New York, Berlin, and Mumbai. Part urban think tank, part community center and public gathering space, the Lab's goal has been

the exploration of new ideas, experimentation, and ultimately the creation of forward-thinking visions and projects for city life. Through the lens of the themes Confronting Comfort, Making, and Privacy and Public Space, this global project has explored how people relate to cities and public space today. (http://www.bmwguggenheimlab.org/what-is-the-lab, July 2013)

The two-month-long Mumbai GL activities included events that focused on violence and gendered and classed spaces. One of these included the public screening on 30 December 2012 of filmmaker Sameera Jain's acclaimed 64 minute documentary *Mera Apna Sheher* (Hindi: *My Own Town/City*) released in 2011 (see Figure 7.1). The screening of the film was part of a prelude to a two-member expert panel commentary and public discussions on gendered urban spaces (see Figure 7.2). The film, shot in Delhi, focuses on the mundane nature of women's relationships with and reclamation of public spaces in the Indian capital. *The Indian Express*, a leading newspaper, describes the film's relevance for the issues it raises across India as follows: 'Even though, the characters [in the film] belong to underprivileged sections of society, the film rises above and can well be applied to women across class and caste in the country' (Krishnamurthy, 2012, http://newindianexpress.com/magazine/article577530.ece?service=print, July 2013).

As this multiscaled analysis indicates, this GL event gets (re)framed within and also highlights larger societal narratives triggered by the rape in Delhi that occurred two weeks earlier. This GL event and specific past

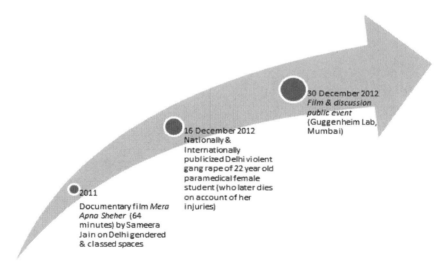

Figure 7.1 Interlinked event flows across time
Source: *Mera Apna Sheher* (Hindi: *My Own Town/City*)

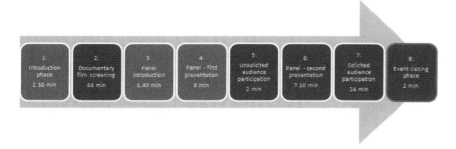

Figure 7.2 Making language and gender (in)visible: Phases of GL event in Mumbai, 30 December 2012

happenings, including two narrative tools that become relevant in this multiscale ethnographic analysis (the documentary film and the December rape), are represented schematically in Figure 7.1.

An overarching analysis of the interactional order, including the primary participants who language or hold the floor, the activity focus, the organization and use of tools and space (see Figure 7.3), across the public event gives rise to eight distinct phases. Figure 7.2 represents this flow of social actions

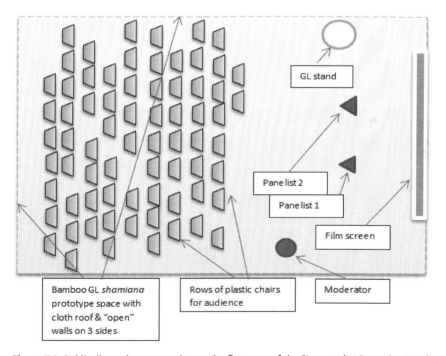

Figure 7.3 Public discussion spaces: Composite floor map of the GL event (30 December 2012)

or the eight identified phases of this GL event that took place in East Mulund, a suburb of the megacity of Mumbai. While the planned structure of this event includes a brief introduction by a female GL representative moderator, a film screening, followed by a two-member expert panel presentation, with a concluding open dialogue with public participation, the analysis of the data shows a different trajectory.

In the introductory Phase 1 (2.5 minutes), the moderator talks into a hand-held microphone in what can be called metropolitan Mumbaiya-Hindi with a smattering of Angresi or Indian-English terms. She presents the rationale behind the event, framing the film screening against the backdrop of both the general issue of women's access to and position in public spaces and the recent rape in Delhi (see Transcript 7.1). The moderator announces the order of the program in her brief introduction, which is followed by the hour-long screening of the documentary film (Phase 2). The languaging during Phase 2 consists of north Indian-Hindi and urban public space sounds from the capital of India.

Phase 3 (1 minute 40 seconds) first sees the moderator, using a hand-held microphone, briefly recapitulate salient points from the film against the backdrop of the GL event agenda, while some male officials reorganize the front part of the event space (schematically represented in Figure 7.3). The moderator then invites the two panelists to this re-configured space. Panelist one, Shilpa Phadke, an assistant professor from Mumbai, is presented as the co-author of an academic book in English titled *Why Loiter. Women and Risks on Mumbai Streets*, takes the floor and presents her reflections in English and Mumbaiya-Hindi during Phase 4 (see Transcript 7.2). Seated on a stool with notes on her lap, she talks into a hand-held microphone facing the audience. Shilpa Phadke marks the end of her contribution in Phase 4 (8 minutes) through a shift in gaze from the audience toward Prasad Shetty, the second panelist, extending the hand-held microphone to him and announcing in English simultaneously, 'I can come back but I will hand over to Prasad now'.

The next phase of the GL event (Phase 5; 2 minutes) is initiated during this turn shift when a male audience member politely but forcibly takes the floor in Mumbaiya-Hindi despite pleas from the moderator and the panelists to wait until the second panelist has presented his reflections. This unsolicited participation from the audience, voiced without the support of the amplifying microphone, receives brief responses immediately from both of the panelists in Mumbaiya-Hindi and Marathi.

Phase 6 (7 minutes 10 seconds) sees the second panelist – who is presented as having multiple professional titles including 'urbanist, architect, city official of the Mumbai Metropolitan Region and teacher' – present comments and reflections in Mumbaiya-Hindi with some Angresi. Phase 6 concludes when Prasad Shetty shifts his gaze from the audience to the moderator and says in English, 'so we can actually open up'.

The moderator now comes forward, with a microphone in hand, and elicits participation from the audience, initiating Phase 7. The languaging during this phase is marked by the use of Marathi (first audience participant) or Mumbaiya-Hindi or both Marathi and Mumbaiya-Hindi. The first participant, a male member of the audience, reiterates (similar to the audience member during Phase 5) the need for using Marathi in Mumbai public spaces. While he holds the floor for 1 minute 25 seconds, the remaining four participants from the audience, all male, take the floor and raise either personal general opinions about women's dress-codes or late working hours or their own daughters' dress-codes and relationships with public spaces. These latter speakers use either Mumbaiya-Hindi or a blend of Marathi and Mumbaiya-Hindi in their renditions.

During the concluding Phase 8 (less than 2 minutes), the moderator ignores a male audience member's repeated requests for the floor. She marks the lateness of the hour, the fact that female members in the audience have dwindled in numbers and that audience participation has only seen male participation. Languaging here occurs primarily in Mumbaiya-Hindi with a smattering of Angresi and the GL event is brought to a close.

The eight phases that emerge in the analysis of the interactional order at the scale of the GL event sees the deployment of different language varieties, modalities and tools in complex and interlinked ways. The public interactional order during the GL event allows all participants to potentially access the languaging broadcast via a microphone as well as the multimodal imagery, sounds and languaging displayed on the film screen. In addition to highlighting the existence of this complex interaction, such an analysis of languaging contributes to a nuanced understanding of what is commonly glossed as multilingualism including multimodalities. Agency is situated and distributed across the actors and tools that include a film, written notes, microphones and also language itself. A visual-manual dimension of agency here highlights the subtle ways in which actors coordinate not only the use of time and space but also gaze and body shift in concert with verbal contributions, for instance when they mark a phase transition turn. Sequentially built upon participants' co-contributions, the collaborative performance in this event cannot be attributed to any single actor.

The ebbs and flows in the deployment of language varieties during the eight phases is representative of metropolitan-languaging in India. During all phases, barring perhaps Phase 5, more than one language variety dominates. The unsolicited audience participation during Phase 5 and the first speaker during Phase 7 both *index the language used for languaging* during the event itself. This discussion is carried out in Mumbaiya-Hindi (Phase 5) and Marathi (first speaker Phase 7). The public challenge of the order of the planned activity during Phase 5 demonstrates an agentic move whereby an audience member takes the floor directly after the first expert commentary, and furthermore refuses to step down when asked to wait with his comments. Interestingly, the challenge is directed toward the GL event and not the individual panelists as such. These challenges act not only upon the issue of language-choice, but also on the very agenda of the event: the focus of the topic of the GL event shifts radically from gendered and class-framed public spaces to appropriate language variety usage in Mumbai. While two successful bids are made for a new agenda and both are acknowledged, they are also counter-challenged by the panelists, the organizers and to some extent other audience members. Issues of access to the interactional order builds upon an institutional frame that is respected, challenged and counter-challenged in dynamic ways.

While it is analytically meaningful to focus on the sequentiality of the interactional order of the GL event against the backdrop of macro-scale happenings across time and space (see analysis related to Figure 7.1), and the trajectory of phases (see analysis related to Figures 7.2 and 7.3), language and identity issues related to this radical turn in topic (RTiT) at this macro-scale are explored through the representation and analysis of data at the micro-interactional scale in the next subsection. The micro-interactional order makes visible actors' languaging and engagement with tools, including resources from different language varieties and modalities, illustrating the situated as well as distributed actor–tool linking further.

Identity marking in and through languaging

Labels used for the geopolitical space *Mumbai* or *Bombay* have been discussed in mass-media and social media sites, since at least the 1990s. Nationalist discussions are said to have shifted the terminology in the mid-1990s from *Bombay* to *Mumbai* (as well as *Poona* to *Pune*; see below). While the appropriateness of these labels are discussed in sentimental, politically charged terms, I have during my fieldwork heard the label *Bambai* being used by the citizenship of the megacity – at the not-for-profit spaces, by taxi drivers, shop keepers, middle class people and at the GL event. While the labels are linked to three language varieties in the popular imagination, the languaging I encounter during fieldwork indicates a more complex picture (see Transcripts 7.1 and 7.2). The term *Bombay* is, in the popular discourse, linked to colonial English, and perhaps also to Hindi, a language that has more recently become indexed as a migrant language from north India. *Mumbai* is framed as being politically driven by proponents of Marathi right-wing factions who succeeded in getting the name of the city replaced in 1996.

Transcript 7.1 highlights, among other issues, how central labels for Delhi and Mumbai are used in the flow of languaging during Phase 1 when the GL female moderator has the floor. Three cities are marked explicitly in Transcript 7.1 – *Dilli* (Mumbaiya-Hindi: *Delhi* or *New Delhi*), *Bambai* (Mumbaiya-Hindi or metropolitan Hindi: *Mumbai*) and *Pune*. The female moderator frames the film that will be screened during Phase 2 by accounting for the similarities and differences between the cities (lines 1.05 onwards) and the shifts in her experiences of the gendering of public spaces in *Mumbai* over the years (lines 1.09–1.20). In addition to identity marking where gender is indexed, this dataset highlights complex ways in which inclusion and exclusion work occurs in the languaging during different phases where class and migration are also explicitly indexed. The labels *Bambai* and *Dilli* are used four times during Phase 1. The city of *Pune*, which also lies in the state of Maharashtra (of which Mumbai is the capital), is also referred to (line 1.05). The moderator displays a fluid orientation to these labels, transcending the boundaries of distinct language varieties to which specific labels are popularly imagined.

Transcript* 7.1: **Dilli–Bambai** and visible violence – quite violence (Phase 1)

0.22: our cities.
   hamare jo sheher hei (.)
0.23: they are so <u>unsafe</u> for women
   vo kitne <u>unsafe</u> hei aurreto ke liye(.)
0.28: taking that idea this <u>film</u> was made in **dilli** (.) last year
   *uss madde ko leke ye <u>film</u> banai gai thi **dilli** me (.) pechele sal.*
0.32: but this <u>film</u> (.) <u>violence</u> (.) that which is visible it is not on that
   par ye <u>film</u> (.) <u>violence</u> (.) jho jho dhikti hai vovo uske uper nahi hai
0.39: but the existent <u>quite violence</u> (.) the ways in which in the city
   par jo <u>quite violence</u> hai (.) jis tere se sheher me
0.44: the loitering of women (.) is considered bad (.) or
   aurato ka mm e eidher udhar e jana (.) boora mana jata hai (.) ya
0.49: and is viewed with anger
   aur phir e gusse se dhekha jata hai
0.52: it is on this topic (.) this <u>film</u> is about what has happened recently
   uske uper hai (.) to ye ye <u>film</u> aaj ke haal me jo hoa
0:54: taking this idea
   uske e uske mudde ko lekar ke
1.01: we can understand from the <u>film</u> how cities have become <u>hostile</u> for women
   <u>film</u> se samadj aata hai ke hamare jo sheher hai to kis tere se aourate ke prati <u>hostile</u> ho chuke hai
1.05: this is not just the case with **dilli** (.) in **bambai** too in **pune** too
   *to ye serif **dilli** ki kahani nahi he (.) **bambai** me yehi hai **pune** me yehi hai*
1.09: where every i have grown up and studied in **bambai**
   ***bambai** me jaha jaha me badi padhi huei hoo*
1.12: and where there were no restrictions about what time one had to return home
   aur jaha khabi koi roak dhok nahi ta ki ghar eetne bajhe tak ana hai
1.16: because there was safety for women in **bambai**
   *kayoki **bambai** mai ek suraksha thi aourateey ke liye*
1.20: but we are seeing that even in **bambai** this safety is becoming less
   *par ham dekh rahe hai ki **bambai** me bhi vo suraksha kam hoite ja rahi hai*
1.29: and why is this happening (.) the ways in which our cities are growing
   aur ye kyo ho raha hai (.) hamare sheher jis tare se bard rahe hai
1.31: the <u>film</u> explores that
   usko leke ye <u>film</u> bani gai hai
1.33: and the <u>film</u> is one hour long
   aur ek ghante ki film he

---

*Transcription notes at the end of the chapter

Furthermore, the use of Angresi words in the flow of the moderators talk-at-work is interesting: 'film' is used six times (lines 0.28, 0.32, 0.52, 1.10, 1.31 and 1.33), and 'violence' (line 0.32), 'quite violence' (line 0.39) and 'unsafe' (line 0.23) once each. Rather than drawing upon a colonial discourse or a deficit argument to explain this display, I will argue that the languaging made visible in Transcript 7.1 constitutes an example of urban metropolitan discourse – here Mumbaiya-Hindi. The use of a smattering of English is in itself a feature of Mumbaiya-Hindi, or if one prefers, metropolitan languaging in India. Second, the female moderator links the recent rape in Delhi with the 'quite violence' that women (particularly women from the lower and lower-middle classes) face in Delhi – a central topic in the film that is screened during Phase 2 – with similar violence in the spaces of Mumbai.

The moderator's languaging links specific and diffuse issues from the topic of the film and her own life across both time and space when she orients toward city labels, spaces where 'violence' (line 0.23) and 'quite violence' (line 0.38) occur, that are 'unsafe for women' (line 0.23) or 'have become hostile for women' (line 1.01). This display and the actors' orientation and indexing of spaces makes relevant the positions women have vis-à-vis public spaces in Mumbai and a city 2000 kilometers to the north. It is in these ways that the micro-interactional order represented in Transcript 7.1 agentically marks and indexes gender and urban spaces in specific ways. Third, facing the audience, the female GL representative frames her narrative, standing and speaking into a hand-held microphone. Her agency here is embodied in her introductory narrative in Mumbaiya-Hindi and cannot be divorced from her tool-mediated languaging.

This micro-interactional analytical scale links into both the phase-scale interactional order of the GL event illustrated in Figure 7.2 and the macro-temporal trajectory of events represented in Figure 7.1. Responding to the classical CA query of 'why this now?' becomes possible through a multi-scaled analysis of both participants' ways-of-being-with-words in situated stretches of languaging (for instance Transcript 7.1) and inter-linked events where these are distributed across actors, tools, time and space. These issues are further illustrated in Transcript 7.2, another micro-scale analysis of talk-at-work from the start of Phase 4 when the female panelist takes the floor to present her reflections.

The expert panelist starts her contribution in English, explicitly marking that she will start in English and move into the two other commonly used language varieties in *Mumbai* during her commentary (Transcript 7.2, line 2.04). Her self-presentation and the announced framing of her language choice resemble, in large measure, the flow of languaging during the interactional order represented through Transcript 7.2. In other words, this is how she languages during her eight minutes of reflective commentary.

There are two significant issues that are salient here: while the panelist announces that she will start her presentation in English and then 'keep moving into e hindi and marathi a little bit' (line 2.04), she first, more or less shifts into Mumbaiya-Hindi (at times completely) and second, does not draw upon Marathi at all during Phase 4. While four turns are in English (lines 2.04, 2.09, 2.24 and 2.41), two are both in Mumbaiya-Hindi and English (lines 2.24 and 2.57). Furthermore, in addition to the marking of the city *Mumbai* (line 2.14) and *Bambai* (lines 2.17 and 2.36), only two items in English can be observed in Transcript 7.2: 'bag' (line 2.46) and 'permission' (line 3.07). Shilpa Padke's co-authored English book uses the label *Mumbai* in its subtitle (see above). Her use of the term *Bambai* in her oral contributions during Phases 4 and 7 of the GL event occurs primarily when she uses Mumbaiya-Hindi and English. Thus, it can be argued that the term *Bambai* perhaps is both a hybrid of the recognized terms *Bombay* and *Mumbai* and is also related to the dominating metropolitan Hindi variety used in the city, that is, Mumbaiya-Hindi.

Transcript 7.2: Languaging and hanging out in **bambai** (Phase 4)

2.04: <u>ok e e I willl start in english and keep moving into e hindi and marathi a little bit</u>
2.09: <u>as as ee sshu shhurbi* just said (.) e we wrote a book call called bh bh why loiter</u>
2.14: <u>women and risk on **mumbais** streets</u>
2.17: this book was about **bambai**
        ke kitab **bambai** *ke bare mei thi*
2.20: but the books ideas are applicable perhaps to other cities too
        lekin uske mudde s shaid doosre shehero me bhi ham deek sakte hai
2.25: one of our ideas was that <u>when women are out in public space</u>
        hamara ek mudda tha ki e
2.30: when a woman is outside on the road pathway she is there because she has some work
        jab mahila bahar raste par saradk par hoti hai jab unko koi kaam hota hai
2.36: like shurbi just explained that is ok in **bambai**
        jese ki sshurbi ne abhi samjaya to ki vo **bambai** *me to vo thek hai*
2.41: <u>it is acceptable for women to be out there with purpose</u> (.)
2.46: and women also [xxx] have big big <u>bag</u> that they take with them
        auur mahila ke bhi [xxx] hai ke apne sat bade bade <u>bag</u> *leke jate hai*
2.49: to show that they are
        ke dhikhane ke liye
2.52: we have work outside (.) we are doing something (.) and (.)
        ki hame bahar koyi kam hai (.) ham koch kar rahe hai (.) aaur (.)
2.57: consider if there is no work <u>if you want to hang out</u>
        smajho koch kam nahi hai
3.02: without any work or reason at night we wish to go for a walk
        hamme kooch kaam bina aaese hi raat ko thehel na hai
3.07: for fun we have no <u>permission</u> completely no
        maauch maajha hai uske liye hamko <u>permission</u> *bilko nahi hai*

---

*The moderator

With this as backdrop let us revisit the unsolicited audience participation during Phase 5 where a case is made for using the label *Mumbai* (and not *Bombay*). While the panelists do not disagree (in fact they explicitly state that they agree with the suggestion), they account for their usage of the Indian-English or the Mumbaiya-Hindi terms for the city as habitual talk. I will argue that the unsolicited audience participation can be understood as a dimension of the interplay between enabling and disabling features of languaging during Phase 4. Could the *Mumbai–Bambai* (ie. the hybrid form of *bam*[bom] plus *bai*) and the panelists' explicit announcement of her language preferences at the start of Phase 4 have contributed to the unsolicited challenge in Phase 5? This issue has relevance given that the panelist uses the challenger's preferred term *Mumbai* in the oral rendering of the subtitle of her co-authored book (line 2.14). As such, the panelist not only *does not use* the targeted term *Bombay*, she explicitly uses the preferred term *Mumbai* when she languages in English (line 2.14). In addition, she uses the term *Bambai* (and not the disprefered *Bombay*) twice (lines 2.17 and 2.36) when she languages in Mumbaiya-Hindi. The female panelists' use of larger chunks of English and her framing of the language varieties she aims to deploy (line 2.04), one of which she does not use during Phase 4, pave the way for the unsolicited audience participation after her expert contribution at the GL event.

This shift in the event agenda during Phase 5 amounts to, as argued above, a rupture, an RTiT where the focus on violence and gendered spaces is made invisible and is replaced by a new agenda: an orientation toward the language variety that should be used in public spaces. This itself can be seen as an important dimension of gendered violence. Irvine and Gal (2000) use the term 'erasure' to highlight processes whereby individuals' or communities' identity positions or linguistic practices are ignored or made invisible. The contestation of the social order that is planned and announced during Phase 1 of the GL event by two men from the public, when they challenge and in part succeed in diverting attention from the event topic, amounts to agency as resistance. The gender of the moderator and the first panelist perhaps also shapes audience participation. The significant point here is that agency cannot solely or categorically be attributed to the male intruder who disrupts the planned, announced order of the event when he takes the floor during Phase 5. The ways-of-being-with-words, both the sequential ordering and the RTiT, re-shape the event itself.

The representation of languaging in Transcript 7.2 reiterates some salient issues highlighted earlier. In addition to features of urban metropolitian discourse, one can identify chaining and translanguaging where English and Mumbaiya-Hindi fold into one another (lines 2.04–2.17, 2.25, 2.36–2.46, 2.57 and 3.07). Gender and public space are foregrounded when the female panelist presents the title of her co-authored book *Women and Risk on Mumbais Streets* (line 2.14). Similar to the languaging work that the moderator has previously accomplished (see Transcript 7.1), the panelist orients toward and brings together different marked and unmarked issues, including tools: her book (line 2.09), names of spaces (lines 2.14, 2.17 and 2.36), spaces that pose 'risk' (line 2.14), 'public space' (line 2.25) and tools like 'bags' (line 2.46) that index 'purpose' (lines 2.30 and 2.41) and thus legitimate women's access to public domains.

The female panelist does explicit gender work in her narrative in a complex manner. In addition to the lexical content of her message where visible tools like 'bags' or work agendas mark women's purposeful entry into and access to public spaces (lines 2.46–2.52) or where a casual walk or a recreational outing at night is forbidden (lines 2.57–3.07), the panelist positions herself initially in a first-person subject position (line 2.04), then a plural 'we' position (lines 2.09 and 2.25), and then a neutral observer position, thus indexing a range of women's ways of relating to public spaces (lines 2.25–2.49). An interesting shift occurs between lines 2.49 and 2.52 when the panelist shifts allegiance: from a neutral observer narrator (line 2.49) to a plural 'we' position (lines 2.52–3.07). Coming center-stage herself at this juncture in the languaging accentuates the gender marking since the panelist introduces a potentially novel and controversial[3] issue (line 2.57) – women hanging out in public spaces 'without any work or reason at night' (line 3.02) – and her own voicing of the societal verdict for such behavior – 'we have no permission completely no' (line 3.02). Invited as an expert to a public event where the topic is gender and public space, and having co-authored a book on the subject, the female panelist's languaging during Phase 4 indexes her skillful navigation of the topic, her role as author and expert but also that of a woman with gendered experiences of urban spaces generally and the megacity of Mumbai particularly.

Finally, Transcript 7.2 indexes agency both explicitly in that the semantic content of the panelists' narrative relates to women's agentic ways-of-being-with-words in accessing public spaces, and also in the panelist's positioning of herself in both a first-person subject position (line 2.04) and a plural 'we' position (lines 2.09, 2.25, 2.52–3.07). Agency also gets marked implicitly in Transcript 7.2 in the panelist's presentation of the diffuse societal framings that enable, but also restrict, women's agentic access to public spaces. Physical tools like a 'big big bag' (line 2.46) support women's agency, as do conceptual tools like 'work' (line 2.30).

The proposed interactional order of the GL event builds upon an institutional genre with specific participatory roles allocated to actors, including tools (like microphones, a film to be screened) and a specific organization of space. Focusing upon the linking of micro-interactional scales and event phase scales allows us to 'see' the intricate ways in which agency is at play across time and space. It allows us both to go beyond specific utterances or happenings, and to recognize actors' interactions with others and tools. The audience is not just made up of individuals who consume the planned order of the event or the ways-of-being-with-words of the expert panelists. Far from being passive, they contribute to the event by defying both the planned event structure (despite resistance from the organizers and the panelists), and more significantly, the topic in focus. The efforts to 'hijack' the event and the topic are actively challenged also, displaying dimensions of the *flow of agency* in public spaces in and through social action.

Furthermore, the boundaries commonly drawn between one language variety and another are not in sync with actors' agentic ways-of-being-with-words. Actors' agency in the uses of these varieties appears, however, to be at odds with how we, analysts situated in the language sciences, not uncommonly conceptualize language in institutional, including educational, contexts. Identity indexing of geopolitical spaces, language varieties and individuals occurs in and through languaging. The analysis presented here highlights the interplay between temporal and spatial scales: across event phases, actors and tools, and language varieties that actors draw upon in everyday life. This complexity, made visible through representations like trajectories of interlinked happenings, processes, maps and transcripts, enables us to understand how agency is a dimension of the actor–tool continuum made relevant in languaging.

Conclusion

The study of communication is a transdisciplinary endeavor and understanding its situated distributed nature generally and its relationship to agency is multifaceted, shaped by disciplinary vantage points. My aim has not been to present a coherent overview of the relationship between languaging and agency, but rather to empirically explore this relationship and offer an outline of what the study of communication reveals about the nature of agency and identity across scales. The action-based sociocultural and postcolonially framed analysis in this chapter focuses on the ways in which languaging occurs in communities of practices. Their situated and distributed *in situ* languaging emerges as the building blocks of agency: actors actively language and their agency is irreducibly linked to tools and the work that other participants do in specific settings. Thus the analysis presented here has tried to make visible the performatory work that actors do with tools through representations of naturally occurring practices and mundane (inter)actions across scales.

Focusing on naturally occurring data allows for contrastive viewings of the dynamic and chained obstacles, resistance, support and meaning-making that characterizes everyday life as well as the unfolding of identity-positions. Representations of the analysis of (inter)action, space and time through the sequential turn-by-turn languaging and use of tools in micro-scale transcripts, trajectories of interlinked interactional order in phases and the organization of space via maps illustrate some of the ways in which multimodal analysis of the actor–tool and human–sign continuum allows us to unpackage agency as a dimension of communicative performance. Conceptualizing actors separated from the affordances offered in and through the communicative practice they co-construct in different settings would therefore comprise a reductionistic view of the practice.

The participants, in their different designated roles at the GL event, collaborate and push interaction forward by both challenging and counter-challenging the topic and the planned event structure. The work they do at the micro-scale with the cultural tools – the terminology for the city, the themes explored in the film – is intricately handled and relates to the *performance of agency* where language is the most central tool. The organization of space and the film screening are other tools. The analysis also highlights that a simultaneity of contact in and between varieties and modalities is not an anomaly. Rather, it is a dominant pattern at both the micro- and macro-scales. One can say that the human condition of languaging is littered with this type of complexity that is only visible to us analysts from the outside – as members of academic tribes that are colored by both Eurocentric understandings of language-use as well as from our etic ivory tower language science lenses.

The representations of languaging and the use of space and tools presented in this chapter illustrate four aspects that are important. First, tools are engaged with in terms of resources that are a regular part of the ongoing interactional order. Agency and languaging cannot be meaningfully understood separately from the use of space and tools. Second, different language varieties, resources and modalities at different scales constitute important dimensions of languaging. These are contingent upon explicit and diffuse associations with happenings and events across time and space and a finely tuned linking in languaging that makes concrete what the actors agentically articulate, irrespective of whether this gets mediated via an actor, a tool, a modality or a film screen.

Third, the oral-language-bias in the reporting of interactionally focused research (Bagga-Gupta, 2012b) is visible also in how literature on agency is framed: what an actor says is explicitly equated with her/his motivations, desires and overt efforts. Such a position is at crossroads with a socioculturally framed action-oriented perspective on communication and learning. I have empirically illustrated that agency needs to be analyzed along the agents–tools continuum and cannot be reduced to what an actor says about 'his or her agency'. While actors' oral contributions are primarily highlighted in much of the research literature that focuses on social interactions, focusing upon the multimodality of (inter)action raises a range of important insights that have a bearing upon our understandings of agency more broadly. Agency, as the analysis in this chapter illustrates, is interlayered and includes embodiment (for instance, pointing and gaze) and oral, textual and haptic dimensions of human conduct.

A fourth aspect of multidimensional (inter)action relates to the term multilingualism (especially in the Global North). The fluidity and interlinking of language varieties and modalities in complex and routine ways-of-being-with-words at different scales exemplify and illustrate an interactional order where tools are deployed as mediational means. The dominant ideology that has framed the language sciences generally and language education specifically has envisaged the 'needs' of children vis-à-vis a specific language variety that is seen as a prerequisite for the later learning of another language variety. This ideology also, commonly, envisages the need for keeping these two language varieties apart from one another in classroom learning settings. A systematic analysis of actors in (inter)action with one another and tools across scales both inside and outside school settings, however, illustrates that this gets played out in quite a different and complex manner (see also Gynne & Bagga-Gupta, 2013; Messina Dahlberg & Bagga-Gupta, 2013; Tapio, 2013). Such analysis can open the way for critically discussing opportunities for participation in meaning-making and learning that are made available for pupils in school environments, rather than the different cultural linguistic systems of meaning.

Appendix: Transcription Conventions used in Transcripts 7.1 and 7.2

abcd	Oral communication in language variety Mumbaiya-Hindi
abcd	Oral communication in language variety English
abcd	Translated Mumbaiya-Hindi talk into English
abcd abcd	focused city labels
[xxx]	unclear talk
(.)	pause

Notes

(1) The ongoing Gender Talk Gender Spaces project is based at the CCD research group at Örebro University, Sweden (www.oru.se/humus/ccd). It builds upon a previous ethnographic fieldwork at a not-for-profit organization during 1991–1993 (see Bagga-Gupta, 1995, 2012b).
(2) The MMC, Mumbai Mobile Creches (http://www.mumbaimobilecreches.org/).
(3) Discussing the ideal Indian woman, Madhok says: 'The woman who gets around, who is free to move about as she chooses, is the antithesis of the ideal Indian [woman] who by definition leads a life that is circumscribed' (Madhok, 1986: 24).

References

Akkerman, S.F. and Bakker, A. (2011) Learning at the boundary. An Introduction. *International Journal of Educational Research* 50, 1–5.
Antaki, C. and Widdicome, S. (eds) (1998) *Identities in Talk*. London: Sage Publications.
Bagga-Gupta, S. (1995) *Human Development and Institutional Practices. Women, Child Care and the Mobile Creches*. Linköping Studies in Arts and Science 130. PhD thesis, Linköping University, Sweden.
Bagga-Gupta, S. (2012a) Challenging understandings of bilingualism in the language sciences from the lens of research that focuses social practices. In E. Hjörne, G. van der Aalsvoort and G. de Abreu (eds) *Learning, Social Interaction and Diversity – Exploring School Practices* (pp. 85–102). Rotterdam: Sense.

Bagga-Gupta, S. (2012b) Privileging identity positions and multimodal communication in textual practices. Intersectionality and the (re)negotiation of boundaries. In A. Pitkänen-Huhta and L. Holm (eds) *Literacy Practices in Transition: Perspectives from the Nordic Countries* (pp. 75–100). Bristol: Multilingual Matters.

Benwell, B. and Stokoe, E. (2006) *Discourse and Identity.* Edinburgh: Edinburgh University Press.

Blommaert, J. (2010) *The Sociolinguistics of Globalization.* Cambridge: Cambridge University Press.

Blommaert, J. and Rampton, B. (2011) Language and superdiversity. *Diversities* 13 (2), 1–20.

Bucholtz, M. and Hall, K. (2005) Identity and Interaction: A Sociocultural linguistic approach. *Discourse Studies* 7 (4–5), 584–614.

Chaiklin, S. and Lave, J. (eds) (1993) *Understanding Practice: Perspectives on Activity and Context.* Cambridge: Cambridge University Press.

Drew, P. and Heritage, J. (eds) (1992) *Talk-at-Work. Studies in Interactional Sociolinguistics 8.* Cambridge: Cambridge University Press.

Gal, S. and Irvine, J.T. (1995) The boundaries of languages and disciplines: How ideologies construct difference. *Social Research* 62 (4), 967–1001.

García, O. (2009) *Bilingual Education in the 21st Century: A Global Perspective.* Malden: Blackwell.

Goodwin, C. (1994) Professional vision. *American Anthropologist* 96 (3), 606–633.

Gynne, A. and Bagga-Gupta, S. (2013) Young people's language usage and identity positioning. Chaining in 'bilingual' educational settings in Sweden. *Linguistics and Education* 24, 479–496.

Hasnain, I., Bagga-Gupta, S. and Shailender, M. (eds) (2013) *Alternative Voices. (Re)searching Language, Culture & Identity.* Newcastle upon Tyne: Cambridge Scholars Publishing.

Hult, F.M. (2004) Planning for multilingualism and minority language rights in Sweden. *Language Policy* 3, 181–201.

Hult, F.M. (2010) Analysis of language policy discourses across the scales of space and time. *International Journal of the Sociology of Language* 202, 7–24.

Hutchins, E. (1993) Learning to navigate. In S. Chaiklin and J. Lave (eds) *Understanding Practice: Perspectives on Activity and Context* (pp. 35–63) Cambridge: Cambridge University Press.

Irvine, J.T. and Gal, S. (2000) Language ideology and linguistic differentiation. In P.V. Kroskrity (ed.) *Regimes of Language: Ideologies, Polities and Identities* (pp. 35–83). SantaFe: School of American Research Press.

Jorgensen, J.N., Karrebaek, M.S., Madsen, L.M. and Moller, J.S. (2011) Polylanguaging in superdiversity. *Diversities* 13 (2), 22–37.

Krishnamurthy, A. (2012) http://newindianexpress.com/magazine/article577530.ece?service=print (accessed July 2013).

Krzyzanowaki, M. (2010) *The Discursive Constitution of European Identities. A Multi-Level Approach to Discourse and Identity in the Transforming European Union.* Frankfurt: Peter Lang.

Lantolf, J.P. (2000) *Sociocultural Theory and Second Language Learning.* Oxford: Oxford University Press.

Lave, J. and Wenger, L. (1991) *Situated learning: Legitimate Peripheral Participation.* Cambridge: Cambridge University Press.

Linell, P. (1998) *Approaching Dialogue: Talk, Interaction and Contexts in Dialogical Perspectives.* Amsterdam: John Benjamin.

Madhok, S. (1986) At the workplace. *Seminar* 318, 24–28.

McIlvenny, P. (2013, October) Refusing What We Are: Communicating Counter-Identities and Prefiguring Social Change in New Social Movements. Paper presented at the Swedish–Norwegian Interdisciplinary International conference Revisiting Identity. Embodied communication across time and space. Örebro, Sweden.

Messina Dahlberg, G. and Bagga-Gupta, S. (2013) Communication in the virtual class-room in higher education: Languaging beyond the boundaries of time and space. *Learning, Culture and Social Interaction* 2 (3), 127–142.

Näslund, S. (2013) Födandets sociala utformning. Språkliga och kroppsliga praktiker i förlossningsrummet [The social organization of birthing. Linguistic and embodied practices in the delivery room]. *Studies from Örebro in Swedish Language 8*. PhD thesis, Örebro Univeristy, Sweden.

Ochs, E. (1992) Indexing gender. In A. Duranti and C. Goodwin (eds) *Rethinking Context: Language as an Interactive Phenomenon* (pp. 336–358). Cambridge: Cambridge University Press.

Perret-Clermont, A.-N. (2009) Introduction. In M. César and K. Kumpulainen (eds) *Social Interactions in Multicultural Settings* (pp. 1–12). Rotterdam: Sense.

Reddington, E. (2013) Membership categorization in action. *Teachers College, Columbia University Working Papers in TESOL & Applied Linguistics* 13 (1), 21–24.

Rogoff, B. (1990) *Apprenticeship in Thinking: Cognitive Development in Social Context*. Oxford: Oxford University Press.

Rosén, J. and Bagga-Gupta, S. (2013) From worker to work oriented discourse in the language training for immigrants. Shifting identities in the development of the educational system 'Swedish for immigrants'. *Language, Culture and Curriculum* 26 (1), 68–88.

Säljö, R. (2012) Literacy, digital literacy and epistemic practices: The co-evolution of hybrid minds and external memory systems. *Nordic Journal of Digital Literacy* 7 (1), 5–20.

Scollon, R. and Scollon, S.B.K. (2004) *Nexus Analysis: Discourse and the emerging internet*. London: Routledge.

Shohamy, E. (2006) *Language Policy: Hidden agendas and new approaches*. London: Routledge.

Speer, S.A. and Stokoe, E. (2011) *Conversation and Gender*. Cambridge: Cambridge University Press.

Stokoe, E. (2000) Toward a conversation analytic approach to gender and discourse. *Feminism and Psychology* 10 (4), 552–563.

Stokoe, E. and Smithson, J. (2001) Making gender relevant: Conversation analysis and gender categories in interaction. *Discourse and Society* 12 (2), 217–244.

Tapio, E. (2013) A nexus analysis of English in the everyday life of FinSL signers: A multimodal view on interaction. PhD thesis, Oulu University, Finland.

van Lier, L. (2004) *The Ecology and Semiotics of Language Learning. A Sociocultural Perspective*. Boston: Kluwer Academic.

Vygotsky, L.S. (1962) *Thought and Language*. Cambridge: M.I.T Press.

Wertsch, J. (1998) *Mind as Social Action*. Cambridge: Cambridge University Press.

Widdicombe, S. (1998) Uses of identity as an analysts' and a participants tool. In C. Antaki and S. Widdicombe (eds) *Identities in Talk* (pp. 191–206). London: Sage Publications

Zimmerman, D. (1998) Identity, context and interaction. In C. Antaki and S. Widdicombe (eds) *Identities in Talk* (pp. 87–106). London: Sage.

8 'He's the Star!': Positioning as a Tool of Analysis to Investigate Agency and Access to Learning Opportunities in a Classroom Environment

Hayriye Kayi-Aydar

Introduction

Drawing on Positioning Theory (e.g. Davies & Harré, 1990, 1999), this chapter aims to explore the tight yet complex relationships among agency, positioning and access to learning opportunities in a language classroom. The main theoretical assumption here is that identities are constructed in the ways people position themselves and are positioned by others in and through discourse. These positional identities, shaped by storylines including one's cultural and subjective experience, emerge naturally from social interactions and shape one's agency by implicitly limiting or allowing certain social actions. This belief is supported by Positioning Theory, which adopts a microanalytic perspective to understand how individuals shape the discourse and are shaped by the discourse through positions that they occupy or construct for themselves. The two main objectives of this chapter are to: (1) introduce Positioning Theory as a method of analysis to explore agency; and (2) describe the analytic procedures used and demonstrate how they have been applied in one qualitative case study. In order to accomplish these goals, I will first unpack the term 'agency' and describe its relationships with positioning. Then I will present a case study that illustrates how Positioning

Theory can be used as a conceptual and methodological tool to understand the 'constitutive force of social interaction in shaping our "power" to make choices' (Miller, 2006: 121).

Positioning and Agency

Positioning Theory (e.g. Davies & Harré, 1999), rooted in discursive social psychology, social constructivism and discourse analysis, is the study of positions created in conversations as well as the social force of what is being said and done (acts and actions). Situated in poststructuralism and narratology and partly built on Austin's work on speech acts (see Austin, 1962), the theory suggests that individuals, through occupying interactionally constructed positions, may implicitly limit or allow certain social actions. Assigning positions to oneself and/or others is called positioning. Through positioning, individuals locate themselves and others with rights, duties and obligations in and through talk.

Two common types of positioning within a discursive event are interactive and reflexive positionings. Interactive positioning is when one person positions another whereas in reflexive positioning one positions oneself. In a conversation, an utterance may involve either reflexive or interactive positioning by one of the speakers. The hearer(s) may respond to this utterance in various forms (e.g. silence, repositioning, reflexive positioning, confirming initial positioning). Eventually, there is an effect achieved by positioning(s). For example, let us imagine that two graduate students have just met at a conference and started to converse about their work. In Table 8.1, in the left column, I provide a hypothetical conversation between the two students, and in the right column, I point out reflexive and interactive positionings.

The positions that these two students assign to each other or themselves might change as the conversation develops. Student A might challenge the knowledge of student B and construct himself as a challenger. He might then bring further information to the conversation and position himself as a contributor or even the superior peer. As seen, positions, unlike social roles, are fluid, dynamic and context-dependent (Davies & Harré, 1990).

Through an analysis of positioning, a small but growing body of research has recently attempted to investigate various issues in a number of contexts involving English language learners. Conducted mostly in primary and secondary school classrooms, these studies illustrated how interactive and/or reflexive positionings of students impacted upon or interacted with their identity development (e.g. Abdi, 2011; Anderson, 2009; Kayi-Aydar, in press; Reeves, 2008), beliefs (e.g. De Costa, 2011) classroom participation (Kayi-Aydar, in press; Martin-Beltrán, 2010; Yoon, 2008), gender (Clarke, 2005; Ritchie, 2002) or second language development and learning (e.g. Menard-Warwick, 2008; Miller, 2006). For example, through a recursive

Table 8.1 Interactive and reflexive positioning in conversation

Student A: What is the topic of your talk?	
Student B: Positioning.	
Student A: Wow, you must be an expert on it. What is positioning?	Interactive Positioning: Here Student A *positions* Student B as a competent or knowledgeable person, possibly hoping that Student A will know and be able to explain the concept of positioning.
Student B: Frankly speaking, I don't know. I am still trying to understand.	Reflexive Positioning: However, because student B is not able to provide an explanation, he rejects the initial position assigned by Student A. Student B then *positions himself* as a learner.
Student A: Well, my understanding of it is that it is about constructing identities in talk.	Reflexive Positioning: Student A takes a turn and *positions himself* as a knowledgeable person on the topic by projecting his knowledge on the concept of positioning.
Student B: I guess you are right.	What happens in the end? Student A's legitimate, more powerful position is accepted and confirmed by Student B.

microanalysis of classroom interaction, Kayi-Aydar (in press) illustrated how two talkative students came to occupy polarized positions in an ESL classroom. One of these students, Tarek, engaged in teacher-like positions, displayed his knowledge and experience whenever possible, and often challenged the authority of his teacher. However, by building friendships with particular students and using humor frequently as a communication strategy, he was able to become an accepted member. The second focal participant, Ahmad, who mirrored Tarek, displayed his competence and dominated classroom conversations by producing long turns. However, unlike Tarek, he was not able to be in the group because his participation behavior was not accepted by his classmates, who positioned him as an outsider. Kayi-Aydar discusses that Tarek did not become a 'helpful', 'funny' classmate in a single day, nor did Ahmad become an outsider all of a sudden. They took up these positional identities because of the ways in which they recursively positioned themselves and the ways in which they were positioned by others over one academic semester. Kayi-Aydar and others (e.g. Menard-Warwick, 2008; Miller, 2006; Yoon, 2008) have emphasized that students do not come into classrooms always marginalized or privileged, but are assigned such positions, and either gain or lose access to classroom participation and language learning opportunities. Although such positioning events can be observed in many classrooms, few scholars have investigated positioning in language classrooms, and fewer studies have explored the link between positioning and agency. Indeed, positioning is a powerful tool to analyze and understand agency in language classrooms as one's agency closely depends on how one is positioned in social interactions.

A number of applied linguists have defined agency as the learner's ability to seek out learning opportunities, carry out various acts and actively participate in the learning process. This understanding of agency is similar to the understanding of agency in traditional sociological theory in which agency is viewed as 'an individual matter in which any individual conceives of a line of action, knows how to achieve it, and has the power and authority and right to execute it' (Davies, 1990: 343). Researchers such as Davies (1990), Fogle (2012) and McKay and Wong (1996), note the pitfalls of this understanding of agency. First of all, they suggest that active participation is not always an indication of agency. Deliberate silence or resistance, which do not lead to active participation, can also be agentic in nature. For instance, one of the ESL students in McKay and Wong's (1996: 592) study, Michael Lee, adopted 'the coping strategy of resistance to counteract his powerless positioning as "ESL student"'. As McKay and Wong described, 'at the first language assessment, he decided not to write on the suggested topics of family or school and instead was the only focal student who chose to write about his hobbies (sports, pets)' (McKay & Wong, 1996: 592). Gaining enough agency and satisfaction from his multiple social identities as athlete and popular friend, Michael did not feel compelled to develop further as a scholar or to please his parents and teachers by perfecting his academic writing skills. In brief, as Fogle (2012: 3) states, agency 'can both afford and constrain language-learning opportunities depending on the sociocultural contexts and the intentions or goals of the learner'.

In this chapter, like Davies (1990) and others, I argue that one's agency depends upon the particular discursive practices in use and the positionings of that individual in those practices. This understanding of agency is consistent with Positioning Theory according to which an individual can only speak from the positions made available within discourses (Davies, 1990). In other words, by being positioned in certain ways, individuals may or may not exercise agency. While certain positions may enable one to become agentic, agents can also actively resist certain positionings. Agency and positioning are therefore closely linked, one influencing the other and vice versa. Examining the 'habitual ways of speaking' (Miller, 2010: 484) in her participants' autobiographical accounts, Miller illustrated how agency was discursively constructed as her participants positioned themselves and were positioned as agents within ideologically defined spaces. For example, one learner positioned herself agentively by going to a community college in order to learn more English. The same participant attributed her inability to continue her education to 'the understandable and socially recognized difficulty of juggling work and school simultaneously' and positioned herself as 'someone who cannot be held responsible for not finishing college' (Miller, 2010: 479). In language classrooms, positioning is an important conceptual and method-ological tool that can help elucidate how communication is constructed and what rights, duties and obligations are available for second language learners to make choices or act. Building on the studies by Miller (2010), McKay and Wong (1996) and others, this chapter aims to investigate the issue of agency by using positioning as an analytical lens in a classroom context, therefore contributing to the limited literature on positioning and agency in language classrooms. This study also adds to the literature by illustrating how agency emerges and is negotiated moment by moment in classroom interactions.

The Study

The case study presented in this chapter comes from a 3.5-month quali-tative study conducted in an academic ESL classroom that focused on listen-ing, speaking and note-taking skills at the advanced level. The ESL class was offered in an Intensive English program at a doctoral granting university in the USA. Four courses – (1) grammar; (2) oral skills (listening, speaking, pronunciation); (3) writing and (4) reading and American culture – were offered in five different proficiency levels – from beginning to advanced. The goal of the oral skills class observed for this study was to give learners experi-ence in using English for academic purposes. Formal lectures by the teacher, student-led discussions, individual student presentations, and listening and note-taking tasks were the major classroom activities.

The ESL class included 11 students who represented nine different nationalities (four females and five males). It was their first time in the USA for all participants. Peggy (all names are pseudonyms), the ESL teacher, was a White American. She had spent more than 30 years teaching English in different contexts at the time of the study. In this qualitative case study, I describe how one focal participant, Mounir, frequently displayed the singu-larity and uniqueness of various aspects of his selfhood to exercise agency and how his peers and ESL teacher responded to his reflexive positionings in classroom activities. My aim is to gain an in-depth understanding of the complexity and peculiarity of Mounir's positioning and agency, and his English language learning experience in a classroom setting. At the time of this study, Mounir was a 19-year-old ESL student from a bilingual country in Central Africa. He spoke French as his native language and had also stud-ied Arabic and German. He held a high school diploma from his native coun-try. In the USA, Mounir was living with his uncle and his uncle's family. He spoke both French and English at home – English with his cousins who were born in the USA. They lived in a neighborhood with a large Hispanic popula-tion, which did not give Mounir many opportunities to use his English out-side the home. However, his interactions with his cousins seemed to have a positive impact on his English as he sometimes used vocabulary that his peers in the oral skills class were not familiar with. In the oral skills class, Mounir was an enthusiastic language learner and active participant. My field notes include many examples of Mounir scaffolding other students' language learning, actively participating in class discussions, dominating classroom talk in teacher–whole class interactions and generally fulfilling the role of a leader in group work.

Since I wanted to observe a communicative-oriented classroom that included peer-led discussions and collaborative work as well as students coming from diverse cultural and linguistic backgrounds, an oral skills class seemed to be the best choice. Furthermore, the participating teacher, Peggy, had expressed interest in my work through informal conversations and she volunteered to participate in the study upon a formal invitation. To explore how agency was negotiated in classroom discourse, I observed the class from late January to early May for five hours per week. Each observation was audio- and video-recorded. In addition to my extensive observations and field notes, I used teacher–student interviews, student diaries and artifacts (e.g. teacher notes, samples of student work) to understand participants' positionings and how those positionings interacted with their agency. The analysis of classroom talk helped me understand how agency was discursively constructed in the oral skills class. Other data sources (e.g. interviews, field notes) enabled me to make sense of *agency* better in this particular setting.

After spending eight weeks in Peggy's class, I chose to focus on the positioning work of two students and considered how their participation differed in terms of both quality and quantity to that of other students in the same class. In this chapter, I present only Mounir as a case with a particular focus on agency. Findings related to the other focal participant are reported elsewhere (Kayi-Aydar, in press). In my observations, my focus was on positioning in classroom talk. While I was reading and expanding my field notes after classroom observations, I constantly looked for recurring patterns or themes. In particular, I looked for positionings that were recursive (e.g. a student frequently positioning himself as a help-seeker across different classroom interactions). After spending almost five weeks in the classroom, I decided to focus on atypical positionings (e.g. a student positioning himself as an interrupter) or unique positionings (e.g. a student positioning herself as a teacher in group work), as such positions seemed to give more or less power and agency to students. Power was particularly important in the analysis as 'agency and power are interconnected, for agency is a major basis for claiming power' (Al Zidjaly, 2009: 179). Because I aimed to understand how positioning interacted with one's agency, I closely looked at not only how students positioned themselves and others but also how those self- and other-positionings were responded to by others in the classroom and what happened at the end of such particular interactions.

I observed Peggy's ESL class for five hours per week for about 14 weeks. Technically, it was not possible to transcribe every class session to code for positioning. Instead, I reviewed my field notes recursively and made notes of the related sections to transcribe later. I then found those sections in audio and video-recordings, watched each segment multiple times and transcribed each. After I had transcribed a number of segments at varying lengths, I compiled the ones that included Mounir's participation or turn-taking. I read through each segment in this group several times and identified self- and other-positionings. Here, I provide one sample excerpt from my data to show what my coding looked like, hoping that the readers can follow what I have done in their own analyses of agency, positioning and classroom interactions:

Storyline 1
   S: Student
   T: Teacher
	Preliminary codes

1 **S**: Teacher, just a quick 2 question.	Interruption/request Reflexive positioning, 'interrupter'
3 **T**: All right.	Response/allows him to take the floor
4 **S**: You know, who told you this 5 intonation?	Inappropriate discourse competence Pronunciation Reflexive positioning, 'help seeker'
6 **T**: Who told me this? (Class 7 laughs)	Confusion
8 **S**: How do you guess to … ? (The 9 teacher waves at the camera)	Clarification Rephrasing Legitimate question Reflexive positioning, 'legitimate student'
10 **S**: Sorry, if I asked the wrong 11 question.	Embarrassment Reflexive repositioning/illegitimate question
12 **T**: Doesn't matter. It's just that I'm 13 surprised that you asked that.	Surprised Supports the student's reflexive, weak position
14 **S**: I mean how did you know that?	Questioning competence Restating the question Resistance and repositioning (legitimate student)
15 **T**: How do I know that?	Clarification Restating the question
16 **T**: By growing up in this culture. 17 [and speaking that language all 18 my life.	Culture Reflexive positioning, 'native speaker of English' Native speaker superiority – power

19 **S**: [Oh, okay.	Confirmation/confirming teacher's superior position
20 **T**: Yeah, but it follows a pattern. It 21 follows a pattern. And it, 22 uhmm, I told you about it, near 23 the beginning of the course. We 24 were working with the word 25 'indiscriminately'.	More detailed explanation/confirming student's legitimate position

I generated a large number of reflexive and interactive positions for Mounir. These positions were words or phrases like *contributor, informer, supporter, less superior group member, more superior classmate, challenger, negotiator, evaluator, manager, interrupter, help-seeker, initiator, promoter, facilitator.* I then compared positions across different segments within the same group to see which ones were recurrent and therefore significant to report. My next question that guided my analysis was 'How does Mounir's reflexive and interactive positionings differ than those of the other focal participant and the rest of the class?'

I followed the same steps in identifying positions in segments where the second focal participant was involved. I did the same for the third group of segments that included conversations in which Mounir and other focal participants were not involved. In each group, I then categorized similar positionings, which led to my themes.

Findings

Reflexive positionings of Mounir

Over the semester, Mounir assigned various unique positions to himself. I describe these positions unique because I have not observed other students assigning these positions to themselves. Such reflexive positionings seemed to give more power to Mounir and enabled him to say more in the interactions or participate more actively than others. In addition to assigning unique positions to himself, Mounir also created frequent opportunities for himself to contribute to classroom conversations. Since Mounir's level of spoken English was slightly higher than that of other students in the class, he used vocabulary or structures that other students found pretty complex and difficult to understand. His higher proficiency also enabled him to say and accomplish more in classroom conversations, giving him more power and making him more agentic.

'I'm a scientist!': Displaying particular aspects of selfhood

Frequently over the semester, Mounir recursively constructed strong aspects of his selfhood. One of these was his reflexive positioning of himself as a scientist. One day, the class engaged in a whole-class discussion. To the question, 'Do you think humans will disappear some day?' Mounir raised his hand and said:

Excerpt 1
1. According to me, I think that humans will disappear some day because it
2. depends on anyone's belief. According to my belief, my religion, it's
3. written in my religion book that humans will disappear some day. And
4. also I'm a scientist. And I'm referring to, I am basing it on facts.
5. One day, it's proven that the Sun, as the source of energy, will run out of
6. energy. With the energy, coming from the Sun, is the source of life.

In his answer to the question whether humans would disappear one day or not, Mounir referred to two sources to support his opinion. He argued that humans would disappear and referenced a religious text he believed in as the evidence for his argument. Later on in the conversation he chose to position himself as a scientist. This way, Mounir supported his argument by referring to facts, which enabled him to establish his claims to knowledgeability as credible. His answer had to be right and accepted by others because he was 'basing it on facts' as a scientist. By constructing an expert identity in the discourse, Mounir was able to establish a degree of autonomy and control, which is one form of agency (Fogle, 2012). When he positioned himself as a scientist, I observed that his peers chose to not continue the argument or support their own views. In a way, while Mounir's positioning of himself as a scientist enabled him some degree of agency, this reflexive positioning limited his peers in achieving agency in interaction. In their discussion of positioning and selfhood, Harré and van Langenhove (1999: 7) claim that 'I' is used not to name or to refer to oneself or to one's body. Rather, 'its use expresses one's personal identity'. It is used to 'display the singularity of our selfhood'. By using first person indexical, *I*, and saying 'I am a scientist', Mounir singularized himself. He made himself unique by bringing up his perceived identity as a scientist, which would give him symbolic power in class.

In addition to positioning himself as a scientist, Mounir took up various similar unique positions that enabled him to exercise agency. The following excerpt, which was taken from Mounir's end-of-term presentation with Takeshi, shows how Mounir portrayed his singularity, individual or unique identity and therefore his superiority over Takeshi. Although all other students had conducted their presentations individually, Mounir and Takeshi co-presented because they both wanted to present on the same topic: Japanese anime. In the warm-up phase of their presentation, Mounir and Takeshi showed a number of pictures and asked the class what was common in them. Once a few people responded saying they were anime, Takeshi introduced their presentation topic:

Excerpt 2

1	**Takeshi:**	So, our topic today is Japanese anime.
2	**Mounir:**	We chose this topic because first of all we are very inter- ested in
3		Japanese anime. For Takeshi, it might be obvious that he chose this
4		topic because he is from Japan, but me I am not from the same
5		country as Takeshi. I'm from (omitted information), but there I'm a
6		drawer. I like drawing and I'm really interested in Japanese anime because
7		I like this style. That's the style that I usually use.

In the introduction of their presentation, right after Takeshi introduced their topic, which was Japanese anime, Mounir continued to explain why they chose it. This was the typical structure of presentations. However, what was interesting in this introduction was Mounir's further explanation. By positioning himself as a 'drawer' and referring to his unique ability and style 'I like this style. That's the style I usually use', Mounir was displaying his expertise which, according to Mounir, Takeshi did not possess. Harré and Van Langenhove (1999: 24, 25) state:

> Having presented oneself as a unique person through one's choice of grammatical devices appropriate to that act, one is then in a position to offer personal explanations of personal behavior. There seem to be at least three distinct ways of explaining personal behavior: by referring to one's powers and one's rights to exercise them, by referring to one's biography (what one did, saw, etc. and what happened to one) and by referring to personal experiences that one has had as legitimating certain claims, for example, 'expertise'. When a person is engaged in a deliberate self-positioning process this often will imply that they try to achieve specific goals with their act of self-positioning. This requires one to assume that they have a goal in mind. Paraphrasing Goffman's concep- tion of 'strategic interaction', this could be called 'strategic positioning'.

With his strategic positioning, that is, positioning himself as a 'drawer', Mounir had a certain goal. He wanted to show his expertise in drawing to others and that he had more symbolic power than Takeshi. Takeshi was positioned as a student who picked that topic (Japanese anime) not because of any unique feature or ability he had, but only because he was from Japan. It was probably the expert position that gave confidence to Mounir to answer most of the questions asked by his classmates after the presentation.

In a similar discursive event, Mounir highlighted where he was from to gain power. This time, Rosemary was the student-presenter. In her presentation, she narrated how she and her cousins got lost in a jungle and then saw gorillas that scared them. After her presentation, she encouraged her peers to ask follow-up questions. The questions were: 'How old were you then?', 'How many people were there?' and 'How long did it take for you to find your home?' The final question came from Mounir:

Excerpt 3

1	**Mounir:**	I'm from Africa and I know that gorillas don't attack people. Did
2		anyone of you did something to offend the gorilla because it will
3		come after you if you did something.
4	**Rosemary:**	Yes, my cousin did.
5	**Mounir:**	What did she do?
6	**Rosemary:**	He was saying, 'hello', 'is everybody there?' 'we're lost' and I
7		think they heard that and
8	**Mounir:**	Did they really come after you?
9	**Rosemary:**	No, no.
10	**Mounir:**	Okay, I knew it.

By saying that he is from Africa and he '*knows* gorillas don't attack people', Mounir positioned himself as someone knowledgeable on the topic and therefore having the right to speak. Mounir's desire to be exceptional and therefore 'visible' to others was also evident in his unforgettable story presentation. Duff (2012: Data analysis section, para. 3) argues that 'nonverbal behaviors, social networks, artistic constructions (photo collages, artwork, plays) or essays created by learners to represent themselves might also be examined more holistically for evidence of how language learners perceive or portray themselves and/or their linguistic and cultural attributes, histories, and futures'. At the beginning of the semester, each student was required to narrate an unforgettable event in their life in the oral skills class. In my field notes, I included a summary of Mounir's story and described the ways he positioned himself in it. A visual representation of his story drawn by Mounir is also provided below.

Excerpt 4. Expanded field notes

Today students continue their presentations on unforgettable events. Today's first presentation is Mounir's. He has one transparency. Here is his story: Mounir's friends organized a 'swimming pool party' in a hotel and invited him. Mounir went to the party where his friends were having lots of fun in the swimming pool. Mounir had a big problem: he did not know how to swim. Everybody was enjoying the party but not Mounir. He sat by the pool for a while watching his friends having fun. Then, 'some of his friends started noticing that he couldn't swim'. Mounir said, 'So, I didn't allow them to know that!' He made a decision, walked toward the pool, and he jumped into the pool 'in order to catch everybody's attention'. By doing so he thought he would be 'the star of the swimming pool party'. He was now very happy. However, since he did not know how to swim, he began drowning. A few minutes later, he became unconscious and was taken to the emergency.

Mounir's desire to be recognized is clearly evident in his story; in his own words, 'I would be the star of the swimming pool party' by diving into the pool. His self-positioning enabled him to act: he jumped into the pool, which resulted in a failure. In addition to unique powerful positions Mounir took up over the semester, he further gained agentic status by displaying his competence, which came mostly in linguistic form. It is his negotiation of this competence that I describe next.

Figure 8.1 Visual representation of Mounir's story

'Coward. I can spell the word. C-o-w-a-r-d': Displaying knowledge

Although placed in the oral skills class because of his proficiency level in listening and speaking, Mounir seemed slightly more advanced than his classmates, especially in terms of his vocabulary use and fluency, which was indeed acknowledged by Peggy several times. Mounir used his linguistic capital quite often during classroom conversations. This usually included using more advanced level vocabulary and checking with classmates if they knew or understood the words he used. I provide one example below.

Excerpt 5

1	**Mounir:**	I think that like Hassan I disagree, because I think, according to
2		me, that's my personal opinion, I am not referring to facts, that's
3		my personal opinion and that you'd be coward, you know?
4	**Xian:**	Coward?
5	**Mounir:**	Coward. I can spell the word c-o-w-a-r-d.
6	**Xian:**	Coward (repeating the word to practice pronunciation).

As the excerpt shows, Mounir used the word 'coward' when he disagreed with others who argued that euthanasia should be provided as an option to seriously ill patients. Xian repeated the word 'coward', signaling that she did not know what it meant or how it was spelled (Line: 4). Xian's lack of knowledge of the word 'coward' became an opportunity for Mounir, who immediately chose to spell the word for Xian and others, thereby showing his knowledge of this particular word. In many other similar instances, Mounir used unfamiliar vocabulary, asked others if they understood, and either spelled the words for them or provided a definition, thereby positioning himself as a competent language learner.

Interactive Positionings of Mounir

Interestingly, Mounir's reflexive positioning of himself in the oral skills class contradicted the positions assigned to him by his classmates and teacher. His more proficient skills and unique reflexive positionings gave him the confidence to actively participate in classroom activities. His frequent turn-taking and complex language use seemed to bother his peers over time as they started to interpret his participation as showing off. Over time, his peers positioned Mounir as an outcast. When Mounir found himself in a marginal position, he actively resisted his marginality. His attempt to reposition himself did not seem to change the interactive positionings of him by his classmates in any obvious way. During the final interview with Mounir, his repositioning of himself became obvious:

Excerpt 6

1. Sometimes people don't understand me. They think that I wanna show off that I
2. know many things so every time I jump in and I am not like that. You know I am
3. very humble. I keep my feet on the ground so the thing is that when I know
4. something, just kind of my head, I just get it out. Sometimes, I calm myself down
5. and just realize that I have to raise my hand. But it depends on the intensity of my
6. when it comes to my head I found it I answer. But I really participate. I answer as
7. many questions as possible. Because I want the teacher to have a good
8. impression of me. Sometimes, when I don't do the homework it's not I don't want
9. to do that. Maybe I had something interfered with that. So, I am really good
10. student. If you ask other my teachers, they will tell you that. All those teachers
11. know my name. They really know me well and they never forget me.

Mounir was aware that others did not perceive him as a humble student, but reflexively positioned himself as considerate and humble. However, his reflexive positioning was in complete contradiction with Peggy's interactive positioning of him:

Excerpt 7

1. Well, he says he's the star (laughs). I think he comes across as arrogant.
2. And you know we've talked about the class. They became obviously quite
3. fond of him (referring to other focal participant) and I think he interacted
4. better and better with them. But Mounir is just pretty full of himself. He
5. (referring to other focal participant) also managed to whether by accident
6. or design to project a little humble attitude. I mean Mounir of course never
7. projects a humble attitude.

These excerpts highlight discrepancies between reflexive and interactive positionings of Mounir. Noted are the stark contrasts that exist between the description of Mounir from his point of view and from the point of view of Peggy. Mounir described himself as a humble person. However, it is clear that Mounir was not so perceived by his teacher. Similarly, he positioned himself as 'funny, nice, cool, respectful, polite' and these adjectives were used by his classmates to describe what Mounir was not.

Indeed, all the students I interviewed at the end of the semester complained about Mounir's participation to exert power and influence others in class. They positioned him as someone who was inconsiderate and showed off his linguistic abilities. These negative interactive positionings of Mounir limited his agency and his access to learning opportunities. Since his peers positioned him as an outsider and an arrogant individual, they started to interact less with him over the semester. Through the end of the academic semester, I observed Mounir's difficulty in finding partners for pair and group activities. Indeed, in the final interview, Mary, one of Mounir's classmates, clearly stated her lack of desire to work with Mounir:

Excerpt 8

1. With Mounir now, at the end, it's just like I don't like working with him
2. anymore. But, just because like today in the presentation, there were
3. Takeshi and Mounir and when Takeshi talks, Mounir then add things and
4. that made Takeshi do worst. But it's not because of Takeshi. Just because
5. of Mounir. That's trying to improve or I don't know. But I think that in
6. our presentation that I don't think that it's a good idea to add things that
7. another one already said. I don't know. He's always like giving long
8. answers. He just get boring. And because in other classes like I am taking,
9. they are not going to listen at him. They are just ignore him and start
10. talking about everything. It's like uncomfortable to stop. He's a nice
11. person but he's trying to be better than the other ones, so that's not good.

Mounir's interactive positioning as an 'arrogant' student who was 'trying to be better than others' is seen in Mary's description of Mounir's participation. By saying that Mounir would be ignored by his classmates if this was a different class, Mary was actually giving an implicit message: it was possible and reasonable to ignore Mounir's contributions. In fact, this is exactly what was happening in the oral skills class as seen in the following excerpt. This excerpt was from Mary's presentation on healthy diet. After each student presentation, the class had 10–15 minutes to ask questions to the presenter as well as answer his or her questions. Hassan, one of the student-participants, asked the first question to Mary:

Excerpt 9

1	**Hassan:**	In fact, I would like to ask question. Are there any methods or
2		way to improve my memory? I mean I don't know maybe you got
3		an idea.
4	**Mary:**	For me, I used to have really bad memory. Really bad memory.
5		But, I start organizing my thought. I (incomprehensible) notes in
6		my desk, things on my cell phone to ring at some time, so I
7		remember things. Well, up to now, is really helpful.
8		(Mounir raises his hand.)
9	**Hassan:**	[Yeah?
10	**Rosemary:**	[I do have another question. Do you think that it's good to take
11		drugs to remember things?
12		(Mounir's hand is still up and then down.)
13	**Mary:**	Well, I don't know I mean. There are people for them is really hard
14		to concentrate, so they took drugs, but I think that I don't know.
15		That's something to ask doctor. But maybe if you have problem to
16		concentrate, maybe is like uhm like uhm some health problem, but
17		I don't know. I really don't.
18		(Mounir raises his hand.)
19	**Mary:**	Yes.
20	**Mounir:**	I would like to answer two questions. First of all, the question
21		about to take drugs how to improve memory. I think most of the
22		time is not a good way to improve the memory because most of the
23		substances that are advised to use to memory are addictive. They
24		are addictive kind of that you come addicted to those substances.
25		And potential that you got stuck. It only depends on the substance.

26		When you like the substance, you won't be able to use your
27		potential high efficiency. And about the second question, I'd like to
28		answer, about Hassan's one about what techniques he can use to
29		improve his memory. I'd like to say there are many techniques. It
30		depends on how good what type of learning you are using. Maybe
31		there are visual learners. There are visual learners. There are people
32		who images to memorize, to memorize the content really well.
33		There are some people who like letters. You know when they read,
34		they feel comfortable when they are reading. And there are people
35		who like just listening. Like just listening. Listening someone
36		talking to...how to memorize something to...So I think it depends
37		on you. You can use diagrams, you can use sticks. People write
38		down what they like to memorize and keep them somewhere so
39		every time they like to remember of what that's something about
40		who just to check those sticks so I will be able to learn what was
41		really important.
42	**Hassan:**	[Thank you. Appreciated.
43	**Mary:**	[Takeshi, you have something to say?

In this exchange, Mary could not fully answer Rosemary's question (lines 13–17) and said it should be addressed to an expert, perhaps a doctor. Mounir joined the conversation in line 20 saying he wanted to answer both questions. He thus positioned himself as knowledgeable. By providing answers to a question that Mary could not answer, Mounir also assigned himself a more powerful position in the discourse. His answer greatly differed in depth and in the amount of detail given in his explanation. As seen, he produced a long turn. Although he tried to join the conversation several times, Mary somehow ignored him. He eventually managed to take a turn and provided his answer, though. Interestingly enough, only Hassan thanked him and no one else responded to his comments. As soon as Mounir's answer was over, Mary moved on and invited Takeshi to the conversation. Here, we can see both interactive and reflexive positionings constructed in the conversation. Mounir was assigning powerful positions to himself, but others did not seem to confirm those positions. In fact, by ignoring his comments, his classmates were assigning him a different, contradictory position: nonvalued, illegitimate speaker.

Discussion

In this paper, I aimed to demonstrate how positioning interacted with agency in a classroom environment. Frequently constructing himself as an expert or knowledgeable person, Mounir was able to say or claim things that others could not, which enabled him to assert agency. In relation to Mounir's reflexive positioning, the exemplars I provided demonstrate Mounir's efforts to construct himself as *knowledgeable* and *special, unique* and *unforgettable* in contrast to his peers. These positions seemed important for him. He could achieve these identities through drawing on what he *knew* from his religion and as a 'scientist', drawing on his talents and personal interests (e.g. 'I'm a drawer'), his *knowledge* as an African, and his linguistic *expertise* in English. These various resources from his biography were brought to bear in his active efforts to construct himself as *smart, knowledgeable* and *confident*. His agency is demonstrated in his strategic positioning. He created positions for himself in the talk in which he was able to cast himself as smart. Although others found him arrogant, Mounir exploited openings in the talk and made them work for him. For example, in responding to a question on whether humans would disappear someday, he used the legitimated opportunity to respond and to give his opinion in a class discussion as an opening to construct his knowledgeable identity. He used the conventional introduction to a presentation as an opening to talk about his ability to draw and his interest in anime, and thus, to construct himself as particularly interesting or unique. By analyzing how this student agentively exploited these openings in the classroom interaction to create identity positions for himself, I was able to explore how agency is actively deployed. That is the power of positioning analysis; it provides us with a way of seeing the dynamic processes of agency in moment-to-moment interactions.

His agentive attempts were not always well received by his peers and teachers. On the one hand, they enabled his strategic positioning by not challenging him. On the other hand, because they were so put off by his seeming arrogance, they blocked his ability to interact collaboratively with others. For example, in the Excerpt 9 above, Mounir positioned himself as a knowledgeable person in the conversation when he answered the questions that Mary could not answer. However, by not responding to his comments or asking follow-up questions, his classmates seemed to not confirm Mounir's powerful positions in the discourse. By positioning him as an outcast, as marginal, they constrained his ability to have others receive him as he wished to be received, identified or understood. As such, his agentive positioning work was always co-constructed, sometimes leading to a position of dominance, but, over time, increasingly leading to a position of marginality. These contradictory positionings, in return, limited his access to learning opportunities as his peers became less willing to collaborate with him in class activities. His agency therefore fluctuated depending on his various reflexive and interactive positionings. The interactions analyzed in this paper demonstrated how powerful positions could be in terms of allowing others to say and do things or limiting them.

Conclusion

The analysis of discourse in this paper suggests that agency emerges and is negotiated in and through interactions. Therefore, as Al Zidjaly (2009: 182) claims, agency is 'collective, interactive, and emergent'. By looking at how language learners position themselves and others and how they are positioned by others, second language scholars and classroom teachers can better understand why some students become agents whereas others cannot. By becoming agents, some students gain the right to speak and act or limit or expand the opportunities for others to speak and act. For example, in this study, the focal participant, Mounir, attempted many claims for agency. By assigning powerful positions to himself in classroom interactions, he managed to exercise agency by gaining the right to 'speak with authority' (Davies, 2000: 67), construct knowledge, and allow others to participate or limit them. On the other hand, it was the very same claims and positions that ultimately positioned him as an outcast even by the teacher. Therefore, his agency was interactive and constantly shaped by the reflexive and interactive positions assigned to him. In this study, Positioning Theory, as articulated by Davies and Harré (1990), helped reveal the complexity related to positioning and agency. Positioning allows selves to say and do things or limits them. In a language classroom, positioning is important because it either constrains or gives agency to students. When students are positioned in agentic ways, they can gain access to language experiences or opportunities that are believed to foster learning in the classroom. For example, positioning himself as a legitimate speaker on topics related to Africa (e.g. gorillas), Mounir initiated the conversation by asking questions of Rosemary and reflecting on her answers during her presentation. Thus, he was able to create conversational opportunities for himself to practice and perhaps improve his English language skills. By critically listening to the voices of students in classroom talk, teachers can get a better understanding of how power and agency are constructed and negotiated in classroom discourse (Clarke, 2006). Such 'interactional awareness' (Rex & Schiller, 2009) will help them not only recognize different dynamics of classroom participation, but also seek ways to create more effective classroom talk through which learners can become agentic selves (Kayi-Aydar, in press). Rex and Schiller encourage teachers to develop interactional awareness in their classrooms to provide equal opportunities for classroom members to speak and be recognized:

> With interactional awareness comes choice in what we and our students can say and how we respond to each other. Developing interactional awareness among teachers means they understand that, depending on the situation, learners want to be recognized by others as particular kinds of people. They believe that for learning to be successful, students need to feel they are capable of handling the academic challenge. They assume that how they construct their classrooms, the discursive choices they make, determines whether or not all their students will be perceived as capable and recognized as worthy of having something to say. (Rex & Schiller, 2009: 154)

Teachers can help foster agency in their classrooms by creating and giving opportunities to each individual to speak up with authority and be heard by minimizing power differentials among students through various conversational strategies. Learners can become agents only when they do not compete for but learn how to create and contribute to classroom discourse in collaborative, meaningful ways.

References

Abdi, K. (2011) 'She really only speaks English': Positioning, language ideology, and heritage language learners. *Canadian Modern Language Review/La Revue Canadienne Des Langues Vivantes* 67 (2), 161–190.

Al Zidjaly, N. (2009) Agency as an interactive achievement. *Language in Society* 38 (2), 177–200.

Anderson, K. (2009) Applying positioning theory to the analysis of classroom interactions: Mediating micro-identities, macro-kinds, and ideologies of knowing. *Linguistics and Education* 20, 291–310.

Austin, J.L. (1962) *How to Do Things with Words.* Oxford: Oxford University Press.

Clarke, L. (2006) Power through voicing others: Girls' positioning of boys in Literature Circle discussions. *Journal of Literacy Research* 38 (1), 53–79.

Davies, B. (1990) Agency as a form of discursive practice: A classroom scene observed. *British Journal of Sociology of Education* 11 (3), 341–361.

Davies, B. (2000) *A Body of Writing: 1990–1999.* Walnut Creek: Altamira Press.

Davies, B. and Harré, R. (1990) Positioning: The discursive production of selves. *Journal for the Theory of Social Behavior* 20 (1), 43–63.

Davies, B. and Harré, R. (1999) Positioning and personhood. In R. Harré and L. van Langenhove (eds) *Positioning Theory* (pp. 32–52). Oxford: Wiley-Blackwell.

De Costa, P.I. (2011) Using language ideology and positioning to broaden the SLA learner beliefs landscape: The case of an ESL learner from China. *System* 39 (3), 347–358.

Duff, P. (2012) Identity, agency, and SLA. In A. Mackey and S. Gass (eds) *Handbook of Second Language Acquisition* (pp.410–426). London: Routledge.

Fogle, L.W. (2012) *Second Language Socialization and Learner Agency*. Bristol: Multilingual Matters.

Harré, R. and van Langenhove, L. (1999) The dynamics of social episodes. In R. Harré and L. van Langenhove (eds) *Positioning Theory* (pp. 1–14). Oxford: Blackwell.

Kayi-Aydar, H. (in press) Social positioning, participation, and second language learning: Talkative students in an academic ESL classroom. *TESOL Quarterly*; doi: 10.1002/tesq.139.

McKay, S.L. and Wong, S.L.C. (1996) Multiple discourses, multiple identities: Investment and agency in second-language learning among Chinese adolescent immigrant students. *Harvard Educational Review* 66 (3), 577–609.

Martin-Beltrán, M. (2010) Positioning proficiency: How students and teachers (de)construct language proficiency at school. *Linguistics and Education* 21 (4), 257–281.

Menard-Warwick, J. (2008) 'Because she made the beds every day': Social positioning, classroom discourse, and language learning. *Applied Linguistics* 29 (2), 267–289.

Miller, E.R. (2010) Agency in the making: Adult immigrants' accounts of language learning and work. *TESOL Quarterly* 44 (3), 465–487.

Miller, E.R. (2006) Learning English, positioning for power: Adult immigrants in the ESL classroom. In M. Mantero (ed.) *Identity and Second Language Learning: Culture, Inquiry, and Dialogic Activity in Educational Contexts* (pp. 119–141). Greenwich, CT: Information Age.

Reeves, J. (2008) Teacher investment in learner identity. *Teaching and Teacher Education* 25 (1), 34–41.

Rex, L.A. and Schiller, L. (2009) *Using Discourse Analysis to Improve Classroom Interaction*. New York: Routledge.

Ritchie, S.M. (2002) Student positioning within groups during science activities. *Research in Science Education* 32 (1), 35–54.

Yoon, B. (2008) Uninvited guests: The influence of teachers' roles and pedagogies on the positioning of English language learners in the regular classroom. *American Educational Research Journal* 45 (2), 495–522.

9 'Crossing' into the L2 and Back: Agency and Native-like Ultimate Attainment by a Post-critical-period Learner

Adnan Ajsic

Introduction

Although introspective learner narratives have been used as a data source in second language acquisition research sporadically throughout its existence as a field of inquiry (e.g. Schumann & Schumann, 1977; Schmidt & Frota, 1986; Neu, 1991; Kramsch & Lam, 1999; Pavlenko, 1998, 2001; Lin *et al.*, 2002), it is only in the last 10–15 years that autobiographical learner narratives, a potentially valuable but sometimes controversial source of data, have become popular (Pavlenko, 2007). At the same time, there is a growing recognition that cognitivist methodology is inadequate for a fuller understanding of the relationship between social identity and success in (post-critical-period) L2 acquisition (e.g. Piller, 2002; Atkinson, 2013). As Block (2012: 203) notes, '[w]e can document what learners do in cognitive and linguistic terms and we can attribute cause to effect as regards a particular task design or a particular discourse feature ... [b]ut there are other causes, or in any case shaping factors, to consider in the process of second language learning'.

Following these developments, I use autoethnography (Chang, 2007) to present and analyze my own linguistic autobiography, with a focus on the underexplored link between agency and ultimate attainment. In particular, I demonstrate a retrospective approach to autoethnography, 'connecting the personal to the cultural' (Ellis & Bochner, 2000: 739) and locating my personal experience in relation to relevant second language acquisition

(SLA) and social theories. Furthermore, I show that well-informed retrospective autoethnography can compensate for analytical weaknesses of third-person research into autobiographic narratives (Pavlenko, 2007) by combining subject, life and text realities in a single autobiographic narrative and approaching them from both macro- and micro-levels of analysis with an *emic* perspective. In the discussion, I point to the importance of identity and *investment* (Norton Peirce, 1995) in the interplay between structure and agency, hypothesizing a confluence of favorable circumstances, which I call 'felicity' conditions, as a factor that makes native-like ultimate attainment by a small minority of late learners possible and best explains the difference between high-level and native-like proficiency. I further contend that native-like ultimate attainment stands in a dialogic relationship with individual agency, which is here understood in broad terms as having the will (Gao, 2010) and capacity to act (Ahearn, 2011) as well as a way for individual learners to overcome structural constraints (e.g. Flowerdew & Miller, 2008).

Legitimizing First-person Learner Narratives

In a pertinent discussion of future challenges for SLA theory, Ortega (2007: 247) points to 'the need to theorize [learner] experience in explanations of SLA'. In her view, traditional SLA theories 'trivialize learner experience as anecdotal and outside the systematic scope of empirical or theoretical understanding, divesting it from any theoretical status' (Ortega, 2007: 247). Pavlenko and Lantolf (2000: 156) note that first-person accounts of learner experience in particular are seen in mainstream SLA research as 'perhaps interesting but potentially incomplete, if not erroneous, unless, of course, they are produced by researchers themselves and even then they are not granted the same legitimacy as third-person accounts'. Pavlenko (2002), in a side-by-side comparison of the sociopsychological and poststructuralist approaches to SLA, critiques the sociopsychological approach to SLA and the role accorded to motivation in particular, pointing to the neglect of the sociohistorical and structural processes as well as issues of power and domination in sociopsychological SLA research.[1] Norton Peirce (1995: 10) similarly challenges the traditional view of motivation, arguing against what she sees as 'artificial distinctions between the language learner and the language learning context' and an exclusive focus in SLA research on one or the other. In her view, SLA research needs to relate the individual learners to the power relations extant in their wider social context. She further draws attention to the role played by the learner's social identity, advancing her concept of *investment* as 'the socially and historically constructed relationship of the [learners] to the target language and their sometimes ambivalent desire to learn and practice it' (Norton Peirce, 1995: 17).

Against this background, Pavlenko and Lantolf propose a program for first-person narrative research,

> While the tradition of hermeneutic research in SLA is rich and longstanding, up until now it has mainly considered the 'here-and-now' or 'in process' descriptions of second language learning process by learners and researchers. Our intent ... is to establish 'retroactive' first-person narratives as a legitimate source of data on the learning process by teasing out in a theoretically informed way insights provided by the life stories of people who have struggled through cultural border crossings. (Pavlenko & Lantolf, 2000: 158)

Ricento (2005: 904) further endorses the first-person learner accounts of 'their experiences "crossing" into other cultures and languages' as a 'methodology that is particularly suited to exploring the topic of identity for L2'. As a result of these and similar contributions, linguistic autobiography is now increasingly seen as 'a legitimate discursive space' (Lin et al., 2002: 299) in SLA research and an attempt 'to theorize learner experience'. Arguably, despite methodological objections against introspective research, it is clear that 'only language learners themselves are in a position to [directly] observe their experiences' (Schmidt & Frota, 1986: 238).

The Ultimate Agency: Learner as Researcher

Objecting to the denial of learner agency implicit in much third-person, observation research, Lin et al. (2002) argue that the first-person narrative accounts of language learners are sociopolitically authentic and therefore preferable to third-person accounts of language-learning histories. Analyzing their own narratives, they attempt 'to create subject positions more complex than and alternative to those traditionally created for us in EFL [English as a foreign language] learning and teaching discourses' (Lin et al., 2002: 299), claiming their voices and providing themselves with a 'foundation for agency' (Vitanova, 2005: 149). Concurring, I argue that (research-trained) learners should exercise agency by appropriating the position of researcher, as an assertion of 'the[ir] ability to reflexively meta-analyze or theorize about what they do' (Lin et al., 2002: 297). SLA theory can benefit from third-person emic qualitative research, cognizant of the learner's point of view and attuned to their intimate experiences of the learning process in order to produce holistic and situated accounts of SLA phenomena under investigation (cf. Pavlenko, 2002: 297). However, when this is done by the learner/user acting as researcher, such agentive theorizing and reflection directly contributes to and helps shape not only learner/user experiences but also the scholarly and public discourses on them, which, I would argue, represents the ultimate form of (learner/user) agency.

(Native-like) Ultimate Attainment and Agency

Unlike traditional critical period hypothesis research, which focuses on the majority of L2 learners who fail to acquire the target language, recent research has focused on advanced post-critical-period L2 speakers whose competence and performance are equivalent to those of native speakers (e.g. Bongaerts, 1999). Such native-like ultimate attainment in adult learners includes the ability in a small minority of L2 speakers' to 'pass' for native speakers, now understood as a temporary, context- and audience-specific performance (Piller, 2002). It is not entirely clear what sets these speakers apart, but some comprehensive empirical accounts point to their above-average language-learning aptitude and professional engagement with the L2 (e.g. Abrahamsson & Hyltenstam, 2008). In addition, Schumann's (1986) acculturation hypothesis, although now out of favor (but see Lybeck, 2002), postulates a direct link between the degree of acculturation to the L2 culture and the level of proficiency attained.

A number of recent narrative studies explore the links between identity, agency and success in language learning. Pavlenko and Lantolf (2000) analyze the autobiographical narratives of 10 American and French authors (nine East European, one Japanese) who learned their second languages (in which they now write) as adults, while Lin et al. (2002) critically analyze their own autobiographical narratives of learning and teaching English in different sociocultural contexts. Similarly, Belcher and Connor (2001) offer personal accounts of formative literacy experiences of highly successful, academic second language users. Learner narratives have also been used to explore the role of individual agency in language learning (e.g. Gao, 2010), and especially as a complex dynamic system (Mercer, 2011), while Block (2012) examines the largely neglected role of class in second language learning on the basis of an adult migrant's life trajectory. However, there is a gap in both the literature on learner narratives and the critical period hypothesis with respect to native-like ultimate attainment vis-à-vis L2 learner/user agency which I propose to address in the present study. In particular, although Pavlenko and Lantolf (2000), for example, do argue that ultimate attainment in second language learning (SLL) depends on individual agency, they also suggest that this involves a process of self-translation from L1 to L2. In contrast, based on my personal experience, I argue that individual agency is a necessary but insufficient condition as well as that native-like ultimate attainment is more about suspending L1 and acquiring L2 identity than self-translation (which may actually be detrimental to this goal).

Autoethnography as Method

Autoethnography is ethnographic inquiry utilizing the researcher's autobiography as the primary data; it 'should be ethnographical in its methodological orientation, cultural in its interpretive orientation, and autobiographical in its content orientation' (Chang, 2007: 208). Chang (2007: 213) notes that there are three principle benefits of autoethnography: researcher- and reader-friendliness; enhancement of cultural understanding of self and others; and a transformational potential for self and others. However, as Pavlenko (2007: 166–167) argues, there are also four major weaknesses of content and thematic analyses of autobiographic narratives: lack of a theoretical premise and established procedures; over-reliance on repeated instances; exclusive focus on text; and uncritical reliance on storytellers' self-interpretation and positioning. By integrating the different aspects of analysis (i.e. subject, life and text realities; Pavlenko, 2007) and interjecting reflective commentary, I show that an autoethnographic approach to learner narratives can mitigate many of the noted methodological weaknesses. My approach to autoethnography emphasizes the self-narrative (cf. Ellis & Bochner, 2000), giving comparatively more weight to a *theory-informed* retrospective account of my personal learning experiences. Thus, in addition to emphasizing 'cultural analysis and interpretation of the researcher's behaviors, thoughts, and experiences in relation to others in society' (Chang, 2007: 207), I make reference to relevant SLA and social theory concepts in order to provide a theoretical framework for an interpretation of my experience. The remainder of this paper, therefore, presents my own theory-informed linguistic autobiography and a theory-based discussion of the links between my experience, individual agency and native-like ultimate attainment.

The Story of my English: A Linguistic Autobiography

Early childhood

I was born and raised in a major urban area in Bosnia–Herzegovina in a predominantly working class community of monolingual speakers of Bosnian, only a few of whom had any knowledge of foreign languages (mostly German). I went to a typical monolingual, Bosnian-medium public elementary school in which almost all children were monolingual speakers of Bosnian. My exposure to foreign languages during childhood was thus limited.

Around age 7, I began learning German by watching a popular German-language soap opera (Lichtenfeld, 1985–1989), which was aired with Bosnian subtitles and the original German dialogue intact. By this age, I was already able to read and write in Bosnian. My learning of German was motivated by my interest in the TV series and it mostly consisted of the memorization of dozens of individual words as heard on the show, which I also recorded in writing together with their Bosnian equivalents, thus effectively creating a glossary. It is perhaps interesting to note at this point that, although my early interest in and apparent aptitude for foreign language learning were fairly unusual in my social environment, they nevertheless went unheeded by my family and community.

The school years

Foreign language instruction was introduced in Grade 4 (age 9–10). In my school, classes were randomly assigned to either German or English instruction. Instruction was limited to two classes per week, 45 minutes per class period; it was based on locally produced bilingual textbooks that combined grammar and translation exercises, and the audio-lingual and communicative methods. Ironically in terms of my later language-learning experiences, I expressed a strong desire to study German, although this would have involved an otherwise undesirable change of class as my class had been assigned English. However, at the insistence of my teacher, who reasoned that English was a more attractive option, I remained in my original class and thus began my study of English, which continued through Grade 8. Lacking further input, my spontaneous learning of German soon began to wither, while I started to make some progress learning English in school; my enthusiasm for German turned into enthusiasm for English, and English became and remained my favorite subject throughout both elementary school and high school.

By the time I started high school (age 14), I had developed a basic competence in English, which, crucially, exceeded that of most of my peers, so I began to view English as a career choice and myself as someone whose future professional identity was tied to English. I attended what was considered an elite grammar school, in which three foreign languages were taught as compulsory subjects. In my case, this meant Latin, English and German. Instruction in the first two years amounted to ten 45-minute class periods per week (two class periods of Latin and four each of English and German), while during the latter two years the number of class periods went down to eight, equally divided between English and German.

Foreign language instruction in high schools relied on textbooks and methodologies similar to those used in elementary schools. Schools were typically understaffed, as English and German departments that trained both elementary and high school teachers existed at only one of the country's four public universities and had an annual output in low double-digits. This meant that often months would go by during the school year without any foreign language instruction. Because I went to high school during wartime, available teachers were even fewer in number and learning materials were scarce. Also, the schools were forced to rely on poorly trained and inexperienced teaching staff, since the better qualified senior teachers had left schools for more lucrative employment as interpreters with the United Nations peace-keeping force, deployed around the country during the war. Arguably, this affected me minimally because I was an independent learner who was interested in aspects of the language and culture (e.g. pop music) that would not have been taught in school anyway.

Outside of school, my primary exposure to English came from my interest in popular music from the English-speaking world, which I developed late in elementary school (age 12–13); this largely consisted of studying lyrics with the help of a dictionary and, sometimes, translation. Not unusually for members of my age group who lived in urban areas during the 1980s, I was part of a youth subculture that revolved around English-language rock music. This culture also served as a discursive space for experimentation with alternative social identities. The need for an alternative social identity was amplified by a drive to rebel against tradition and an inability and/or unwillingness to occupy any of the available social positions,[2] which often led to escapism and a fetishization of the subculture that made such identity transformations possible. In combination, then, my relative success in learning English at school and my membership in a subculture conducive to the development of alternative social identities led me to construct multiple identities for myself based on a close identification with English and, increasingly, an idealized, mythical image of America as a place of material prosperity, social justice and unconstrained individual freedom.

A crucial event happened during my senior year in high school (age 17–18), when I took part in a school translation project in which students were asked to produce a translation of a book from English to Bosnian in exchange for a donation of a computer laboratory for the school. When my classmates elected me to lead the project, insisting that I was the most competent person among them, my self-identification as an 'expert' English user received social validation, while my English-based self-identity was strengthened by the realization that other people had come to see me in similar terms. Paradoxically, in a (linguistic) culture that proverbially holds that 'one's worth as a person is proportional to the number of (foreign) languages one is able to speak',[3] and quite unlike many postcolonial settings where proficiency in English continues to be a prerequisite for success, even a socially recognized competence in English did not entail prestige since an ability to speak a foreign language had long been ancillary to rather than essential for socioeconomic advancement. Indeed, this explains why a highly judgmental high school cohort would spontaneously elect as their leader someone who was otherwise hovering on the social margin: leadership in this case meant all the responsibility and only modest (and short-lived) symbolic distinction (Bourdieu, 1991).

Enter felicity conditions

Importantly, the course of historical events that followed immediately thereafter changed this aspect of the national linguistic culture (and economy) in my favor. The end of the war, which came in December 1995, saw the arrival of tens of thousands of foreign troops, mostly American, whose task was to implement the newly signed peace agreement. The resulting explosion of demand for Bosnian-to-English interpreters and translators, in a country ravaged by war with unemployment at more than 50%, gave proficiency in English a whole new meaning. Moreover, as a consequence of the peace agreement, an English-using international coalition was now in control of the country's political life, which automatically accorded English enormous prestige, while emigration to the prosperous Anglophone world, of course, was greatly facilitated by an ability to speak English. For me, now aged 18, this massive macro-social change meant an instantaneous leap from a working-class life on the social margin to a quasi-elite status that came with pay that, for a time, was higher than that of the country's president, and a social intimacy with the powerful foreigners, even if at first my accent resembled British more than American English. In an additional stroke of good luck, I was assigned to a coveted position that involved the translation into English of selected regional media output, with an emphasis on accuracy. Based on a US Army and NATO open-source intelligence agenda, I helped produce a news-digest that included radio and TV news broadcasts and news articles from regional dailies and magazines.

Unlike virtually all other people who found employment as English interpreters or translators at this time, however, I was more interested in the opportunity to advance my command of English through interaction with native speakers than I was in momentary financial gain. Having resolved on my choice of career years earlier, I now sought to combine exposure to authentic input and the opportunity to practice language skills daily with formal, university-level language instruction. However, this would have to wait another two years as the sole English department, housed in the national university in the Bosnian capital, Sarajevo, admitted as few as 20 candidates per year, and the prestige associated with a competence in English had by now made such education exclusive and therefore accessible only to the children of political and business elites.

In the meantime, I continued employment as a linguist with the US Army on several military installations, which were modeled on those in the USA and therefore represented a fairly authentic, if limited, cultural space, effectively turning what otherwise would have been a typical EFL situation into a quasi-ESL one. This involved sustained exposure to a wide range of formal and informal registers and styles very similar to those normally encountered in authentic work and social environments (e.g. daily office communication, business meetings and trips, but also social functions and wide-ranging downtime conversations), as well as the availability of expert informants and, in the early days of the internet and before video streaming, ready access to authentic cultural production. In the absence of instruction but with plenty of robust authentic input and both positive and negative feedback, I was now acquiring rather than merely learning (in the sense of Krashen, 1981) English rapidly. Acquisition was further greatly advanced by my insatiable interest in nearly all aspects of American culture and a psychological disposition toward its members that went from a favorable attitude to a nigh-complete identification. After a series of failed attempts to either gain admission to the one program in English available nationally or to get a scholarship for study in the USA, I finally decided to enroll in a BA program in economics at the local university. My score on the TOEFL PBT (paper-based test), taken in preparation for study in the USA after roughly two years of employment with the US Army (age 20), was 600; my accent had begun to resemble the broad American English accent strongly. I was now well on my way to meeting my goal, which was to speak American English in a way indistinguishable from native speakers. (Somewhat predisposed toward a binary worldview, I had always strongly believed that one should either learn to speak a foreign language as a native speaker or not at all.)

Take-off

During the ensuing year-long study of economics (in Bosnian), however, I found that I was still far more interested in English, so when, in response to the newly created demand, the local university decided to start a BA program in English, I jumped at the opportunity. Over the course of the next two years, I experienced a dramatic surge in proficiency as I was now enjoying a felicitous confluence of high-quality university-level formal instruction in all aspects of the English language and daily exposure to a native-speaker environment. Although my proficiency in English had already improved immensely owing to exposure to authentic input and daily interaction with native speakers, with the addition of formal, university-level instruction, the process of acquisition simply took off. This was reflected in increasingly positive feedback I was receiving from native speakers as well as in my class performance and my own assessment of my proficiency. Figure 9.1 charts my learning/acquisition experience up to this point (approximate age 22).

In terms of performance, I was now rapidly leaving behind everyone who had the same benefit of exposure to an authentic L1 environment in the quasi-ESL settings described above (i.e. other locals employed as linguists by the US Army or US civilian contractors), and even those few others who managed to combine such exposure with formal instruction in the same way I did, that is, by enrolling in a degree program in English while working for the military or its US civilian contractors. My native-like proficiency was finally confirmed during my first visit to the USA at age 22, where I was

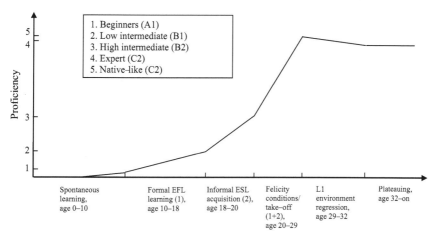

Figure 9.1 My English language-learning and using trajectory (labels A1–C2 indicate the Common European Framework of Reference for language proficiency levels)

often able to 'pass' for a native speaker despite experiencing a mild culture shock and having only a superficial familiarity with the intricacies of everyday American life.[4]

A career in English ensues

Feeling stuck in a dead-end job despite all the felicity conditions and the progress toward a BA degree in English, I decided to take up an offer to move to the Netherlands to work for the United Nations International Criminal Tribunal for the Former Yugoslavia as a 'language assistant' (i.e. interpreter/ translator) for Bosnian and English. The new job was in many respects similar to the old one, but the social and professional environments were completely different. I now found myself in a truly international setting exposed to a large number of both native and non-native varieties of English, including many other languages and the language of the host country, Dutch. Yet even in this context, which included many people proficient (or native) in two or more languages, judging by my superiors' and my colleagues' comments as well as my own assessment, my English proficiency exceeded that of all but the most competent L2 professionals with degrees in translation/ interpretation and years of experience and exposure to authentic L1 settings.

Although I was working in a general service position as I still lacked a university degree, I fared reasonably well on account of my (surprisingly) high proficiency in English. At the same time, I also felt that this new environment often failed to challenge me linguistically and even caused my proficiency in English to deteriorate somewhat as I was unable to continue my studies. I would thus often jokingly refer to the variety of English spoken within the UN as 'unEnglish'. In reaction to my new multilingual environment, I now also began to feel that my linguistic repertoire needed expansion by at least one other language, so I enrolled in a beginners' Dutch course offered in-house for the UN staff. However, despite a promising start and further demonstration of an apparently high degree of language-learning aptitude,[5] because of frustration with short-term employment contracts combined with a lack of motivation, as English is spoken widely in the Netherlands and therefore Dutch is not at all necessary to get by, I soon dropped out of the course.

In order to better understand an important aspect of my investment in English, it is necessary at this point to briefly draw attention to the general circumstances I was facing together with other Bosnians during this period of time. After the war broke out in the early 1990s, many Bosnians sought refuge throughout Europe and globally. By the time I arrived in the Netherlands in 2000, hundreds of thousands of Bosnian refugees had been scattered throughout the countries of the European Union, unwanted but unable to return. Coupled with the incessant news of wartime atrocities, this presence of large numbers of Bosnian refugees throughout Europe put all Bosnians in the position of a foreign minority that was empathized with but also despised. Dissociation from the Bosnian identity was thus often desirable and sometimes necessary. Faced with this 'soft' form of discrimination, I responded by appropriating English and an American identity, which now for a second time instantaneously propelled me from a relatively disadvantageous position to a quasi-elite status, as American English carried very prestigious connotations in most of pre-9/11 Europe. Having passed for a native speaker among native speakers themselves, it was easy for me to pass for one among most non-native speakers.

After nearly four years in the Netherlands, I decided it was time to go back to school and get a degree. I chose to go to Austria as it offered a number of advantages: a free education on account of historical (i.e. colonial) ties with Bosnia, an opportunity to learn German and a reunion with my only sister who, similar to many other Bosnians, was also getting an education there. I continued my study of English at a major Austrian public university, and began learning German again. An apparently high degree of language-learning aptitude helped here again, so I was able to pass the compulsory test of academic German after only one semester of study. Now, although English is not used as widely in Austria as it is in the Netherlands, the Austrian (linguistic) culture being considerably more conservative and autarchic in comparison, appearing to be an American who was beginning to learn German was much more advantageous than being a Bosnian who spoke limited German. Indeed, a local realtor advised my wife (who speaks five languages fluently) and me to use English rather than German in our communication with the locals as this 'would make things easier'. During my stay in Austria, I continued to profit from my proficiency in English, becoming a minor celebrity in the department of English and American studies[6] despite a somewhat slow progress toward fluency in German (the medium of instruction in my department was almost exclusively English so I did not feel hardpressed to master German quickly). However, since the academic setting proved to be generally more tolerant and accepting, my appropriation of English had a different meaning here: rather than enabling me to pass for a native speaker, my proficiency in English now portrayed me as an exceptionally talented individual. This alternative mode of appropriation would continue after I left Austria and moved to the USA.

Things fall apart (somewhat)

Nearing the end of my degree program at the Austrian university (age 30), I accepted a scholarship offer for an MA program at a private American university. I had always wanted to study in the USA and this was my (somewhat belated) opportunity. This was followed by a similarly belated offer from my Austrian university to stay and enroll in a PhD program in English and American literature, which I turned down. I thus spent the next two years as a graduate student in Pan-African studies in upstate New York. I also worked as a teaching assistant in the department and was exposed to African American and African varieties of English daily. I briefly studied Kiswahili and then spent one month on an externship in South Africa. In these settings, I found my proficiency in English enormously beneficial yet again, but the appropriation would take a somewhat ironic turn as it made dissociation from the American identity more difficult when I felt the need or desire to do so. This was especially true during my stay in South Africa, where such dissociation was often met with palpable incredulity and where my Caucasian extraction turned into an inescapable signifier that 'spoke' more quickly and more convincingly than the tongue ever could. For example, whenever I talked to any Black South Africans, it was obvious to me that I was being treated as a 'White person' and thus with a certain amount of suspicion and incredulity, particularly when I demonstrated an interest in the obviously sensitive local language issues. These encounters were thus less about me speaking to my Black South African interlocutors than they were about the whole discriminatory colonial history speaking for all of us (Bourdieu, 1991: 144, cited in Blackledge & Pavlenko, 2002: 126), even if I was never in any way (by ancestral or personal involvement) a part of that history. It was around this time that I realized that my attitude toward English had begun to change.

After years of diligent study of the English language and linguistics, British and American literatures and civilizations, as well as the role English played and continues to play in the colonial and postcolonial world, I was now capable of a more critical understanding of the language, its history and its associated cultures, and last but not least, my own relationship to them. The 'idealized, mythical image' I once harbored was shattered as I experienced a bout of disillusionment and self-doubt: was all that investment a giant error in judgment? I now decided to keep both the language and my 'English' self at an arm's length. There was nothing to prove anymore either to myself or to others, and the constant vigilance that a flawless performance of a second identity through language demands had become a nuisance. From this point on, I chose to occupy a legitimate peripheral position (cf. Lave & Wenger, 1991), stressing the performative nature of my L2 identity but sometimes asserting my right to full participation in the L2 culture (e.g. in discussions of US politics or culture with American colleagues and friends). In terms of my spoken L2 performance, this meant a slight intentional regression from 'peak performance' and deliberate plateauing at a near-native level;[7] because it is only indirectly related to self-identity and because it is indispensable in my professional life, written L2 performance would be exempt from this adjustment. Figure 9.1 charts the learning/acquisition dynamics and my English-learning and -using trajectory in its entirety.

Discussion

My language-learning and -using experiences accord well with a number of findings from previous studies, but also offer some contradictory evidence and possibly novel theoretical insights. Nevertheless, my overall experience is highly idiosyncratic and must be understood in its context, without undue generalizations to other learners or contexts. Clearly, my L2 proficiency developed in a series of distinct phases resulting from changing circumstances and conscious choices. This lends support to Mercer's (2011: 435) view of learner agency as a complex dynamic system 'continually developing and adapting to changes in different parts of a wider system ... and also varying across parameters, such as language domains and contexts'. I began as a sensitive learner in a typical EFL situation and later became an intrinsically motivated learner with an integrative motivation, seeking to develop an additional identity and 'cross' into the L2. However, this trajectory was complicated in subsequent phases by my evolving attitude, ultimately resulting in ambivalence toward identitary implications of native-like ultimate attainment, which accords quite well with Norton Peirce's (1995: 17) concept of investment as 'the socially and historically constructed relationship to the target language and [the] sometimes ambivalent desire to learn and practice it'. Whereas initially I was willing to fully identify with and quite eager to assimilate into the L2 community, as I learned more about and experienced more of the L2 community life and culture I began to realize that there were aspects of both that I was not interested in or that I felt the need to distance myself from. The most obvious are the consequences of the colonial history, both in the USA and elsewhere in the anglophone world, which, as Pennycook (1998: 195) has noted, have a tendency to 'adhere to English' and, I should add, also to people who appear to be native speakers of it. Having been born and raised in a socialist country, not only did I have a strongly anti-colonial outlook, but I also began to realize that I too, although 'a white European', had been a kind of colonial subject. Related to this was my ultimate disappointment with the role that the Western powers, particularly the USA, had played during and after the Bosnian War. Their obvious unwillingness to uphold, in Bosnia as well as elsewhere, many of their own self-proclaimed principles, such as respect for human rights, effectively made it impossible (and undesirable) for me to continue to identify fully. In any case, I had never rescinded my Bosnian identity, nor did I ever desire to do so; for me, the development of an L2 identity was largely an exercise in self-development, a kind of psychosocial experiment. Yet there remained numerous aspects of the L2 culture such as cosmopolitanism and individual autonomy that were not only attractive but which had become a *sine qua non* for me. As a result, I find myself unable and unwilling to fully identify with the L2 community, but I (happily) remain quite at home in it.

Further, my ability to 'pass' for a native speaker on different occasions and in different contexts lends credence to Piller's (2002: 201) contention that 'personal motivation, choice and agency' rather than age 'seem to be more crucial factors in ultimate attainment'. Similarly, my integrative motivation-based success seems to support Lybeck's (2002: 184) finding that '[t]hose learners who [a]re engaged in supportive exchange networks within the target culture [a]re provided meaningful frameworks within which they [can] access and acquire both linguistically and culturally appropriate behaviors, effectively reducing their cultural distance'. Although the notion of investment, as noted above, has complicated our conception of motivation, I would argue that motivation continues to have importance within the realm of individual agency. Obviously, my overall learning circumstances have been incomparably more favorable than those of many other successful learners (see, e.g. Gao, 2010), but the point to note here is that highly motivated learners operate autonomously and seek opportunities to learn on their own, which ultimately results in a certain degree of serendipity.

Native-like ultimate attainment in my case seems to be a product of the confluence of a number of factors, that is, a set of 'felicity' conditions. These include a high degree of language-learning aptitude; exposure to robust native-speaker input and ample opportunities for interaction; a favorable attitude toward the L2 speakers and their culture, and an accordingly high level of intrinsic motivation; an ability and willingness to suspend L1 identity and a desire to adopt L2 identity; and access to high-quality formal instruction and a professional engagement with the L2. For me, the question of native-like ultimate attainment has thus been a question of acquisition of an additional social identity (i.e. acculturation) as well as professional success and self-validation.

Although the concept of acculturation is often criticized as conducive to assimilation (e.g. Norton, 1998), deliberate, appropriative acculturation, whereby the learner gains 'ownership' of the L2 but retains an (evolved) L1 identity, is key to nonassimilative native-like ultimate attainment. Whereas expert L2 use as performance is always contextual, attaining a level of proficiency that enables any sustained passing beyond a single utterance in a service context necessarily entails at least some identitary implications, Piller's (2002: 198) claim that 'the passing of expert L2 users is contextual rather than identity related' notwithstanding. Perhaps the most interesting aspect of my entire experience of learning and using English has been my ability to appropriate English as well as an American identity and use it to overcome multiple disadvantages inherent in my starting position by 'access[ing] some of the privileges associated with native speaker status' (Piller, 2002: 200). This shows the extent to which individual agency can be successfully deployed to overcome the often daunting structural constraints such as class, nationality and, to a lesser extent, race. However, the relationship between agency and ultimate attainment is dialogic as full individual agency can only be attained with a sufficiently high degree of acquisition. In a world dominated by language ideologies that continue to celebrate demonstrations of high language-learning aptitude as intellectual prowess, native-like ultimate attainment is arguably the most desirable (because highest in linguistic capital and thus most useful) possible outcome for subaltern learners, despite the reservations expressed above.

Individual agency notwithstanding, structural constraints remain and can be quite disempowering and discouraging in the absence of a native-like proficiency, as even the simplest service encounters, for example with gatekeepers such as supermarket cashiers in the German-speaking world, attest.[8] Furthermore, even native-like ultimate attainment and successful appropriation of the position of researcher by learners themselves, which I have called the ultimate form of agency, cannot save one from the gate-keeping function of entry visa requirements. In addition, the flip-side of a successful appropriation of a dominant L2 identity, as evidenced by my experience in South Africa, is that the appropriating agent's agency may be constrained by some of the sociohistorical implications of that identity. I had seen evidence of this already in my interactions with my peers as well as the faculty in my African studies department, but there the issue was less language proficiency and rather more the implications of race, which were similarly difficult to deal with as I was compelled to work against an unwanted ascribed identity ('White person') and assert a chosen identity that explicitly rejected some of the implications of the ascribed identity (i.e. 'Whiteness' as an ethnicity with all of its sociohistorical implications in the US context).

I hope that I have demonstrated that, informed by theory, autoethnography can be an effective methodological approach to SLA phenomena. Retrospective autoethnography certainly enhanced my cultural understanding of myself and others by forcing me to reconstruct, revisit and critically re-examine my experiences and trace their evolution over time. With respect to agency, it made possible a reconstruction of both the structural contexts of my language learning and the use of experiences and the opportunities for individual action available within them. Furthermore, it enabled me to approach my experiences in a systematic, theoretically grounded way, which I had wished for all along, for what good is any research if it does not help us explain our experiences to ourselves?

Finally, a comparison with some of the autobiographical accounts in Belcher and Connor (2001) and Pavlenko and Lantolf (2000), as well as learner narratives in Lybeck (2002) and Piller (2002), suggests that, despite many similarities between native-like L2 users who began acquisition in the post-critical period (e.g. formal academic training in the L2, see also Abrahamsson & Hyltenstam, 2008), there is no one road to native-like ultimate attainment. Although, as Mercer (2011: 435) notes, such experiences 'do not provide easy formulas or advice for pedagogy', it seems that native-like ultimate attainment implies at least some degree of identitary transformation as well as a confluence of favorable circumstances. More importantly, such experiences can help expose the lingering 'native speaker fallacy' and 'set up more realistic goals, and support SLL by presenting students with realistic role models of successful L2 users rather than the monolingual native speakers they can never be' (Piller, 2002: 201). Perhaps the most important pedagogical implication of first-person narratives by successful learners and users, then, is that English language teaching (ELT) practitioners can and should strive to contribute to the creation of learners' felicity conditions while simultaneously empowering them by upholding the image of the successful L2 user, with native-like ultimate attainment or without it.

Notes

(1) This re-examination has paralleled a wider debate in the field between cognitivists and socioculturalists over epistemological as well as methodological approaches to SLA which is of considerable concern here (for detailed and rather insightful discussions, see Hulstijn, 2013; Swain & Deters, 2007; and Zuengler & Miller, 2006).
(2) Part of this was simply youthful rebellion, but part of it was a lack of identification with the available social positions and a feeling of constraint and a need/desire to be different.
(3) As elsewhere in Europe, this is an expression of the valuation of individual rather than societal multilingualism.
(4) My 'passing' experience began on the US military bases in Bosnia where I was working as a translator when military personnel would sometimes mistake me for an American. On my first visit to the USA, I had an episode sharing a taxi with a group

of strangers in Los Angeles who expressed disbelief at my telling them I was a foreigner.

(5) I was asked by my Dutch instructor to return on several occasions on account of my (perceived) aptitude.

(6) This is reflected in numerous positive comments by my professors (and my peers) and a somewhat special status I enjoyed vis-à-vis other students. For example, one of my peers found it shocking when my professors asked my opinion on a translation controversy related by a visiting Austrian author during her talk to the English department. The last such instance happened fairly recently, at the end of the final examination in my MA program, when one of my professors (an Oxford University graduate) commented on the 'superiority of your English'.

(7) 'Regression' here means that I simply do not attempt to appear native anymore, although I do retain a native-like command of English most of the time. My command of English has always been performative and now I find I prefer the role of an exceptional individual to that of a 'quasi' native speaker.

(8) In my experience and that of my wife, sister and many acquaintances/foreigners to Austria, not all of whom are Bosnian, service personnel seem to be particularly alert to and negatively predisposed toward foreignness, and, with some exceptions, are quick to let their views be known in subtle and sometimes not so subtle ways.

References

Abrahamsson, N. and Hyltenstam, K. (2008) The robustness of aptitude effects in near-native second language acquisition. *Studies in Second Language Acquisition* 30, 481–509.

Ahearn, L.M. (2011) *Living Language: An Introduction to Linguistic Anthropology.* Malden, MA: Wiley-Blackwell.

Atkinson, D. (2013) Language learning in mindbodyworld: A sociocognitive approach to language acquisition. *Language Teaching* First View Article, 1–17.

Belcher, D. and Connor, U. (eds) (2001) *Reflections on Multiliterate Lives.* Clevedon: Multilingual Matters.

Blackledge, A. and Pavlenko, A. (2002) Introduction. Language ideologies in multilingual contexts. [Special Issue.] *Multilingua* 21 (2/3), 121–140.

Block, D. (2012) Class and SLA: Making connections. *Language Teaching Research* 16 (2), 188–205.

Bongaerts, T. (1999) Ultimate attainment in L2 pronunciation: The case of very advanced late L2 learners. In D. Birdsong (ed.) *Second Language Acquisition and the Critical Period Hypothesis* (pp. 133–160). Mahwah, NJ: Lawrence Erlbaum.

Bourdieu, P. (1991) *Language and Symbolic Power.* Cambridge, MA: Harvard University Press.

Chang, H. (2007) Autoethnography: Raising cultural awareness of self and others. In G. Walford (ed.) *Methodological Developments in Ethnography: Studies in Educational Ethnography* (pp. 207–221). Oxford: Elsevier.

Ellis, C. and Bochner, A.P. (2000) Autoethnography, personal narrative, and personal reflexivity. In N. Denzin and Y. Lincoln (eds) *Handbook of Qualitative Research* (2nd edn) (pp. 733–768). Thousand Oaks, CA: Sage.

Flowerdew, J. and Miller, L. (2008) Social structure and individual agency in second language learning: Evidence from three life histories. *Critical Inquiry in Language Studies* 5 (4), 201–224.

Gao, X. (2010) Autonomous language learning against all odds. *System* 38, 580–590.

Hulstijn, J. (2013) Is the second language acquisition discipline disintegrating? *Language Teaching* 46 (4), 511–517.

Kramsch, C. and Lam, W.S.E. (1999) Textual identities: The importance of being non-native. In G. Braine (ed.) *Non-native Educators in English Language Teaching* (pp. 57–72). Mahwah, NJ: Lawrence Erlbaum.

Krashen, S. (1981) *Second Language Acquisition and Second Language Learning*. Oxford: Pergamon Press.

Lave, J. and Wenger, E. (1991) *Situated Learning: Legitimate Peripheral Participation*. Cambridge: Cambridge University Press.

Lichtenfeld, H. (1985–1989) *Die Schwarzwaldklinik*. Mainz: ZDF.

Lin, A., Wang, W., Akamtsu, N. and Riazi, A.M. (2002) Appropriating English, expanding identities, and re-visioning the field: From TESOL to teaching English for glocalized communication (TEGCOM). *Journal of Language, Identity, and Education* 1 (4), 295–316.

Lybeck, K. (2002) Cultural identification and second language pronunciation of Americans in Norway. *The Modern Language Journal* 86 (2), 174–191.

Mercer, S. (2011) Understanding learner agency as a complex dynamic system. *System* 39, 427–436.

Neu, J. (1991) In search of input: The case study of a learner of Polish as a foreign and second language. *Foreign Language Annals* 24, 427–442.

Norton, B. (1998) Rethinking acculturation in second language acquisition. *PROSPECT: Australian Journal of TESOL Associations* 13 (2), 4–19.

Norton Peirce, B. (1995) Social identity, investment, and language learning. *TESOL Quarterly* 29 (1), 9–31.

Ortega, L. (2007) Second language learning explained? SLA across nine contemporary theories. In B. VanPatten and J. Williams (eds) *Theories in Second Language Acquisition: An Introduction* (pp. 225–250). Mahwah, NJ: Lawrence Erlbaum.

Pavlenko, A. (1998) SLA learning by adults: Testimonies of bilingual writers. *Issues in Applied Linguistics* 9 (1), 3–19.

Pavlenko, A. (2001) In the world of the tradition, I was unimagined: Negotiation of identities in cross-cultural autobiographies. *International Journal of Bilingualism* 5, 317–344.

Pavlenko, A. (2002) Poststructuralist approaches to the study of social factors in second language learning and use. In V. Cook (ed.) *Portraits of the L2 User* (pp. 277–302). Clevedon: Multilingual Matters,.

Pavlenko, A. (2007) Autobiographic narratives as data in applied linguistics. *Applied Linguistics* 28 (2), 163–188.

Pavlenko, A. and Lantolf, J. (2000) Second language learning as participation and the (re) construction of selves. In J. Lantolf (ed.) *Sociocultural Theory and Second Language Learning* (pp. 155–177). Oxford: Oxford University Press.

Pennycook, A. (1998) *English and the Discourses of Colonialism*. London: Routledge.

Piller, I. (2002) Passing for a native speaker: Identity and success in second language learning. *Journal of Sociolinguistics* 6 (2), 179–206.

Ricento, T. (2005) Considerations of identity in L2 learning. In E. Hinkel (ed.) *Handbook of Research in Second Language Teaching and Learning* (pp. 895–911). Mahwah, NJ: Lawrence Erlbaum.

Schmidt, R.W. and Frota, S.N. (1986) Developing basic conversational ability in a second language: A case study of an adult learner of Portuguese. In R. Day (ed.) *Talking to Learn: Conversation in Second Language Acquisition*. Rowley, MA: Newbury House.

Schumann, J. (1986) Research on the acculturation model for second language acquisition. *Journal of Multilingual and Multicultural Development* 7 (5), 379–392.

Schumann, F. and Schumann, J. (1977) Diary of a language learner: An introspective study of second language learning. In H. Brown, C.A. Yorio and R.H. Crymes (eds) *Teaching and Learning: Trends in Research and Practice* (pp. 241–249). Washington, DC: TESOL.

Swain, M. and Deters, P. (2007) 'New' mainstream SLA theory: Expanded and enriched. *The Modern Language Journal* 91, 820–836.

Vitanova, G. (2005) Authoring the self in a nonnative language: A dialogic approach to agency and subjectivity. In J.K. Hall, G. Vitanova and L. Marchenkova (eds) *Dialogue with Bakhtin on Second and Foreign Language Learning: New Perspectives* (pp. 149–169). Mahwah, NJ: Erlbaum.

Zuengler, J. and Miller, E.R. (2006) Cognitive and sociocultural perspectives: Two parallel SLA worlds? *TESOL Quarterly* 40 (1), 35–58.

10 Analyzing Learner Agency in Second Language Learning: A Place-based Approach

Peter W. Stanfield

Learner Agency and the Construct of Place

This chapter explains how researchers can access second language learners' assumptions about the agency available to them in their learning processes. Learner agency emerged from a recent study (Stanfield, 2013) as the key to understanding why various places are significant for language-learning effectiveness. I regard agency as 'people's ability to make choices, take control, self-regulate, and thereby pursue their goals as individuals leading, potentially, to personal or social transformation' (Duff, 2013: 15). My study indicated that assumptions about agency vary significantly between learning processes that occur in classrooms, interim educational places such as college libraries, cafeterias and sports fields, and the broader community.

My focus on the construct of *place* emerged from an etymological analysis of the word *curriculum*. This showed that the suffix *cule*, which is affixed to the stem *currere* to form the modern English word, has been largely ignored. In Latin *cule* converts verbs into nouns to denote either a *means* by which an action is performed or a *place* appropriate to an action (Dictionary. com, 2009). Curricula as *means* toward predetermined language-learning ends are common (e.g. Brown, 1995: 104–105). The semantic potential of *place*, the question of *where* knowledge is most appropriately acquired is, however, rarely recognized. An exception is Pinar (1991), who introduced place-oriented learning into his general education curricula. Hedegaard and Chaiklin (2005) and Osberg and Biesta (2008) have also applied similar approaches. However, while these theorists seek to make education relevant to daily life, they persist in physically situating the learners themselves in classrooms. Knowledge is thus shifted from the social relations of the places where it is constructed to those of educational institutions. This *recontextualization* (Bernstein, 1996) has consequences for second language learning because it strips discourse of its indexicality (Ochs & Schieffelin, 2008) to real-world communities of practice. The result is classroom discourse that merely *refers* to the concerns of learners without giving them opportunities to construct meaningful solutions to them through target language use. Indeed, Foucault (1977) and Bernstein (1996) have argued that the rationale for such recontextualization is not *education* in the sense of generating new knowledge but the *regulation* of unequal power over knowledge in favor of dominant social interests. My study confirms this because participants systematically assume the classroom to be controlled by educational agents rather than themselves.

In contrast, postmodern educators such as Umphrey (2005) and Slattery (2006) and a growing number of place-conscious educators from various political perspectives recognize that learning beyond the classroom offers greater learner agency (see Gruenewald, 2003a; Sobel, 2004; McLaughlin & Blank, 2004; Bowers, 2005; Gruenewald & Smith, 2008; Lanas, 2011). Although Blackburn (1971) recognized the potential of place-oriented second language learning decades ago, contemporary language curriculum designers continue to assume that learning will *take place* in the classroom (e.g. Brown, 1995; White, 1998; Richards, 2001; Nation & Macalister, 2010). It was the exploration of this lacuna in place-based second language learning that led to the analysis of learner agency below.

Operationalization of the Construct of Place

Human beings are fundamentally *place makers* (Gruenewald & Smith, 2008). Through engagement in communities of practice, members come to possess mental constructs about the order of their societies that divide total geographical *space* into so many institutional *places* (Soja, 1989). A set of ideal *situation types* are distributed within each of these places (Fairclough, 1989: 150). The linguistic features of discourse are deployed and interpreted as people compare these ideal types with the actual situations in which they find themselves (Fairclough, 1989: 151). In other words, we must necessarily ask, 'Where am I?' *before* we begin to participate in discourse. Our answer to this question will differ according to our commonsense assumptions about the order of society and its power relations (Fairclough, 1989: 140).

Ideal situations in educational institutions, especially the classroom, are shaped by a limited set of interests vested in educational agents (Foucault, 1977: 167 and 184–192; Willis, 2011: 62–77). In recognition of this, a new place-oriented educational movement has emerged (Umphrey, 2007) that is breaking down barriers between the classroom and community (Slattery, 2006). Not satisfied with *placeless* curricula (Gruenewald, 2003b: 8) that focus on acquiring standardized knowledge produced at a distance, place-oriented educators systematically situate students and the learning process within local communities of practice. This approach increases learner agency to the extent that it allows students to participate in the co-construction of *new* knowledge (Gruenewald & Smith, 2008: xvi; Umphrey, 2007: 71). My study sought to explore the potential of this approach in second language learning.

The Research Context

My research was conducted in a tertiary college in the Western Region of the United Arab Emirates (UAE), known as Al Gharbia. Al Gharbia is a desert region containing 9% of the UAE population but producing 46% of its gross domestic product. Extensive oil and gas reserves were discovered there in the 1960s, leading to economic growth in the urban centres of the UAE but not Al Gharbia where, until recently, traditional lifestyles have persisted owing to its geographical remoteness and security concerns over its mineral reserves.

Emiratis comprise approximately one-fifth of the UAE population, with expatriates from India, Pakistan and Bangladesh making up much of the remainder along with smaller communities from the Philippines, Afghanistan, the USA, the UK and North Africa. The expatriate segment is continuing to grow at an increasing rate (Groth & Sousa-Poza, 2012). These demographics are reflected in Al Gharbia, where linguistic diversity has significance for second language learning. Owing to the social coherence it offers and the perceived need to empower the population with Anglicized global knowledge, English is the medium of instruction in tertiary education and is taught as a second language in the region's schools. English teaching has, however, achieved poor results until now with 90% of secondary school leavers required to spend several semesters studying English at foundational level before entering degree programs.

The Participants

I selected 15 participants from whom to collect reflections about their English language-learning processes. I chose participants who possessed good spoken communication skills: five college students, five teaching faculty from a range of cultural backgrounds and five Emirati managers from within the local community. Twelve participants had Arabic as their mother tongue, two French and one a dialect of Farsi, although all participants were fluent and literate in Arabic. I maintained a balance between males and females in order to avoid any gender bias in the results (see Appendix).

Table 10.1 The broad domains of place

Classrooms	Interim educational places	Community places
Less-communicative classrooms	Beyond-classroom	Home and work *e.g. bedroom/office*
		Service encounters *e.g. clinic*
Primary	*Formal, e.g. library*	Social meeting places *e.g. café*
Secondary	*Informal, e.g. corridors*	Virtual Places *e.g. Google*
Tertiary	Peripheral	Places of recreation *e.g. campsite*
More-communicative classrooms	*Formal, e.g. work placement*	Places of entertainment *e.g. cinema*
		Cultural places *e.g. art gallery*
Secondary	*Informal, e.g. sports fields*	Industrial places *e.g. oil field*
Tertiary		International places *e.g. International Fair*

The Research Method

I interviewed each participant twice, generating 10 hours of recordings. My initial purpose was to ascertain an overall picture of individual learning processes, identify specific places of learning and assess the degree to which participants were aware of any benefits or disadvantages of learning in various places. The subsequent interviews sought deeper insight into the assumptions participants held about the characteristics of specific places of learning. The places in which English was learned emerged across three broad domains as in Table 10.1.

I employed a form of Critical Discourse Analysis (CDA) adapted to place-oriented research (Stanfield, 2013: 80–81) to discover how the properties of these places were embedded in participant language choices. The key common factor for language learning effectiveness that emerged was the level of learner agency assumed to exist.

Preliminary Analysis

Two linguistic elements began to emerge that indicated that learner agency might be a significant factor for effective acquisition. First, learners consistently tended to reflect negatively on their classroom experiences compared with interim educational places and community places of learning. Some, like Ghareeb, metaphorized them with profoundly negative images:

When you're in the classroom you think and you feel like this is, it's a learning environment it's a, you know, **it's not natural**. But when you're outside, you know, you're not thinking about the language. It's a natural thing. It's, you know, you're trying to get certain things across to the other person and trying to make your, you know, get your needs or like get a conversation going and talking about different things so you're – it becomes a part of like seamlessly you've integrated the language into a topic. You're trying to discuss. So it doesn't become a **burden** on you. Like in the classroom it's a **burden**, you know. You like oh! I **have to** learn this and I **have to** and so it's, it's on the back of your mind; you're always thinking like I **have to** learn something.

I noted how the use of the quasi-modal *have to* appeared to denude learner agency over mental transitivity processes; *I have to learn this* is not a transparent declarative phrase in which having to learn is predicated about the subject. It is a grammatical metaphor for the passive voice because teachers and other text external educational administrators are opaquely embedded in the quasi-modal, forcing Ghareeb to learn. Ghareeb experiences their power as loss of control over his learning, which is metaphorized as a psychological weight he feels constrained to bear, hindering rather than facilitating English language learning. Such use of the quasi-modal emerged systematically in the data as participants reflected about classroom learning.

Second, most participants cordoned off their classroom experiences from what they perceived to be the *real, actual, natural, life itself* of the community. These *in vivo* terms begged the question as to what the properties of the classroom were by implication that led participants to regard it as utterly distinct from their quotidian life. Could the lack of agency embedded in Ghareeb's quasi-modalized burden metaphor be generalized across classroom experiences?

As I interrogated the reflective texts at the level of vocabulary and grammar with the battery of questions adapted from Fairclough (1989: 110–111), five linguistic features emerged that systematically embedded participant assumptions about agency in various places of learning. These were: (1) the use of grammatical metaphor; (2) the choice of transitivity processes; (3) the loss of Actor role within the tripartite subject; (4) quasi-modalization; and (5) metonymical clustering.

I use the term *grammatical metaphor* in the Hallidayan sense of employing a syntactic structure to carry a meaning that is incongruent with common expectations (Romero & Soria, 2013). In many cases the unmarked meaning continues to be assumed by discourse participants while the marked meaning remains opaque. By metonymical clustering I mean an accumulation of closely related terms, each of which carries slightly different connotations about a common activity. These features are interwoven within participant discourse but can be separated for purposes of analysis. Before presenting this in detail it is necessary to discuss two other theories I have employed.

The Tripartite English Subject

I used Eggins's (2004) tripartite perspective on the English subject to gain an understanding of how assumptions about agency are embedded in participant discourse. Eggins delineates three constitutive layers of the English subject. First is the *thematic* subject where the participant may be fronted in a clause and prioritized, or delayed and therefore distanced within the organization of the text (Eggins, 2004: 320). Second is the *grammatical* subject where something is stated or argued about the participant in a predicate. Third, the role of *Actor* may be assigned to the participant such that she has sufficient agency to carry out material transitivity processes, for example, writing. I use the term *Actor* generically to encompass other participant roles such as Sensor, Sayer, Carrier, Beneficiary and Possessor, etc., which in Systemic Functional Linguistics are associated with a range of transitivity processes. The unmarked subject is one where participants inhabit all three layers of the subject position simultaneously. However, different combinations of these elements can be configured to change the level of agency available to the participant. Analysis showed that, largely by dint of the social power relations prevalent in educational institutions, classroom-based English language learners were constructed as assuming subject positions that deprived them of the Actor role and attenuated their agency.

Some examples may serve to illustrate this place-dependent hermeneutic. Consider the contrastive meaning of the transitivity process *started* referring to *school* as opposed to *home* learning of English in the following:

I started studying English at school. (Saeeda)
I started ... watching movies ... (Fakhra, about the university library)
I started reading myself at the age of thirteen. (Hadi, about the home)
I started to read a first story. (Abdullah, about the home)
I started picking up a lot of vocabularies. (Ghareeb, about the football pitch)

In the first *school*-based case we cannot regard the subject position inhabited by Saeeda as fully tripartite; she forfeits the Actor role because it is agents of the school who decide when pupils begin learning English. In the second case, even moving a short distance to the interim place of the library, we must restore the Actor role to Fakhra because, while the institution provides and vets the movies available, it is Fakhra who decides to watch them. In the two *home*-based cases we must interpret the subject positions inhabited by Hadi and Abdullah as fully tripartite because their participant role as Actor is unalloyed by opaquely embedded educational agents.

In Ghareeb's community-based case there is a subtle agentive effect indicated by *picking up*, a material process that metaphorizes English acquisition as a side effect akin to dust accumulating on one's shoes. While participation in a football community of practice occurs from the position of Actor and is, therefore, fully tripartite, the learner has little direct agency over language acquisition *per se*. As Ghareeb puts it elsewhere, '*You're not thinking about using the language but you are using it actually*'. It is this combination of social engagement and subliminal acquisition that participants consider to be the most effective.

A place-dependent hermeneutic is further supported by considering the meaning of *identical* phrases. For example:

I <u>started learning</u> English in grade 4. (Eva)
I <u>started learning</u> English OK … in the school when I was in Grade 4. (Fakhra)
I <u>started learning</u> words. I <u>started</u> also <u>learning</u> some very simple sentences … like, 'Made in USA'. (Hadi, home)

In the first *school*-based cases, neither Eva nor Fakhra inhabit fully tripartite subject positions. The Actor role is removed because they had no decision-making rights over attending school or at which point English was introduced. The declarative phrase functions as a grammatical metaphor for the passive, '*I was started in learning English by (opaque, discourse external) agents of the school*'. However, merely by dint of a shift of place, in the two *home*-based cases of an *identical surface structure* the interpreter must restore the Actor role to Hadi because the decision to learn English is transparently his alone.

Legitimate Peripheral Participation

I have also used situated learning theory (Lave & Wenger, 1991) to achieve an understanding of learner agency. This regards learning as a way of being-in-the-world-with-others (Heidegger, 1962) rather than merely coming to know about it from afar. It shows how a new member of a community of practice is first allowed to participate at the periphery before gradually taking on roles carrying more responsibility and risk, moving toward the center in a process theorized as *legitimate peripheral participation* (Lave & Wenger, 1991: 104–105). Thus learning necessarily implies the incremental acquisition of sufficient agency to construct an identity by participating in the power relations of specific communities of practice.

A vignette of legitimate peripheral participation, which illustrates its significance for English language learning, occurred in Saif's numinous reflection about camping with his host family in the USA.

It was a fantastic trip and I enjoyed it a lot. Till now I still remember this event. There was like a conversation. They were talking to each other. I was listening. Sometime I joined them and they explain. They were helpful. They explained for me this is how do we, you know, cook. This how do we you know do things. This is our culture and, you know, I learned also their culture because it's informal, you know. I see how they deal with each other, you know.

An analysis of the transitivity processes and participant roles shows how peripheral participation increases learner agency and facilitates language acquisition. First, Saif is the silent *observer* of the *sayers* in the verbal process of talking (Toolan, 1988). Next, informal social relations allow him to shift from passive observer to more agentive roles, sometimes listening and sometimes joining conversations. Later, Saif is the *beneficiary* of verbal processes when his American interlocutors *explain* their specific actions, general manner of camping and culture. Subsequently, Saif is an active participant in the *mental* processes of *learning* about his hosts' culture and metaphorically *seeing* (understanding) how they relate to each other.

The dynamics of legitimate peripheral participation show Saif moving from the outer fringe of silent observation, through the intermediate realm of benefaction, to the inner circle of participation and finally to the center of understanding. Throughout, Saif inhabits a fully tripartite subject position playing agentive participant roles toward the transitivity processes of *enjoying, listening, joining, learning* and *seeing*. This is in stark contrast to Ghareeb's opaque loss of agency through quasi-modalization and negative metaphorization of his *classroom* experiences.

Even brief episodes of legitimate peripheral participation appear to have considerable significance for learner agency and effective language acquisition. For example, Hadi reflects on participating in English conversation for the first time in an encounter at an international trade fair in Tehran.

A cousin of mine who has a clothes workshop was interested in a couple of those, you know, equipment and sale from a Swiss or I don't know European company and then he was there and he, he, he pushed me into talking to that guy, getting some information for him. And I remember that in the first place even though my language level was quite high, it wasn't easy because again I was put in a completely different situation. But of course it was, you know, sort of like I say a leap forward to be able to actually talk to someone.

Hadi was thrust toward an English-speaking representative by his cousin who also lacked spoken competence but had a social imperative to communicate. The passive voice *I was put in a completely different situation* does not, therefore, refer to an opaque agent but rather to given familial relations. It was the challenge involved in this mildly humorous encounter that advanced acquisition for Hadi as he moved from periphery to participation. The effectiveness of such increased agency is highlighted by Hadi, who says,

These were like a couple of minutes compared with the hundreds or thousands of hours when I was learning in class but those were important minutes.

Legitimate peripheral participation appears to promote English language learning out of proportion to time spent in the classroom which, largely controlled by teachers, denies learners opportunities for incremental growth toward agency within a range of communities of practice and associated power relations (Lave & Wenger, 1991: 104).

Five Linguistic Features

A radical bifurcation of the classroom from the community was constructed in interview accounts by more than 80% of participants. To further investigate this, I applied the place-based adapted CDA methodology to the whole dataset. Five linguistic features emerged as being systematically employed to signal assumptions about the levels of learner agency available to second language learners in the classroom, interim educational places and the community. We now deal with each in turn.

Grammatical metaphor

An example of the place-determined shift in assumptions about learner agency realized primarily through grammatical metaphor is found in Hadi's reflection on his school learning.

> English **didn't used to be** a subject in elementary school. We only started doing English once we **stepped into** what we call their middle school which is sort of equivalent to grade 6 or grade 7 actually. At that age we only started English and that **was** just, you know grammar and vocabulary; quite like the old grammar translation method.

The material transitivity process *stepped into* masks agency over the social construction of time, place and teleology. It refers to decisions about starting Middle School (*place*) related to age (*time*) and theories of child development (*teleology*). Although the pupils (*we*) appear to inhabit a tripartite subject position including participant roles as Actors of the *physical* process of entering a new building, the deep structure of the transitivity process indicates a juncture of *ideational* processes determined by an educational bureaucracy rather than pupils or parents. We must interpret it as, *when we were required to step into what they call our middle school* such that the active process becomes a grammatical metaphor for the passive voice.

This embedding of bureaucratic agency is further re-enforced in Hadi's reflections by his use of various forms of the verb *to be*. For example, *English didn't used to be a subject in elementary school.* The negated infinitive expressing past habit naturalizes the lack of English at elementary school as a familiar pattern of behavior and becomes a metaphor for the passive voice masking the decision-making agents who have determined it. Lack of English at elementary school is not a *natural* disposition but the result of *political* decision-making.

Hadi's choice of the existential verb *was* has a similar effect. This apparently inevitable choice is determined by the fact that Hadi is talking about school. A range of grammatical features is available to Hadi but the social relations of the school channel him into the choice of the existential verb because it lacks any recognizable agency for the use of grammar translation methodology. The apparently vacant agency is replaced by the adverbial *just* to suggest the mere existence of such methodology. This is emphasized by the filler *you know*, which invites the interviewer to help account for this agent-free existence of traditional teaching methods. The declarative structure, *that was just* is thus a grammatical metaphor for the learner's decision-making rights over teaching methods being usurped by text external agents of the school.

Hadi's discourse about the home exhibits quite different features and concomitant agentive effects. For example, after his cousin had visited from the capital and started to teach him the English alphabet he reflects:

> I was left with six letters of English so what I did was that I started looking around just reading things on the boxes and occasionally on some walls and other things, looking at the letters **that were familiar to me**; the six letters and then picking some words which had those six letters and which also had some other letters and then I asked, kept asking people around me. So, for instance, when I saw a word like 'dad' well of course I could read it because D, A, D, I had learned already but then I saw another word, ah! Then I started asking what the other letters are and asking people.

Hadi now inhabits a fully tripartite subject position, including the Actor role, in the processes of *doing, looking, reading and asking*. The existential verb *were* no longer embeds opaque agents who usurp the learner's rights as in the school because the agent of Hadi's familiarization with the alphabet is transparent to us as his cousin.

A similar case occurs when Hadi describes his first discoveries about the English language:

> For some reasons I came to that conclusion very early that (it) looks like the letters do not necessarily sound as they should. That **was** one of my first understandings, things I understood about English.

The existential verb is associated with the possessive pronominal, indicating that the lack of direct correspondence between phonetics and orthography does not merely exist but is actively possessed by Hadi.

The systematic place-based shift in our interpretation of these linguistic features as grammatical metaphors for opaque passives in the classroom but transparent declaratives tracing active agency in the home is one way in which the classroom and community are bifurcated.

Choice of transitivity processes

A representative example of cases where a systematic shift in transitivity processes is the key feature realizing differential assumptions about agency occurs in Mohamed.

Interviewer: it seems to me that students need, that they need both opportunities to practice outside the classroom (exactly). What kind of balance do you feel that you had in that? Was it just a progression from one to the other or is one more important than the other?

Mohamed: I would consider it, it's one chain you know, in ... anyway the, what do they call it – the academic year? Basically at the class we learn, you know, literally, you know words and vocabularies but when, whenever we are out at the you know, devoting our time in the society there are so many words that we need to use whether from the academic life or from the, you know, from the society. At the class you **become** more of a listener but when you get outside the class there are so many efforts you need to **think** of; when to **become** a listener when to become a speaker.

Mohamed selects the transitivity process *become* when reflecting about both the classroom and the community. However, he distinguishes between these otherwise identical processes by interspersing the mental process *think* when reflecting about acquisition in the community. In the first classroom case, the learner is the subject within a declarative phrase of his becoming a participant in the receptive act of spoken communication. In the second community case he is the subject of the mental process of thinking about how and when to choose between receptive and productive acts. This assumes an increase in learner agency over acquisition processes within the community where judgment and choice over the mode of participation are both possible and necessary.

Grammatical metaphor is associated with transitivity choice and further denudes learner agency within the social relations of the classroom which assume decision-making rights for the teacher. In the classroom the declarative phrase, *you become more of a listener*, must be interpreted as a grammatical metaphor for the passive *you are constrained to be more of a listener*. This underlying passive opaquely places the teacher in the participant role of Actor toward the transitivity process, ousting the learner and tracing his attenuated agency.

In contrast, within the community, the mental process *think* is introduced in a declarative phrase that does not insinuate the passive but places the learner in the participant Actor role in relation to the mental process of thinking about his mode of participation in spoken discourse. Different assumptions about the levels of learner agency available are embedded in the identical process of *becoming* either a listener or speaker and are determined by whether the participant is reflecting about the classroom or the community.

The interrelations of the transitivity processes *force* and *involve* further illustrate the subtle manner in which assumptions about learner agency are embedded in participant discourse. For example, when reflecting on classroom learning Ghareeb says:

> I've learned the vocabulary yes, from the rules and the guidelines and procedures like vocabularies, grammar and, you know, of course, you know, you, you would learn. But I, I really do believe again you know English as a language it needs to be somehow – sometimes you need to **force** it on people – you should not leave them other options to speak other languages.

In reflecting about learning in the community in the USA he says:

> We went to America. We were not placed all together even though, you know, many of us like including myself didn't know any English so it, like English was like **forced** in a way. Like the environment we were in we were **forced** to make mistakes, speak the language, you know, the word we learned in the classroom or outside, you know, we were using it.

In the classroom the material transitivity process *force* in infinitive mode metaphorizes language policy as a physical threat to learner agency. The difficulty of achieving such enforcement is recognized in the hedge *somehow* but the injunction nevertheless assumes the desirability of maintaining teacher agency over students' language rights. In contrast, although in the community-based excerpt *force* is explicitly in passive mode, learner agency seems less threatened. This is because in the community it is the learner's desire to participate in meaningful communication that channels his acquisition processes rather than opaque social agents who determine language policy.

A similar bifurcation occurs in Saif's reflections in which he uses *force* and *involve* in his proposal for English-only classroom policy in the schools of Al Gharbia.

Interviewer: You've started to contrast between the different places you went to with your host family and the classroom. You were saying that you would like the classroom to be more practical. Can you draw out little bit of that? What do you mean by practical teaching?

Saif: I'm not sure about now, old teaching method used very strutical (sic) you know, method. And the only, they are giving the, or feeding the student, not giving them the the opportunity to participate. They should **involve** them, you know, by **force**, you know, (laugh) because there they don't speak Arabic (yeah). We have no other choice, no translation.

I laughed instinctively in the interview and Saif smiled suggesting a conflict between the underlying assumptions he was making about language learning and his more liberal experience in the USA. Saif has control over passive structures in his interlanguage and could have chosen *They should be forced to use English* but this seems not to be his intent. His decision to thematically front the process of *involvement* and postpone *enforcement* as the means by which this may be achieved appears deliberate. Having gained an understanding of the importance of participative community-based learning in the USA, he wants to bring this about in the classrooms of Al Gharbia and make this the theme of his utterance. The double use of the filler *you know* is an appeal to the interviewer to try to understand that reconciling participatory pedagogy with the normal agency rights of the classrooms of Al Gharbia, which give majority power to the teacher, is difficult.

Saif attempts to do this by selecting the material transitivity process *involve*, but rather than placing the students in the Actor participant role they are objectified (*them*) and agents of the school (*they*) instead take up this role while remaining nameless and opaque. Saif further undermines student agency by modalizing the school agents' role (*should*) in an exophoric reference to his own advisory rights as a local authority educational manager. The combined discourse features of transitivity choice, allocation of Actor role and modalization go beyond metaphor to create a grammatical *euphemism*. With a sleight of hand recognized only by Saif's quizzical smile, the participative learning he enthusiastically proposes is replaced by teacher enforcement, which robs learners of the agency necessary for such participation. A place-based interpretation reads the utterance as:

Teachers and key stakeholders of the school with agency rights over the curriculum and classroom methodology, as advised by me, an experienced learner and member of local government, are recommended to force students to participate in classroom activities in English for their benefit.

The contradictions inherent in this attempt at bringing about communicative English language learning in authoritarian classrooms illustrates how the bifurcation of *learning* in school from *acquisition* in the *real life* of the community is marked by assumptions about differential levels of learner agency and traced in systematic linguistic choices.

Loss of Actor role

Examples where loss of Actor role within the tripartite subject position is employed to limit agency can be found in Eva's interviews. These are associated with grammatical metaphor, emphasizing the interrelatedness of the linguistic features that systematically embed learners' place-based assumptions about their agency.

Firstly, when reflecting about her school learning in UAE secondary schools, Eva employs possessive *had*:

> OK first of all I, I had all my education in a governmental school we were w ... We had all the education in Arabic and only, we took only six periods a week in English and I started learning English in grade 4.

The choice of being educated in an Arabic-medium government school with only six English periods per week was determined by agents of the government and the school who opaquely inhabit the subject position as Actor participants. The declarative mode of the transitivity processes *had, took and started*, therefore, functions as a grammatical metaphor for the passive voice such that the underlying structures are: *I was given my education in a government school*; *I was given all the education in Arabic*; *I was given only six periods a week in English*.

When the gerund is used to emphasize active participation, opacity of agency remains. Whilst the surface structure of *I started learning English in Grade 4* positions Eva as an Actor participant, a place-based interpretation indicates that the power relations of the school remove this role. Eva (*I*) is only the theme of the verb phrase and grammatical subject about whom something is predicated, not an *Actor* because agents of the school decided to introduce English at Grade 4.

Quasi-modalization

Quasi-modalization was one of the initial signposts to the significant variable of learner agency noted above. A representative example is Eva's reflection about the use of English in the community in the early learning years:

> Sometimes my mother tell us to go; when we go out to a restaurant she will ask us to order and she will notice how we spell (say) the word and everything. Then she will come back and say OK, you made a mistake

in this word. You have to say this not to say this and what expressions **we have to** use in this. That's why um we know these expressions from my mum.

This *in situ* encouragement, correction and advice enabled the acquisition of everyday expressions through social participation, with Eva's mother playing an advisory role. Here in the community *have to* does not function as a grammatical metaphor for the passive as it might in the classroom. In the early learning years the collective pronominal *we* constructs a dual but transparent Actor within the subject position, Eva and her mother.

In contrast, when transposed to the classroom, the quasi-modalization indicates *loss* of agency. Consider the following from Maha:

Maha: So um, yeah, I think it, it's the teacher and her methods and um, yeah, and the, the, the variety she brought in the classroom wasn't just music. Sometimes we had um magazines. She, we had to cut up some pictures and put pictures, It was art, It was, you know. It wasn't a just the language (um). It was um the variety she brought in the classroom that made a big difference.

Interviewer: So it was the … would you say it was the inspiration of the teacher there that got you interested in English (yeah) and then you, you took it from there (oh yeah) yourself?

Maha: Ah, yeah! She did something to me (laughing).

Interviewer: Yeah.

Maha: I cannot explain but she did something for me. She impacted me in so many ways.

This passage describes a richly communicative English language classroom run by a charismatic teacher who had a profound effect on Maha the learner. Music and art were utilized as conduits for English language learning, which Maha greatly enjoyed. Charisma and a communicative approach, however, do not change the power relations of the classroom. Grammatical analysis indicates that Maha continues to assume limited agency. The students (*we*) are the fronted theme of the phrase *we had to cut up*. The material transitivity process *cut up* is predicated about them so they are also the grammatical subject. However, they do not inhabit the third constituent of the subject position because here in the classroom the quasi-modal *had to* opaquely embeds the teacher's decision-making rights over the choice of activity and ousts the learners from the participant Actor role within the subject, significantly reducing their agency.

Greater learner agency is, however, sometimes assumed in college and university classrooms where the learner has confidence, low risk-aversion and sufficient spoken communication skills. Eva possessed these characteristics while most of her colleagues in their final years at college did not, as we witness in the following extract:

Interviewer: What places in Jordan did you have the opportunity to speak English and, because if you went to a restaurant there you would order in Arabic wouldn't you?

Eva: Yes, of course. It was only in my final year in college we had two Russian teachers. They came from Russian and they were speaking in English and we had ...

Interviewer: They came from where?

Eva: From Russian.

Interviewer: Russia, yeah.

Eva: Yeah! And they were speaking in English. We were listening to a lecture for the first time in English. It was a big difference but I for myself I didn't struggle with that because I used to speak in English. I found it an opportunity to speak with a teacher in English and **try to run a conversation** and ask questions **but I found that my friends sometimes they will not**[1] **they will prefer to not understand the point rather than raising their hand and try to speak in public** and in front of others in English and sometimes if they have um a ... wrong mark on their exam paper they will not go that teacher and ask him to correct the mark that or they deserve better marks or something because simply **they can't go and speak with him and try**[2] to defend their rights.

Here the quasi-modal *had to* is systematically replaced by the transitivity process *try* with Eva transparently in an Actor participant role assuming significant agency. Her colleagues, however, who lack confidence and sufficient spoken communication and are risk-averse, exhibit severely limited agency to the extent that they are unable to defend their academic rights, as indicated by negation of the transitivity process *try* with *will not* in the elided case[1] and *can't*[2] above.

Metonymical clustering

There are clusters of metonyms for the manner in which English is learned that are quite different for the classroom and the community. In the classroom we find *learning, studying, practicing, doing exercises* and *memorizing* whilst in the community beyond we find *participating, sharing, using, practicing, communicating, conversing, judging, negotiating, implementing, self-managing, self-auditing, anticipating* and *collaborating*. All of the latter presuppose greater agency except the neutral term *practicing*, which is the only category common to both domains.

A key example of metonymic bifurcation, exhibited by two-thirds of the participants, is the differential choice of *learn* and *use* with reference to English in the classroom and community respectively. For example, Mohamed says of his time in the USA:

> We had chance, you know, in the high school to practice some and to learn some of the basic or the main like structures of the English language and then me and my friend had been scholared (sic) through the government of Abu Dhabi to, you know, to continue our postgraduate in the states. This was the ... I would call it, you know, the main or the most important period in our life of learning the English language because, you know, **we had the chance to learn and then use whatever have been gained** or obtained through the materials and practice them on the society or the community.

Learn is coordinated with *use* by the temporal adverbial *then*, tending to assume a linear relationship between classroom *learning* which occurs first, and subsequent *use* in the community. Ghareeb cuts the classroom off from the community in a similar manner:

> We were forced to make mistakes, speak the language, you know, the word we learned in the classroom, outside, you know, we were using it.

Again classroom learning of lexis precedes its use in the community, where the active process of trial and error is necessitated.

Abdullah's reflections about learning English through online gaming make similar assumptions:

> I didn't even feel like I was learning you know. For example, when I go to the school I feel like I'm forced to learn, you know, but in home when I use this language in games and stuff I feel like I'm using it. I don't feel myself being forced you know. I, like from inside, me it's coming out, you know.

Language *learning* in the classroom is passivized in the phrase, *I feel like I'm forced to learn.* This enforcement is contrasted with Abdullah's acquisition in the virtual world of gaming where he has direct agency over the material process of language *use* with the progressive aspect emphasizing this in *I feel like I'm using it.* This agency is made explicit in the negatively orientated statement that subsequently denies a passive role for language acquisition in the virtual context: *I don't feel myself being forced.*

Conclusion

The metonymical clustering constructed by participants systematically assigns low levels of agency to the classroom, cordoning it off from the rest of the world. Similarly, their use of grammatical metaphors for the passive, differential selection of transitivity processes, embedding of opaque agents in quasi-modals and removal of the Actor role from within the subject positions they inhabit show how they assume learner agency to be denuded within the classroom. Conversely, a place-based interpretation shows how participants assign significant agency to the learner in interim educational places and the community.

Increasing learner agency through place-based learning has been shown to be a primary factor for successful general education pedagogy (Sobel, 2004; Bartsch, 2008; Cameron, 2008; Dubel & Sobel, 2008; Sorensen, 2008; Lanas, 2011). Learner agency is re-emerging as a vanguard issue in second-language learning, and my recent study confirms the importance given to it by researchers such as Gao and Zhang (2011) and Fogle (2012). The application of CDA to the reflective discourse of English language learners indicates that learners' assumptions about agency vary considerably between their places of learning.

I, therefore, argue that the sociological construct of place (Gruenewald, 2003b: 619) might usefully become a primary organizing principle of second language curriculum design. This can be achieved by applying a postmodern approach (Slattery, 2006) to curricula alongside classroom experiences such that second language learners are systematically assisted to participate in real-world communities of practice as an integral part of their learning processes. The resultant breaking down of barriers between the classroom and community is likely to increase levels of learner agency and help transform the effectiveness of second language learning.

Appendix: The Participants

	Place of birth	Role	Language	Place of education
Faculty				
Eva	Al Gharbia	IT teacher	Arabic	UAE/Jordan
Maha	North Africa	English teacher	French	North Africa
Saeeda	Al Gharbia	English teacher	Arabic	UAE
Ghareeb	Lebanon	Academic chair	French	USA
Hadi	Rural Iran	English teacher	Farsi	Iran/UAE
Community				
Budoor	Al Gharbia	HR manager	Arabic	UAE

	Place of birth	Role	Language	Place of education
Fakhra	Abu Dhabi	Local Government	Arabic	UAE
Ghaleb	Al Gharbia	Local health	Arabic	UAE/USA
Mohamed	Al Gharbia	Local education	Arabic	UAE/USA
Saif	Al Gharbia	Local Government	Arabic	UAE/USA
Students				
Delilah	Al Gharbia	Current student	Arabic	UAE/USA
Mariam	Al Gharbia	Current student	Arabic	Al Gharbia
Shamsa	Al Gharbia	Current Student	Arabic	Al Gharbia
Abdullah	Al Gharbia	Current Student	Arabic	UAE
Khalil	Al Gharbia	Current Student	Arabic	Al Gharbia/UAE

References

Bartsch, J. (2008) Youth as resources in revitalizing communities. In D.A. Gruenewald and G.A. Smith (eds) *Place-based Education in the Global Age* (pp. 65–83). New York: Lawrence Erlbaum.

Bernstein, B. (1996) *Pedagogy, Symbolic Control and Identity*. London: Taylor and Francis.

Blackburn, M. (1971) English for foreign students goes out on the streets. *TESOL Quarterly* 5 (3), 251–256.

Bowers, C.A. (2005) *False Promises of Constructivist Theories of Learning: A Global and Ecological Critique*. New York: Peter Lang.

Brown, J.D. (1995) *The Elements of Language Curriculum: A Systematic Approach to Program Development*. Boston, MA: Heinle.

Cameron, J.I. (2008) Learning country: A case study of Australian place-responsive education. In D.A. Gruenewald and G.A. Smith (eds) *Place-based Education in the Global Age: Local Diversity* (pp. 283–307). New York: Lawrence Erlbaum.

Dictionary.com (2009) *Curriculum*, http://dictionary1.classic.reference.com/browse/Curriculum (accessed 15 May 2009).

Dubel, M. and Sobel, D. (2008) Place-based teacher education. In D.A. Gruenewald and G.A. Smith (eds) *Place-based Education in the Global Age* (pp. 49–64). New York: Lawrence Erlbaum.

Duff, P.A. (2013) Identity, agency, and second language acquisition, http://educ.ubc.ca/faculty/pduff/personal_website/Publications (accessed August 2013).

Eggins, S. (2004) *An Introduction to Systemic Functional Linguistics*. New York: Continuum.

Fairclough, N. (1989) *Language and Power*. New York: Longman.

Fogle, L.W. (2012) *Second Language Socialization and Learner Agency: Adoptive Family Talk*. Bristol: Multilingual Matters.

Foucault, M. (1977) *Discipline and Punish: The Birth of the Prison*. New York: Penguin.

Gao, X. and Zhang, L.J. (2011) Joining forces for synergy: Agency and metacognition as interrelated theoretical perspectives on learner autonomy. In X. Gao and T. Lamb (eds) *Identity, Motivation and Autonomy in Language Learning* (pp. 25–41). Bristol: Multilingual Matters.

Groth, H. and Sousa-Poza, A. (eds) (2012) *Population Dynamics in Muslim Countries: Assembling the Jigsaw*. London: Springer.

Gruenewald, D.A. (2003a) The best of both worlds: A critical pedagogy of place. *Educational Researcher* 32 (4), 3–12.

Gruenewald, D.A. (2003b) Foundations of place: A multidisciplinary framework for place-conscious education. *American Educational Research Journal* 4 (3), 619–654.

Gruenewald, D.A. and Smith, G.A. (2008) *Place-based Education in the Global Age: Local Diversity.* New York: Lawrence Erlbaum.

Hedegaard, M. and Chaiklin, S. (2005) *Radical-local Teaching and Learning.* Aarhus: Aarhus University Press.

Heidegger, M. (1962) *Being and Time.* Oxford: Blackwell.

Lanas, M. (2011) *Smashing Potatoes; Challenging Student Agency as Utterances.* University of Oulu, Faculty of Education.

Lave, J. and Wenger, E. (1991) *Situated Learning: Legitimate Peripheral Participation.* Cambridge: Cambridge University Press.

McLaughlin, M. and Blank, M. (2004) Creating a culture of attachment: A community-as-text approach to learning. *Education Week* 24 (11), 34–35.

Nation, I.S.P. and Macalister, J. (2010) *Language Curriculum Design.* New York: Routledge.

Ochs E. and Schieffelin, B.B. (2008) Language socialization: An historical overview. In P. Duff and N. Hornberger (eds) *Encyclopedia of Language and Education (2nd edn), Volume 8: Language Socialization* (pp. 2580–2594). New York: Springer.

Osberg, D. and Biesta, G. (2008) The emergent curriculum: Navigating a complex course between unguided learning and planned enculturation. *Journal of Curriculum Studies* 40 (3), 313–328.

Pinar, W.F. (1991) Curriculum as social psychoanalysis: The significance of place. In J.L. Kincheloe and W.F. Pinar (eds) *Curriculum as Social Psychoanalysis: The Significance of Place* (pp. 165–186). Albany: State University of New York Press.

Richards, J.C. (2001) *Curriculum Development in Language Teaching.* Cambridge: Cambridge University Press.

Romero, E. and Soria, B. (2013) The notion of grammatical metaphor in Halliday, http://www.ugr.es/~bsoria/papers/Grammatical/metaphor (accessed August 2013).

Slattery, P. (2006) *Curriculum Development in the Postmodern Era.* New York: Routledge.

Sobel, D. (2004) *Place-based Education: Connecting Classroom and Community.* Great Barrington: Orion Society.

Soja, E.W. (1989) *Postmodern Geographies: The Reassertion of Space in Critical Social Theory.* New York: Verso.

Sorensen, M. (2008) STAR: Service to all relations. In D.A. Gruenewald and G.A. Smith (eds) *Place-based Education in the Global Age* (pp. 49–64). New York: Lawrence Erlbaum.

Stanfield, P.W. (2013) *An Exploration of Place-based TESOL.* Saarbrücken: Lambert Academic.

Toolan, M. (1988) *Narrative: A Critical Linguistic Introduction.* New York: Routledge.

Umphrey, M.L. (2007) *The Power of Community-centered Education: Teaching as a Craft of Place.* Lanham: Rowman and Littlefield Education.

White, R.V. (1998) *The ELT Curriculum; Design, Innovation and Management.* Oxford: Blackwell.

Willis, P. (2011) *Learning to Labour; How Working Class Kids get Working Class Jobs.* Farnham: Ashgate.

Part 3

Pedagogical Practices for Agency

11 Agency, Anxiety and Activity: Understanding the Classroom Behavior of EFL Learners

Christina Gkonou

Introduction

The prominence of learner-centered curricula and the focus on social constructivist views of language learning largely characterize current approaches to second language acquisition (SLA) theory, research and practice. In light of these developments, language learners are viewed as active agents, whose learning in classrooms is contextualized, and is both ecologically and dynamically influenced by their personal histories and by the range of settings in which they interact (Benson, 2005; Block, 2003; Lantolf & Pavlenko, 2001; Larsen-Freeman, 2001; Mercer, 2011a, 2011b; Mercer *et al.*, 2012; Ushioda, 2009; Williams & Burden, 1997). Personal and socially constructed agency exert a significant influence on the control learners have over their own learning, and, ultimately, on the levels of attainment of proficiency in a second or foreign language.

This chapter reports on a study designed to explore the relationship between learner agency and language anxiety (LA). The research reported here was part of a larger four year investigation into the origins of English as a foreign language (EFL) learners' anxiety and their strategies for coping with LA in private language schools in Greece. Learner agency was found to exert both a positive and a negative influence on the participating students' levels of LA, revealing the complex nature of both constructs. Given that links between agency and LA have not been established in the literature to date, the present study supplements previous findings and discusses possible future directions for research into language learner agency. The mutually constitutive influence of agency on LA and vice versa was one of the serendipitous insights that the study uncovered.

Learner Agency

In anthropological research, agency is viewed as 'the socioculturally mediated capacity to act' (Ahearn, 2001: 112). Given the fact that one's capacity to act is likely to be influenced by their cognitive and motivational affordances, agency can refer to an individual's will and capacity to act in SLA research (Gao, 2010). More recently, Mercer (2012: 42) defined agency as being composed of two dimensions that cannot be meaningfully separated:

> Firstly, there is a learner's sense of agency, which concerns how agentic an individual feels both generally and in respect to particular contexts. Secondly, there is a learner's agentic behaviour in which an individual chooses to exercise their agency through participation and action, or indeed through deliberate non-participation or non-action. Agency is therefore not only concerned with what is observable but it also involves non-visible behaviors, beliefs, thoughts and feelings; all of which must be understood in relation to the various contexts and affordances from which they cannot be abstracted.

Thus, learners may feel that they want and are able to act (i.e. sense of agency), and then proceed to real action and participation (i.e. exercise of agency). At the same time, their refusal to act or participate in specific contexts for specific reasons is also an indication of their sense and exercise of agency.

Agency can therefore have a major impact on learning outcomes and, as van Lier (2008) put it, successful language learning depends on the activity and initiative of the learner. Lantolf and Pavlenko (2001: 145) emphasized that learners are 'people with human agency who actively engage in constructing the terms and conditions of their own learning'. However, as Mercer (2012: 41) argued, 'before a learner engages their agentic resources and chooses to exercise their agency in a particular learning context, they have to hold a personal sense of agency – a belief that their behavior can make a difference to their learning in that setting'. Much in the same vein, Bown (2009: 580) explained that 'to effectively manage learning and regulate emotional responses, learners must be aware of their own agency and must believe themselves capable of exercising that agency'. Hence, effective language learning depends on learners' awareness of themselves as active agents, capable of exerting influence on and of shaping their own language learning experiences.

Therefore, emphasis on the role of the individual and of his or her cognition in shaping learner agency has gained ground in SLA research. However, equal importance is now assigned to both the individual and the context, and agency is viewed as being largely mediated from a range of settings surrounding the students, as well as from the temporal and spatial dimensions associated with those settings. As Carter and Sealey (2000: 11) argued,

> Too great an emphasis on structures denies actors any power and fails to account for human beings making a difference. Too great an emphasis on agency overlooks the (we would claim) very real constraints acting on us in time and space. And reducing each to merely a manifestation of the other ... necessarily results in a theory which is unable to capture the complex relations between them.

Thus, contextual and personal factors should not be ignored, but should rather be seen as interacting with each other in order to lead to desirable results. Bandura (1989, 2008) attached importance to the interplay between environmental and intrapersonal (e.g. cognitive, affective and motivational) factors, and posited that individuals should not be merely viewed as agents reactive to their contexts, but should also be viewed as proactive agents who are able to change them. Investigating how learners exercise their agency in their selection and use of strategies, Gao (2010) concluded that the interaction of context and agency can initiate strategy use, and that the concept of learner agency needs to be extended to include aspects other than a learner's metacognition and self-regulation.

Thus, learner agency should not be seen as a monolithic variable, but rather as a latent construct that is shaped by numerous contextual, sociocultural and intrapersonal factors influencing the students. This echoes Lantolf and Pavlenko's (2001: 155) call for 'a more complex view of second language learners as agents'. Consistent with these views, the present chapter seeks to explore the relationship between learner agency and anxiety about language learning.

Anxiety and Language Learning

Generally speaking, anxiety in both the psychology and the language learning literature is characterized as a negative emotion with a negative impact on learning. In SLA research, the definitions and conceptualization of LA have been significantly influenced by the field of cognitive psychology, yet drawing on this discipline has not reduced the difficulty of capturing the nature of this psychological construct. Brown (1994: 141) argued that anxiety 'is almost impossible to define in a single sentence'. Arnold and Brown (1999: 8) opted for a qualitative description, claiming that anxiety 'is associated with negative feelings such as uneasiness, frustration, self-doubt, apprehension and tension'. Much in the same vein, Spielberger (1983: 3) defined anxiety as 'the subjective feeling of tension, apprehension, nervousness, and worry associated with an arousal of the autonomic nervous system'.

The great majority of early LA research falls into two broad approaches to identifying anxiety (Horwitz & Young, 1991). The first approach views LA as a transfer of anxieties from other domains, for example, stage fright or test anxiety. In the second approach, researchers claim that there is something unique about language learning that makes LA a unique experience too. However, as MacIntyre (1999: 26) suggested, 'these two approaches are not necessarily opposing positions but represent different perspectives from which to define language anxiety'.

In their seminal research into foreign language classroom anxiety, Horwitz *et al.* (1986: 128) defined LA as 'a distinct complex of self-perceptions, beliefs, feelings, and behaviors related to classroom language learning, arising from the uniqueness of the language learning process'. An important difference in approaches to LA is the extent to which it is regarded as dynamic or stable. SLA researchers have suggested that it is not a question of either/or, and that LA could best be conceived of as situation-specific (Ellis, 2008; Horwitz & Young, 1991; MacIntyre, 1999), given that there is something unique about the language learning process that makes students anxious about it. Specifically, LA may be stable over time but not necessarily applicable to all situations, as it only refers to the specific context of learning and using a foreign language. Students anxious about language learning may be confident and resilient in most other contexts, for example, their history or math classes. Thus, a combination of both trait/stable and situation-specific/dynamic dichotomies of LA is needed to appreciate learners' anxiety in EFL classrooms.

MacIntyre and Gardner (1989, 1991a, 1991b) suggested a model that could potentially be applied to the emergence and maintenance of LA as a latent variable, and that illustrates how LA can best be conceived of as situation-specific. At the initial stages of language learning, anxiety as perceived by the learner constitutes an undifferentiated, stable personality trait, which is not specific to the language learning situation. Students who are still at those stages of learning a language are therefore not expected to be able to differentiate their anxiety, 'because their experiences in language class have not had sufficient time to become reliably discriminated from other types of anxiety experiences' (MacIntyre & Gardner, 1991b: 303). However, after repeated experiences with the second language environment, students may begin to associate feelings of anxiety with the language class. If the learner has negative experiences in the classroom, foreign language anxiety is likely to develop.

Some of the most frequently cited sources of classroom LA include competitiveness and peer pressure (Bailey, 1986; Horwitz *et al.*, 1986), speaking in a foreign language and a subsequent fear of negative evaluation (Aida, 1994; Gregersen & Horwitz, 2002; Horwitz *et al.*, 1986; Kitano, 2001; Mak, 2011), and weak self-concepts (Kitano, 2001; MacIntyre *et al.*, 1997). The study reported here aims at exploring the conceptual links between learner agency and LA in an attempt to open up new directions for an interdisciplinary approach to researching agency and anxiety within language education settings.

It is noted that Benson (2007: 30) contended the theorization of 'agency ... as a point of origin for the development of autonomy', while Gao and Zhang (2011: 26) associated agency with metacognition as 'prerequisites for learners' autonomous learning'. However, the developments in research on agency could also inform, and even transform, theoretical and methodological conceptualizations of other aspects of the psychology of language learning, such as classroom LA. Possible links between learner agency and LA have not been identified in the existing literature, partly because it was not within the scope of that research. The study of the agentic system of highly anxious language learners can indeed provide further insights into the complexity of the constructs of both agency and anxiety. It also suggests new directions for pedagogical practices that can strengthen learners' sense and exercise of agency and concomitantly alleviate their stress over language learning.

In order to gain insights into students' sense and exercise of agency, the study posed the following two research questions:

(1) What are the main components of the participating students' agentic systems?
(2) How does learner agency influence learners' LA levels?

Method

Research design

This chapter draws on the qualitative dataset of a larger study of the LA of students learning EFL in private language schools in Greece. The first step in this mixed-methods study involved administering a quantitative survey (Foreign Language Classroom Anxiety Scale; Horwitz *et al.*, 1986) to 128 students in order to test relations among variables (e.g. correlations between student age and LA, or level of proficiency and LA) and identify a percentage of those students who received the highest LA scores on a numerical scale. The results obtained from this quantitative phase informed the collection of data for the second, qualitative phase by identifying highly anxious participants. The subsequent qualitative data collection involved interviewing these highly anxious students and collecting weekly diary entries from them. This step was taken in order to understand the reasons why this specific group of students deviated significantly from the rest.

The sequential explanatory design that was adopted for this study, like all mixed-methods designs, aimed at triangulating data. However, it differs from triangulation designs, as the purpose in collecting data through different instruments is not to compare and contrast the different findings, but rather to help to inform one stage through the other.

Participants

Seven adult Greek EFL learners who were enrolled in general English classes in two private language schools in northern Greece participated in the qualitative strand of the study. Their level of proficiency ranged from B1 (pre-intermediate) to C1 (upper-intermediate) (Common European Framework of Reference for Languages; Council of Europe, 2001). The minimum length of exposure to English was two years with a maximum length of six years. The participants were classified as highly anxious on the basis of their total anxiety score on the Foreign Language Classroom Anxiety Scale. All students gave their consent to participating in the study. Table 11.1 summarizes the information about the participating students (the students' names in the table are pseudonyms).

Instruments

Students were asked to write a learner diary on their computers on a weekly basis, and return it to me electronically at the end of each teaching week. The diary study spanned two months. Participants attended a training session prior to the commencement of diary keeping, and were provided with a list of prompts to have an idea of the aspects of their EFL learning experience that they were expected to comment on in their diary entries. Examples of prompts included questions, such as 'What is the most/least anxiety-provoking aspect of the lesson?', or 'How do you feel when you work in pairs or groups in class?' Students were given the option to write

Table 11.1 Information about the student participants

Participant	Total LA score (minimum = 33, maximum = 165)	Age	Proficiency level	Reasons for learning English
Natassa	147	26	C1	Job prospects
Sophia	144	19	B1	Importance of English as an international language
Nikos	126	30	B2	Job prospects
Kiki	113	35	C1	Job prospects
Zoe	112	27	B2	Academic goals abroad
Danae	107	18	B1	Importance of English as an international language
Maria	93	23	C1	Love for foreign languages

Table 11.2 The interview guide

1. How would you define anxiety?
2. What makes you anxious about English?
3. Why do you learn English?
4. Do you think that the reasons for learning English influence your learning? In what way/ways?
5. Do you view yourself as an experienced language learner? Why/Why not?
6. Do you think that your language learning experience influences your learning? In what way/ways?
7. As an adult, how do you see language learning?
8. What are your strengths at English? Why do you think so?
9. What are your weaknesses at English? Why do you think so?
10. Is there anything else you would like to comment on?

their entries in English or Greek, although the benefits of writing a diary in the target language were emphasized, as this was considered as a means of urging students to persist with the study.

An in-depth, follow-up, semi-structured interview was conducted with each diarist in Greek. An interview guide formed the basis of this phase of the study. However, the guides were slightly modified to ensure that interesting points made by each student in their diary entries were covered, and to account for themes that were of particular significance to each student. Table 11.2 includes the main questions of the interview guide.

Data analysis

The interview and diary data were analyzed combining deductive and inductive approaches (Lincoln & Guba, 1985; Strauss, 1987). A categorical scheme for analyzing these data was created based on the quantitative analysis of students' questionnaires and by drawing on existing LA frameworks from the literature (e.g. Horwitz *et al.*, 1986). The scheme consisted of themes, such as fear of negative evaluation, concern over errors, self-concepts and team work, which helped to develop an awareness of possible themes that may emerge from the data. However, given that qualitative data analysis should be dialectical and not just an application of the theory (Lincoln & Guba, 1985), the data were also analyzed in line with an inductive approach, which does not rely on preconceived assumptions, but rather on an analysis that takes into account the situated nature of the data and any themes that are constructed as meaningful to the diarists/interviewees with regards to the topic under investigation. The data were coded in two stages: (1) first-level coding, where themes were created, revised, and defined; and (2) pattern (or, second-level) coding, which allowed the researcher to group the already identified codes into manageable sets (Miles & Huberman, 1994).

The themes of the categorical scheme, which were generated through the analysis of the quantitative data collection instrument and through the review of the literature, were compared and contrasted to the codes identified during the process of first- and second-level coding. Certain themes that were part of the categorical scheme, such as team work, were not mentioned by any of the interviewees as concepts associated with learner agency, and were therefore eliminated from the final list of codes. Creating a categorical scheme and comparing it with the final codes facilitated the process of understanding if and how the findings of the present study resonated well with the existing literature.

Findings

The most important characteristic of the participating students' agentic system was that it was composed of a range of dimensions that, although occasionally contributing toward increasing their levels of LA, often helped them to develop internal mechanisms to control it. Therefore, learner agency was found to play a dual role in LA. Table 11.3 summarizes the components of the students' agentic system, dividing them into two categories, namely those that influence LA positively, by reducing it, and those that exert a negative influence on LA, by increasing it.

Metacognitive knowledge about oneself, mostly gained through self-evaluation, appeared to be a crucial part of the students' agentic system, affecting their levels of LA positively. Accounts related to metacognition surfaced in the interviews and diaries:

> I try to think of why I get anxious. Then I consider all the possibilities, for example if this happens, it will result in this and that etc. I try to come up with a rational explanation to any result, and choose the result I like. To feel that I have found a solution to whatever might happen in the end. And I think I am not anxious this way.[1] (Zoe, interview)

Table 11.3 Components of the participating students' agentic system and how they influence their LA levels

Positive influence	Negative influence
• Metacognition	• Self-regulation and attempts to prioritize tasks and needs
	• The status of English language learning in Greece
	• The Greek foreign language education system
	• Self-perceived competence
	• Age

When I am anxious, I avoid thinking about my anxiety and try to shift my focus to the task itself. For example, the teacher once asked us to do some writing in class. At that moment I was feeling that I couldn't write a word. But in the end I did very well. I tried to forget my anxiety. (Sophia, interview)

I am trying not to focus on my anxiety. I know I want to learn English and I will do it. (Maria, diary)

I worry if I get a low mark. I then review the class lessons to make sure I know what has been covered. Then I feel like I know everything, I feel more competent. And I aim for a higher mark next time. (Danae, diary)

If I am very anxious, and what I've been asked to do is something I really have to do and can't avoid, I will do it because I will have no other choice. You need to take risks at some point. I believe that anxiety is a kind of fear and something we have to get over. If there is no other way out, we will overcome our fears and whatever will be, will be. (Natassa, interview)

Metacognition through self-evaluation influenced students' decisions about what they needed to focus on, and how and when to act. Thus, it is clear that learner agency is associated with metacognition, the latter being used as a strategy for coping with LA by the participating students.

At the same time, learner agency was found to have a negative impact on LA. The first component of the students' sense and exercise of agency concerned their strong sense of self-regulation and their attempts to prioritize tasks and needs. Students mentioned that, as independent adults, they had to balance their agentic resources skillfully in order to achieve their goal to master the target language. Concerns over time management, work–life balance, responsibility to cover their English language lesson tuition fees and studying English to become proficient were daunting tasks that increased the learners' fear of failure and LA. These concerns can be seen in Nikos's and Sophia's comments.

When you are an adult, you work, you may not have much time to study and you would wish to be able to study more, you have to pay your bills, your tuition fees, the books you are using in class. You have to be a conscious individual who cares about the English classes and wants to succeed. You have to learn English because at this age you don't want to waste your time and also you don't want to pay all over again in case you fail. So my anxiety results from all this effort I am expending, both in financial and ethical terms. (Nikos, interview)

Well, when you are young, you don't really understand why you are learning English. It's almost always your parents' decision to attend lessons in the language school. But as you grow up, you realize that it is something useful and that you have to expend effort on it if you want to achieve something. It's the realization that you have to do well in English, and this may increase your anxiety about English in class. And it's not just that. It's difficult to study and work at the same time. I am not always happy with my performance, because I know that I couldn't study. I didn't have time to study because of the hectic schedule I have at work. This really makes me anxious. (Sophia, interview)

Both interviewees explained that their anxiety stemmed from their fear that they would fail the course, which in turn seemed to stem from the realization that having to balance work, life and studying is difficult and may lead to failure. An interesting connection emerges here between attributions that learners make for their possible failures and the way these attributions mediate the effect of possible failures on LA. Learners' sense and exercise of agency were affected by contextual factors, such as the difficulty of having to work and study at the same time and, thus, their occasional inability to act increased their LA.

Another way that learner agency was found to exert negative influence upon LA concerned students' realization that English language learning is necessary for professional advancement. This realization emanated from the structure of the Greek foreign language education system, which actually imposes a set of success-oriented beliefs on students. One of the requirements for admission to various posts in the public sector concerns certified knowledge of English, and this broadly dictated that failure was not an option for the students. Danae and Kiki emphatically demonstrated their concerns regarding these issues in their interview comments:

> When I was younger, I was lazy and I wasn't studying English. I can now understand how important having certified knowledge of English is. I mustn't fail. I need the points to have more chances to get a job in a state school. (Danae, interview)

> My anxiety stems from all the effort I am expending and from the possibility of failure. The reason why I am learning English, apart from the fact that I like it, is also connected with my profession, because quite often employers ask for an excellent knowledge of the English language. And this again relates with failure. It means that if you fail, you will not get the certificate, and therefore you will not meet the personnel specification criteria for that specific job that requires that certificate. (Kiki, interview)

The fact that certified knowledge of English is a prerequisite for getting a good job in the public sector seemed to motivate Danae and Kiki to work toward completing their goal, and increased their sense and exercise of agency, as they realized that they had to act and study in order to succeed in English language learning and secure a good job with the public sector. At the same time, the requirement for an English language certificate for jobs and the subsequent high sense of agency increased their fear of failure and their anxiety about failing the course.

Self-perceptions of one's ability in the target language were another principal component contributing to learners' sense and exercise of agency. Certain students appeared to hold weak self-concepts that made them avoid studying harder. Thus, in this case, they exercised their agency through non-participation and nonaction, which led to mounting levels of anxiety. The extracts below illustrate this point:

> Being a perfect student is not what I am aiming for. I have never been the best student in the class and I am not expecting to be the best either, but I think that my anxiety stems from the fact that I am filled with remorse for not being good enough. It happens unconsciously I think. (Sophia, interview)

> I know I am not good at listening and what's more I don't like it. So I don't want to work on it, but I should make some progress in my listening skills. On the one hand, I don't like it, and on the other hand I have to do well. This really makes me anxious. (Maria, interview)

It should be noted, however, that students' self-perceived abilities do not always reflect their actual abilities. Given that the study did not include any objective measures of the participants' actual performance and achievement in EFL other than information about their Common European Framework of Reference for Languages scores, the reliability of their comments on their self-perceived performance could not be tested.

Another insightful comment that the majority of the students made concerned the complex interplay between learner agency, age, and LA. Students argued that older learners (i.e. adults) are active agents in their own learning, and in most cases, have developed a sense of need for achievement and internal attributions, which in the case of the highly anxious EFL learners in this study, ignited feelings of LA. This was illustrated by Sophia and Zoe in the following excerpts:

> When you are young, you don't really understand why you are learning English. It's almost always your parents' decision to attend lessons in the language school. But as you grow up, you realize that it is something useful and that you have to expend effort on it if you want to achieve something. Not only are you learning English out of your own volition, but it's also the realization that you have to do well in it, and this may increase your anxiety about English in class. It's also the fact that things

are more difficult, the input is getting harder and you need to study more. And this makes me anxious. (Sophia, interview)

The younger we are, the more naive we also are, and therefore the less anxious. While growing up, we have to be responsible individuals and manage language learning satisfactorily. That's why I think I am more anxious about English now than when I was younger. (Zoe, interview)

Notably, the findings reveal that age could impact on differential levels of LA, as well as on how learners shape their sense and exercise of agency. With adult learners, foreign language learning is a conscious decision, thus incentivizing them to act and participate in the process, but it also makes them more nervous and concerned about their performance and success.

Discussion

The important perspective that emerged from this study is that the student interviewees' high sense and exercise of agency led to differential levels of classroom LA. The findings illustrate that learner agency and anxiety influenced each other and consisted of a range of dimensions that on the one hand contributed toward increasing students' anxiety, and, on the other, often helped them to develop effective strategies to cope with it. The findings of the present study therefore posed questions of directionality between classroom LA and learners' sense and exercise of agency. Since research into the relationship between LA and learner agency is scarce, this study aimed to reach a better understanding of this connection, with the hope of identifying practices that language educators could put in place to help students develop a strong sense of agency to better deal with their classroom LA.

One of the most salient components of the informants' agentic system was metacognitive knowledge gained through self-evaluation and self-perceptions of ability in EFL. As was mentioned above, the participating students were frequently constructing their self-evaluative judgments and were aware of their skill development. Clearly, self-regulation will influence agency as well as students' decisions about 'how to allocate their agentic resources' (Mercer, 2011b: 433) and thus what they need to focus on. Mercer (2011b: 431) also stressed that self-perceived competence 'will affect decisions about how to exercise agency as well as the degree to which a learner feels able to direct their agency in ways to enhance their learning'. Metacognitive knowledge can therefore lead to 'healthy reflection and evaluation of one's thinking which may result in making specific changes in how one learns' through a targeted and well-defined agentic behavior in the classroom (Anderson, 2012: 170). Metacognition and agency should thus be considered complementary to each other in revealing the process and goals of autonomous learning (Gao & Zhang, 2011).

Although this aspect of agency seems to promote learner self-regulatory processes toward planning for effective learning, increasing self-confidence and hence reducing LA, it may also determine an adverse outcome. Dörnyei (2005) claimed that students will tend to compare their self-perceived performance with future goals, and if they notice any gap they will be motivated to act. However, any gaps between students' perceived competence and the accomplishment of future goals may also accentuate their potential fear of failure in their studies and maximize their anxiety over academic achievement. On the one hand, therefore, students should be encouraged to set goals and exercise their agency toward achieving them. On the other hand, EFL learners' failure or even reluctance to exercise their agency and exhibit self-regulatory behavior can often ignite more anxiety.

Another particularly noteworthy dimension of the informants' agentic system concerns their time management skills in an attempt to prioritize tasks and personal needs. Given that this study was conducted with adult learners who have to balance their goal to become proficient in the language and their other life goals, such as going to work and attending other classes, it becomes clear how learner agency influences classroom LA. As age increases, learners go through a maturation phase where they feel that they understand the significance behind learning English, take a proactive role and continuously build their sense of agency. Students generally felt that they needed to prioritize concurrent needs and goals, and as far as EFL learning was concerned, they thought that their goal to master the language should be attained. As Nikos said, an adult needs to oversee a number of different tasks on a daily basis; therefore, she or he does not 'want to waste [their] time' in the EFL classroom. Thinking that mastering the language is a goal to be pursued, an increasing fear of failure accompanied by high LA emerges, and students feel that mastering the L2 is not well within their means.

Students' high levels of fear of failure and their strong desire for high achievement also appeared to pressure them to exercise their agency in the EFL classroom. An explanation for the participating students' fear of failure and subsequent exercise of agency could be their fixed set of success-oriented beliefs, which could in turn be attributed to the structure of the Greek foreign language education system. Strong claims, such as 'I mustn't fail' (Kiki, interview), reveal that failure is not an option for the students. In the absence of a longitudinal, developmental study, it is unclear whether these success-oriented beliefs were initially externally formed and imposed, and then gradually internalized by the students, or whether they formed an integral part of the students' beliefs about the scope of language learning in general. In fact, when certain beliefs are dominant within one's immediate sociocultural environment, individuals tend to internalize them unconsciously and spontaneously. This dynamic relationship between what individuals believe (i.e. their self-concept) and what others impose on them to believe (i.e. their ideal self or their ought-to self; Dörnyei, 2009) is demonstrated in the fact that one's ideal or ought-to self can change one's self-concept. As Dörnyei and Ushioda (2011: 82) commented,

> it is not always straightforward to decide at times of social pressure whether an ideal-like self state represents one's genuine dreams or whether it has been compromised by the desire for role conformity. Indeed, group norms, as their name suggests, impose a normative function on group members and because humans are social beings, most of us adhere to some extent to these norms. This means that there is a pressure to internalize our ought selves to some extent, resulting in various degrees of integration.

Thus, the internalization of social values and identities conditions one's personal values and preferences. The process of internalization helps to explain how specific external orientations can be assimilated into one's self-concept. Different people and different contexts can play a significant role in how students internalize beliefs about success in language learning. Therefore, we can better understand how 'aspects of context shape the learner's experience, and, reciprocally, ... the learner shapes the context to meet her needs and aspirations' (Noels, 2009: 299).

Internalization of success-oriented beliefs could, on the one hand, lead to negative consequences in academic environments, given that students may consider English simply as an academic subject that one has to study in order to succeed, or graduate, or be given a promotion, before moving on to more personally relevant pursuits. Thus, students may not view the English class as an opportunity to become proficient speakers of the language and acquire and develop specific skills, but rather as a place that will guarantee them success in English for better employment prospects. This belief could endanger their intrinsic interest in the language, if there is one, or prevent them from gradually developing one.

On the other hand, internalization of these beliefs could serve educational purposes in the sense that students could be encouraged by their teachers to appropriate learning goals that they see as personally relevant. To make this process feasible, students' needs and interests should be reflected in the learning program. Teachers can guide students to exercise their agency through identifying their personal learning goals, developing strategies to achieve them, monitoring their goals, evaluating the progress made and refining or developing new goals.

Three important insights follow from these findings. First, developments in research on agency can inform, and even transform, theoretical and methodological conceptualizations of LA. The study of the agentic system of highly anxious EFL learners can indeed provide insights into the complexity of the constructs of both agency and LA. This leads to a call for more studies of the interconnection between LA and learner agency.

Second, enhancing learners' metacognitive knowledge is indispensable not only for effective language learning in the long run, but also to give students the opportunity to speculate on and analyze the ways they think about language learning in an attempt to identify how they can diminish the anxiety they experience in the classroom. As Anderson (2012: 172) argued, 'rather than focusing students' attention only on issues related to learning content, effective teachers structure a learning atmosphere where thinking about what happens in the learning process leads to stronger learning skills'. Asking students questions that lead them to examine and assess their learning strategies could help toward effective metacognition training. Questions such as 'When you start to work on an activity, what do you need to think about first?' or 'What have you learned, and how can you transfer this to other situations in the English classroom?' could be incorporated into the English lessons. Pajares (1993: 50) suggested that teachers 'become models of the thinking they seek to encourage'. To put it simply, language educators should demonstrate the process of engaging in metacognitive thinking in order to provide students with concrete examples of what metacognition in action means. At this stage, learners could also benefit from discussing their own thoughts and actions with peers.

Self-assessment could also help students to see how efficient their learning is. Asking students to reflect on the way they approached a reading passage or a written task increases their awareness of themselves as agentic language learners, helps them to progress in their study skills, and calls attention to what they should concentrate on in order to continue to improve. In addition, students should be made aware of the marking criteria before they start to work on an activity. Teachers could give students the rubrics they have devised for writing or speaking tasks, and encourage them to complete the tasks taking the rubrics into account. This could help toward having students appraise their own work before turning it in. In this way, specific learning activities motivate learners to exercise their agency and gain better control over their LA.

Finally, language learners should be viewed and understood as people 'who are necessarily located in particular cultural and historical contexts' (Ushioda, 2009: 216), and who have a variety of social roles and are proactive agents and moderators of their own learning. The contexts surrounding the students, ranging from sociocultural, out-of-class settings to formalized learning contexts such as the language classroom, shape their behavior and emotions in class, thus contributing to the complex, dynamic and nonlinear nature of LA. Therefore, learners' needs, interests, perspectives and backgrounds should all be reflected on in the learning and teaching program.

Conclusion

The present study was undertaken to explore the interrelationship between learner agency and LA. First, the study analysed the components of the agentic system of highly anxious EFL learners in private language schools in Greece. Second, the influence that those components exerted on LA was examined. On the basis of the findings, metacognition was found to have a positive impact on learner agency and LA, as opposed to success-oriented beliefs, self-perceived competence, self-regulation and age, which, although contributing toward building a strong sense of learner agency, appeared to influence LA negatively.

Taken together, the findings reveal the highly interconnected and complex nature of a range of agentic dimensions and their impact on LA. It is clear that LA should not be seen as a monolithic variable, but as a construct that functions within a larger system of interrelated contextual influences and learner responses. This study is a first attempt to address the connection between learner agency and anxiety about language learning, taking a fresh look at how the latter could be re-conceptualized. Follow-up studies could supplement the above findings by investigating the link between the two constructs in different settings and with different groups of students.

Note

(1) The interview extracts are all translated from Greek.

References

Ahearn, L.M. (2001) Language and agency. *Annual Review of Anthropology* 30, 109–137.
Aida, Y. (1994) Examination of Horwitz, Horwitz, and Cope's construct of foreign language anxiety: The case of students of Japanese. *The Modern Language Journal* 78 (2), 155–168.
Anderson, N.J. (2012) Metacognition: Awareness of language learning. In S. Mercer, S. Ryan and M. Williams (eds) *Psychology for Language Learning: Insights from Research, Theory and Practice* (pp. 169–187). Basingstoke: Palgrave Macmillan.
Arnold, J. and Brown, H.D. (1999) A map of the terrain. In J. Arnold (ed.) *Affect in Language Learning* (pp. 1–24). Cambridge: Cambridge University Press.
Bailey, K. (1983) Competitiveness and anxiety in adult second language learning: Looking at and through the diary studies. In H.W. Seliger and M.H. Long (eds) *Classroom Oriented Research in Second Language Acquisition* (pp. 67–103). Rowley, MA: Newbury House.
Bandura, A. (1989) Human agency in social cognitive theory. *American Psychologist* 44 (9), 1175–1184.
Bandura, A. (2008) Toward an agentic theory of the self. In H.W. Marsh, R.G. Craven, and D.M. McInerney (eds) *Self-processes, Learning, and Enabling Human Potential: Dynamic New Approaches* (pp. 15–49). Charlotte, NC: Information Age Publishing.
Benson, P. (2005) (Auto)biography and learner diversity. In P. Benson and D. Nunan (eds) *Learners' Stories: Difference and Diversity in Language Learning* (pp. 4–21). Cambridge: Cambridge University Press.
Benson, P. (2007) Autonomy in language learning and teaching. *Language Teaching* 40 (1), 21–40.
Block, D. (2003) *The Social Turn in Second Language Acquisition*. Edinburgh: Edinburgh University Press.

Bown, J. (2009) Self-regulatory strategies and agency in self-instructed language learning: A situated view. *The Modern Language Journal* 93 (4), 570–583.

Brown, H.D. (1994) *Principles of Language Learning and Teaching*. Englewood Cliffs, NJ: Prentice Hall.

Carter, B. and Sealey, A. (2000) Language, structure and agency: What can realist social theory offer to sociolinguistics? *Journal of Sociolinguistics* 4 (1), 3–20.

Council of Europe (2001) *Common European Framework of Reference for Languages: Learning, Teaching, Assessment*. Cambridge: Cambridge University Press.

Dörnyei, Z. (2005) *The Psychology of the Language Learner*. Hillsdale, NJ: Lawrence Erlbaum.

Dörnyei, Z. (2009) The L2 motivational self-system. In Z. Dörnyei and E. Ushioda (eds) *Motivation, Language Identity and the L2 Self* (pp. 9–42). Bristol: Multilingual Matters.

Dörnyei, Z. and Ushioda, E. (2011) *Teaching and Researching Motivation*. Harlow: Longman.

Ellis, R. (2008) *The Study of Second Language Acquisition*. Oxford: Oxford University Press.

Gao, X. (2010) *Strategic Language Learning: The Roles of Agency and Context*. Bristol: Multilingual Matters.

Gao, X. and Zhang, L.J. (2011) Joining forces for synergy: Agency and metacognition as interrelated theoretical perspectives on learner autonomy. In G. Murray, X. Gao and T. Lamb (eds) *Identity, Motivation and Autonomy in Language Learning* (pp. 25–41). Bristol: Multilingual Matters.

Gregersen, T. and Horwitz, E.K. (2002) Language learning and perfectionism: Anxious and non-anxious language learners' reactions to their own oral performance. *The Modern Language Journal* 86 (4), 562–570.

Horwitz, E.K. and Young, D.J. (eds) (1991) *Language Anxiety: From Theory and Research to Classroom Implications*. Upper Saddle River, NJ: Prentice Hall.

Horwitz, E.K., Horwitz, M.B. and Cope, J. (1986) Foreign language classroom anxiety. *The Modern Language Journal* 70 (2), 125–132.

Kitano, K. (2001) Anxiety in the college Japanese classroom. *The Modern Language Journal* 85 (4), 549–566.

Lantolf, J.P. and Pavlenko, A. (2001) (S)econd (L)anguage (A)ctivity theory: Understanding second language learners as people. In M.P. Breen (ed.) *Learner Contributions to Language Learning: New Directions in Research* (pp. 141–158). Harlow: Pearson Longman.

Larsen-Freeman, D. (2001) Individual cognitive/affective learner contributions and differential success in second language acquisition. In M.P. Breen (ed.) *Learner Contributions to Language Learning: New Directions in Research* (pp. 12–24). Harlow: Longman.

Lincoln, Y.S. and Guba, E.G. (1985) *Naturalistic Inquiry*. Beverly Hills, CA: Sage.

MacIntyre, P.D. (1999) Language anxiety: A review of the research for language teachers. In D.J. Young (ed.) *Affect in Foreign Language and Second Language Learning: A Practical Guide to Creating a Low-anxiety Classroom Atmosphere* (pp. 24–45). Boston, MA: McGraw-Hill.

MacIntyre, P.D. and Gardner, R.C. (1989) Anxiety and second language learning: Toward a theoretical classification. *Language Learning* 39 (2), 251–275.

MacIntyre, P.D. and Gardner, R.C. (1991a) Investigating language class anxiety using the focused essay technique. *The Modern Language Journal* 75 (3), 296–304.

MacIntyre, P.D. and Gardner, R.C. (1991b) Language anxiety: Its relation to other anxieties and to processing in native and second languages. *Language Learning* 41 (4), 513–554.

MacIntyre, P.D., Noels, K.A. and Clément, R. (1997) Biases in self-ratings of second language proficiency: The role of language anxiety. *Foreign Language Annals* 47 (2), 94–111.

Mak, B. (2011) An exploration of speaking-in-class anxiety with Chinese ESL learners. *System* 39 (2), 202–214.

Mercer, S. (2011a) Language learner self-concept: Complexity, continuity and change. *System* 39 (3), 335–346.

Mercer, S. (2011b) Understanding learner agency as a complex dynamic system. *System* 39 (4), 427–436.

Mercer, S. (2012) The complexity of learner agency. *Apples – Journal of Applied Language Studies* 6 (2), 41–59.

Mercer, S., Ryan, S. and Williams, M. (eds) (2012) *Psychology for Language Learning: Insights from Research, Theory and Practice*. Basingstoke: Palgrave Macmillan.

Miles, M.B. and Huberman, A.M. (1994) *Qualitative Data Analysis: An Expanded Sourcebook*. Thousand Oaks, CA: Sage.

Noels, K.A. (2009) The internalization of language learning into the self and social identity. In Z. Dörnyei and E. Ushioda (eds) *Motivation, Language Identity and the L2 Self* (pp. 295–313). Bristol: Multilingual Matters.

Pajares, M. (1993) Preservice teachers' beliefs: A focus for teacher education. *Action in Teacher Education* 15 (2), 45–54.

Spielberger, C. (1983) *Manual for the State-Trait Anxiety Inventory (Form Y)*. Palo Alto, CA: Consulting Psychologist Press.

Strauss, A.L. (1987) *Qualitative Analysis for Social Scientists*. Cambridge: Cambridge University Press.

Ushioda, E. (2009) A person-in-context relational view of emergent motivation, self and identity. In Z. Dörnyei and E. Ushioda (eds) *Motivation, Language Identity, and the L2 Self* (pp. 215–228). Bristol: Multilingual Matters.

van Lier, L. (2008) Agency in the classroom. In J.P. Lantolf and M.E. Poehner (eds) *Sociocultural Theory and the Teaching of Second Languages* (pp. 163– 186). London: Equinox.

Williams, M. and Burden, R.L. (1997) *Psychology for Language Teachers*. Cambridge: Cambridge University Press.

12 Verbalizing in the Second Language Classroom: Exploring the Role of Agency in the Internalization of Grammatical Categories

Próspero N. García

Introduction

This chapter explores the role of learner's agency in the development and internalization of the grammatical concept of aspect (in Spanish, using *pretérito* 'preterite' and *imperfecto* 'imperfect') in the second language (L2) classroom from a Sociocultural Theory (SCT) approach to SLA (Lantolf, 2000). The notion of learner's agency in language learning plays a fundamental role in SCT research (Ahearn, 2001; Lantolf, 2013; Lantolf & Thorne, 2006; van Lier, 2008; Wertsch *et al.*, 1993). However, there is very little research addressing the role of learners' agency in the development and internalization of grammatical (i.e. conceptual) categories in the L2 classroom or of the pedagogical approaches that foster its emergence and development.

Using an analytic approach based on Vygotsky's (1978) genetic method, this chapter intends to fill the aforementioned gap in the literature by examining the case study of Catalina, a student enrolled in an advanced Spanish conversation course. The following analysis documents her developing agency over a 12-week period, during which multiple sets of data, including the learner's definition of the grammatical concept of aspect, performance (i.e. written narrations), verbalization and personal reflection data were collected. This chapter also introduces the notion of concept-mediated agency (CMA), proposing that the development of the learners' conceptual agency promotes awareness of and control over the concept of aspect, as seen in the students' qualitative changes in mediation when solving verbalization tasks.

Agency in the L2 Classroom

One of the paramount constructs in SCT is the notion that the human mind is mediated (Vygotsky, 1978), that is, human beings do not interact directly with the world, but through physical and psychological tools (Lantolf, 2000). These tools and symbolic systems are socially constructed, ever evolving and passed on to future generations who continue to reshape them. In this view concepts, as symbolic tools, become the essence of mediation in verbal thinking during verbalization activities (García, 2012).

Yet what is agency, and how is it enacted in L2 learning and acquisition? Lantolf (2013), drawing from Vygotsky (1978), implies that the individual agent is a sociocultural being whose individuality comes from social relationships, culturally organized activities and the use of artifacts or tools. In other words, a human agent is an individual who operates with meditational means (Wertsch *et al.*, 1993), and who exhibits a 'sociocultural capacity to act' (Ahearn, 2001: 118). Agency from an SCT perspective is a complex construct that has been redefined on several occasions over the last two decades. Some of those definitions, as van Lier (2008: 213) points out, fail to pin down important questions, such as the nature of sociocultural mediation and the types that might be involved in human agency. Lantolf and Pavlenko (2001) fill this gap by proposing that agency can be unique to an individual or co-constructed with others, being shaped by the agent's history and mediated by tools and social interactions. However, it is necessary to remark that, regardless of its construction, agency in SCT is situated, that is, it is an action in a particular context rather than an individual characteristic or trait. Lantolf and Thorne (2006: 143) argue that agency is 'about more than voluntary control over behavior', and that it also 'entails the ability to assign relevance and significance to things and events'. In this respect, van Lier (2008: 172) adds that agency also includes 'an awareness of the responsibility for one's own actions'. These definitions were recently revisited and synthesized by Lantolf (2013: 19), who argues that from an SCT perspective agency can be seen as 'the human ability to act through mediation, with awareness of one's actions, and to understand their significance and relevance'. Although complete, Lantolf's definition does not acknowledge that learners' agency is situated (van Lier, 2008), meaning that agency depends and is affected by the learner's initiative as well as the specific context in which an activity is taking place.

Indeed, agency is a multilayered concept that is often related to other notions such as volition, intentionality, initiative, intrinsic motivation and autonomy (van Lier, 2008: 171). It is precisely this status of agency as an umbrella term that hinders the identification and analysis of the different types of learners' agency in the L2 classroom. Even though there have been several studies examining L2 agency from an SCT perspective (Donato, 2000; Kramsch, 2000; Lantolf, 2013; Lantolf & Pavlenko, 2001; Pavlenko & Lantolf, 2000; van Compernolle & Williams, 2013; van Lier, 2000, 2004, 2008; Yáñez-Prieto, 2008), there is still limited research on its emergence and development and the role it plays in the internalization of grammatical categories in the L2 classroom.

Concept-mediated Agency

From a Vygotskian perspective, the goal of education is to help the learner develop into a fully agentive being, one who is able to adapt to the world and also 'change it through conscious intentional activity' (Lantolf, 2013: 27). In his pedagogical theory, Vygotsky (1978) considers learning and development as two different and interconnected processes, where carefully organized instruction bridges the connection between learning and development. Thus, learners' agency is understood here as a situated, relevant, conscious, intentional and mediated process that develops through carefully designed activity aimed at fostering the development and internalization of conceptual categories. This succinct definition allows the researcher to focus on the kind of mediated agency that emerges in the development of conceptual categories: CMA. This construct can be defined as the socioculturally mediated ability of consciously recognizing, interpreting and using conceptual categories to create new meanings in specific contexts. Hence, in the present work, CMA is interpreted as the use of the grammatical concept of aspect as a meditational tool for the development of complex L2 grammatical meanings (i.e. the contrast between the Spanish *preterite* and *imperfect* tenses). Considering van Lier's (2008: 12) understanding of L2 development as 'the development of agency through the L2', I argue that L2 conceptual development is the development of conceptually mediated agency through the L2. CMA is not a notion that precedes or results from activity, but a process that emerges with it. Learners' CMA develops as they start to consciously manipulate concepts to create new meanings in socioculturally situated communicative contexts. It is proposed that CMA can be captured during learning when the learner uses the concept as a meditational tool to create new meanings and internalize the notion of aspect.

CBI: Promoting learners' agency through concepts

The heuristics of understanding L2 conceptual development as the learner's development of CMA over the grammatical concept of aspect emerge from an SCT perspective on concept development (Vygotsky, 1986). In this approach, the relation between form and meaning in language development is based on the notion that, when the form is almost ready to emerge in speech, the concept begins to emerge as well. In other words, the emergence of form marks the beginning of L2 development as a conceptual process. Therefore, and as discussed by Negueruela (2003), it seems essential to implement a pedagogical model in the L2 classroom based on conceptual meanings that foster the emergence of forms during performance. Learners cannot be expected to develop coherent and complete conceptualizations of complex grammatical concepts – such as aspect in the L2 classroom – unless they have a clear understanding of their underlying semantic complexities and are able to use them in concrete communicative activities (e.g. verbalizations). In Vygotsky's (1986) understanding of development, if an individual cannot concretize something into language, he does not understand it.

Negueruela and Lantolf (2006) argue that concept-based instruction (CBI) helps learners develop awareness and control over conceptual categories through explicit grammatical instruction. In the case of aspect, the key for development is not so much mastering the morphological forms and endings as understanding how this concept allows learners to adopt a range of temporal perspectives that they can manipulate according to their communicative intentions. Taking this into account, Negueruela and Lantolf (2006: 82) propose that:

> The concept that is the object of instruction and learning (i.e. aspect) must be organized into a coherent pedagogical unit of instruction. This unit must have two fundamental properties: It must retain the full meaning of the relevant concept and be organized to promote learning, understanding, control, and internalization.

In other words, the quality of the conceptual explanation matters. Unfortunately, most traditional textbook approaches to the teaching of the Spanish *preterite* and *imperfect* rely on rules of thumb that fail to reflect the full meaning of the concept, and they are not organized in a way that promotes understanding, control and internalization (Negueruela & Lantolf, 2006). As Salaberry (2008: 228) points out, there is a general dissatisfaction among researchers and instructors with the way in which textbooks traditionally present rules for the use of the *preterite–imperfect* contrast in Spanish. Indeed, the way in which the aspectual dichotomy is presented in Spanish textbooks seems to be inconsistent, and in most cases, inaccurate (Whitley, 2002).

Table 12.1 illustrates different grammar presentations for *preterite* and *imperfect* from *Revista* (2nd edn) (Aparisi *et al.*, 2007: 38–39), the textbook used in the course in which the study was conducted. An analysis of the values presented reveals that this characterization is problematic on many levels. On the one hand, the two categories are subdivided into a random number

Table 12.1 Uses of the *preterite/imperfect* according to Aparisi *et al.* (2007)

Uses of the preterite	Uses of the imperfect
• Expresses the beginning and the end of an action	• Describes an action with no beginning or end
• Describes completed actions	• Describes habitual actions in the past
• Narrates a series of actions	• Describes a mental, physical or emotional state
	• Tells the time and describes the scene
• Used to narrate actions that tell what happened and imply movement in the narration. It has an informative goal	• Gives the narration a feeling of completeness by providing descriptive details (people, landscape, etc.). This description provides an expressive and lyric value to the narration

In summary: the *preterite* narrates and the *imperfect* describes.

of arbitrary and poorly described uses: four in the case of the *preterite* and six in the *imperfect*. These descriptions, however, are not very illustrative of the contexts where these tenses are actually used, since they are reduced to a simple set of ambiguous coordinates (i.e. narratives) that do not represent their real distribution. On the other hand, and borrowing Whitley's (2002: 109) argument, some rules and decisions present in the L2 classroom might sound capricious to the students, since all seem to be applicable and, thus, conflicting. Additionally, rules such as those in Table 12.1 are based on very different criteria: some are semantic (*preterite* for completed actions), others functional (describes background) and the rest rely on arbitrary decisions (*imperfect* for telling time). As has been observed, rules of thumb have the potential to do more harm than good when 'they depict the language as a sediment that appears to have a life of its own independent of people' (Whitley, 2002: 83), which may confuse learners.

In a CBI approach to instruction, it is essential to develop adequate didactic models that represent a grammatical concept but avoid oversimplification (Engeström, 1991). Didactic models have to be as simple yet as sophisticated as possible, representing structural, procedural, functional and content properties of the concept of study (Karpova, 1977). The idea is that students engaged in CBI become fully agentive learners, ones who can actively use concepts as meditational tools to mediate their performance and facilitate L2 conceptual development. According to Negueruela and Lantolf (2006), when creating didactic models in the form of charts, we must take into account the empirical and theoretical quality needed to raise awareness of the linguistic resources available to the learners to solve a linguistic task, and their presentation (from more to less prefabricated in terms of learner participation). Didiactic models must allow learners to justify their communicative intentions in actual performances (Negueruela & Lantolf, 2006). In this study, Bolinger's (1991) formal accounts of aspect and Bull's (1984) pedagogical recommendations were implemented to develop explanations and supporting visual representations to foster learners' conceptual understanding of the uses of the *preterite* and the *imperfect* in Spanish.

Grammar in CBI is not taught in a mechanical way but is presented in a coherent, systematic way that allows the learners to activate their agency through the manipulation and creation of new conceptual meanings in the L2.

The Study

The present study was conducted over a 12-week period at a university in the northeast of the USA, involving 32 students enrolled in two sections of an advanced Spanish 16-week conversation course (Spanish 301). The class followed the standard syllabus but incorporated communicative activities, group work and assessment from a CBI approach to L2 instruction. The researcher, García, also served as course instructor and interviewer.

The analysis provided in this chapter follows the case study of one of these 32 students, and it includes four types of data: definition, performance, verbalization and personal reflection data. Each one of these is connected to the learner's agency and L2 conceptual development in a different way. While definition data shows awareness of the grammatical concept of aspect and may be used by the learner as a tool for orienting his production, performance data is more concerned with the morphological accuracy involved in the production of *preterite* and *imperfect* forms in written discourse. Verbalization data show the dialectical relation between understanding and performance. They allow the researcher to see the process of concept formation through the learner's ability – or inability – to solve tasks and construct new meanings related to the grammatical concept of aspect. Finally, personal reflection data provide insightful information regarding the learner's perception of the implementation of CBI to the teaching of L2 grammatical concepts.

Definition, performance and verbalization data were collected twice: the first time at three weeks into the semester, and the second time a week and a half before the end of the course. Personal reflection data, however were only collected once. In the next sections I will analyze and discuss the data, and their relation to learner agency and L2 conceptual development.

The learner's background

Catalina (pseudonym) was a second-year comparative literature undergraduate student thinking about minoring in Spanish. She had previously taken four years of Spanish in high school and an accelerated intermediate course in college before enrolling in the advanced conversation class. Although Catalina had been exposed to instruction in Spanish *preterite* and *imperfect* several times prior to the beginning of the course, her pre-test results showed that she was unable to fully use either of them consistently. Additionally, when asked to justify her aspectual choices in the story retelling, she notably resorted to 'rules of thumb', indicating that she had not yet internalized the concept. For all the above reasons, Catalina was considered an ideal candidate for this study.

Notes about abbreviations and transcription conventions

The data analysis in this chapter includes excerpts from the transcriptions of the learner's assessment before and after CBI. Whenever Spanish was used during the collection of data, an English translation is provided below. All translations given are literal in order to capture the full meaning of the learner's production as well as the awkwardness of her Spanish sentences. The transcription conventions are adopted from Negueruela (2003), and they intend to capture particular aspects of the learner's discourse: words marked in bold indicate coherent use of relevant aspect morphology, and underlined words indicate incoherence. Italics are used when the learner is conveying the information in the target language. Crucially, an asterisk (*) marks that there has been an agentive event on the learner's part during the verbalization activity.

Definition data

As part of the course, Catalina was asked to define and explain her understanding of the main grammatical points tackled in the course before instruction. These definitions included topics such as *ser/estar*, *preterite/imperfect* and *indicative/subjunctive*. Only data related to the grammatical concept of aspect will be reported in this study. Although group discussion was frequently used in class to generate a basic understanding of these concepts, learners were asked to provide written definitions individually. This type of data was collected twice over the course of the semester, the first time during the fourth week of classes and the second time a week and a half before the end of the semester. Participants were allowed to write their conceptual definitions either in English or in Spanish. Catalina chose to discuss hers in English.

Although definition data by itself does not show the whole picture of learner's agency and its relation to L2 conceptual development, I argue in this chapter that it is complementary to other types of data (i.e. performance and verbalization data) in ascertaining both notions. Definition data shows the orienting quality of the concept available for the learner during communicative activity. Valsiner (2001: 87) suggests that being able to fully define a concept does not necessarily translate into a perfect linguistic performance. However, it plays a critical role in guiding the learner's development of performance ability by showing them the meaning-making possibilities available in the target language. Catalina provided the following definition of aspect before CBI:

> The preterite is used to describe specific events that happened in the past, that occurred only once, with a set beginning and end. These are actions that move the story along. The imperfect is used to describe habits in the past, things that happened more than once or events that have no clear beginning or end. It is also used for background information and description.

During the last week of classes, in her second and last data collection, Catalina provided the following description of verbal aspect:

> The preterite is used with actions that have a definite beginning or end. It is also used with cyclic verbs that have an implied beginning and end because they only happen once, such as 'close the door'. The imperfect is used to describe actions that occurred habitually in the past or that are ongoing in the past. It is also used to add detail and descriptions such as feelings in the past.

Looking at both definitions, changes in the learner's understanding of the concept of aspect seem apparent. In her first explanation, Catalina categorizes the *preterite* as a nonspecific event completed in the past that is used in narration, while the *imperfect* can be used in a variety of ways (description of habits, repeated events, actions in which beginning or end is unclear and background information). It seems clear that her rationale is based on rules of thumb to which she was exposed several times before CBI. Catalina's definition data after CBI, on the other hand, shows an emergence of a more coherent semantic understanding of the grammatical concept of aspect, especially in her understanding of the lexical aspect (i.e. acknowledging cyclic verbs). In her second definition, Catalina also points out the importance of establishing a point of reference (i.e. *preterite* marks either beginning or end of an action vs *imperfect* describing ongoing actions). Even though this definition is more coherent and semantically functional, there are still traces of her previous instruction in the shape of rules of thumb in her understanding of the notion of *imperfect* (i.e. habitual actions or descriptions in the past).

As mentioned before, these changes do not show a complete picture of L2 conceptual development – nor development in Catalina's CMA – by themselves. Indeed, even a very sophisticated notion of a concept is not useful if it cannot be used to mediate her performance in communicative activity. From a Vygotskyan perspective, definition data must be complemented by performance and verbalization data to actually ascertain changes in a learner's agency and L2 conceptual development.

Performance data

In this section, I explore the link between written performance data and its connection to learner's agency and L2 conceptual development. Analyzing performance data allows the researcher to observe the connection between the learners' understanding of the grammatical concept of aspect and the activation of learners' CMA as a psychological tool to orient their performance, helping them to produce a richer and more coherent use of the morphological forms.

In this section, I argue that, if the learner's understanding of the concept of aspect becomes functional in its orientation and execution after CBI, the aspectual morphology should also experience an improvement. However, it is important to point out that I am not trying to make a causal relation between definition data and performance data. Learners' development of conceptual understanding can be reflected in discourse but is not directly related to their ability to define the grammatical concept of aspect.

Performance data: Analysis

Performance data include Catalina's use of *preterite* and *imperfect* morphological forms in a written narrative before and after CBI. These narratives are based on a comic strip taken from the activity 'El accidente de Miguel' ['Miguel's accident'] in the Spanish textbook *Dos Mundos* (5th edn) (Terrell *et al.*, 2002: 422). These images present a sequence of events in which a boy riding his bike is run over by a car. The story was complemented with a word bank, which served as a tool for the participant's individual mediation.

Assessment of the learner's written performance before and after CBI is carried out in relation to the total number of accurate uses of *preterite* and *imperfect* forms throughout the narration. In other words, I observed Catalina's developing CMA in relation to the emergence and consistency in her use of the aspectual morphology in Spanish. Catalina's first written performance protocol was collected three weeks into the semester and her second one in week 14. All translations given are literal in order to capture the full meaning of the learner's production as well as the awkwardness of some of her Spanish sentences, when relevant.

Excerpt 1. Catalina's written performance before CBI

C: *Era un niño que **tenía** 10 años y que se **llamaba** Jimmy. Un día Jimmy **estaba** montando en bicicleta en Amherst. Jimmy **paró** en una esquina y entonces un coche **chocó** a su bici, a su bicicleta porque el hombre en el coche **estaba** manejando muy rápido. El hombre **salió** del coche para ayudar a Jimmy. Tres personas **vieron** el accidente y también **ayudaron**, una mujer lo **llamó** a la policía. Un policía **llegó** a la escena y **habló** con el hombre del coche mientras Jimmy <u>fue</u> al jos, al hospital en ambulancia. El hombre lo **dijo** al policía que <u>ocurrió</u>, **tenía** mucho miedo porque <u>era</u> un accidente y el hombre **estaba** muy preocupado de Jimmy. Jimmy **fue** al hospital y <u>tenía</u> que dejar en hospital por* *una semana. Cuando Jimmy **salió** del hospital <u>era</u> un gran celebración, Jimmy solamente **tenía** un cicatriz y una bicicleta rota.*

[Once upon a time] There was a 10 year old child named Jimmy. One day Jimmy was ridding his bike in Amherst. Jimmy stopped in a corner and a car crashed into his bi, bike because the man in the car was driving too fast. The man came out of the car to help Jimmy. Three people saw the accident and also helped, a woman called the police. A policeman arrived to the scene and talk with the man of the car while Jimmy went to the hos, hospital in an ambulance. The man told the policeman what happened. He was very afraid because of the accident and the man was worried about Jimmy. Jimmy went to the hospital and had to stay at the hospital for a week. When Jimmy left the hospital there was a big celebration, Jimmy only had a scar and a broken bike.

Excerpt 2. Catalina's written performance after CBI

C: *Un día, un niño que se **llamaba** Pablo **decidió** a montar en su bicicleta por la calle. **Era** un día hermoso y Pablo **estaba** muy contento. Pablo **estaba** parado enfrente de una señal de pare cuando de buenas a primeras un coche **chocó** contra su bicicleta. Pablo **gritó** y **cayó** al suelo. Su bicicleta **estaba** rota. El hombre se **asustó** porque Pablo <u>quedaba</u>(*) en el suelo. El hombre **salió** del coche y **trató** de ayudar a Pablo. Tres personas **vio**(*) el acontecimiento y una mujer **llamó** a la policía por su móvil. La policía **respondió** rápidamente y **animó** a Pablo. Cuando Pabló **entró** a la ambulancia el hombre **contaba** lo que **ocurrió** a la policía, **explicó** que no **vio** a Pablo y su velocidad **era** muy rápida por eso no **pudo** parar. El hombre **era** muy preocupado sobre Pablo y **fue** al hospital a decir lo siento. Pablo **perdió** mucho sangre y **necesitaba** un tratamiento muy caro. El hombre **pagó** por todo el tiempo que Pablo <u>estaba</u> en el hospital y por su generosidad Pablo solamente <u>quedaba</u> (*) en el hospital una semana.*

One day, a kid called Pablo decided to ride his bike in the street. It was a beautiful day and Pablo was very happy. Pablo had stopped in front of a stop sign when all of a sudden a car crashed into his bike. Pablo yelled and fell into the floor. His bike was broken. The man got scared because Pablo stayed in the floor. The man came out of the car and and tried to help Pablo. Three people saw what happened and a woman called the police with her cellphone. The police answered quickly and encouraged Pablo. When Pablo went into the ambulance the man was telling what happened to the policeman. He explained that he didn't see Pablo and his speed was very fast, and that's why he could not stop. The man was very worried about Pablo and went to the hospital to say that he was sorry. Pablo lost a lot of blood and [because of that] he needed a very expensive treatment. The man paid for all the time that Pablo spent at the hospital and, because of his [the man's] generosity, Pablo only stayed at the hospital for a week.

Catalina's written performance shows improvement in the use of *preterite* and *imperfect* morphology after CBI in terms of morphological accuracy. Before CBI, utterances using *preterite* and *imperfect* are used accurately in 84.6% ($N = 11/13$) and 72.7% ($N = 8/11$) of the cases, respectively. After CBI, *preterite* is used accurately 100% of the time ($N = 19/19$), and the *imperfect* 75% of the time ($N = 10/13$). Whereas her total aspectual accuracy in the first written protocol is 79.1% (19 out of 24 aspectual utterances), Catalina's total aspectual accuracy in the final protocol is of 90% (28 out of 31 utterances).

As can be recalled from her definition data, Catalina's understanding of verbal aspect before CBI was diffuse and based on the notion of event completion complemented by some rules of thumb. This becomes evident in sentences such as '*mientras Jimmy fue al jos, al hospital en ambulancia*' (while Jimmy went to the hos, hospital in an ambulance), or '*Cuando Jimmy salió del hospital era un gran celebración*' (When Jimmy left the hospital there was a big celebration). Based on Catalina's definition of verbal aspect, the misuse of the *preterite* '*fue*' could be explained by her interpreting the event as a completed action that happened only once. Her choice of '*era*', in the second example could be related to the rule of thumb that links the use of *imperfect* to the presentation of background information. Understanding learner agency as situated and constructed through activity implies that it is 'intrinsically related to individuals' histories and habitus' (Yáñez-Prieto, 2008: 292). Hence, Catalina had no choice but to make the decisions documented in the previous examples. Her agency was constrained by the rules of thumb resulting from her L2 learning experience. As Vygotsky (1987) points out, learners find it difficult to regulate their behavior when it is outside of their awareness.

After CBI, Catalina's understanding of verbal aspect displayed a movement toward a more semantic notion incorporating lexical aspect into her conceptual understanding. This became evident in her increased control over her production of *preterite* forms. However, her definition at that point did not show a complete internalization of the concept of aspect, presenting traces of perceptual understanding of the uses of the *imperfect* and some rules of thumb (e.g. using the *imperfect* for habitual actions). Towards the end of her second excerpt she writes '*El hombre **pagó** por todo el tiempo que Pablo estaba en el hospital*' (The man paid for all the time that Pablo spent at the hospital). At that point her control over *preterite* morphology is marked (as in '*pagó*'); however, her choice of *imperfect* in '*estaba*', suggests that the concept of aspect had not been fully developed yet. Nevertheless, Catalina's performance data shows a marked improvement in her overall control of aspect morphology after CBI. This suggests a gain in her CMA by developing the necessary meaning-making tools to become a self-regulated learner, oriented by her own intentionality.

From a Vygotskyan perspective, the key to understanding L2 conceptual development comes from studying the quality of the learners' concepts from the earliest stages of their formation as mediational tools for development (understood here as awareness and control over the features of the grammatical concept of aspect). Connecting L2 conceptual development with the emergence of CMA implies that learners' L2 conceptual development is a process of conscious creation and transformation through activity. I will discuss this issue in relation to CMA in the next section.

Verbalizing data

In this section, I explore the role of learner's agency as a mediator in the potential internalization of the grammatical concept of aspect in the context of verbalizing (i.e. using concepts as mediational tools for understanding). To do so, I will analyze Catalina's verbalization data collected during two oral interviews before and after CBI. I argue here that verbalizing data complement definition and performance data in relation to learner's agency as a mediator in the potential internalization of the grammatical concept of aspect. In addition to allowing the researcher to study conceptual development in its formation, verbalizations provide evidence for the development of the learner's CMA.

While definition data after CBI showed Catalina's awareness of the concept in its orienting quality, performance data displayed the learner's control over the morphological forms. An analysis of her verbalization data allows me to fully explore this learner's agency and its role in L2 conceptual development as a dialectical connection between understanding and execution. In my view of L2 development as a conceptual process, a learner's agency in communication plays an essential role in the process of internalization of the grammatical concept of aspect. For that reason, verbalization activities used in the classroom and in the data collection (before and after CBI) were specifically designed to allow for mediation in the definition, execution, and conceptualization of the target concept. In what follows, I bring up a series of excerpts from the interviews conducted before and after CBI to argue that verbalizing fosters CMA, helping the learner establish dialectical links between conceptual definition and execution which, in turn, are a key factor to explore and explain L2 conceptual development. While Excerpts 3 and 4 belong to the first interview, Excerpts 5 and 6 were collected during the second one.

Learner's verbalizations before CBI

In the verbalization activity before CBI, Catalina was asked to read her narrative out loud, and was allowed to take notes and make corrections. Then, she was requested to provide an explanation and make changes, when necessary, on a number of verbs. Additionally, Catalina was asked to produce a rationale for the use of *preterite* and *imperfect* in all the excerpts, and she was provided with mediation whenever it was required.

Excerpt 3

I: *Ok. Una pregunta, ahm, en la, en tu composición decías 'mientras Jimmy fue al hospital en ambulancia', ¿por qué usas Pretérito ahí?*
      Ok, question, in your essay you said 'while Jimmy went to

[preterite] to the hospital in an ambulance', why are you using preterite there?

C: *Ahm ... [pauses] No, [pauses] no sé si ...*
Uhm ... [pauses] No, [pauses] I don't know if ...

I: *Aha ...*
Uhu ...

C: *No, yeah, no sé si era pretérito y, o imperfecto ...*
No, yeah, I don't know if it was preterite and, or imperfect ...

I: *Y, ¿por qué piensas que escogiste pretérito?*
And, why do you think that you picked preterite?

C: I just guessed ...
I just guessed ...

I: *Aha, Bueno, vale ...*
Uhu, well, ok ...

C: It just sounded right. [laughs]
It just sounded right. [laughs]

I: *Pero entonces, no, que quiero decir ... porque dices 'un policía llegó a la escena y habló con el hombre del coche mientras Jimmy fue al hospital en ambulancia'*
But then, no, what do I mean ... Why do you say 'a policeman arrived to the scene and talked to the man in of the car while Jimmy went to the hospital in an ambulance?'

C: *Ahm ...*
Uhm ...

I: *¿No?*
No?

C: *Imperfecto ... probablemente ...*
Imperfect ... probably ...

I: *¿Por qué?*
Why?

C: *Porque no, no tenía un fin y ... ah ...*
Because it didn't, it didn't had an end and ... uh ...

I: *¿Ni un principio?*
Nor a beginning?

C: *Sí ...*
Yes ...

I: *Puedes hablar en inglés si quieres también ...*
You can also speak in English if you want ...

[The conversation shifts into English]

C: Uhm, yeah, it's imperfect because it was ongoing while the other man was doing something else

I: Uhu ...

C: There wasn't a set beginning and end ...

In Excerpt 3 Catalina is requested to reflect on her incorrect use of the *preterite 'fue'* within the context of a sentence, but she is unable to provide a coherent rationale for her aspectual choice (i.e. 'I just guessed'). When the interviewer insists by repeating the whole sentence, she changes her mind and decides that her aspectual choice should have been *imperfect* instead. As can be observed in this excerpt, Catalina requires some mediation on the part of the interviewer and uses her L1 as a meditational tool to arrive to a conclusion. Her final reflection, however, does not seem to be an agentive move mediated by a semantic understanding of the concept of verbal aspect. Rather, it appears to be triggered by the interviewer's insistence, or her own (mis)understanding of the uses of the *imperfect* based on her previous history as a learner memorizing rules of thumb. Catalina's agency appears to be constrained by her previous history as an L2 learner. Her dependency on rules of thumb to explain the contrast between Spanish *preterite* and *imperfect* tenses seems to make her unable to understand events lying outside this constraining, agency-less, instructional technique.

Excerpt 4

I: *Ok, está bien y, por último, ah, decías 'Jimmy solamente tenía una cicatriz y una bicicleta rota'. Would you keep it like that?*
Ok, it's ok and, finally, ah, you said 'Jimmy only had [imperfect] a scar and a broken bike'. Would you keep it like that?

C: Uhm, yeah, cos it was a description in the past.

In Excerpt 4, Catalina is requested to rationalize her incorrect use of the *imperfect* form *'tenía'*. In her response, Catalina bases once again her aspectual choice on her understanding of verbal aspect as a set of rules of thumb. In this case, her answer shows an even less agentive rationale, as she merely repeats the rule that indicates that one must use the *imperfect* in Spanish to describe actions in the past. The problem of reducing the teaching of verbal aspect to simple rules of thumb is that these descriptions are based on specific contexts rather than on general meanings, depriving learners of agency to emerge through personal intent and mediated subjectivity. According to Yáñez-Prieto (2009: 281), this occurs because rules of thumb 'confine language within a set of parameters which language learners then react to when they are prompted by linguistic cues'. These cues range from words such as *'mientras'* [while], which generally trigger the use of the *imperfect* tense, or events happening once, which are associated with the *preterite* form.

Learner's verbalizations after CBI

In the verbalization activity that took place after CBI, Catalina was asked to read her narrative out loud, and to take notes if any corrections were needed. As in previous sections, Catalina's awareness and control over verbal aspect during her written performance improved noticeably after CBI. By purposely using the grammatical concept of aspect to mediate her performance while reading her narration out loud, Catalina was able to correct the ungrammatical forms *quedaba(*), vio(*)* and *quedaba (*)* to their grammatical counterparts *quedó, vieron* and *quedó*. These changes illustrate a developing CMA not only in the realm of verbal aspect (i.e. she corrects two incorrect *imperfect* forms, providing the correct aspectual choice), but also in the concept of number (i.e. noticing that the Spanish verb *ver* should be third-person plural, as in *vieron*).

After the initial reading, Catalina was requested to provide a rationale for the general use of *preterite* and *imperfect*, receiving mediation when required. At this stage of the study, Catalina's developing CMA allowed her to solve tasks individually that she had not been able to complete without mediation before. The following excerpts show Catalina's rationale for the use of *preterite* and *imperfect* in the context of verbalizing as a tool to explore her developing CMA.

Excerpt 5

I: *Ahm, vale. Una pregunta, por qué, en la última línea de la primera, de la primera página pones 'quedaba', por qué, ¿por qué imperfecto?*
Uhm, ok. One question, why, in the last line of the first, the first page you wrote 'stayed'[imperfect], why, why imperfect?

C: *Ahm, [pauses], Ahm no, es, ah, quedó.*
Uhm, [pauses], Uhm no, it's, uh, stayed [preterite].

I: Aha ...
Uhu ...

C: *... Ah, porque es una acción completa, tiene un fin o ... y, no es cíclico ... pero no es 'ongoing'.*
... Uh, because it is a completed action, it has an ending or ... and, it's non cyclic ... but it's not ongoing.

In her definition data after CBI, Catalina's understanding of the grammatical concept of aspect had already become more semantic in nature (i.e. She was able to recontextualize her definition in a wide variety of tasks). In Excerpt 6, Catalina's CMA becomes visible as she consciously uses her conceptual understanding of aspect to appropriately mediate her performance and rationalize her choice of *preterite* morphology in a particular context. Catalina's CMA allows her to consciously mediate and justify her performance.

Excerpt 6

I: *Bien, vale, ahm... También en la última línea 'estaba', ¿por qué imperfecto?*
Well, ok, uhm... Also in the last line 'estaba', why imperfect?

C: *Ahm ... [Pauses], ah, pretérito, lo mismo [que el anterior] ...*
'Uhm ... [Pauses], Uh, same [than the previous one] ...
I: *Aha ...*
Uhu ...
C: *Si, Ahm, no es cíclico pero, ah, es una acción completa, no es*
ah ... ¿'ongoing'?
Yes, Uhm, it's not cyclic but, uh, it is a completed action, it's
not uh ... 'ongoing'?
I: *Sí, continua ...*
Yes, ongoing ...
C: *¡Continua! [Laughs]*
Ongoing! [laughs]

In Excerpt 6 Catalina's CMA is in full motion when she consciously uses her understanding of the grammatical concept of aspect to mediate her performance and correct her initial choice of *imperfect*. As observed in the previous example, Catalina's verbalizations after CBI exhibit a qualitative development in her understanding and control over the concept of aspect, which in turn, are guided by her CMA.

Personal reflection

This section examines Catalina's personal reflection data, which were collected at the end of the second interview. This type of data provides insightful information regarding her perception of the implementation of a CBI approach in the L2 classroom, and it documents her developing CMA throughout the whole process.

Excerpt 7. Personal reflection data

C: You know, this was actually really helpful.
I: Mmm ... What do you mean?
C: Well, this way of looking at the preterite and the imperfect
I: Uhu ...
C: Yeah, I mean, I have seen rules a thousand times but they never quite clicked with me. Uhm, like, [pauses] seeing the differences between cyclic and non cyclic verbs really helped me understand those little differences. Like, all of a sudden, in my mind, uhm, it all made sense. Uhm (pauses), and I know that some people [in the class] had problems using the diagram, but like, for me, I think that it is a great way to explain the differences between the *preterite* and the *imperfect*.

Catalina's reflection in Excerpt 7 reveals a positive reaction toward the implementation of this pedagogical approach in the classroom. She claims that being exposed to conceptual instruction allowed her to understand the nuances behind the grammatical concept of aspect, advocating for the usefulness of introducing more semantically complex notions such as cyclic–noncyclic during instruction. In her opinion, abandoning mechanical rules – as shortcuts to solve aspectual tasks – to focus on a more conceptual explanation helped her to develop a better understanding of the concept (e.g. 'all of a sudden, in my mind, uhm, it all made sense'). These comments suggest that fostering self-mediation in the context of a more agentive type of assessment allowed for the development of Catalina's CMA, which in turn favored the construction of new contextual meanings based on the concept of aspect.

Catalina explicitly acknowledges that, while other learners seemed to struggle when using conceptual explanations (in the form of a diagram), that was not the case for her. As observed in her performance, definition and verbalizing data after CBI, she managed to mediate her execution by using the conceptual tools provided.

Discussion and Conclusion

Catalina's personal reflections can be connected to her developing CMA throughout the learning process. Her definition data after CBI showed a qualitative improvement in her understanding of the grammatical concept of aspect, which became more conceptually sophisticated in post-CBI reflections. The concept of aspect also became functional in its orientation and execution after CBI. Catalina's performance data showed a notable increase in aspectual accuracy, and her control over the definition and the morphology of the target tenses also improved considerably. I argue that these changes in performance point to an emerging CMA, which can be observed in Catalina's appropriation of the meaning-making tools needed to become a self-regulated learner.

These findings also suggest that a learner's agency in the context of verbalizing is a key factor to ascertain L2 conceptual development, allowing the researcher to have a more comprehensive picture of the learner's development. Additionally, the construct of agency is seen as a meditational tool that fosters L2 learners' internalization of grammatical concepts. In particular, the verbalizations analyzed in this study indicate that agentive learners are able to: (1) promote the development of a more sophisticated semantic understanding of conceptual categories; and (2) foster control over grammatical concepts during L2 communicative interaction. While engaged in this communicative activity, the student becomes an agentive learner who is able to reflect upon her own performance through her understanding of the grammatical concept of aspect.

As seen in Catalina's data, L2 development and internalization of a grammatical concept are linked directly to CMA in that the learner needs to be consciously aware of the concept and its uses in communication to mediate her performance. The aim of education in SCT is developing fully agentive learners who are not only able to interact with the world, but to transform it. The learner engages in CMA by consciously manipulating the concept during communicative activity, which in turn allows her to become aware of its meaning and uses, and most importantly, to construct or co-construct new meanings and eventually regulate her performance in the context of communication. Exposing the learner to a CBI approach achieves precisely that goal. By introducing conceptual categories in the context of communicative activity, students become fully agentive learners, and the concept gains meta-mediational properties that allow the learner to understand it and internalize it through verbal manipulation. Verbalizing not only helps in developing the learner's CMA to mediate her understanding (awareness), performance (control) and the creation of new meanings, but it also gives the researcher the opportunity to ascertain the learner's agency and L2 conceptual development from a new and more complete standpoint. In other words, verbalization data allows the researcher to analyze the multiple layers that constitute the notion of agency and foresee the learner's potential L2 conceptual development.

References

Ahearn, L. (2001) Language and agency. *Annual Review of Anthropology* 30, 109–137.

Aparisi, M.C., Blanco, J. and Rinka, M.D. (2007) *Revista*, 2nd edn. Boston, MA: Vista Higher Learning.

Bolinger, D. (1991) *Essays on Spanish: Words and Grammar*. Newark, NJ: Juan de la Cuesta.

Bull, W.E. (1965) *Spanish for Teachers*. Malabar, FL: Robert E. Krieger. [Originally published 1984.]

Donato, R. (2000) Sociocultural contributions to understanding the foreign and second language classroom. In J.P. Lantolf (ed.) *Sociocultural Theory and Second Language Learning* (pp. 27–50). Oxford: Oxford University Press.

Engeström, Y. (1991) Non scolae sed vitae discimus: Toward overcoming the encapsulation of school learning. *Learning and Instruction* 1, 243–259.

García, P. (2012) Verbalizing in the second language classroom: The development of the grammatical concept of aspect. PhD thesis. University of Massachusetts, Amherst.

Karpova, S.N. (1997) *The Realization of the Verbal Composition of Speech by Preschool Children*. Paris: Mouton.

Kramsch, C. (2000) Social discursive construction of self in L2 learning. In J.P. Lantolf (ed.) *Sociocultural Theory and Second Language Learning* (pp. 133–153). New York: Oxford University Press.

Lantolf, J.P. (2000) *Sociocultural Theory of Language Learning*. Oxford: Oxford University Press.

Lantolf, J.P. (2013) Sociocultural theory and the dialectics of L2 learner autonomy/agency. In P. Benson and L. Cooker (eds) *The Applied Linguistic Individual: Sociocultural Approaches to Autonomy, Agency and Identity* (pp. 17–31). London: Equinox.

Lantolf, J.P. and Pavlenko, A. (2001) (S)econd (L)anguage (A)ctivity theory: Understanding second language learners as people. In M. Breen (ed.) *Learner Contributions to Language Learning: New Directions in Research* (pp. 141–158). London: Longman.

Lantolf, J.P. and Thorne, S.L. (2006) *Sociocultural Theory and the Genesis of Second Language Development*. Oxford: Oxford University Press.

Negueruela, E. (2003) Systemic–theoretical instruction and L2 development: A sociocultural approach to teaching-learning and researching L2 learning. PhD thesis. The Pennsylvania State University.

Negueruela, E. and Lantolf, J.P. (2006) Concept-based pedagogy and the acquisition of L2 Spanish. In R.M. Salaberry and B.A. Lafford (eds) *The Art of Teaching Spanish: Second Language Acquisition from Research to Praxis* (pp. 79–102). Washington, DC: Georgetown University Press.

Pavlenko, A. and Lantolf, J.P. (2000) Second language learning as participation and the (re)construction of selves. In J.P. Lantolf (ed.) *Sociocultural Theory and Second Language Learning*. New York: Oxford University Press.

Salaberry, M.R. (2008) *Marking Past Tense in Second Language Acquisition: A Theoretical Model*. London: Continuum.

Terrell, T., Andrade, M., Egasse, J. and Munoz, E.M. (2002) *Dos Mundos*. New York: McGraw-Hill College.

Valsiner, J. (2001) Process structure of semiotic mediation in human development. *Human Development* 44, 84–97.

van Compernolle, R. and Williams, L. (2013) Reconceptualizing sociolinguistic competence as mediated action: Identity, meaning-making, agency. *The Modern Language Journal* 96 (2), 234–250.

van Lier, L. (2000) From input to affordance: Social-interactive learning from an ecological perspective. In J.P. Lantolf (ed.) *Sociocultural Theory of Language Learning* (pp. 245–259). Oxford: Oxford University Press.

van Lier, L. (2004) *The Ecology and Semiotics of Language Learning: A Sociocultural Perspective*. Boston, MA: Kluwer Academic.

van Lier, L. (2008) Agency in the classroom. In J.P. Lantolf and M.E. Poehner (eds) *Sociocultural Theory and the Teaching of Second Languages* (pp. 163–188). London: Equinox.

Vygotsky, L.S. (1978) *Mind in Society: The Development of Higher Psychological Processes*. Cambridge, MA: Harvard University Press.

Vygotsky, L.S. (1986) *Thought and Language*. Cambridge, MA: MIT Press.

Vygotsky, L.S. (1987) Thinking and speech. In R.W. Rieber and A. Carton (eds) *The Collected Works of L. S. Vygotsky, Volume 1: Problems of General Psychology*. New York: Plenum Press.

Wertsch, J.V., Tulviste, P. and Hagstrom, F. (1993) A sociocultural approach to agency. In E.A. Forman, N. Minick and C.A. Stone (eds) *Contexts for Learning. Sociocultural Dynamics in Children's Development* (pp. 336–356). New York: Oxford University Press.

Whitley, M.S. (2002) *Spanish/English Contrasts: A course in Spanish Linguistics*. Washington, DC: Georgetown University Press. [Originally published 1986.]

Yáñez-Prieto, C. (2008) On literature and the secret art of the invisible words: Teaching literature through language. PhD thesis. The Pennsylvania State University.

13 Critical Discourse Analysis in a Medical English Course: Examining Learner Agency through Student Written Reflections

Theron Muller

Introduction

This chapter presents a pedagogical investigation of three students' written reflections on a short Medical English course taught at a Japanese public university. This research has several complimentary objectives. One is to examine what insights the students' written reflections offer into their agency as enacted in (and in response to) the course. Another is to determine whether and to what extent the course goals of promoting criticality were accomplished. A final objective is to evaluate the efficacy of the research methods employed here – examination of students' reflective assignment writing as a means of revealing in-course, in-context agency and development, particularly over short spans of time.

This investigation is multidisciplinary in the sense that it intends to engage conversations from English for Specific Purposes (ESP), from the language-learning agency and motivation literature and from the doctor–patient discourse analysis literature. In ESP, contexts discussed tend to describe classrooms where language learners will go on to complete the majority of their coursework in English, or where their workplaces will require the use of English in particular circumstances (see, e.g. Belcher, 2006; Flowerdew, 2005). Contexts such as Japanese medical education, where students have English as a foreign language coursework but where their content classes are taught in their first language, are less well represented and can present unique challenges to ESP teachers and course designers, as the English needs that learners have can be ambiguous or seem distant from the students' everyday experiences. This chapter shares the solution to this dilemma implemented at one institution, where criticality in ESP course design (Belcher, 2006; Fairclough, 2010) has been used to help raise students' awareness of the unequal power relationships inherent in doctor–patient communication.

With respect to the language learning motivation literature, the trend in recent years has moved from positivistic frameworks of learner motivation and autonomy to research methods that emphasize individual variation among groups of learners (Dörnyei & Ushioda, 2011). Recently research has tended to employ longitudinal, ethnographic style investigations over extended periods of time (see, e.g. Deters, 2011). An issue for language teachers with these new trends is how to incorporate the insights offered by this sociodynamic turn in agency and motivation research into the language classroom, or how to go about focusing 'on the agency of the individual person as a thinking, feeling human being, with an identity, a personality, a unique history and background, with goals, motives and intentions' and 'the interaction between this self-reflective agent, and the fluid and complex web of social relations, activities, experiences and multiple micro- and macro-contexts in which the person is embedded, moves and is inherently part of' (Ushioda, 2011: 12–13). While Murphey and Carpenter (2008) share a pedagogy based around the incorporation of such principles into the language classroom, they describe learners responding to a syllabus centered around the exploration and discussion of issues of language-learner agency. In contexts where the course theme is institutionally prescribed, such as with the Medical English course described here, while exploring and promoting student agency remains important, the course syllabus also needs to take into account the expectations of the institution and students. Thus, this investigation describes an effort to incorporate issues of agency into the ESP curriculum and evaluates the effectiveness of these pedagogical tasks to reveal students' developing agency during the course.

Finally, the medical ESP literature has tended to focus on the needs of learners to perform specific tasks, but has tended not to cite investigations from the medical literature of interaction between doctors and their patients. To address this gap, this chapter describes how literature from the medical field was incorporated into my medical English classroom. As ESP is inherently multidisciplinary, it is hoped that the adaptation of themes from specialist literature for the ESP classroom described here will be of interest to ESP practitioners more generally.

Literature Review

This literature review is divided into three parts. It begins with a discussion of current issues in ESP course design. This is followed by a discussion of the current state of the field regarding investigations of learner agency. Finally the medical discourse literature used in the class is reviewed.

Critical pedagogy in ESP

ESP has traditionally presented itself as a largely pragmatic field, investigating what language learners need in order to function in particular contexts or to accomplish particular tasks, evaluating what language abilities learners currently have, and then helping to bridge the gaps between their current language knowledge and that which they need (Belcher, 2006). Relatively recently issues have been raised from within ESP with respect to the unequal distribution of power and the role language plays in the perpetuation of such power imbalances, what Bourdieu (1999) refers to as *habitus*. Pennycook (1997: 253) goes so far as to accuse ESP of 'vulgar pragmatism' in this respect, and in response to such criticisms, discussion of ESP syllabus design has come to include calls for criticality to be incorporated into the ESP curriculum in order to 'empower students by helping them to develop a critical awareness of ... institutions in order to facilitate change' (Flowerdew, 2005: 136). The Medical English course described in this chapter takes as its starting point a desire to incorporate such criticality into the pedagogic design of the class syllabus.

Another issue in ESP is that it has traditionally focused on what to teach, rather than on the methods of instruction (Belcher, 2006; Flowerdew, 2005; Watson Todd, 2003). Sensitive to this discussion, the course content, and the way in which it was introduced to students, was intended to bridge the 'what' and the 'how' (Watson Todd, 2003: 148) of ESP course design, introducing critical discourse analysis, a topic not covered in students' regular curriculum (a strategy encouraged by Belcher, 2006), in a way that encouraged criticality among students in their engagement with the themes covered in class. There was the potential for at least three levels of student criticality: in discussion and analysis of doctor–patient interaction from the medical discourse analysis literature; in assessing models of doctor–patient interaction from the doctor–patient discourse analysis literature; and finally, through teaching the course in English, as learning content in English was a first for many of the students on the course, and this offered students an avenue through which to critically reflect on their approach to language learning. Criticality as a component of the ESP curriculum is promoted by Fairclough (2010) and it is hoped gives students an analytical perspective that can benefit them in their future careers as medical doctors, in both their Japanese and English consultations.

Recent developments in student agency and motivation research

Recent trends in investigation of learner agency and motivation have turned from positivistic models of general tendencies and preferences across populations or subsets of populations toward acknowledging the importance of the individual in modeling learner motivation and behavior (Dörnyei & Ushioda, 2011). Termed the sociolinguistic turn in language learning motivation research by Dörnyei and Usioda (2011), this relatively recent development seeks to explore how the local classroom context and the people who participate in the classroom influence the way students interact with and participate in learning. In this conception of the social nature of the classroom and its participants, learner agency and learner identity are not seen as attributes that learners possess, but as enacted through language, where 'languaging' (Swain, 2006: 96) embodies learning with learner agency and identity enacted and formed through the use of language. This makes it difficult or impossible to separate the language learners produce from their agency and motivation; rather than assuming identity is independent of an individual's actions, treating learners in this way assumes that their actions construct their identity in practice, and this constructed identity is what should be engaged when investigating agency and seeking to improve language learner motivation (Ushioda, 2011).

This relatively recent turn in classroom research, while welcome, raises several issues that require attention. One is how teachers can take advantage of the insights gained through viewing the classroom as a social environment, and another is the practical means for incorporating a view of classrooms as communities into the curriculum. Murphey and Carpenter (2008: 17) accomplished this quite elegantly in a project where they had students complete 'language learning histories', which formed a basis from which their learners could exercise agency in their English-learning experience, expressing their identity in terms of how they reacted and responded to their past education and in considering alternative ways to learn language. Murphey and Carpenter (2008), along with their students, then analyzed these reports, identifying common issues arising from the students' accounts of their experiences and demonstrating how, through these reports, the students came to envision preferable alternatives to the negative experiences related in their reflections. While the curriculum described in Murphey and Carpenter's (2008) investigation of their learners' language learning histories offers a means for making students' experiences of identity and motivation explicit in the classroom, it is not possible to center the curriculum around such investigations in all contexts. Returning to my classroom, the institution and students expect a focus on medical English in class, making a course concentrating on language-learning histories problematic. Thus this chapter is a description of a pedagogical design that intends to incorporate models of learners as individuals exercising their personal agency and motivation within the constraints of what is possible and practical in my ESP classroom, with the hope that the description provided here is of interest to ESP practitioners more generally.

Furthermore, the methods used in the sociolinguistic turn in motivation and agency research tend to be longitudinal, ethnographically oriented investigations (Dörnyei & Ushioda, 2011). While such research paints a rich picture of the learner as a unique individual responding to, transforming and being transformed by the social contexts in which they find themselves, it is difficult to envision classroom teachers being able to apply similar techniques to investigate the experiences of all of the students in their classrooms. Also, the emphasis on longitudinal research may discount the possibility of changes in attitudes and beliefs over the course of short time spans, particularly when students find themselves in new circumstances or experiencing learning styles that are new to them. For example, Kern (1995) notes how more than 50% of the 180 university students in his investigation experienced some shift in their attitudes toward learning French as a foreign language over the course of an academic semester, and Guilloteaux and Dörnyei (2008) explore micro-shifts in student learning motivation in response to different teaching methods, noting how student motivation varies even within single classes. The short six week course used for this investigation presents a means through which to investigate whether and how students' agency and motivation as expressed in their reflective writing change over short timescales.

The medical discourse analysis literature

Positivist paradigms remain the standard for medical interventions, although within medicine there is an important tradition that emphasizes the importance of dialogue in the doctor–patient relationship. Mishler (1981) notes how medicine should treat the whole person, which requires engaging with patients' lived experiences in medical consultations. Mishler (1981), drawing on concepts from Habermas (1984), labels this lived experience lifeworld and posits that engaging the lifeworld allows a person to present a coherent picture of their self, while the emphasis in medicine tends to be on the medical voice, which leads to a disjointed, inconsistent representation of the self, as it is constructed by the medical professional and the patient has little or no control over its contents or composition. Mishler (1981) contends that medical practice that engages the lifeworld is 'humane and effective' (Barry et al., 2001: 489) while consultations that only engage the voice of medicine are 'inhumane and ineffective' (Barry et al., 2001: 489). While Mishler's (1981) argument is largely theoretical, Barry et al. (2001) use it as a basis from which to evaluate interactions between doctors and patients to determine the extent to which medical professionals engage the lifeworld in medical interactions. Barry et al. (2001: 493) conclude that the most problematic medical interactions are those where the lifeworld is 'blocked' or where patients try to share information from their life experience they feel is relevant to their treatment and the doctors they are interacting with fail to acknowledge or engage this nonmedical discourse. Of relevance to my medical English classroom is that Barry et al. (2001) include a number of doctor–patient consultation transcripts, which were used to raise my students' awareness of the issues discussed above.

Of further relevance to patient representations of their lifeworld experience are issues of patient autonomy in medical encounters. One investigation of patient autonomy that offers a contrasting perspective to the strong case for incorporating the lifeworld, and thereby strong patient autonomy, into the medical consultation outlined above is Nessa and Malterud's (1998) analysis of a consultation with a patient recently released from a psychiatric ward, her husband and her family doctor. In the consultation there are places where the doctor defers to the patient's requests to not explore an uncomfortable topic more deeply, and there are other places where the doctor retains autonomy, such as in the selection and prescription of medicine to treat the patient. As their paper includes the consultation transcript, it offers an excellent way to engage issues important to doctor–patient interaction more generally while still offering my students the opportunity to work with authentic doctor–patient dialogue.

Returning to the ESP literature, as Belcher (2006) acknowledges, ESP practitioners face the issue of needing to have sufficient subject specialist knowledge to select content appropriate for the ESP classroom. In the case of the Medical English course described here, one reason why I incorporated the medical discourse analysis literature cited here into my classroom is because the authors of the papers cited are themselves medical doctors and the papers used were published in medical journals, thus adding a degree of external validation of the issues they raise as important and relevant to my students' education.

Pedagogic Context

In contrast to North American medical education, in Japan the medical curriculum is a six year undergraduate program that culminates in students sitting for the national medical doctor licensing exam at the end of their program. Medical English is taught in the students' third year, as they are taking specialist classes in Japanese in preparation for an examination that is a prerequisite for them to begin their clinical clerkships. The course described here is a short course consisting of six 90 minute sessions that students take as part of a larger Medical English program. The Medical English program is the last required English that students have on their curriculum, and they go on to complete their additional education in Japanese. The institutional expectation is for the classes to cover medical themes in English, and students tend to expect the classes to teach English as content rather than content in English.

Unfortunately, the literature on language-learning autonomy, while it calls for treating learners as unique selves with interests and identities that extend beyond the classroom, has yet to describe in detail what goals learners should ultimately be aiming for. The standard in the second language acquisition literature, despite being much maligned and contested (see Canagarajah, 1996), is native speaker proficiency as a goal of language learning. ESP has largely managed to skirt this debate, focusing on functional competencies necessary for learners to achieve goals based on occupational or academic requirements (Watson Todd, 2003), although this concentration on function and backgrounding of critical stances toward teaching methodology is increasingly being questioned, with Fairclough (2010) from ESP and Turner (2011) from English for Academic Purposes encouraging greater reflection on the part of educators regarding how standards and expectations are communicated to students.

The issue of what particular institutions and societies expect learners to become are foregrounded when thinking about the training of licensed professionals such as medical doctors. While it is certainly necessary to consider what learners desire to become, focusing exclusively on their individual goals and desires may downplay other factors influencing pedagogical goals in particular contexts. Perhaps here, as in the model of learners as individuals, context plays an important part in understanding what the goals of particular programs and courses should be, goals that can be described in terms of the actions of specific power relationships. Taking such a stance, and describing the different goals for learners included in the language curriculum could itself go some way to promoting the agency of students, for without description to make explicit the hidden forces working on the classroom, it is difficult for students and teachers to take those forces into account.

In this case, with respect to my classroom, I have described some of these forces: students desiring practice of doctor–patient dialogues and university expectations for the course to cover 'medical English'. Other factors, more distant, include a drive by Japan's Ministry of Education, Culture, Sports, Science, and Technology to promote the increased use of English in Japanese universities in general, increased communicative competence in English among Japanese university graduates and increased internationalization of Japan's universities (see, e.g. Commission on the Development of Foreign Language Proficiency, 2011). Also acting on my pedagogy are the classroom pedagogies of the other professors at the university, both within and outside the English faculty, who help to shape students' expectations of what the university classroom and the university English classroom should be. Furthermore, students bring with them to class a considerable history of educational experience, particularly experience of having studied English, which acts on their expectations and identities in the classroom. Finally, there is my own experience of having been a learner and teacher, which I bring with me to the classroom, and which shapes what I feel is appropriate teaching practice. Rather than considering these factors separately, it is perhaps more fruitful to consider how they intersect and interact in the language classroom described here, specifically through students' languaging in their written reflections.

While students appear to expect practice of patient–physician dialogues in English, as the instructor I hope to avoid the kind of artificial, classroom language described and criticized by Ushioda (2011), where students, given the chance to speak freely, reproduce textbook-like dialogues distant from issues of everyday importance to them (Legenhausen, 1999), and where a teacher is more interested in correcting a student's grammar than in the fact that a student is sharing a story of a relative having passed away (Scrivener, 1994). Thus, I incorporated medical discourse analysis of doctor–patient consultation literature into the course, in the hope that this would meet student expectations of covering doctor–patient dialogues while also including the criticality that I as instructor desired. This chapter is partially an evaluation of the degree of success achieved in trying to realize these goals.

Methods

Pedagogic methods

The first concepts covered in the course used the doctor–patient encounter described and discussed by Barry *et al.* (2001: 495) between a patient with angina, 'Krystof', and his physician. In the encounter, Krystof speaks using the lifeworld voice while his physician uses the medical voice, leading to a situation where Krystof's lifeworld story is cut off and he is noticeably uncomfortable with his condition and the interaction. During class, the issues arising from this dialogue and potential alternative dialogues between doctor and patient were proposed and discussed. Next the voices of lifeworld and medicine were described and students were asked to reflect on Mishler's (1981) assertion that the voice of the lifeworld is integral to effective medical treatment. Covering the Barry *et al.* (2001) material and Mishler's (1981) concepts spans the first three of the six classes. During the third class, the second theme to be covered is introduced, which explores issues of patient autonomy as theorized and discussed by Nessa and Malterud (1998), first reviewing their transcript of an interaction between a psychiatric patient, her doctor and the patient's husband. Here issues of the veracity of patient statements and the possibility of patients withholding information from their doctors are discussed and explored, and the hidden meanings embedded in the transcript are discussed.

Research methods

After each class students were asked to write one A4 page of reflection, answering the questions, 'What did you learn in today's class? What was new to you? What did you already know?' Students' written reflections form the languaging that is analyzed in this chapter. These written reflections are similar to the reflections collected and analyzed by Murphey and Carpenter (2008), although in this study students were asked to write about themes from their current course rather than retrospective histories of their language-learning experience. Methodologically, the use of written reflections is not very common in the motivation and agency literature, where there is currently a preference for ethnographically inspired field observation and reflective interviewing. These methods, however, were not practical in the research context described here because the course was quite short – only six classes over six weeks – and because one of the objectives of this investigation is to explore a means for practicing teachers to examine their students' in-course agency and motivation. Thus, the stance taken here is that students' written reflections represent a dialogue between them and the course instructor (also the researcher) about their experience in the course, what they are learning and the degree to which they are able to comment on and critique the themes covered in the course. This stance has antecedents in sociolinguistics, where Lillis (2013) argues that the distinction between speech and writing as separate modes of communication overlooks the reality that both represent the use of language to enact identity and agency, and thus written communication is at least as legitimate a representation of an individual's thoughts as speech.

The written reflections were examined for evidence of 'critical incidents' (Flanagan, 1954: 327) which demonstrated changes in stance and position between attitudes and beliefs going into the course and those attitudes and beliefs as they were shaped by the concepts covered in the course. Critical incidents have traditionally been used in professional development to help participants identify difficulties they have had and to examine the issues at play behind those difficulties in order to better understand their practice and how to operate more efficiently and effectively in their local context (Tripp, 1993). The difference between more traditional critical incidents research and the research conducted here is that this research examined participants' reflections for evidence of the classroom themes challenging and changing their beliefs and, once identified, examined how those beliefs appeared to change.

Data

Out of a possible 259 critical reflection reports for 62 students, 162 reports were collected. Included in my dataset were reports from students who had completed at least three-quarters of all of the assigned reports. These reports were examined for evidence of critical engagement with the class themes, particularly where students noted changes in beliefs and attitudes. Of these 14 sets of reports, the majority were quite positive toward the class and the issues discussed. Preference for selection for inclusion in this chapter was given to reports that were more critical of the course or showed signs of students struggling with the course themes, which resulted in the three report cases discussed below. For an example of a much more positive student reaction to the same course contents, see Muller (2012), which discusses student reactions to an earlier version of the course.

With the knowledge that grammatical errors and misspellings can lead to language being 'marked' (Lillis *et al.*, 2010: 783) with identities that authors do not necessarily intend to convey in their writing, I have corrected obvious errors in the extracts shared here. For similar reasons, I have also intentionally typed students' handwritten reflections, conscious of how the typed mode of this book format conveys different connotations than if students' reflections were presented as scanned images in their original handwritten form. All names used here are pseudonyms. The gender balance in the classes is about half male and half female, but the extracts discussed below are all from male students, as their writing seemed to show more evidence of changing beliefs. This is perhaps reflective of the fact that in Japan language learning is 'feminized' (Kobayashi, 2002: 188), meaning that the study of English tends to be a predominantly female endeavor and women tend to see more value in the pursuit and exercise of English proficiency. Thus, perhaps the female students in the course were more comfortable learning content in English, while the male students struggled more to adapt to the style and focus of the course, struggles that manifested in their written reflections on the class. Also, as discussed in the implications section, one of the limitations of collecting data in the way described here is that it is dependent on students completing the assigned work. One way in which students, female and male, could have exhibited some resistance to the themes introduced during class is through not completing the assignments, and thus their views would not be reflected in the data collected. This is partially evident in Yuto's reflections, the third of the students discussed below, who shows some resistance or reluctance to engage the classroom themes from the course and instead addresses topics that are of more immediate importance to him in his writing.

Student reflection case one: Drawing on past experience

In this first reflection Aki approaches his studies in Medical English in a similar way to how he has studied English as a subject previously, concentrating on new vocabulary in his first reflection report in Extract 1.

Extract 1. Relating past experience to current circumstances

> I think that this class is very new to me because English classes I have participated in [before] only [involve] learning words and grammar. Explaining 'discourse' or 'discourse analysis' is difficult for me, so I must

> train my discourse skills. What I found interesting is the dialogue between doctor and patient. As they speak [with] each other, the position up to the present is reversed. This is very new to me. I should know that there will be the same [kind of] things in my future.

In Extract 1, Aki relates his experience of the first class of Medical English to his past history as a language learner, noting that in the past the focus of his classroom English learning has been on learning language rather than using language to accomplish communicative goals, such as explaining the definition of 'discourse' and 'discourse analysis', both tasks from the first session of the class. He also notes the relevance of the themes covered in class to his own future as a doctor. This is an illustration of students' past language-learning experiences influencing their expectations of how they should learn in their current classes, a theme noted by Liu and Littlewood (1997), although it is important to point out that this type of class being 'very new' to Aki is not a negative evaluation, particularly since some literature on the Japanese context asserts that new methodologies are unwelcome or incompatible with student expectations of the language-learning classroom (see, e.g. Sato, 2009).

In Extract 2, Aki's reflection after the second class, he continues to relate his experience of the class as one of learning language, rather than dealing critically with the concepts being covered in the course.

Extract 2. Medical English as language study

> New things to me [from] today's class is how to express [myself]. For example, when we correct a patient's mistake, we should use a word, 'Actually'. This is very practical. I will use this word in my future.
>
> And second thing is slang words ... I have never learned slang words, so I [don't] know the words' meanings. I want to be a person who can handle these words.
>
> This class is very interesting.

Aki's reflection appears to enact an identity as a student of English (rather than as a user of English to learn content) that he is familiar with from his earlier language studies, evidenced through his reflecting on the vocabulary learned in class that he finds useful to his future self as a medical professional. His last line in the reflection appears to be an indirect acknowledgment of this, noting that the class and its contents are 'interesting' despite the fact that his reflection is primarily concerned with language he learned rather than concepts covered.

However, in his third report (Extract 3), written after the third class, Aki begins to deal with the themes being covered in the class, moving beyond his past experience and his conceptualization of himself as a learner of English to someone capable of discussing ideas and theorizing in English.

Extract 3. From language learner to language user

> [In] today's class, what is new to me is the experiment 'subject's choice and experimenter's choice'. I thought that the subject choice [group would] perform better than the experimenter choice [group]. But, in fact, the experimenter choice [group] performed better than the subject choice [group], so I'm interested in the results. I think the reason is mental power. Perhaps, the subjects believe the experimenters, so [they] perform better.
>
> I think this topic is very important in drug experiments. I'm glad [to have listened to] this topic.

To offer some background, in discussing patient autonomy, students felt it important to offer patients choices of treatment, and as instructor, while acknowledging that medical ethical policies call for physicians to offer patients treatment options, I wanted to challenge the assertion that more choice is always preferable. To do this, I summarized the results of research by Shiv and Fedorikhin (1999), who demonstrated that giving subjects choice before a challenging cognitive task resulted in poorer performance compared with subjects who were not given a choice before the task. In Extract 3 Aki shares his reaction to the conclusions of the research and offers some critical critique, considering variables that could have influenced subject performance that the researchers may not have accounted for (e.g. the study may not have involved double blinding). Evaluating the accuracy of Aki's speculations is not of interest here, but what is of interest is Aki's shift from concentrating on language learning in Extracts 1 and 2 to discussion of the issues covered in class in Extract 3. In Extract 3 Aki is constructing himself as critical of the research shared, building agency for himself as someone who does not simply accept the conclusions of research but rather raises questions of validity of research methods. While this does not show Aki transformed from uncritical to critical in the week between classes three and four, what it does show is that he is now applying his critical capacity to information that has been shared in, and which he is discussing, in English, a promising development in terms of student agency.

Student reflection case two: Enacting Japanese identity

The second student to be discussed, Tomo, interprets the information covered in class through an expression of his Japanese identity, as presented in Extract 4, his first written reflection after the first class of the semester.

Extract 4. Languaging a Japanese identity

> It was the first time that I hear[d] the word 'discourse analysis', so I studied about discourse analysis on the internet. Discourse analysis is used by linguistics. It is not the way to see a word but the way to see the whole sentence. And we can recognize information that isn't recognized if we see only a word.
>
> Discourse analysis is applied to a lot of situations. Doctor and patient conversation is one of these situations. Discourse analysis is a very effective method because doctors have to get a lot of information from patients.
>
> In Japan, besides discourse analysis, we use 'guessing'. We Japanese guess the emotion of the person who we are talking to, not by using a word or discourse analysis, but by guessing from our conversational partner's expression, voice, motion, and so on. It is [a] characteristic style [unique] to Japanese and a lot of foreigners confuse the style.
>
> I think the style is made up through long years, and is caused by Japan's island country characteristic.

There are several interesting agentive strategies enacted in this transcript. First, Tomo shares some ownership and responsibility for learning by noting 'I studied about discourse analysis on the internet'. He then languages his own definition of discourse analysis, demonstrating comprehension of the concepts covered. He also evaluates and legitimizes study of doctor–patient discourse analysis as relevant to cover in the course as such analysis 'is a very effective method'.

The most interesting part of the extract comes with the paragraph starting, 'In Japan'. Rather than noting the personal relevance of discourse analysis to him and his learning trajectory, Tomo performs an interesting 'othering' move – establishing his Japanese identity with 'In Japan', 'we use' and 'we Japanese'. This rhetorically sets him apart from me as his non-Japanese (nonexpert on Japan) teacher and allows him to assume a position of expert on Japan addressing a non-Japanese nonexpert. This also shows him building the concepts covered in class, ideas about discourse analysis and evaluating the language people use in communication, into his understanding of his everyday lived experience. In addition to setting himself apart from me, this othering move also appears to be othering the discussion of discourse analysis from class, saying that, while as a tool discourse analysis may be applicable to interaction in English, in his experience as a Japanese speaker there are other issues at play in conversation that he feels are outside the purvey of discourse analysis. Tomo's second reflection in Extract 5 shows how, through the class discussion in the second class, his understanding of the way people interact outside of Japan and Japanese has developed since his first reflection.

Extract 5. Internalizing new analytical models

> I'm interested in soft language. For example, 'Actually' means soft 'No'. Japanese also has a lot of soft language, and we use them to keep out of trouble. I checked on some other soft language. I used the word euphemism to search for some expressions on the internet. There are a lot of euphemisms. For example, we use bathroom or restroom instead of toilet [four more examples are shared]. It is interesting to me that in English they also use euphemism and take a hint. Guessing is not only characteristic of Japanese. All people use guessing.

Here Tomo again illustrates agency through conducting an independent investigation of themes from class of interest to him through his internet search for euphemisms (only one example of which is included in Extract 5). While his identity is still enacted as a speaker of Japanese and not English (note the 'they also use' instead of 'we also use'), he demonstrates that he has come to understand that discourse analysis is more nuanced an analytical methodology than he had originally thought in his original reflective report, and that 'all people' use ambiguity of meaning in ways similar to those he thought unique to Japanese in his original reflection in Extract 4.

Student reflection case three: Avoiding association with classroom themes

This final discussion considers Yuto's reflection reports, and how he avoids internalizing and connecting with the themes discussed during class, enacting a disassociation from the content covered in the course. Extract 6 shares his first reflection report.

Extract 6. Resisting internalizing pedagogy

> At first, before I reflect, I want to introduce myself [shares several lines of personal information]. By the way, it was easy to listen to what you said, so I enjoyed taking lessons from you. And everything I heard was new to [me]. [So] I learned the meaning of 'angina', 'discourse' and the difference between 'chronic' and 'acute'.

Yuto's self-introduction, which comprises more than half of his first reflection report after the first class, indicates his interest in the interpersonal student–teacher relationship over the contents of the classroom discussion, and a disassociation from or misunderstanding of the pedagogical goals of the course. This may be a manifestation of 'resistance' (Swain & Deters, 2007: 826) to the agenda set by the instructor (me) from the outset of the course or could represent an unarticulated assumption on Yuto's part that courses taught by non-Japanese instructors should be conversational and interpersonal in nature. Also, similar to Aki's initial reflections in Extracts 1 and 2, Yuto is concentrating on the language covered in class rather than the concepts. Extract 7 shares Yuto's second reflection report, where he engages with the ideas covered rather than simply the language learned, similar to Aki's shifting depiction of what he learned from the course, although in Yuto's case the extent to which he identifies with the information reviewed is more limited.

Extract 7. Limited identification with course themes

> I learned when I want to know patient's symptoms and understand them very well, I have to talk with the voice of medicine and the voice of the lifeworld. But if I talk only in the voice of the lifeworld, it is bad, so I think the ratio of the voice of medicine and the voice of the life-world is important.
>
> In last class, I couldn't understand the English you spoke. What should I do when I want to understand it perfectly? However, I enjoyed taking [the] lesson.
>
> By the way, I am interested in bowling . . .

Extract 7 shows that Yuto understands the main themes covered in the lesson but has had some difficulty in comprehension. However, the common themes here carried over from Extract 6 include an evaluation of enjoyment as important to his experience of the lesson and an interest in sharing about topics of more interpersonal importance to him.

Implications

This section turns to some of the implications of the reflection reports discussed here, first considering student agency as expressed in the reflection reports, then moving on to some of the pedagogical implications for my classroom, and finally commenting on the efficacy of using reflective written reports for examining student agency in the classroom.

Student agency as expressed in their reflective writing

The varied nature of the three reflection reports discussed here exhibit a number of dimensions of student agency enacted in their writing. First, there is evidence of their responding to course themes in ways that are consistent with what the English language classroom has been for them in the past, with all three students concentrating on lexis learned (when the class themes are mentioned at all in Yuto's case) during class in their initial two reports. In Yuto's case there is also evidence that he is attempting to language a classroom that fits with an image of language classrooms as places where interpersonal communication is emphasized, as he devotes most of his reflections to getting-to-know-you themed discourse, a trend he continued throughout his written reflections on the course.

There is also evidence of shift in students' handling of course themes in their writing in later classes. In this respect, Aki's reflections are the most compelling, as he shifts from a focus on the language learned in class in his initial two reports to a critical commentary on the results of research shared during class in his final report. Yuto demonstrates a similar shift, but to a less critically analytical extent than Aki.

The agency Tomo languages is compelling because he constructs for himself an identity as Japanese in his first report, and the teacher as a non-Japanese nonexpert on Japan, which is a powerful rhetorical move in that it gives him a domain of knowledge in which he can act as more expert than his language teacher. He then proceeds, in English, to share information he feels is important for his non-Japanese teacher to understand, which he possesses and his teacher lacks.

Pedagogical implications – student agency and criticality in the reflection reports

Pedagogically, the reflective reports discussed here demonstrate that these three students started the course paying attention to the language items discussed, but that there was some shift toward critical consideration of the larger themes introduced in class. The three reflections shared here were chosen for this purpose, as many of the other student reflections started with deeper levels of criticality in their commentary, and as the teacher I wanted to examine whether students who seemed to avoid grappling with the more complex concepts discussed in the course came to incorporate such commentary into their reflections. The answer to this question is a tentative yes, although in the end some students (Aki) appeared to be more successful at engaging with the issues raised in class than others (Yuto). Whether this is because Yuto is uninterested in or does not comprehend the deeper themes discussed is not clear from his written reflections, which is one limitation of using this method to assess the success of the course – these reflections represent student languaging intended for consumption by the instructor, and so it is possible that they avoid saying things that could lead to a negative evaluation of their performance on the course, or that would be face-threatening for the teacher, such as complaining that they are unable to understand the purpose of the class or that they feel the course themes are inappropriate.

Along these lines, separate from this research, the coordinator of the Medical English curriculum spoke with some students about their experiences of the full curriculum and shared that the students with weaker English skills noted difficulty following the course and attributed this to shortcomings in their language abilities rather than shortcomings in the contents of the course or the way it was taught. It is these voices which are perhaps marginalized in this investigation of students' reflective writing, as students with weaker English skills will by extension have more trouble expressing the difficulties they are having on the course while writing in a language they are not confident in. Furthermore, students who did not complete the reports did not have their perspectives represented in the data that was collected and analyzed.

Finally, Tomo's reflections indicate the promising potential for the pedagogy described here to help broaden students' understanding of how language is used for communication regardless of where it is spoken and in what language people are speaking. In his initial reflection he describes a picture of Japanese as unique in the way they express themselves, attributing this to Japan's geographical and historical context. That these 'myths' of Japaneseness have been roundly critcized is of academic interest (see Dale, 2012), but in terms of pedagogy, it is interesting that, after further elaboration about the nature of discourse analysis and the way language is used in doctor–patient consultations, Tomo revises his understanding of how language is used to convey unspoken meaning, relanguaging his initial beliefs that such characteristics are limited to communication in Japanese to acknowledge 'All people use guessing'. It is particularly important to note that Tomo underwent this shift without me as the teacher directly confronting the initial beliefs he expressed, which shows some of the potential benefits of the pedagogy described here.

Research implications

With respect to research into student agency, this investigation suggests that students, even in the short course used for this investigation, do indeed show surprising potential for demonstrating agentive change in response to their language-learning experiences. In particular, Aki demonstrates a shift from language as content learner to learning of content using English. Tomo illustrates a different, but equally important, shift from a perspective of Japanese as unique to a more inclusive understanding of how language is used. His initial reflection also demonstrates the kind of quite complex agentive positioning that students are capable of in their languaging with their teachers, as he 'others' his instructor in order to establish a domain of expertise which he is the expert on relative to his language teacher. Yuto, while showing some signs of resistance, also comes to show some understanding of the critical themes introduced during the course.

For teachers interested in exploring issues of student motivation and agency in intact classes, the methods outline here, if implemented with some understanding of their limitations, offer a means to access responses of students to the themes and contents of a class that are otherwise difficult to examine. Limitations include the fact that students who do not complete the assignments will not have their voices included in the data gathered and that the students' written reports are themselves performances of being students intended for their teacher, which influences the kind of themes engaged in their writing. Thus, it is important for teachers to remember that the perspectives students share do not necessarily represent the full range of their opinions and feelings about the course. Therefore, teachers interested in gaining a more complete picture of their classrooms should also keep in mind the more in-depth instruments available, such as interviewing and observations of lessons, where practical. That said, in the busy world of education work, student written reflections do offer a means of accessing student perspectives that would otherwise be unavailable.

Conclusion

To return to the objectives of this research, the students' written reflections offered some insight into their agency as enacted in response to the course, and demonstrated that the three students discussed here responded to the class themes in different ways and with varying degrees of criticality. This seems to indicate that the course goals of promoting a more critical understanding of language and its use were at least partially accomplished with respect to these three students, although the amount of uptake of the ideas discussed in the course in students' reflective writing varied according to the individual. Finally, for teachers interested in accessing students' understanding of the materials covered and gauging how their students respond to concepts introduced in class, the investigation here shows that analyzing student reflective writing, while it does not offer a complete picture of student agency and motivation, does allow a glimpse into how students are responding to materials while the course is still in session, and thus allows teachers to make adjustments and address students' needs.

References

Barry, C.A. Stevenson, F.A. Britten, N. Barber, N. and Bradley, C.P. (2001) Giving voice to the lifeworld. More humane, more effective medical care? A qualitative study of doctor–patient communication in general practice. *Social Science and Medicine* 53, 487–505.

Belcher, D.B. (2006) English for specific purposes: Teaching to perceived needs and imagined futures in worlds of work, study, and everyday life. *TESOL Quarterly* 40 (1), 133–156.

Bourdieu, P. (1999) Language and symbolic power. In A. Jaworski and N. Coupland (eds) *The Discourse Reader* (pp. 502–513). [Reprinted from Raymond, G. and Adamson, M. (transl.) and J.B. Thompson (ed.) *Language and Symbolic Power* (1991).] Abingdon: Routledge. [Originally published 1988.]

Canagarajah, A.S. (1996) 'Nondiscursive' requirements in academic publishing, material resources of periphery scholars, and the politics of knowledge production. *Written Communication* 13, 435–472.

Commission on the Development of Foreign Language Proficiency (2011) Five proposals and specific measures for developing proficiency in English for international communication (provisional translation), 30 June, www.mext.go.jp/component/english/__icsFiles/afieldfile/2012/07/09/1319707_1.pdf (accessed 3 July 2013).

Dale, P. (2012) *Myth of Japanese Uniqueness*. Abingdon: Routledge

Deters, P. (2011) *Identity, Agency, and the Acquisition of Professional Language and Culture*. London: Continuum.

Dörnyei, Z. and Ushioda, E. (2011) *Teaching and Researching Motivation* (2nd edn). Harlow: Pearson Education.

Fairclough, N. (2010) *Critical Discourse Analysis: The Critical Study of Language* (2nd edn). Harlow: Pearson ESL.

Flanagan, J. (1954) The critical incident technique. *Psychological Bulletin* 51, 327–58.

Flowerdew, L. (2005) Integrating traditional and critical approaches to syllabus design: The 'what', the 'how' and the 'why?' *Journal of English for Academic Purposes* 4, 135–147.

Guilloteaux, M.J. and Dörnyei, Z. (2008) Motivating language learners: A classroom-oriented investigation of the effects of motivational strategies on student motivation. *TESOL Quarterly* 42 (1), 55–77.

Habermas, J. (1984) *The Theory of Communicative Action, Reason and the Rationalization of Society*, Vol. 1. London: Heinemann.

Kern, R.G. (1995) Students' and teachers' beliefs about language learning. *Foreign Language Annals* 28 (1), 71–92.

Kobayashi, Y. (2002) The role of gender in foreign language learning attitudes: Japanese female students' attitudes towards English learning. *Gender and Education* 14 (2), 181–197.

Legenhausen, L. (1999) Autonomous and traditional learners compared: The impact of classroom culture on attitudes and communicative behaviour. In C. Edelhoff and R. Weskamp (eds) *Autonomes Fremdsprachenlernen* (pp. 166–182). Ismaning: Hueber.

Lillis, T. (2013) *The Sociolinguistics of Writing*. Edinburgh: Edinburgh University Press.

Lillis, T. Maygar, A. and Robinson-Pant, A. (2010) An international journal's attempts to address inequalities in academic publishing: Developing a writing for publication programme. *Compare: A Journal of Comparative and International Education* 40 (6), 781–800.

Liu, N.-F. and Littlewood, W. (1997) Why do many students appear reluctant to participate in classroom learning discourse? *System* 25 (3), 371–384.

Mishler, E.G. (1981) Viewpoint: Critical perspectives on the biomedical model. In E.G. Mishler, L.R. Amara Singham, S.T. Hauser, R. Liem and N.E. Waxler (eds) *Social Contexts of Health, Illness and Patient Care* (pp. 1–24). Cambridge: Cambridge University Press.

Muller, T. (2012) Critical discourse analysis in ESP course design: The case of medical English. *Professional and Academic English* 40, 25–28.

Murphey, T. and Carpenter, C. (2008) The seeds of agency in language learning histories. In P. Kalaja, V. Menezes and A.M.F. Barcelos (eds) *Narratives of Learning and Teaching EFL*. New York: Palgrave Macmillan.

Nessa, J. and Malterud, K. (1998) Tell me what's wrong with me: A discourse analysis approach to the concept of patient autonomy. *Journal of Medical Ethics* 24, 394–400.

Pennycook, A. (1997) Vulgar pragmatism, critical pragmatism, and EAP. *English for Specific Purposes* 16 (4), 253–269.

Sato, R. (2009) Suggestions for creating teaching approaches suitable to the Japanese EFL environment. *The Language Teacher* 33 (9), 11–14.

Scrivener, J. (1994) *Learning Teaching*. Oxford: Heinemann.

Shiv, B. and Fedorikhin, A. (1999) Heart and mind in conflict: The interplay of affect and cognition in consumer decision making. *Journal of Consumer Research* 26 (3), 278–292.

Swain, M. (2006) Languaging, agency and collaboration in advanced second language proficiency. In H. Byrnes (ed.) *Advanced Language Learning: The Contribution of Halliday and Vygotsky* (pp. 95–108). London: Continuum.

Swain, M. and Deters, P. (2007) 'New' mainstream SLA theory: Expanded and enriched. *The Modern Language Journal* 91, 820–836.

Tripp, D. (1993) *Critical Incidents in Teaching*. London: Routledge.

Turner, J. (2011) *Language in the Academy*. Bristol: Multilingual Matters.

Ushioda, E. (2011) Motivating learners to speak as themselves. In G. Murray, X. Gao and T. Lamb (eds) *Identity, Motivation and Autonomy in Language Learning* (pp. 11–24). Bristol: Multilingual Matters.

Watson Todd, R. (2003) EAP or TEAP? *Journal of English for Academic Purposes* 2, 147–156.

14 Toward a Relationship-oriented Framework: Revisiting Agency By Listening to the Voices of Children

Man-Chiu Amay Lin

Adult: Why do you want to learn Truku?
Nine-year-old girl: I want to protect my grandparents.
From the first village assembly meeting,
February 2012

Introduction

In an age when one's linguistic needs, rights and values are subject to the economics of the linguistic marketplace (Bourdieu & Wacquant, 1992), interaction between structure and agency plays a critical role in creating a space for heritage language maintenance. In particular, as many Indigenous children worldwide are learning their ethnic languages as second languages, agency has been conceptualized as reconstructing transformative practices in studies on indigenous language shift (e.g. Hinton & Hale, 2001; Hornberger & Swinehart, 2012; Joseph & Raman, 2012; McCarty *et al.*, 2012; Patrick *et al.*, 2013). Some of these studies further emphasize communities' ambivalent attitudes to the competing ideologies of development and decolonization (e.g. Baéz, 2013; Howard, 2009; Kamwangamalu, 2009; Lopéz, 2009; Messing, 2009; Recendiz, 2009). Language shift/ revitalization is an extremely complex phenomenon that offers a unique opportunity to further our understanding of the possibilities and nature of agency (Ahearn, 2001).

In the meantime, although past studies in Indigenous language education have increasingly prioritized the voices of community members, including those of the parents and the youths (e.g. Curdt-Christiansen, 2013; McCarty & Wyman, 2009; Romero-Little, 2006; Romero-Little *et al.*, 2011), what remain excluded are the voices of the children. In contrast to Fishman's (1991) intergenerational language transmission model that positions children as passive learners (Reynolds, 2009), current language socialization research has shown that children and their peers are active socializing agents to each other and to their adult caretakers (e.g. Baéz, 2013; Luykx, 2005; Ren & Hu, 2013). In early childhood educational research, critical researchers also advocate for the need to research 'with' children and value their voices to generate 'culturally relevant, dialogic practices' that better meet their needs (Malewski, 2005: 220; also see Bucholtz, 2002; Cameron et al., 1992).

Concerned with the primacy of praxis and the much-needed inclusion of children's voices in Indigenous language learning, I privilege the voices of the children and discuss how an ethnographic understanding of children's theory of Truku language and learning can illuminate and advance the praxis of Indigenous language revitalization as a recursive process of action and reflection. Inspired by Brayboy's (2013) illustration of the close relationship between stories and theories, I explore the following questions in this ethnographic study:

(1) What do children's stories and participation tell us about their theories of language and learning?
(2) How can we make use of children's voices to inform pedagogical practices?

To answer the questions above, I draw on social theories of learning (Wenger, 1998), poststructuralist theories of identity and language learning (Norton Peirce, 1995; Norton, 2000; Norton & Toohey, 2011) and language ideologies in linguistic anthropology (Kroskrity, 2000; Field & Kroskrity, 2009) to argue that agency as 'the socioculturally mediated capacity to act' (Ahearn, 2001: 112) should be understood as a collective in the context of Indigenous language education. This means that agency results from an emergent process of attaining mutuality and rebuilding relationships among different communities of stakeholders, between elders and children, between children and the researchers, and between children themselves. Such a relational take on agency also implies the need for the effort to respectfully position one's interests and needs in relation to others in praxis.

The present study contributes to contemporary studies of language learning, identity and agency by bringing in a praxis-oriented empirical case in an Indigenous language learning site and highlighting the affective and relational dimension of language learning and local activism. It also advances the scholarship of Indigenous language policy and planning (McCarty & Warhol, 2011) by including 'the child perspective' (Hedegaard, 2008).

In the following sections, I first introduce the present research context and then elaborate on the theories that guided the research design and data analysis. I will then discuss how children's social identities and theory of learning recursively inspired adults to critically re-examine the language revitalization praxis. I conclude with a critical reflection on the nature of agency and the possibility of collective agency in indigenous language education praxis.

Truku Language Loss and Revitalization

The Truku people, one of the Indigenous groups in Taiwan, used to dwell in the mountains, practicing subsistence hunting and farming. They have experienced involuntary migration and drastic sociocultural changes several times over the centuries. During the Japanese colonial period (1895–1945), the government created 'imperial subjects assimilated into the Japanese national polity' (Ching, 2001: 137) through compulsory education in Japanese. Growing up bilingual (i.e. acquiring Truku and learning Japanese), therefore, is a common childhood memory among the Truku great grandparents aged around 80. After the Second World War, the KMT Party from China replaced the Japanese regime and formed the new colonial government, 'the Republic of China'. This time, in order to remove traces of Japanese and other vernacular cultural influence, a rigid Mandarin-Chinese-only language policy was imposed on all students in school (Friedman, 2010; Chun, 1994). A 60-year-old grandfather shared, 'At home our parents spoke both Japanese and Truku. In school, if I spoke in Truku, we would be shamed to wear two wooden plates "SPEAK THE NATIONAL LANGUAGE" in the front and on the back', an experience that resonated with all the people of his generation (personal communication, 4 April 2012).

Additionally, since the national modernization project began in 1960s, many young Truku men have been forced to shift away from a mountain-land-based way of living to one that depends highly on the market and money. The drastic change of cultural practices and decades-long Chinese-dominant education have further resulted in changes to child socialization practices (Yang, 2001) and limited the traditional domains of use for the Truku language. One Truku elder's words of wisdom vividly explain the current situation of language endangerment: 'Our language is like a child beaten by two adults' (personal communication, 17 June 2012). Indeed, during more than 100 years of two colonial regimes, the Indigenous people have not been given sufficient cultural space to practice, experience and/or develop their cultural knowledge from their ancestors.

As a non-Truku scholar accepted by the some Truku elders as 'our Truku daughter' (太魯閣的女兒) (field notes, 26 December 2012), I have been drawn to Truku language education through my genuine friendship with some of the villagers and children in Qowgan Village, an administrative unit composed of several relocated Truku clans from the past. In 2012, the Genographic Legacy Fund granted the villagers the financial resources to allow them to establish a community-based Truku language classroom for the children.

The project features the establishment of a free Truku language program for children on Saturdays. Currently, there are around 20 children attending the program regularly. With my close friendship with the project manager (a local Truku scholar in linguistics) and academic interests in community activism, since February 2012, I have been involved in this local endeavor as an engaged ethnographer (Low & Merry, 2010), and continue to facilitate the reflective space for the project by bringing in ethnographic findings to dialogue with the team. In the process, one of the major challenges encountered by the project team was children's lack of motivation in learning Truku. The study reported in this chapter therefore evolved in response to the immediate local demand for understanding children's theory of language and learning to improve the pedagogical practice.

Theoretical Framework

Sociocultural approaches to learning

The study draws on Wenger's social theory of learning to conceptualize the dynamics of learning as communities of practice (CofP). According to Wenger (1998: 159–160), people are always in 'a nexus of multimembership', that is, engaged in multiple communities; consequently, members may deal with conflicting forms of identities or individuality as defined by different communities. A CofP therefore cannot be designed; instead, it slowly emerges with sustained interpersonal engagement and substantial negotiation of meanings. With conflicts being inevitable, what makes a CofP possible, Wenger argues, partly lies in the development of mutual engagement through participation. 'In this experience of mutuality, participation is a source of identity. By recognizing the mutuality of our participation, we become each other' (Wenger, 1998: 56). Thus, participation, broader than engagement, suggests both action and connection among community members. It (re)shapes not only the praxis but also one's identity by creating a space for collective belonging.

In a CofP, 'mutuality' is used as an alternative concept to 'agency'. Similarly, other sociocultural approaches to learning conceive agency as 'socially distributed or shared' (Wertsch et al., 1993: 352) or as 'a relational construct, a relationship that is constantly co-constructed and renegotiated with those around the individual and with the society at large' (Lantolf & Throne, 2006: 239). Adopting a sociocultural approach to agency, I define agency as a relational construct, a network of relationships that is constantly negotiated among the members in the communities of practice.

Nevertheless, although Wenger's social theory of learning reminds educators to acknowledge learners' dynamic identification and negotiation of meanings in CofP, its analytical framework has been critiqued for overlooking the micro-aspects of discourse and power in social interactions

(Barton & Tusting, 2005). Additionally, it does not necessarily address the specific context of language learning. I therefore utilize two other bodies of literature in the following to foreground the construct of 'identity' and 'language ideologies' in the communities of practice of language learners and educators for the investigation.

Language and identity

Norton (Norton Peirce, 1995; Norton, 2000) builds on feminist post-structuralist Weedon's (1987) concept of subjectivity or social identity to conceptualize identity as occupying multiple, contradictory and changing subject positions to discourses in a variety of sites. Seeing language as a site of identity struggle and reconstruction, Norton argues that one's motivation to language learning is 'not a fixed personality trait but must be understood with reference to social relations of power that create the possibilities for language learners to speak' (Norton Peirce, 1995: 26). Compatible with Wenger's CofP, Norton's theory of social identity emphasizes the diverse subject positions or multiple identities that socioculturally mediate one's motivation to learn. Nevertheless, agency from this theoretical lens is constructed on an individual basis and viewed as the human capacity to resist imposed subject positions and language ideologies and/or to create new ways of being as well as new possibilities of future (Yashima, 2012).

Although I do not stop at understanding agency as personal identity negotiation and move to reconstruct a mutuality of identity in the communities of practice in the study, the former and the latter do not necessarily differ from each other. In fact, I argue that Norton's poststructuralist take on identity can enrich the analysis of CofP by problematizing the inherent power relations among the stakeholders, which is less discussed in traditional CofP research (Barton & Tusting, 2005). Furthermore, it highlights the role of language as resources to fulfill one's identity needs.

Language ideologies

I also draw on the construct of language ideologies from linguistic anthropology to locate the site of ideological struggle in the communities of practice. Kroskrity (2000: 7) conceptualizes language ideologies as 'a cluster of concepts consisting of a number of converging dimensions'. First, they are a form of discourse constructed in the interests of particular social groups. They are also best conceived as multiple because different sociocultural groups (e.g. based on class, gender, generation, etc.) may have divergent perspectives about the role of language in their lives. Lastly, they are displayed through diverse local speakers' varying degrees of ideological awareness and mediate between people's sociocultural experiences (social structure) and language use (forms of talk). The attention to the heterogeneous and incongruous nature of language ideologies suggests that it can cause symbolic dominance when the dominant group takes its own language ideologies for granted. In the present research context, it has guided the adult educators (including the researcher) to highlight the work of power in praxis and recognize the incongruity of language ideologies between the children and some adult educators.

Bringing together and building on the above-mentioned theories, I intend to locate the space of identity work and language ideological struggle in pedagogical praxis. Furthermore, I have also undertaken conscientious efforts to learn from and establish mutuality with the children in order to make the communities of practice possible. The process of action and reflection itself is seen as an attempt of collective agency.

The Praxis

In the following, I reflect on how children's theories of language and learning have unpacked and engaged adults' own in changing pedagogical contexts. I first drew on my ethnographic data (from observation field notes, survey, informal discussions with children and their parents, and bi-weekly home visits) to understand children's language ideologies. The reflective process further inspired the exploratory design of a five week curriculum titled 'Caring for the Elderly', in which Truku language learning was combined with children's visits to the elderly. I then revisited this process by transcribing the video recordings of the implementation and closely examining the verbal turn-taking as well as the nonverbal aspects of the interaction. In analyzing 'identity', I consistently pursued the social constructionist underpinnings of the study and examined how children positioned themselves and were positioned by the adults and their peers in interactions (Bucholtz & Hall, 2005). The analytical process revealed how the dynamics of children's identity construction had challenged adult educators' language ideologies and reshaped the communities of practice.

It is important to note that, ideally, the research design should have resonated with Hymes' 'ethnographic monitoring' in which ethnographical research and teaching practices inform each other in an iterative process (Hymes, 1980; Van der Aa & Blommaert, 2011). Nevertheless, in reality, the emotional labor and intellectual demands of functioning as both a practitioner and a researcher often left me with little time to generate rigorous analysis and facilitate collective reflection at the time of curriculum implementation. The theoretical discussion in the latter part of the chapter serves more as personal hindsight for future reference.

Children's theory of language

Although at school children have been told that 'if you don't know to speak Truku, you are not Truku' (field notes, 10 April, 2012), the ideological connection between language and ethnic identity (Field & Kroskrity, 2009) has not proven to be effective in creating an immediate context of learning to engage the children. Part of the reason is because the children in the village are predominantly Truku and they do not have frequent contact with other ethnic and racial groups until middle school. Adults' discourses regarding the language-and-ethnicity connection remains abstract from children's point of view. As a result, in the beginning two months of the language program, we as adult educators were constantly challenged by how to actively engage children until one day when the improvised performance of three children (Sukin, Tapang, Yuyuh) shed light on our understanding of their theory of language:

In late afternoon, two third-graders, Sukin (pseudonym) and her cousin Tapang (pseudonym), dropped by my place, still with their school bags. 'Tapang and I came to see "Bubu" (Truku meaning: mother)'. They like to call their 86-year-old great grandmother 'Bubu' as they have heard their own grandpa call Great Grandma 'Bubu' for years. After greeting the great grandma in Chinese 'Bubu we came to see you', they started giggling amongst themselves in the hallway. I asked if they would like to speak in Truku to 'Bubu'. They responded with interest and went back to Great Grandma's bedroom. Tapang started with a greeting in Truku 'Embiyax su hug?' ('How are you?') Great Grandma smiled and replied 'Embiyax ku!' ('I am fine!). Then the conversation started to fade into awkward silence and Tapang looked back at me with uncertainty. Soon Tapang's older sibling Yuyuh came and now there were three of them. Sukin initiated, 'Why don't we sing for Bubu?' Having learned many Truku traditional songs in the past two months, they devised among themselves what songs to sing as I observed from the background. Right before they presented the first song, Yuyuh rushed to me and asked, 'Teacher, what should we say? I don't know how to speak in Truku'. I told her they could start with the sentence 'Mha nami mgrig' ('We're going to dance'). She repeated the sentence several times with me before returning back to the group. I was quite surprised as she had not been such an active learner of Truku earlier in class. During their performance, Great Grandma laughed a lot, clapping her hands and moving her toes along with the melody. The children ended their performance with a bow, saying 'Mhuway su balay' ('Thank you very much'). Then they sat bouncing on the edge of her bed giggling. Yuyuh tenderly held and shook Great Grandma's right hand and called 'Bubu Bubu Bubu' rhythmically. Great Grandma asked where they were going next and asked if they could stay a bit longer. Repeatedly she asked in Truku, 'Iyah tuhuy duri ha!' ('Come back again, all right?') Before departure, Yuyuh turned to Great Grandma, whispered in her ear in Chinese 'Bubu, I want to tell you a secret', and unexpectedly gave her a kiss on the cheek. Great Grandma chuckled lightly. I praised the children and asked what brought them here today. Yuyuh said to me, 'Because Bubu asked us to come visit her. We promised her. Let us take care of it. We are the police. We are the detectives!' I asked if they would like to form a team to visit the elderly. They cheerfully agreed and said they would start recruiting their friends at school the next day. (Refined field notes, 3 September 2012)

In this vignette, the three children Sukin, Tapang and Yuyuh demonstrated the kind of motivation to learn and use Truku that was not shown
in community class: they actively asked questions about the Truku language
and voluntarily organized their Truku song performance. They used their
body language (e.g. holding hands, kissing, sitting close by) to complement
their limited Truku and bring communication alive. As children, they had
not been unaware of Great Grandma's loneliness and deteriorating health. In
adopting the subject position of being an affectionate, faithfully protective
great grandchild in relation to their 'bubu', children naturally found it worthy
to speak in Truku. I argue that these children's motivation to learn Truku
intersects with their Grandma's need and is closely connected to the ongoing
production of their social identity as loving and caring grandchildren.
Yuyuh's final account – 'let us take care of it' – suggests her willingness to
be responsible for Great Grandma's well-being. The metaphorical self-
positioning of 'being the police and detectives', which connotes a protective and competent persona in the local context, suggests that this subject
position – as caring grandchildren – is relatively more empowering.

The next day, without being reminded or asked by any adults, the three
children voluntarily invited three other playmates to join the team and on
another afternoon they completed visits to four elders' homes that they
selected themselves. During these visits, Yuyuh, the oldest child, would initiate discussion with the others of what songs and dances they wanted to
perform. The songs and dances had been taught to them in the community
language program. Children preferred the songs that had a cheerful musical
rhythm (e.g. *'Mqaras Ku Bi Yaku'* – 'I Am Very Happy'; *'Tndahu Hariruya'* –
'Praise God') and the songs that they had memorized and could sing fluently
(e.g. *'Wow Pnkari Ta Truku Hug'* – 'Wow Let's Speak in Truku'). These songs
seemed interesting to them because they were fun ('很好玩'), expressed a
positive ambience and brought joy to the audience. One child even asked me
to review one Truku song with her because she 'wanted to be able to sing it
for her grandma and wished her good health' (personal communication, 6
September 2012).

Holland *et al.* (2001: 276–277) note that, in locating spaces of agency, we
should pay attention to improvisations that 'piece together existing cultural
resources opportunistically to address present conditions and problems'.
From a language ideological approach, I argue that, to the children, the Truku
language, instead of being an autonomous system of linguistic competence,
is more of relationship-oriented knowledge that constructs their relational
ways of being with their Truku-dominant grandparents. These children's
linguistic improvisations also suggest that it is not so much *being Truku* (indi-
geniety) as *being loving grandchildren* that is made relevant in these moment-
by-moment interactions.

Field and Kroskrity (2009: 20) contend that 'people are likely to adopt,
maintain, or modify language ideologies that reflect their sociocultural

perspective and rational views from that vantage point'. Children's relation-ship-oriented language ideology and natural bond with the elders here needs to be understood in the larger family and sociocultural context of the village where the majority of the children have grandparents living together with their families or close by. One may argue that the grandparents offer oppor-tunities to immerse the children in Truku; however, asking Truku-dominant grandparents to play an active role in socializing the children is too difficult a task. First, formal education has replaced traditional Truku child socializa-tion practices (i.e. working with the adults outdoors) and occupies more than two-thirds of children's waking time. Second, the grandparents are often physically weak and not as mobile as the children. From my ethnographic observations, I have noticed that, when cross-generational communication is not contextualized in their daily routines, communication often breaks down and results in children's 'confusion' and 'embarrassment' (personal communication, 14 September 2013).

To validate my observation of children's language practices and ideolo-gies, I did a follow-up survey with the second-to-fifth graders ($N = 75$) in the village elementary school. More than half of the children expressed that they were 'often' or 'sometimes' unable to comprehend when adults spoke in Truku at home. When asked if they liked learning Truku, all the children answered 'very much', and more than half of the children in Grades 3–6 linked their motivation to their aspiration to be able to communicate with the grandparents and/or other adult figures (e.g. 'because I want to under-stand what Grandma said', 'because I want to know how to respond when elders talk to me', 'because I can talk to Grandma and Dad', 'because I can communicate with Grandma and Grandpa', etc.). With my increasing under-standing of the home language dynamics and children's relational take on language, I shared my ethnographic findings with the other adult villagers in the curriculum meeting for community language class. The proposed idea of combining Truku language learning with visits to the elderly was well received. We started designing and implementing a five week curriculum in which children would learn the social language needed on their planned visits to the elders.

'Caring for the Elderly' in practice

In the newly designed curriculum 'Caring for the Elderly', each session of class time was divided into four parts: (1) learning a new song or a prayer (whole class); (2) rehearsal in small groups; (3) actual visit to an elder's home (still in small groups); (4) and whole-class reflection on that day's visit. Even though the children's improvisation inspired us to highlight the connection between language and relationship-building, in retrospect, we as adult educa-tors had remained enclosed in the metaphor of language acquisition or acqui-sition planning (Cooper, 1989) and considered generational ties as a way to motivate children rather than an end to itself. For example, when teaching children a new song, we started from assuming language learning as acquisition of in-context performance competence through repeated practice. We took children to visit the elderly partly because we considered language learning as (1) proficiency achieved through practices in meaningful contexts and (2) transmission from competent learners to novices.

The curriculum spanned five consecutive weekends (three hours per week), involving 17 children and 11 elders (aged between 65 and 89) in total. Children were taught to initiate a semi-structured interaction with the elderly, accompanied by four adult teachers (Kimay, Ribih, Gingay and the researcher) who served as facilitators and guides. The interaction began with a greeting in Truku, followed by each child's self-introduction and group performance of Truku songs, and concluded with a prayer of blessing for the elder's good health. We borrowed one of the children's creative expression – 'We are the angels for Grandma' ('母語大使的使就是天使'), and discursively positioned all the children as 'angels of light' ('光明的天使') for the elders we visited. Interaction between the children and the elders in Truku was semi-structured. The degree of interactiveness and improvisation varied partly depending on the elder's response. For example, some elderly women we visited were extremely friendly, initiated holding children's hands and responded positively to children' self-introduction by nodding, smiling and calling the children by their names. As the children were positioned by an elder as being very likeable, more children would also willingly linger. Some children who looked shy in normal class started to speak loudly enough to be heard. In a few cases where some of the children were already acquainted with the elder we visited, they would comfortably sit down by the elder's side, initiate 'nonscripted' interaction, and possibly ask questions in Chinese. For instance, in the following excerpt, a group of children and one adult facilitator, Kimay, surrounded Grandma Lituk. Giku, a fourth-grader, asked what Grandma meant by saying 'Kmbiyax smluhay'. Code-switching between Chinese and the Truku language occurred, the children negotiating meanings with and learning Truku from the adults. (Transcription conventions: *italics* signal speech in Truku, which is spelled using the local writing system; pictorial characters 中文 indicate Chinese speech; (parentheses) contain descriptions of nonverbal activity and English translations.)

1 **Grandma Lituk:** *Kmbiyax smluhay* ('Learn diligently!').
2 **Child Giku:** 他說什麼? (turning to the teacher Kimay, 'What did she say?').
3 **Teacher Kimay:** *Kmbiyax smluhay* ('Learn diligently!').
4 **Child Rabay:** (looking at the ceiling, trying to think).
5 **Child Mijang:** *Smluhay* ('learn').
6 **Teacher Kimay:** *Smluhay* 這個字是什麼 ('What dose the word '*smluhay*' mean?').

7   **Child Mijang:**   學 ('learn').
8   **Child Giku:**   要好好學習? ('Learn diligently?').
9   **Teacher Kimay:**   嘿!要好好學習 *Kari Lituk* ('Yes, learn diligently
                         – that is Grandma's message).

In line 6, Kimay did not immediately take the role of the teacher or the knowledge-giver, but built on Mijang's turn and brought the question back to the children. The question then led to an active co-construction of meaning from the group. Quite different from our earlier teacher-directed learning in class, in such pedagogical practices it is the children's social identity as 'angels for Grandma' that takes precedence, and one's identity as a Truku learner emerges out of one's genuine need for communication. This analysis can be supported by children's collective reflections in which they tended to recall the experience using emotional expressions to foreground their connection with the elderly: 'When we danced and prayed, we could see the elder's smiling face'; 'I feel touched when seeing the elder's face'; 'It's great we can sing for her'; 'I could see the elder's smiling face'. Children's accounts again suggest their implicit ideology of language as relationship, which offers children a more powerful subject position because they are able to make a positive impact on the elderly.

Additionally, in successful group-visit contexts, the metaphor of learning as participation (Sfard, 1998; Wenger, 1998) is reflected in children's cooperative peer dynamics and mediates children's opportunities to learn. Children who were still hesitant to speak up would listen to their peers many times until they were ready to initiate their own turn. Children who were not familiar with the lyrics would still dance along. Cooperative peer dynamics can potentially expand the zone of proximal development (Vygotsky, 1978) for all the children as it allowed children of various competency levels to participate in the communicative event. In the later stage of the curriculum, we noticed that some children gradually shared the role of a facilitator by reminding their peers to cooperate ('Hurry up! We're going to start!'; 'It's your turn to introduce yourself!'; 'Come, Tapang, it's your turn!'; 'Don't climb onto Grandma's bed. Come down!') or carrying on the agenda ('We haven't prayed!'; 'Let's sing the song again!'). Subsequently, the accompanying teacher could really take a step back, taking on the role of a teacher only when needed or requested.

I argue that over time children and adult educators gradually reached mutual engagement in the community of practice and children started to develop 'relations of mutual accountability' with adult educators (Wenger, 1998: 81). That is, over time, children and adults came to agree on 'what is important and why it is important, what to do and not to do, what to pay attention to and what to ignore, what to talk about and what to leave unsaid' (Wenger, 1998: 81). Truku language education in the CofP becomes a bi-directional, co-constructive process between adults and children.

Conflicts

What about the not-so-successful visits? Rather than glossing over the process of the curriculum implementation, I highlight the challenges involved when teachers want to enhance 'the range of identities available to the [their] students' (Norton & Toohey, 2011: 429). In the following analysis, I pay attention to moments of resistance and frustration from children when communication broke down and conflicts of interests arose in group dynamics. Below is an instance in which we visited an 87-year-old elder, who used to be a teacher of the Truku language himself. Prior to the excerpt, the children greeted the elder and the adult facilitator Ribih invited the children to start their self-introductions. Four children actively raised their hands, including the first-grader Kumu, who had progressed in speaking in the preceding weeks.

(Three children, Yabung, Yudaw, Kumu, and two adult teachers/facilitators, Amay and Ribih surrounded the elder.)

1	**Child Yabung:**	*Yaku o Yabung ka hangan mu. Payi mu o Tumi. Pnaah ku alang Gowgan* ('My name is Yabung. My grandmother is Tumi. I am from Qowgan Village').
2	**Teacher Ribih:**	*O Tayal suyang!* ('Oh how great!').
3	**Elder:**	*Inu?* ('Where?').
4	**Child Yabung:**	*Gowgan* ('Qowgan!').
5	**Elder:**	*Pnaah su alang Qowgan. Q q q q q Qowgan* ('You are from Qowgan Village. Q q q q q Qowgan').
6		(Kumu looked at Yabung and turned to the other teacher Amay. Yudaw stared at the elder intently. Yabung hunched her back and withdrew two steps.)
7	**Teacher Ribih:**	(laughing and turning to Yabung) *Iq, ksa.* ('say yes').
8		(Child Yabung covered her mouth, smiling with embarrassment).
9		(Kumu withdrew two steps and left the scene).

In line 3, instead of responding to the girl's name identity and calling her 'Yabung', the elder asked Yabung again where she was from. In line 5, the elder corrected Yabung's pronunciation of the village name, emphasizing it was a uvular plosive 'q' rather than a velar plosive 'g'. The elder's ideology of linguistic purism or perfectionism inevitably positioned Yabung as an incompetent learner or speaker of the Truku language. In line 7 the teacher Ribih tried to mitigate the tension by helping Yabung to respond appropriately. Yabung's body language (e.g. hunching her back, covering her mouth in embarrassment) signaled her withdrawal.

The video camera also captured the first-grader Kumu immediately sneaking out of the scene. Later on Kumu was called back to introduce herself and she did not say it loud enough to be heard, even though she was able to do so in some other elders' homes. In other similar contexts where children were restrictively positioned as learners whose pronunciation needed to be fixed, or when the communicative event was co-constructed more like a language proficiency test, some children resisted speaking up and others just went through the agenda quickly without any improvisation. Children's changing language performance and motivation across contexts highlight the interrelationships of identity needs, language ideologies and children's motivation to participate. Rather than assuming that children can immediately take on the role of caring grandchildren, the analysis illuminates that children have been assigned dual subject positions by adults (e.g. as an 'angel for Grandma', and as a learner) in the task and that their desired social identity may not be made relevant all of the time. Kumu's resistance to speak, therefore, can be positively reinterpreted as her passive renegotiation of the meanings of the activity rather than as being incompetent or merely shy.

Peer dynamics

The complex relationship between identity and learning is also played out in peer dynamics. Because quite a few elders in the village highly approved of the curriculum, they started sending their grandchildren to the program. The new students' legitimacy to participate was not taken for granted but needed to be negotiated (Wenger, 1998), as they were not necessarily welcomed by the existing members in the program. At one time, I had hoped that the more competent, experienced student members could mentor the newcomers and therefore assigned them to be leaders of different groups. There was an air of dissatisfaction among the older members because they did not want to be separated from their original clique. My decision was rationalized under the metaphor of language transmission, whereas the children's theory of learning was more about participation through affinity to their bounded community. Another instance of negotiation of meaning in communities of practice is that, in my retrospective examination of the video recording, I was surprised to notice constant, implicit exclusion of a new first-grade member, Ikay, from participation by some older members. For example, she was constantly excluded from the circle during the group performance. When she finally got the chance to cut in, the boy next to her refused to hold her hand. Such implicit bullying occurred a few times and resulted in Ikay's rage , which subsequently disrupted the class order. Although none of the adult teachers was aware of the whole picture at that moment, thankfully it was the positive response from the 89-year-old elder we visited that opened the door for Ikay to participate. Through conducting this analysis, I have also come to realize that, if we, as adults, continue to consider language learning as a politically neutral process of knowledge transmission, we could misinterpret Ikay's class performance as lack of attention or interest. Wenger's metaphor of learning as participation in communities of practice inspires an alternative reading of the class disturbance.

Reflecting on the curriculum design, I realized that our original idea of 'engaging children's social identity as caring children for the elderly' overlooks the mediating role of peer dynamics in communities of practice. In these above-mentioned incidents, I, as a language revitalization activist and educator, unconsciously confined my perspective to the idea of language transmission and acquisition, using language proficiency as a defining criterion to restructure class dynamics. In contrast, for children, it is more about being around their good friends than about transmitting their knowledge to new members. Drawing on Wenger's communities of practice to make sense of the mismatches of language learning ideologies, I have come to better empathize with children's emotional and identity needs in learning, and appreciate their implicit ideology of language as relationship, which has been applied to both family relations and friendship. Their stories piece together a more complex picture of motivation and learning, which is more like a rubber sheet that is constantly being stretched and shaped by pulling from existing social relationships, situated identity construction and opportunities to participate.

Discussion

By focusing on an empirical, praxis-oriented case from one of the Truku villages in Taiwan, I present how children's multiple identity positions and language performances work to mutually develop one another with implications for praxis. Specifically, children's dominant social identities of being members of existing social networks (e.g. being a grandchild, being a friend) mediate their own and their peers' learning processes. The focus on the identity label 'Indigenous' to build unity and support for Indigenous revitalization in the previous literature may have overlooked the need to explore how other identities are made relevant in children's learning trajectories. The complex language–identity–motivation nexus from children's situated performance and participation further humbles me to recognize the limitation of our academic language ideologies of 'acquisition' and 'transmission'. Children's motivation to learn Truku also needs to be understood as a process dynamically mediated by their existing and emerging social relationships with others.

How does this pedagogical experience contribute to our understanding of agency? I argue that considering agency as resistance to dominant language ideologies through community-based language revitalization does not fully capture the dynamism of praxis. Our project team has experienced numerous challenges in reconstructing language practices from the bottom up where different stakeholders' theories of language and learning diverge on both conscious and unconscious levels. Aligning with Wenger's emphasis on the importance of 'mutual engagement' and 'negotiation of meanings' in the CofP, I argue that agency from minority language activists or educators' perspectives can be understood as a conscientious attempt to relate oneself to students and their communities, to address their needs and interests and to build mutuality of seeing, learning and being. Additionally, instead of seeing mutual engagement as the precondition to 'create relationships among people' in the CofP (Wenger, 1998: 76), these Truku children's stories inspire us to value the relationships that pre-exist in the village. For future community-based language revitalization initiatives, the present study suggests the potential of a relationship-oriented framework – one that values and incorporates existing social relationships in praxis, and one that requires the dominant group (e.g. adults) to humbly recognize the work of power in social relations and develop a trusting, reflective, nondiscriminatory bond with the nondominant group (e.g. children) before rushing to impose agendas. As community language revitalization can be a very emotional struggle, especially when we deal with frustrations resulting from conflicting local perspectives, it is as caring grandchildren that children become our teachers. It is as good friends that children become good teammates. It is as understanding adults that we become learners and educators. It is from focusing on immediate identity needs that we understand the workings of language ideologies. It is the bond of love – the valuing of relationship and people over ideas – that makes genuine listening and dialogue possible.

Norton and Toohey (2011: 435) note that, 'an understanding of identity and SLA [second language acquisition] processes must be enriched by research conducted in postcolonial and indigenous sites'. Situated in an Indigenous community in Taiwan, the present pedagogical experience illuminates an expansive understanding of Norton's social identity theory of language as I rethink the appropriateness of the pervasiveness of the economic metaphors in our time, for example, 'capital' and 'investment' (Bourdieu, 1977; Norton Peirce, 1995). In contemporary society, when language is increasingly commodified (Heller, 2010), the capital of Indigenous language can hardly survive if we continue to theorize the value of language using the economic metaphor. The children's genuine improvisation inspires us to highlight the *heart* to speak – viewing language as a way to reconnect, to rebuild and enrich relationships, to value family and lives regardless of their market capitals. When we start to put human relationships at the center of our endeavors, we are also learning to redefine success. We see success when a young Truku lady told us, 'I was touched to see when children pray for my grandmother. I had assumed you guys only focused on the Truku language'. We see success when a female elder came to tell us, 'My granddaughter initiated to pray for me in Truku a few days ago when seeing me ill in bed'. We see success when children would voluntarily perform traditional songs and dances for the elderly in their neighborhood at sunset. Children's various forms of improvisations in the following months continue to offer us glimpses of hope on this journey, where we as adults are learning to celebrate the moments of love – a journey that is more than revitalization of the language, but the restoration of humanity as we rethink what gives life to languages.

Conclusion

In this chapter, I brought together ethnographic work and an innovative pedagogical experience to reflect on the possibility of agency in community-based Indigenous education. I have necessarily strived for a middle ground along the dimension of theory, on the one hand, and praxis, on the other. The study makes a strong case for extending the relevance of linguistic anthropological research to practical activities and advances the theoretical tradition of second language studies by bringing in an Indigenous, postcolonial context in Asia. It is my sincere hope that the present study encourages researchers to extend this type of work and continue to listen to the hearts of our children, which shine glimpses of hope and light in our time.

Acknowledgments

I would like to thank all the Truku children and my Truku colleagues – Bowtung Yudaw, Apay Yuki, Tien-Mu Chen, Tumun Kingjiang, Ciwas Uming, Ciming Miki and many others – without whom the project would not have been possible. I also want to thank the reviewers, Dr Ping Deters and Dr Kate Anderson for their valuable insights on the manuscript.

References

Ahearn, L.M. (2001) Language and agency. *Annual Review of Anthropology* 30, 109–137.
Baéz, G.P. (2013) Family language policy, transnationalism, and the diaspora community of San Lucas Quiavini of Oaxaca, Mexico. *Language Policy* 12, 27–45.
Barton, D. and Tusting, K. (eds) (2005) *Beyond Communities of Practice: Language Power and Social Context*. New York: Cambridge University Press.
Bourdieu, P. (1977) The economics of linguistic exchange. *Social Science Information* 16, 645–668.
Bourdieu, P. and Wacquant, L.J.D. (1992) *An Invitation to Reflexive Sociology*. Chicago, IL: University of Chicago Press.
Brayboy, B.M.J. (2013) Tidemarks and legacies: Building on the past and moving to the future. *Anthropology & Education* 44 (1), 1–10.
Bucholtz, M. (2002) Youth and culture practice. *Annual Review of Anthropology* 31, 525–552.
Bucholtz, M. and Hall, K. (2005) Identity and interaction: A sociocultural linguistic approach. *Discourse Studies* 7 (4–5), 585–614.
Cameron, D., Frazer, E., Harvey, R., Rampton, M.B.H. and Richardson, K. (1992) *Researching Language: Issues of Power and Method*. London: Routledge.

Ching, L. (2001) *Becoming Japanese: Colonial Taiwan and the Politics of Identity Formation.* Berkeley, CA: University of California Press.

Cooper, R.L. (1989) *Language Planning and Social Change.* New York: Cambridge University Press.

Chun, A. (1994) From nationalism to nationalizing: Cultural imagination and state formation in postwar Taiwan. *The Australian Journal of Chinese Affairs* 31, 49–69.

Curdt-Christiansen, X.L. (ed.) (2013) Family language policy: Sociopolitical reality versus linguistic continuity. *Language Policy* 12, 1–6.

Field, M.C. and Kroskrity, P.V. (2009) Introduction: Revealing native American language ideologies. In P.V. Kroskrity and M.C. Field (eds) *Native American Language Ideologies: Beliefs, Practices, and Struggles in Indian Country* (pp. 3–30). Tucson, AZ: The University of Arizona Press.

Fishman, J. (1991) *Reversing Language Shift: The Theoretical and Empirical Foundations of Assistance to Threatened Languages.* Clevedon: Multilingual Matters.

Friedman, P.K. (2010) Entering the mountains to rule the aborigines: Taiwanese aborigine education and the colonial encounter. In A. Heylen and S. Sommers (eds) *Becoming Taiwan: From Colonialism to Democracy* (pp. 19–32). Wiesbaden: Harrasowitz.

Hedegaard, M. (2008) A cultural–historical theory of children's development. In M. Hedegaard and M. Fleer (eds) *Studying Children – A Cultural–Historical Approach* (pp. 10–30). New York: Open University Press.

Heller, M. (2010) The commodification of language. *Annual Review of Anthropology* 39, 101–114.

Hinton, L. and Hale, K. (eds) (2001) *The Green Book of Language Revitalization in Practice.* San Diego, CA: Academic Press.

Holland, D., Lachicotte, W., Skinner, D. and Cain, C. (2001) *Identity and Agency in Cultural Worlds.* Cambridge, MA: Harvard University Press.

Hornberger, N.H. and Swinehart, K.F. (2012) Not just 'situaciones de la vida': Professionalization and Indigenous languages in the Andes. *International Multilingual Research Journal* 6 (2), 35–49.

Howard, R. (2009) Education reform, indigenous politics, and decolonization in the Bolivia of Evo Morales. *International Journal of Educational Development* 29 (6), 583–593.

Hymes, D. (1980) *Language in Education: Ethnographic Essays.* Washington, DC: Center for Applied Linguistics.

Joseph, M. and Raman, E. (2012) 'Glocalization': Going beyond the dichotomy of global versus local through additive multilingualism. *International Multilingual Research Journal* 6 (1), 22–34.

Kamwangamalu, N.M. (2009) Commentary from an African and international perspective. Can school save languages? In N.H. Hornberger (ed.) *Can School Save Indigenous Languages? Policy and Practice on Four Continents* (pp. 136–151). New York: Palgrave Macmillan.

Kroskrity, P.V. (ed.) (2000) *Regimes of Language: Ideologies, Polities, and Identities.* Santa Fe, NM: School of American Research Press.

Lantolf, J.P. and Throne, S.L. (2006) *Sociocultural Theory and the Genesis of Second Language Development.* New York: Oxford University Press.

Lopéz, L.E. (2009) Top-down and bottom-up: Counterpoised visions of bilingual intercultural education in Latin America. In N.H. Hornberger (ed.) *Can School Save Indigenous Languages? Policy and Practice on Four Continents* (pp. 42–65). New York: Palgrave Macmillan.

Low, S.M. and Merry, S.E. (2010) Engaged anthropology: Diversity and dilemmas, an introduction to supplement 2. *Current Anthropology* 51, 203–226.

Luykx, A. (2005) Children as socializing agents: Family language policy in situations of language shift. In J. Cohen, K.T. McAlister, K. Rolstad, and J. MacSwan (eds) *ISB4:*

Proceedings of the 4th International Symposium on Bilingualism (pp. 1407–1414). Somerville, MA: Cascadilla Press.

Malewski, E. (2005) Epilogue: When children and youth talk back: Precocious research practices and the cleverest voices. In L.D. Soto and B.B. Swadener (eds) *Power and Voice in Research with Children*. New York: Peter Lang.

McCarty, T.L. and Warhol, L. (2011) The anthropology of language planning and policy. In B.A.U. Levinson and M. Pollock (eds) *A Companion to the Anthropology of Education* (pp. 177–198). Malden, MA: Wiley-Blackwell.

McCarty, T.L. and Wyman, L.T. (eds) (2009) Indigenous youth and bilingualism: Theory, research, praxis. *Journal of Language, Identity, and Education* 8 (5), 279–290.

McCarty, T.L., Nicholas, S.E. and Wyman, L.T. (2012) Re-emplacing place in the 'global here and now': Critical ethnographic case studies of Native American language planning and policy. *International Multilingual Research Journal* 6 (1), 50–63.

Messing, J.H.E. (2009) Ambivalence and ideology among Mexicano youth in Tlaxcala, Mexico. *Journal of Language, Identity, and Education* 8 (5), 350–364.

Norton, B. (2000) *Identity and Language Learning: Gender, Ethnicity and Educational Change*. Harlow: Pearson Education.

Norton Peirce, B. (1995) Social identity, investment, and language learning. *TESOL Quarterly* 29, 9–31.

Norton, B. and Toohey, K. (2011) Identity, language learning, and social change. *Language Teaching* 44 (4), 412–446.

Patrick, D., Budach, G. and Muckpaloo, I. (2013) Multiliteracies and family language policy in an urban Inuit community. *Language Policy* 12, 47–63.

Pavlenko, A. and Blackledge, A. (eds) (2003) *Negotiation of Identities in Multilingual Contexts*. Clevdon: Multilingual matters.

Recendiz, N.R. (2009) Learning with differences: Strengthening Hnahno and bilingual teaching in an elementary school in Mexico city. In N.H. Hornberger (ed.) *Can School Save Indigenous Languages? Policy and Practice on Four Continents* (pp. 99–124). New York: Palgrave Macmillan.

Ren, L. and Hu, G. (2013) Prolepsis, syncretism, and synergy in early language and literacy practices: A case study of family language policy in Singapore. *Language Policy* 12, 63–82.

Reynolds, J.F. (2009) Shaming the shift generation: Intersecting ideologies of family and linguistic revitalization in Guatemala. In P.V. Kroskrity and M.C. Field (eds) *Native American Language Ideologies: Beliefs, Practices, and Struggles in Indian Country* (pp. 213–237). Tucson, AZ: The University of Arizona Press.

Romero-Little, M.E. (2006) Honoring our own: Rethinking of Indigenous languages and literacy. *Anthropology & Education Quarterly* 37 (4), 399–402.

Romero-Little, M.E., Ortiz, S.J. and McCarty, T.L. (eds) (2011) *Indigenous Languages Across the Generations – Strengthening Families and Communities*. Tempe, AZ: Arizona State University Center for Indian Education.

Schieffelin, B.B., Woolard, K.A. and Kroskrity, P.V. (eds) (1998) *Language Ideologies: Practice and Theory*. Oxford: Oxford University Press.

Sfard, A. (1998) On two metaphors for learning and the dangers of choosing just one. *Educational Researcher* 27 (3), 4–13.

Van der Aa, J. and Blommaert, J. (2011) Ethnographic monitoring: Hymes's unfinished business in education research. *Anthropology & Education* 42 (4), 319–334.

Vygotsky, L.S. (1978) *Mind in Society: The Development of Higher Psychological Processes*. Cambridge, MA: Harvard University Press.

Weedon, C. (1987) *Feminist Practice and Poststructuralist Theory*. London: Blackwell.

Wenger, E. (1998) *Communities of Practice: Learning, Meaning, and Identity*. New York: Cambridge University Press.

Wertsch, J., Tulviste, P. and Hagstrom, F. (1993) A sociocultural approach to agency. In E.A. Forman, N. Minick and C.A. Stone (eds) *Contexts for Learning: Sociocultural Dynamics in Children's Development.* New York: Oxford University Press.

Yang, S.T. (2001) Sejiq 族群的傳統教育 [Traditional education of the Sejiq(Truku) people]. In N.T. Yang (ed.) 太魯閣國家公園原住民文化講座 [*Taroke National Park – Panels on Indigenous Cultures*]. Hualien: Taroko National Park Headquarters.

Yashima, T. (2012) Agency in second language acquisition. In C.A. Chapelle (ed.) *The Encyclopedia of Applied Linguistics*, Vol. 5 (pp. 49–56). Oxford: Wiley-Blackwell.

15 Afterword

Anna De Fina

Let me start this afterword by thanking the curators of this volume for giving me the opportunity to read such an interesting set of chapters. In these brief notes I will not attempt an exhaustive evaluation of each contribution – an enterprise that would be impossible in the space afforded – but rather, discuss some of the general themes and issues that emerge from the works collected here and I will make reference to individual chapters only in so far as they relate to such discussion.

Even though the contributors pursue different objectives and make use of a wide variety of theoretical–methodological instruments, there are some unifying threads that connect their work. First, all the chapters demonstrate the vitality and strength of the so-called 'sociolinguistic turn' (Dörnyei & Ushioda, 2011) in applied linguistics and second language acquisition. Indeed, the questions asked and the theoretical stances taken by all authors reveal a focus away from the positivistic and experimentally driven orientation that has dominated the field in the last two decades and the search for alternative paradigms that are capable of accounting for the social aspects of language acquisition and learning. From the vantage point of such new perspectives, language learning and acquisition are highly complex, individualized and context-bound processes that cannot be studied merely through tests measuring the accuracy of grammatical or pragmatic performances. Rather, the learning and acquisition of languages are seen as deeply embedded in intricate social interactional encounters and practices in which learners participate, often carrying the baggage of highly personal backgrounds, complex motivations, anxieties and desires. These practices are, in turn, part of wide social processes and networks that underlie them in a variety of ways.

As a consequence of this shift in focus, the chapters also share an orientation to and preference for qualitative and ethnographic methods that allow for an appreciation of the uniqueness of the different learning contexts, the specificity of practices in which learning is embedded and the emic perspectives expressed by participants. Qualitative and ethnographic instruments proposed in the volume encompass participant observation, introspective autoethnography, forms of action research, the use of diaries, narratives and learners' biographies: all tools devised to get a glimpse of the individual ways in which learners make concrete uses of their full repertoire of linguistic resources, evaluate their knowledge, face new tasks, deploy cultural under-standing and awareness, and develop identities and a sense of self in relation to the processes of coming into contact with language users and linguistic varieties. All of this, again, represents a far cry from methods of study that look at learners as objects of experimentations, rather than as subjects of learning with agency, dispositions and unique personal histories.

Agency is indeed the main focus of this volume. The concept is proposed as a sort of unifying theme around which all authors coalesce in an effort to provide models of language learning and development that can account for the intricate and multifaceted intersections between individual and social processes. Yet the profound differences in definitions and ways of operation-alizing the concept also alert us to the complexity of the task. As under-scored by the editors in their introduction to the volume, agency is still a highly controversial construct and it is precisely its complex nature that has led one of the main scholars in the field, Laura Ahearn (2001: 112), to look for the simplest possible definition. In her words: 'Agency refers to the socio-culturally mediated capacity to act'. However, the chapters in this volume demonstrate little convergence on conceptualizations of agency. While some authors equate agency with capabilities to act or to react revealed in specific behaviors, others regard it as a construct that involves feelings, beliefs, thoughts and cognitive processes. Yet in other definitions, such as the one by Lantolf and Thorne (2006: 143) quoted in García's chapter, agency is 'about more than voluntary control over behavior' in that it 'entails the ability to assign relevance and significance to things and events'. Agency is related in the chapters to a host of concepts: from capability, to awareness, from con-trol to motivation, to autonomy. While in the definitions of some, agency requires reflexivity, the consciousness of one's behavior and the undertaking of actions, in other views, agency may be connected to internal processes that take place in the mind of learners and to which researchers have no direct access. For example, in Mercer's (2012: 42) definition, quoted by Gkonou, agency is 'not only concerned with what is observable but it also involves nonvisible behaviors, beliefs, thoughts and feelings' – hence the dilemmas that emerge from the reading of the contributions. Can agency be associated with observable behavior and expressed intention and volition, or does it involve unobservable thoughts and feelings? Does agency imply con-crete action, be it positive or negative (see resistance as proposed by Canagarajah, 1999; or Fogle, 2012), or not necessarily? These different theo-retical stances also carry divergent methodological choices because, if agency is conceived as somewhat observable, ethnographic methods and participant observation represent the right instruments for the study of the phenome-non. However, if agency is regarded as involving cognitive and unobservable processes, then introspective methods are a more adequate choice. It seems to me that the latter position and methods involve greater difficulties. Indeed, adopting a 'weak' definition of agency, implying, for example, conscious understanding of linguistic categories (as in García's chapter) or self-reflection on linguistic experiences (as in Muller's chapter), carries the risk of diluting the concept to a point at which it may become indistinguishable from many other forms of conscious (as opposed to automatic) behavior.

Another, significant dilemma raised by the chapters in this volume refers to the possible conflict between individual and social agency. The issue is very lucidly analyzed by Block, who summarizes the opposition as involving a privileging of individualism and free agency against a recognition of the weight of 'structure' (or better said, different kinds of structures) in the realization of social action. Block argues that the excessive emphasis on individual free agency is a product of a general tendency in postmodern theorization to exaggerate the role of the individual. As an antidote to this tendency, he proposes 'critical realism', that is, an approach that recognizes both the existence of 'a real world' out there (composed of objective structures) and the socially constructed nature of knowledge and identities.

The debate over individual vs social determination or individual vs structure is certainly not confined to studies of agency, but represents one of the fundamental dilemmas in identity research in general. In narrative analysis, for example, interactional approaches (see De Fina & Georgakopoulou, 2012) regard identity as socially and interactionally constructed and therefore inscribed and embedded within structures of social action, as opposed to biographic orientations (see for example McAdams, 1997) that conceive of identities as stemming from individual processes of self-construction. Indeed, researchers have taken very different approaches when it comes to defining the role of the individual vs social processes. Such divergences also underlie debates over the concept of positioning (Davies & Harré, 1999; Bamberg, 1997), one of the most important tools for the analysis of identity in interaction (for a discussion see De Fina, 2013), and a widely used methodological approach also in the analysis of agency. The concept and its development closely mirror the dilemma discussed by Block. Indeed, in the Foucauldian interpretation (see Foucault, 1969), subjects' positions pre-exist individual action and discourse and are made available to individuals through dominant discourses, thus fundamentally limiting their possibility of choice. Even within more recent theories, such as the one proposed by Davies and Harré (1990: 47), speakers are assumed to take positions through emerging 'storylines' that create 'our own sense of how the world is to be interpreted from the perspective of who we take ourselves to be'. In this formulation, we get another glimpse of a conception in which individuals are negotiating ready-made models involving representations and roles. Thus, the debate about the concept of positioning prefigures a number of issues and questions that are relevant to the study of agency as well: first of all, whether social structures and power relations constrain individual action and, if so, in what ways; second, to what extent individuals have a choice and how they exert it; third, what the role of local discursive processes and practices is within other (wider or different-scale) contexts and how links between such different levels can be conceptualized.

Discussing positioning and identity in narrative, Depperman (2013: 2) states: 'We are in need of a concept which can capture how identities are deployed in situated narrative interaction. This concept . . . has to be sensitive to structural properties of narratives (and other genres figuring in narrative interaction), to their situated construction in the context of practical action, and to the emergent, recipient-designed co-construction of narratives in interaction'. In my view, the same approach can be applied to the analysis of agency, in the sense that an interactionally based and socially sensitive orientation to agency needs to take into account both social structures (at all levels, but starting from the local) and individual action, both the limitations imposed by power relations and structures and the creativity and ability to force and break them by individuals and communities. Even though the doubts and critiques expressed by Block need to be taken in serious account, it seems to me that the authors of the contributions collected in this volume propose some interesting ways of overcoming the individual/structure dilemma. In most chapters agency is not seen in individualistic terms, but as the outcome of a complex net of relations and actions. As noted by Gkonou in Chapter 11, 'emphasis on the role of the individual and of his or her cognition in shaping learner agency has gained ground in SLA research. However, equal importance is now assigned to both the individual and the context, and agency is viewed as being largely mediated from a range of settings surrounding the students, as well as from the temporal and spatial dimensions associated with those settings'. Contributors resort to a number of constructs to explain and problematize these complex interactions. For example, one trend that emerges in different papers is the idea of looking at agency not so much as stemming from the individual but as 'socially distributed', shared and negotiated within communities. The concept of communities of practice (Lave & Wenger, 1991) is of course, central to these endeavors. Thus, Lin, in her chapter, puts forth 'mutuality' as a form of agency that implies relationality and a constant renegotiation of individual actions and evaluations with other members of a community involved in specific practices. Lin concretely shows how agency is distributed and collectively exerted by the children she studied in the process of language revitalization and re-evaluation. She demonstrates that a focus on collective and socially exerted agency can allow for the emergence of voices (such as those of children) that are otherwise often ignored. Yet other chapters focus on Bakhtinian dialogism (see Bakhtin, 1981) as an antidote against individualism and Cartesian views of the self. For example Dufva and Aro underscore Bakhtin's contribution to our understanding of human agency as emerging through processes of confrontation with the voices of others, but also as the outcome of a polyphony of voices stemming from the same individual at different moments and in different contexts. Dufva and Aro, and other authors in this volume (e.g. Muller and Duran) draw attention to the historically situated nature of social interactions and to the configurations of time and space in which concrete events are embedded. They note how ethnographies are more and more often taking into account the development in time of agentic behavior and the evolutions and changes brought about by different experiences with learning. Duva and Aro put forth the Bakhtian notion of 'chronotope' as a frame for grasping the profound connectedness of space/time/place and ideologies within concrete contexts.

Another important construct proposed by authors to account for the socially and interactionally grounded nature of agency is the concept of 'mediation'. As noted by Bagga-Gupta, a theoretical frame that recognizes agency as being mediated and situated in time, space and social context is another antidote against a view of the self based on individual intentionality and cognition. Mediation involves both the embedding of human action within contexts and a consideration of the historical and ideological dimension of mediating tools. In Bagga-Gupta's study of language use in public space, for example, the expression and embodiment of gendered identities takes place through the mediation of particular tools (such as microphones, written notes and other media) and of the space and time constraints imposed by the format of the public debate. Language has, of course, a privileged role among these media, but it is precisely the embedding of linguistic resources within other media and the practices that they help constitute that provides a deeper understanding of how such resources are deployed to serve agentic behaviors. In this kind of approach to agency, language use is better understood as 'languaging' since the emphasis is on the observation of concrete social and discursive practices. Language resources (be they languages or linguistic elements) themselves, as Bakhtin has taught us, have their own histories and therefore one cannot explain the role of languaging within social practices without considering issues of culture and ideology. In this sense, again, agency cannot be seen as operating only on individual intentions, but always represents a point of intersection between habitus, iterative practices and personal invention and volition.

Bagga-Gupta's chapter also demonstrates the need to look at the interconnection of different scales (see Blommaert, 2010; Collins *et al.*, 2009) in the analysis of agency, as local interactional events are tied with other events, processes and actors that can be far removed in time and space or connected in many other ways to what is happening in the here-and-now. Thus local expressions of identity, or agency, in our globalized world are less and less explainable exclusively through the lenses of the here-and-now.

In my view, the implications of the theoretical-methodological stances expressed in the contributions to the book are clear: modern approaches to agency within sociocultural linguistics need to fundamentally incorporate notions and constructs such as dialogism and relationality, social and discursive practices, mediation, scales. The pedagogical and practical implications are even more far reaching as they point to a consideration not only of learners' personal agency and individuality, but also of the full contexts in which learning happens, of the histories of cultural tools and linguistic resources and of the embedding of all of these within interconnected chains of events in time and space in the design of instruments for teaching languages or for propelling language change. The contributions in this volume definitely represent a step in this direction.

References

Ahearn, L. (2012) *Living Languages*. Chichester: Blackwell.

Bakhtin, M.M. (1981) *The Dialogic Imagination. Four Essays*, (trans. C. Emerson and M. Holquist). Austin, TX: University of Texas Press.

Bamberg, M. (1997) Positioning between structure and performance. In M. Bamberg, (ed.) *Oral versions of personal experience: three decades of narrative analysis* (pp. 335–342). *Journal of Narrative and Life History* 7, 1–4.

Blommaert, J. (2010) *The Sociolinguistics of Globalization*. Cambridge: Cambridge University Press.

Canagarajah, A.S. (1999) *Resisting Linguistic Imperialism in English Teaching*. Oxford: Oxford University Press.

Collins, J., Slembrouck, S. and Baynham, M. (eds) (2009) *Globalization and Language Contact*. London: Continuum.

Davies, B. and Harré, R. (1990) Positioning: The social construction of selves. *Journal for the Theory of Social Behaviour* 20, 43–63.

De Fina, A. (2013) Positioning level 3: Connecting local identity displays to macro social processes. *Narrative Inquiry* 23 (1), 40–61.

De Fina, A. and Georgakopoulou, A. (2012) *Analyzing Narrative: Discourse and Sociolinguistic Perspectives*. Cambridge: Cambridge University Press.

Depperman, A. (2013) Editorial: Positioning in Narrative Interaction. *Narrative Inquiry* 23 (1), 1–15.

Dörnyei, Z. and Ushioda, E. (2011) *Teaching and Researching Motivation* (2nd edn). Harlow: Pearson Education.

Fogle, L.W. (2012) *Second Language Socialization and Learner Agency: Adoptive Family Talk*. Bristol: Multilingual Matters.

Foucault, M. (1969) *L'archéologie du savoir*. Paris: Gallimard.

Lantolf, J.P. and Thorne, S.L. (2006) *Sociocultural Theory and the Genesis of Second Language Development*. Oxford: Oxford University Press.

Lave, J. and Wenger, E. (1991) *Situated Learning: Legitimate Peripheral Participation*. Cambridge: Cambridge University Press.

McAdams, D.P. (1997) *The Stories we Live by: Personal Myths and the Making of the Self*. New York: The Guildford Press.

Mercer, S. (2012) The complexity of learner agency. *Apples – Journal of Applied Language Studies* 6 (2), 41–59.

Author Index

Subject Index